D0093168

OUR KIDS

The American Dream
in Crisis

ROBERT D. PUTNAM

SIMON & SCHUSTER

New York   London   Toronto   Sydney   New Delhi

Simon & Schuster
1230 Avenue of the Americas
New York, NY 10020

First Simon & Schuster hardcover edition March 2015

SIMON & SCHUSTER and colophon are registered trademarks of Simon & Schuster, Inc.

For information about special discounts for bulk purchases,
please contact Simon & Schuster Special Sales
at 1-866-506-1949 or business@simonandschuster.com.

The Simon & Schuster Speakers Bureau can bring authors to your live event.
For more information or to book an event, contact the
Simon & Schuster Speakers Bureau at 1-866-248-3049
or visit our website at www.simonspeakers.com.

Interior design by Ruth Lee-Mui

Manufactured in the United States of America

5   7   9   10   8   6   4

Library of Congress Cataloging-in-Publication Data has been applied for.

ISBN 978-1-4767-6989-9
ISBN 978-1-4767-6991-2 (ebook)

Rosemary, for remembrance

Contents

OUR KIDS

Chapter 1

THE AMERICAN DREAM: MYTHS AND REALITIES

I went back to Ohio, but my city was gone.[1]

If I can get to the heart of Dublin I can get to
the heart of all the cities in the world.
In the particular is contained the universal.[2]

MY HOMETOWN WAS, IN THE 1950S, A PASSABLE EMBODIMENT OF
the American Dream, a place that offered decent opportunity for all the
kids in town, whatever their background. A half century later, however,
life in Port Clinton, Ohio, is a split-screen American nightmare, a community in which kids from the wrong side of the tracks that bisect the
town can barely imagine the future that awaits the kids from the right
side of the tracks. And the story of Port Clinton turns out to be sadly
typical of America. How this transformation happened, why it matters,
and how we might begin to alter the cursed course of our society is the
subject of this book.

The most rigorous economic and social history now available suggests that socioeconomic barriers in America (and in Port Clinton) in
the 1950s were at their lowest ebb in more than a century: economic
and educational expansion were high; income equality was relatively
high; class segregation in neighborhoods and schools was low; class barriers to intermarriage and social intercourse were low; civic engagement

and social solidarity were high; and opportunities for kids born in the lower echelon to scale the socioeconomic ladder were abundant.

Though small and not very diverse racially, Port Clinton in the 1950s was in all other respects a remarkably representative microcosm of America, demographically, economically, educationally, socially, and even politically. (Ottawa County, of which Port Clinton is county seat, is the bellwether county in the bellwether state of the United States—that is, the county whose election results have historically been closest to the national outcome.[3]) The life stories of my high school classmates show that the opportunities open to Don and Libby, two poor white kids, and even to Jesse and Cheryl, two poor black kids, to rise on the basis of their own talents and energy were not so different from the opportunities open to Frank, the only real scion of privilege in our class.

No single town or city could possibly represent all of America, and Port Clinton in the 1950s was hardly paradise. As in the rest of America at the time, minorities in Port Clinton suffered serious discrimination and women were frequently marginalized, as we shall explore later in this chapter. Few of us, including me, would want to return there without major reforms. But social class was not a major constraint on opportunity.

When our gaze shifts to Port Clinton in the twenty-first century, however, the opportunities facing rich kids and poor kids today— kids like Chelsea and David, whom we shall also meet in this chapter—are radically disparate. Port Clinton today is a place of stark class divisions, where (according to school officials) wealthy kids park BMW convertibles in the high school lot next to decrepit junkers that homeless classmates drive away each night to live in. The changes in Port Clinton that have led to growing numbers of kids, of all races and both genders, being denied the promise of the American Dream—changes in economic circumstance, in family structure and parenting, in schools, and in neighborhoods—are surprisingly representative of America writ large. For exploring equality of opportunity, Port Clinton in 1959 is a good time and place to begin, because it reminds us of how far we have traveled away from the American Dream.

• • •

June 1, 1959, had dawned hot and sunny, but the evening was cooler as 150 new graduates thronged down the steps of Port Clinton High School in the center of town, clutching our new diplomas, flushed with Commencement excitement, not quite ready to relinquish our childhood in this pleasant, friendly town of 6,500 (mostly white) people on the shores of Lake Erie, but confident about our future. It was, as usual, a community-wide celebration, attended by 1,150 people.[4] Family or not, the townspeople thought of all the graduates as "our kids."

Don

Don was a soft-spoken white working-class kid, though no one in our class would have thought of him that way, for he was our star quarterback.[5] His dad had only an eighth-grade education. To keep the family afloat, his dad worked two jobs—the first on the line at the Port Clinton Manufacturing factory, from 7:00 a.m. to 3:00 p.m., and the second, a short walk away, at the local canning plant, from 3:30 p.m. to 11:00 p.m. His mom, who had left school in the 11th grade, "lived in the kitchen," Don says, making all of their meals from scratch. Every night, she sat down with Don and his two brothers for dinner. They got used to eating hash, made by frying up everything left in the house with potatoes. The boys were in bed by the time their dad got home from work.

They lived on the poorer side of town, and did not own a car or television until Don went off to college, by which time 80 percent of all American families already had a car, and 90 percent had a TV. Their neighbors drove them to church every week. The family had no money for vacations, but Don's parents owned their home and felt reasonably secure economically, and his dad was never unemployed. "I didn't know that I was poor until I went to college and took Economics 101," Don recalls, "and found out that I had been 'deprived.'"

Despite their modest circumstances, Don's parents urged him to aim for college, and, like many other working-class kids in our class, he chose the college-prep track at PCHS. His mom forced him to take piano lessons for six years, but his true love was sports. He played basketball and football, and his dad took time off from work to attend every single one of Don's games. Don downplays class distinctions in Port Clinton. "I lived on the east side of town," he says, "and money was on the west side of town. But you met everyone as an equal through sports."

Although none of his closest friends in high school ended up going to college, Don did well in school and finished in the top quarter of our class. His parents "didn't have a clue" about college, he says, but fortunately he had strong ties at church. "One of the ministers in town was keeping an eye on me," he says, "and mentioned my name to the university where I ended up." Not only that, the minister helped Don figure out how to get financial aid and navigate the admissions process.

After PCHS, Don headed off to a religiously affiliated university downstate (where he also played football) and then on to seminary. While in seminary, he developed doubts about whether he could "hack it" as a minister, he says, and came home to tell his parents he was quitting. Back home, he stopped by the local pool hall to say hello. The owner, a longtime friend of his dad's, referred to him as "a future minister," and a customer asked Don to pray for him—which Don interpreted as signs that he should continue on his path.

Immediately after college, Don married June, a high school teacher, and they had one child, who became a high school librarian. Don had a long and successful career as a minister and retired only recently. He still helps out in local churches and has coached high school football for many years. Looking back, he says he has been blessed with a very good life. His rise from a poor but close-knit working-class family to a successful professional career reflected his native intelligence and his gridiron grit. But as we shall see, the sort of upward mobility he achieved was not atypical for our class.

Frank

Frank came from one of the few wealthy families in Port Clinton. In the late nineteenth century, his maternal great-grandfather had started a commercial fishing business, and by the time of Frank's birth the family had diversified into real estate and other local businesses. His mother graduated from college in the 1930s and then earned a master's degree at the University of Chicago. While in Chicago she met Frank's father, a college-educated minister's son, and they soon married. As Frank grew up, his father managed the family businesses—fishing, a shopping center, farming, a restaurant, and so forth—and his mother did charity work.[6]

Port Clinton's social elite has long made the Port Clinton Yacht Club its hub. While Frank was growing up, his grandfather, father, and uncle each served a term as the club's "Commodore," and his mother and aunt were elected "Shipmates Captain"—pinnacles of local social status. In short, Frank's parents were the wealthiest, best educated, and most socially prominent parents of the class of 1959.

Nevertheless, the social distance between Frank's family and those at the bottom of the socioeconomic ladder was much shorter than is common in America (even in Port Clinton) today. Frank (who lived only four blocks away from Don) recalls his neighbors as "a nice mix of everyone"—truck driver, store owner, cashier at the A&P, officer at a major local firm, fire chief, gas station owner, game warden. "We played baseball out in the backyard or kick-the-can down at the corner," he says. "Everybody just got along."

Despite his family's affluence, Frank worked summers at the family restaurant, starting at fifteen, scraping paint and doing cleanup work with his high school buddies. And his family carefully downplayed their social status. "If you're in Port Clinton with a group of boys who can afford a Coke, that's what you are to order," Frank's grandfather had memorably warned Frank's uncle. "If we're in Cleveland or New York, you can order whatever you want, but when you're with kids in Port Clinton, you do what they can do."

In high school, Frank interacted with his classmates as a social equal—so ably, in fact, that many of us were unaware of his exceptional family background. But signs of it did appear. He was the first in our class to wear braces. In elementary school he spent winter months at a family home in Florida, attending school there. His grandfather was on the school board. Frank's parents once invited a teacher over for dinner. Afterward Frank chided his mom, "Why did you embarrass me in front of the whole class?" The suggestion that his parents might ever have intervened to try to alter a grade strikes Frank as absurd: "Are you kidding? Oh, jeez, as far as we kids knew, the teachers are always right."

Frank was an indifferent student, but that didn't mean his parents neglected his educational prospects. "My life was programmed from the time I was born until I was through college," he says. "You knew you were going to go to college, and you better graduate." With financial support from his parents, he attended a small college in Ohio, graduating with a major in journalism. After college, he enlisted in the Navy and for seven years navigated Navy transport planes around the world. "I loved it," he recalls.

After his naval service, Frank worked for about twenty-five years as an editor for the *Columbus Dispatch*, until he objected to some personnel decisions and was fired. At that point he returned to Port Clinton, semi-retired, to work in the family businesses—the fish-cleaning operation, dock rentals, and the boutique. He has been helped financially through some difficult years by a trust fund that his grandfather created for him at birth. "It's not a lot of money," he says, "but I'll never starve." Frank's family fortune has cushioned him from some of life's hard knocks, but it was not a trampoline that boosted him ahead of his peers from less affluent homes, like Don.

Class Disparities in Port Clinton in the 1950s

Class differences were not absent in Port Clinton in the 1950s, but as the lives of Frank and Don illustrate, those differences were muted.

The children of manual workers and of professionals came from similar homes and mixed unselfconsciously in schools and neighborhoods, in scout troops and church groups. The class contrasts that matter so much today (even in Port Clinton, as we shall shortly see)—in economic security, family structure, parenting, schooling, neighborhoods, and so on—were minimal in that era. Virtually everyone in the PCHS class of 1959, whatever their background, lived with two parents, in homes their parents owned, and in neighborhoods where everyone knew everyone else's first name.[7]

Our parents, almost universally homemaker moms and breadwinner dads, were not especially well educated. Indeed, barely one in 20 of them had graduated from college, and a full third of them hadn't even graduated from high school. (For the most part, they had completed their schooling before high school education became nearly universal.) But almost everyone in town had benefited from widely shared postwar prosperity, and few of our families were poverty-stricken. The very few kids in town who came from wealthy backgrounds, like Frank, made every effort to hide that fact.

Some dads worked the assembly lines at the local auto part factories, or in the nearby gypsum mines, or at the local Army base, or on small family farms. Others, like my dad, were small businessmen whose fortunes rose and fell with the business cycle. In that era of full employment and strong unions, few of our families experienced joblessness or serious economic insecurity. Most of my classmates, whatever their social origins, were active in sports, music, drama, and other extracurricular activities. Friday night football games attracted much of the town's population.

Seen a half century later, my classmates (now mostly retired) have experienced astonishing upward mobility. Nearly three quarters of us obtained more education than our parents, and the vast majority made it higher up the economic ladder. In fact, some kids from less well-off backgrounds have climbed further up that ladder than kids from more comfortable, better-educated backgrounds. By contemporary standards, our class's absolute level of upward educational mobility was remarkable, a reflection of the high school and college revolutions of the twentieth century. Half the sons and daughters of high school dropouts went on to college. Many of those who were the first in their family to complete high school ended up also being the first to complete college—a remarkable jump in a single generation. Even more striking, although the two black students in our class contended with racial prejudice (as we shall shortly see) and came from homes in which neither parent had completed grade school, both earned postgraduate degrees.

In 1950s Port Clinton, socioeconomic class was not nearly so formidable a barrier for kids of any race, white or black, as it would become in the twenty-first century. By way of comparison, the *children* of the members of the class of 1959 would, on average, experience *no* educational advance beyond their parents.[8] The escalator that had carried most of the class of 1959 upward suddenly halted when our own children stepped on.

This high absolute mobility of my class of 1959 could have been consistent with low relative mobility, if everyone had moved upward in lockstep, but actually, even relative mobility was high. In fact, upward mobility among the kids from the lower half of the socioeconomic hierarchy was almost as great as among the most privileged kids. In short, lots of upward mobility from the bottom and a modest amount of downward mobility at the top.

To be sure, less educated parents, with narrower cultural horizons and less familiarity with advanced education, sometimes had lower educational aspirations for their kids. However, if they, or our teachers, or informal mentors in the community (like Don's pastor), or our friends encouraged us to attend college, we *invariably* did—with virtually no trace of economic or financial or neighborhood bias in our college going.[9] Low costs at public and private institutions across Ohio were supplemented by a wide array of locally raised scholarships—from the Rotary Club, the United Auto Workers Union, the Junior Women's Club, and the like. Of all college grads in the PCHS class of 1959, two thirds of them were the first in their families to attend college, and one third were the first in their families even to graduate from high school. As the 1960s opened in Port Clinton, a single modest reform—better counseling for talented kids from poor backgrounds—would have seemed to hold the key to a truly remarkable degree of equality of opportunity, but instead (as we shall see) social history was about to reverse course.

Of the kids from lower- and middle-class backgrounds who did not immediately attend college, roughly one third later found on-ramps to postsecondary education, such as community college, with no trace of bias against kids from humbler backgrounds. The net effect of these late-blooming successes was to weaken still further the link between family background and eventual educational attainment.

This evidence from a survey of my classmates proves beyond a reasonable doubt that Port Clinton in the 1950s was a site of extraordinary upward mobility. Because the transmitters of socioeconomic status that are so potent today (economic insecurity, family instability, neighborhood distress, financial and organizational barriers) were unimportant in that period, the transmission process from generation to generation was weaker, and thus mobility was higher. Over and over again members of the class of 1959 use the same words to describe the material conditions of our youth: "We were poor, but we didn't know it." In fact, however, in the breadth and depth of the community support we enjoyed, we were rich, but we didn't know it.

But how about gender and race? To open our discussion of those critical issues, let's listen first to the stories of three more of my classmates.

Libby

Libby's father worked as a farmer and a skilled craftsman at Standard Products, while her mother was a full-time housewife. Both parents had left school in tenth grade. The family lived in a large hardscrabble farmhouse outside town. Libby, the sixth of ten children, often wore hand-me-downs. With many mouths to feed, money was tight. Libby never learned to bike or skate: "those things," she says, "were not in the family budget." On the other hand, with thirty acres, hardworking parents, and strong young arms, the family raised vegetables, kept chickens and cows, and was never destitute.

Libby's parents were good role models and nurtured an unusually cohesive family unit. The family always ate supper together, praying before the meal. Her parents insisted that the kids say "please" and "thank you," and stay at the table until everyone had finished. That spirit of togetherness has endured: Libby says that as septuagenarians she and her siblings still "circle the wagons and take care of each other" when adversity strikes.

Social life for this close-knit family revolved around school and church. Libby's parents were involved in the PTA and the kids' extracurricular pursuits, and each week the family sat together in church. Students from the church youth group occasionally took responsibility for adult services, and after Libby preached, she received cards from congregation members telling her what a good job she'd done. She was hired on the spot for her first job when a downtown store owner recognized her from the pulpit.

Academically, Libby's parents set high expectations for their children, and Libby lived up to them: she was an honors student in the college-prep track. Equally important, she made friends easily and could be counted on to get things done. "If you find enough people to help," she recalls her mother saying, "you can accomplish just about everything." A natural politician, Libby was elected president of the German Club, the Future Teachers of America, the Honor Society, and the Junior Class. Nearly 60 years later, Libby remembers high school as one of the most rewarding periods in her life. "I was in my element," she says.

When the time came for college, an English teacher helped Libby win an academic scholarship to the University of Toledo. Libby planned to become a teacher, but almost as soon as she arrived at college, she and her high school sweetheart found themselves overwhelmed by how much they missed each other. And so, like so many of her female peers, Libby dropped out of college, returned home, got married, started a family, and settled down as a civic-minded housewife.

When the marriage ended after 20 years, however, Libby was left on her own. Suddenly, she found her lack of a college degree and work experience, and society's pervasive gender bias, were holding her back. For the only time in her life, she became frightened about her future.

She proved resilient, however. Libby's decades in the social life of this small town had given her a wide reputation for dependability and congeniality. Beginning as a clerk in the lumberyard, she quickly became a writer for the local newspaper and then the head of a nonprofit group. Libby's father, always supportive, encouraged her to enter electoral politics, and within little more than a decade she had been elected to the county-wide office that she still holds, nearly thirty years later. As Libby's track record in PCHS demonstrated, her emotional intelligence and civic spirit were well matched for public life.

As she entered her 70s, Libby had become widely respected statewide as a public official and a quiet power in local party politics. Still feeling the call of service, she began training as a minister and now also serves as a part-time pastor in several area churches.

This farm girl with hand-me-down clothes and exceptional people skills was, beyond doubt, held back by the cultural norms of the 1950s, particularly after she left high school. Born a few decades later, Libby would probably have trained for a profession and might well have risen to the top of Ohio politics. Libby's gender was a serious impediment to upward mobility. But her modest class origins were not.

Libby's experience was typical of women in the class of 1959. Men and women in our cohort were equally likely to attend high school, equally involved in academic and nonacademic activities, equally qualified in terms of academics and extracurriculars, equally likely to aspire to college, and equally likely to attend college. Until we left PCHS, our class experienced no gender differences in opportunity for advancement.

Gender massively affected who *completed* college, however, and thus just like Libby, the women in my high school class were deprived of what would turn out to be the most important credential for upward mobility—a college degree. Equal numbers of men and women of the class of 1959 went off to college, but 88 percent of the men got a degree, compared to 22 percent of the women! In short, no gender winnowing at all until college, and then extreme gender winnowing.

Exactly as in Libby's story, that extraordinary difference was due almost entirely to women dropping out of college to get married. Women in my class were three times more likely to marry during college than men, and marriage was six times more of a barrier to finishing college for women than for men. Men were less likely to marry, and if they did, they stayed in school. Half a century later, my female classmates explain that whatever their academic or professional inclinations, they followed the social norms of the era—marriage, home, and a family. Of course, their world would change dramatically in the ensuing decades, as Libby recounts, but most of them (including Libby) say they don't regret leaving college to start a family.[10] On the other hand, self-imposed or not, the personal and social costs of having to choose between family and career were extraordinary.

The contrast with educational winnowing in twenty-first-century America could not be starker. Nowadays, women are *more* likely to graduate from college than men. On the other hand, 50 years ago family background had very little to do with who finished college, and nowadays it makes a huge difference, as we shall see in Chapter 4.

What about race, then and now?

Jesse and Cheryl

"Your then was not my then, and your now isn't even my now."

Even in a group that collectively experienced remarkable upward mobility in life, two of our 1959 classmates stand out—the only two black students, Jesse and Cheryl. Their experiences were in many respects parallel.

- Both arrived in Port Clinton as children of families fleeing physical violence in the South, part of what historians call "the Great Migration."[11] Jesse's family fled Mississippi after his sister was killed, while Cheryl's family were forced to leave Tennessee after an altercation between her father and a white man.
- Though none of their parents had a formal education beyond elementary school in the Jim Crow South, both Jesse and Cheryl benefited from tightly knit, hardworking, religiously observant, two-parent families.
- Both lived in poorer sections of town. Jesse's father loaded boxcars for a local manufacturer, while his mother worked as a seasonal maid in a nearby hotel. Cheryl's father worked in the gypsum mines and in a fruit-packing plant, while her mother cleaned houses. However, neither considered their families poor. "When we got to Ohio," Jesse recalls, "my dad always had a job, so we always had food and a place to live."
- Both excelled in high school. Jesse, perhaps the best all around athlete in school, was named MVP of the football team and was elected president of the student council. Cheryl was an elected officer of our senior class and ranked very near the top academically.
- Immediately after graduation, both went to good nearby colleges on partial scholarships, obtained graduate degrees, entered the field of public education, and recently retired after long and successful careers. That leap from elementary-school-educated laborers to graduate-school-educated professionals in a single generation is a remarkable testament to their native talent and fortitude, and also to the relative weakness of class barriers to advancement in that era.

This bare biographical recital might suggest that Jesse and Cheryl lived trouble-free childhoods in Port Clinton and achieved their successes in life relatively easily. But they were two black kids living in a predominantly white small town in the pre–Civil Rights 1950s, and inevitably race became the most salient part of their identities, imposed on them by their social environment.

When Jesse first arrived in Port Clinton, he was stared at by classmates who had never gone to school with a black person, just as he had never gone to school with a white person. But he soon began to make friends, especially after he turned out to be good at sports. The son of Jesse's father's white supervisor at work persuaded his father, a Little League coach, to invite Jesse to join their team. "I got on the Little League team," he says, "and started making friends. When you become an athlete, and you're good, and you help the team, people start liking you. I felt welcome on my team, but the other teams didn't like me being on the team."

A talented four-sport athlete, Jesse focused on athletics in high school. Aside from his parents, the most influential person in his life was his football coach—but not because he was particularly sympathetic or close to Jesse. "He was a figurehead," Jesse says, "whose values you wanted to emulate—the hard work, discipline, drive, work together, win. Given where he came from, this guy didn't particularly care to interact with me, but he liked me because of my skills. He could give me an assignment, and I would do it."

Jesse was even-tempered and avoided confrontations. "That's the way you had to be in Mississippi to survive," he says. "If I had responded to white people in Mississippi, I probably wouldn't be here talking with you." In high school, Jesse recalls, "I had such a good personality that they elected me president of the student council." He recalls with pleasure that the candidate he defeated was the author of this book.

During high school Jesse assumed he would not go to college, because his family had no money, but a football coach from a nearby college showed up at his home during his senior year to offer him a generous scholarship. When Jesse discussed the offer with his parents, his father told him, "Son, if you don't get an education, you'll have to work as hard as I work." His father agreed to loan him the $500 in costs not covered by the scholarship, and Jesse went off to college.

After college Jesse hoped to go to law school, but he didn't have the money. He hitchhiked to California, where he was only able to find a job as a utility worker in an electronics company. A friend suggested that he seek a teaching job and work for his teaching credentials. In the end he got a master's degree and spent more than four decades as a teacher, dean, vice principal, principal, and regional director in the Los Angeles education system.

Reflecting on his childhood in Port Clinton, Jesse notes that although he felt uncomfortable about entering a few business establishments, his experience in town was generally positive. "There were so many nice people in Port Clinton," he says, "some of the most pleasant, accepting, and tolerant I ever met. We would go fishing, and they would let us take out the boat."

His family lived in a poor, racially mixed neighborhood. "We had a lot of white neighbors who we walked to school with every day," he recalls, "and we were friends. We never had problems. Everybody was trying to live, and it wasn't about what color you were." A white teammate on the football team who knew that Jesse's family didn't have money took to inviting Jesse over to his house for lunch.

On the other hand, the backdrop to Jesse's good relations with his closest peers was racial prejudice and polarization in the wider society. "The hardest part was not being accepted as a human being. Some people would like you, but others would ostracize you when you never did anything to them."

Jesse says he lived between "two worlds—a black world and a white world. Black kids didn't like it because I got along so well with white kids, [and] when I was with the black kids, the white kids was mad. I'm out there trying to appease both sides and trying to get them to understand that we are all human beings. My white friends would want me to go to a white party in a nearby town, but other kids there, or their parents, might not be so tolerant. My friends were welcome, but I was not welcome, all because I was black."

Cheryl has a different story. Her strong role model was her mother, a savvy and competent woman who insisted that Cheryl not use the word *can't*. "From watching Mama," she says, "I grew up knowing I could do anything. Some things are more caught than taught."

Cheryl's family had first moved to a village near the gypsum mines, where they lived in company housing without indoor toilets. When that housing was closed as unhealthy, the family bought a lot in Port Clinton at the edge of a mostly black neighborhood and moved an older house onto it, though in response to neighbors' protests they were forced to shift the house on its foundation so that it would face away from the adjacent white neighborhood. Subsequently, one of her mother's house-cleaning clients arranged for them to buy a better house in a nearby white area, but the sale was aborted after somebody erected a cross in the yard.

Cheryl says she encountered little overt racism as she grew up. She doesn't recall hearing racial epithets. "You could go anywhere and no one was going to bother you," she says. She could ride her bike all over town and take books out from the public library on her own.

What did bother her was the lack of socializing across racial lines. "Port Clinton had a wonderful education system that prepared people [including her, she adds] for college, but 50 percent of high school is socializing," she says, "and that's what we missed. When I was at school with my white classmates, we talked, and after that it was over. I didn't go home with them; they didn't come home with me. So whatever I had to do, I did by myself." A white friend in elementary school once refused to acknowledge her when Cheryl encountered the girl and her mother on the street. "I was happy to see her," Cheryl recalls, "but she acted like she didn't even know who I was. I was really hurt by that."

Cheryl and her older sister wanted to join a girls' majorettes group, but they knew they couldn't, because the group traveled to places that wouldn't be so tolerant as Port Clinton. "We never tried to join," she says, "because there's some things you just know that you can't be part of." She and Jesse double-dated with a popular white couple, but they couldn't go to the local skating rink, because they expected to be refused admittance—a reasonable fear, a white classmate would much later confirm. "It wasn't like anybody stood outside and said you couldn't come," she says. "You just knew that you don't even try."

An avid and precocious reader, Cheryl got good grades, and wound up in college prep at PCHS, she says, "because my white friends were going to college." Her parents did not particularly encourage her to pursue higher education, however. "It wasn't on their radar screen. They didn't ever talk much about school." At one point, she wrote to a business school in Cleveland, but her mother shut that down, saying, "We don't have any money for you to go to college"—a response that stung.

A turning point came for Cheryl during her senior year in high school, when a white woman for whom she and her mother worked as housecleaners and who had come to respect Cheryl's work ethic learned about her outstanding academic record, and was shocked to discover that nobody at school had talked to her about college. This woman—the wife of the CEO of one of Port Clinton's largest firms—energetically took up Cheryl's case. "I wouldn't have gotten anywhere without that lady going to bat for me," she recalls, "putting on that fur coat of hers and marching down to the principal's office. Twice!" The reluctant principal finally agreed to take Cheryl to visit a nearby state university.

She was admitted to that university, got a partial academic scholarship, and worked summers for four years in menial jobs to cover the rest of the cost. She enjoyed college much more than high school, she says, because there were more blacks, so that "the social part that was missing in high school was available in college." Still, looking back at her time in college, Cheryl regrets that she didn't explore careers beyond teaching or social work. "Some kids say, 'I'm going to be a lawyer, because my dad's a lawyer,'" she says. "If I had had some exposure, I would not have been a teacher, because there are so many other things that you could do. But not in the 1960s."

Cheryl's brothers had more trouble navigating Port Clinton than she did. "If you didn't cross the line, which I never did," Cheryl says, "you could avoid trouble, but if you did cross the line, you would run into some problems." That happened to her younger brother, she recalls. In a history class on slavery, "he went ballistic and got in real trouble," she says, after his teacher said that black people don't have souls. The teacher had made the same remark when Cheryl had been in this class, but she had seethed in silence. For one of her older brothers, simply trying to buy a house upon his return from the Korean War amounted to crossing a line. "I don't care how much money you have," the most prominent real estate agent in town told him, "you're not going to buy a house here."

Her sense of not belonging still haunts Cheryl when she looks back on Port Clinton, even though she emphasizes that she was helped and befriended by individual white people in town. "*Invisible Man*, by Ralph Ellison, best describes my experience at PCHS," she says. "As an African American student in the graduating class of 1959, I participated in but never felt a part of the student body." America, for her, is a deeply racist system that did not—and still does not—allow her or her family to participate fully in economic and social life. For white kids, Port Clinton in the 1950s was a great place to grow up, but she tells me, amicably but accurately, "Your then was not my then, and your now isn't even my now."

There was much racism in Port Clinton in the 1950s, less violent and more subtle than in other parts of America at the time, but painful and deeply wounding nonetheless, as Jesse and Cheryl make clear. Port Clinton, like America, has made hard-won, halting progress toward racial equity in the last half century, and we must not sugarcoat race relations in the 1950s. On the other hand, as Jesse and Cheryl also emphasize, in Port Clinton of the 1950s humble class origins did not prevent them from using their talents and work ethic to achieve great upward mobility, any more than comparably modest family backgrounds prevented Don and Libby from gaining success in life.

In the half century since Libby, Cheryl, and Jesse came of age, the power of race, class, and gender to shape life chances in America has been substantially reconfigured.[12] Inequality in the United States increasingly operates through education—a scarce resource in our knowledge-based economy and a measure that is closely correlated with parental socioeconomic status. Gender inequality, very high in the 1950s, has fallen sharply, so that women are now more likely to graduate from college than men, and gender gaps in pay are shrinking, though still present.

Progress on racial difference has been less encouraging. To be sure, controlling for education, racial gaps in income are modest, and racial gaps in family structure and test scores, though high, are falling. On the other hand, racial gaps in schooling and involvement with the criminal justice system remain immense. Black parents in America remain disproportionately concentrated among the poor and less educated, so black children continue to be handicapped from the start. Whether their parents are rich or poor, black children live in poorer neighborhoods than white children at that income level, and black children experience less upward mobility and more downward mobility than their white counterparts who started at the same income level.[13]

So, gender and racial biases remain powerful, but as barriers to success they would represent less burdensome obstacles for Libby, Jesse, and Cheryl today than they did in the 1950s. By contrast, in modern America one barrier would loom much larger than it did back then: their class origins. That nationwide increase in class inequality—how the class-based opportunity gap among young people has widened in recent decades—is the subject of this book.

Class Disparities in Port Clinton in the Twenty-first Century

As my classmates and I marched down the steps after graduation in 1959, none of us had any inkling that change was coming. Almost half of us headed off to college, and those who stayed in town had every reason to expect they would get a job (if they were male), get married, and lead a comfortable life, just as their parents had done. For about a decade those expectations were happily met.

But just beyond the horizon an economic, social, and cultural whirlwind was gathering force nationally that would radically transform the life chances of our children and grandchildren. For many people, its effects would be gut-wrenching, for Port Clinton turns out to be a poster child for the changes that have swept across America in the last several decades.

The manufacturing foundation upon which Port Clinton's modest prosperity had been built in the 1950s and 1960s began to tremble in the 1970s. The big Standard Products factory at the east end of town had provided nearly 1,000 steady, well-paying blue-collar jobs in the 1950s, but in the 1970s the payroll was trimmed to less than half that, and after more than two decades of layoffs and givebacks, the plant gates on Maple Street finally closed in 1993. Twenty years later, only the hulking ruins of the plant remain, with EPA signs on the barbed wire fence warning of environmental hazard. But the closing of the Standard Products factory, the Army base, and the gypsum mines were merely the most visible symbols of the town's pervasive economic collapse.

Manufacturing employment in Ottawa County, of which Port Clinton is by far the largest town, plummeted from 55 percent of all jobs in 1965 to 25 percent in 1995 and kept falling.[14] Unemployment rose and fell with the national economic tides, but the local booms were never as good as the national booms, and the local hard times were much worse. As late as the 1970s, real wages locally were slightly above the national average, but during the next four decades they fell further and further behind, bottoming out at 25 percent below the national average. By 2012 the average worker in Ottawa County had not had a real raise for nearly half a century, and is now paid 16 percent less in inflation-adjusted dollars than his or her grandfather (or grandmother) was in the early 1970s.

The Port Clinton population, which had jumped 53 percent in the three decades prior to 1970, suddenly stagnated in the 1970s and 1980s, and then fell by 17 percent in the two decades after 1990. Commutes to jobs got longer and longer, as desperate local workers sought employment elsewhere. Most of the downtown shops of my youth stand empty and derelict, driven out of business partly by the Family Dollar and the Walmart on the outskirts of town, and partly by the gradually shrinking paychecks of Port Clinton consumers.

The social impact of those economic hammer blows was initially softened by the family and community bonds that had been so strong in my youth. But as successive graduating PCHS classes entered an ever-worsening local economy, the social norms that had undergirded Port Clinton's community in the 1950s and 1960s gradually eroded. Juvenile delinquency rates had been just about at the national average in the 1980s but then began to skyrocket, and by 2010 were three times the national average. Increasingly, any PCHS graduate who could escape did. Net departures from Ottawa County among 30-somethings more than doubled from the 1970s to the 2010s, from 13 percent to 27 percent.

Not surprisingly, given the economic stresses and strains, single-parent households in Ottawa County doubled from 1970 to 2010, from 10 percent to 20 percent, and the divorce rate quintupled. The incidence of unwed births in the county rose sharply between 1990 and 2010, from less than 20 percent to nearly 40 percent, outpacing a similar increase among whites nationwide and portending a continuing increase in single parenting in the years ahead. In Port Clinton itself, epicenter of the local economic collapse of the 1980s, the rate of unwed births absolutely exploded in little more than a decade. Between 1978 and 1990, the rate jumped from 9 percent (about half the race-adjusted national average) to about 40 percent (nearly twice the national average). And in the decades that followed, child poverty skyrocketed from less than 10 percent in 1999 to nearly 40 percent in 2013.[15]

But the story of Port Clinton over the last half century—like the history of America over these decades—is not simply about the collapse of the working class, because the same years have witnessed the birth of a new upper class.

Port Clinton occupies a lovely site on the shores of Lake Erie. In my youth, small summer cottages and modest resorts and fishing camps dotted those shores, interspersed among fruit orchards, and the shoreline felt available to us all. In the past two decades, however, while the traditional economy of Port Clinton was imploding, wealthy lawyers and doctors and businesspeople from Cleveland and Columbus and other major cities of the Midwest have discovered the charms of the lakeshore and the nearby offshore islands and have begun to take these areas over—for second homes, for retirement, and occasionally even for a better quality of life, at the expense of longer commutes to their well-paying jobs back in the city.

Joined by some fortunate local developers, the newcomers have built elaborate mansions and gated communities. These now line the shore almost uninterruptedly for 20 miles on either side of town. Luxury condos ring golf courses and lagoons filled with opulent yachts. One home along the shore in the upscale Catawba area includes an indoor theater and an athletic court. Nowadays you can read ads in adjacent columns of the real estate pages of the *Port Clinton News-Herald* for near-million-dollar mansions and dilapidated double-wides, and it is possible to walk in less than ten minutes from wealthy estates on the shoreline to impoverished trailer parks inland.

The distribution of income in Ottawa County, once among the most egalitarian in the country, began to skew over these decades: the number of residents at both the top and the bottom increased, and the middle slumped. In 2010, the median household income in the Catawba Island area was more than twice the median household income in the adjoining census tract. Moreover, the pace and concentration of the transformation has been stunning, as the maps in Figures 1.1 and 1.2 reveal. Census tracts with relatively more poor kids are darker, so the maps show that Port Clinton itself (especially outside the immediate downtown) had many more poor kids in 2008–2012 than two decades earlier, but the Catawba residential area along the shore experienced virtually no such change over those decades. In 2011 in the aftermath of the Great Recession, if you drove east from downtown Port Clinton along East Harbor Road, the census tract to your left along the Catawba lakeshore had a child poverty rate of 1 percent, whereas the census tract on the other side of the road had a child poverty rate of 51 percent.

Let's explore what life is like today for two white kids who live on different sides of that road.

Figure 1.1: Child poverty in Port Clinton, Ohio (1990)

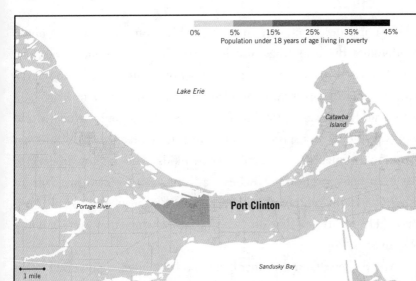

Source: Census 1990 data as compiled by Social Explorer, accessed through Harvard University Library.

Figure 1.2: Child poverty in Port Clinton, Ohio (2008–2012)

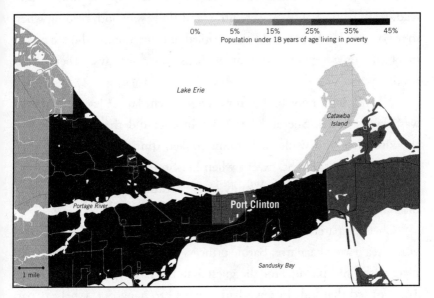

Source: ACS 2008–2012 (5-year estimates) data as compiled by Social Explorer, accessed through Harvard University Library.

Chelsea

Chelsea and her family live in a large white home with a wide porch overlooking the lake. They also have an expensive second home in a nearby small town, where Chelsea and her older brother went to school. Chelsea's mother, Wendy, comes from an affluent family in Michigan, where her father was a prominent lawyer. She has a graduate degree and works part-time as a special educator in private practice. She values her flexible schedule, because raising her two kids (who are now in college) has been her top priority. Chelsea's father, Dick, is a sales manager for a major national corporation, and he travels a great deal for his business. "He wasn't real big on being a father when they were young," Wendy says.

Wendy herself, on the other hand, has been intensely involved in her children's lives growing up. "I probably pushed my kids a lot more than my parents ever pushed us," she says. "I was a real grade hound [with my kids]. I really pushed them through high school, and then I just continued. I read to them [as infants]. That's the biggest thing—read, read, read, read when they were little, and they were both reading when they got into kindergarten." She is critical of other moms who are not so involved. "I see so many kids that are just so lost," she says. "Their mothers don't care."

When Chelsea got home from school each day, at least one parent was always home. She and her older brother did their homework at the kitchen island while their mom cooked dinner. The whole family ate together every night, except when her brother was playing football. "Family dinner is critical," Wendy says, "because the kids learn how to discourse with other people."

Chelsea's parents threw fancy themed birthday parties for her every year—tea party at age five, Barbie princess at six, Academy Awards (complete with limo pickups for the guests) at 11, Las Vegas casino night at 16. Worried that kids in town had nowhere to hang out, Chelsea's parents installed an elaborate 1950s-style diner in their basement. "I'm the cook at the 1950s diner," Wendy says, "which was good, because all their friends would talk to me about stuff, and I knew where they were."

Wendy is proud of standing up for her kids at school. When a seventh-grade teacher claimed that Chelsea's older brother had not completed an assignment, she proved to the teacher that he had—and when the teacher then refused to change his grade to reflect that, she appealed first to the principal and then to the school board. The school board changed the grade and moved the teacher to a different position. Another case in point: Chelsea worked hard on her high school yearbook for four years, and served as its editor-in-chief during her senior year, anticipating that she would get the annual yearbook-based college scholarship. When the teacher in charge declined to nominate Chelsea for the scholarship, her mother went to the principal. He knew immediately why she was there. "You know me," she said. "I will go to the school board. . . . Just tell the teacher to write the [fellowship] check, and let's get this over with." The check arrived next day.

Chelsea describes herself as "the most active person" in her high school—student body president, yearbook editor, National Honor Society, president of the book club, "and a whole bunch of other stuff." Her parents pitched in for school events, even more than other parents. They helped build a giant King Kong float out of chicken wire, because the kids did not know how. When Chelsea was in charge of the prom, and other students failed to show up to construct the scenery, Wendy was there, hot-gluing in the middle of the night.

Although the family is comfortable financially, Wendy doesn't see herself or her affluent peers as "old money" gentry. "Most parents around here are Midwest parents who work for their money," she says. "It's not like Beverly Hills and the Hamptons." She encourages her kids to have part-time and summer jobs. "You have to work if you want to get rich," she insists. She's skeptical about special funding for educating poorer kids. "If my kids are going to be successful, I don't think they should have to pay other people who are sitting around doing nothing for their success."

Asked about times of stress in her life, Chelsea responds, "There's never really been any financial problem." When a friend of her family committed suicide, it was emotionally very stressful, but she was able to talk with her mom and dad about her feelings, and describes them as good role models. "The people I surround myself with have always tried to help me and push me in the right direction," she says. "I am content with what I'm doing in my life."

Chelsea always knew that she'd go to college. Her parents encouraged good grades by promising her and her brother to pay the full ticket for college if they graduated in the top 10 percent of their high school classes. Both did, and both now attend the same Big Ten university. Chelsea is aiming for law school, following in the footsteps of her grandfather.

David

David was a scrawny 18-year-old in jeans and a baseball cap when we first encountered him in a Port Clinton park in 2012. His father had dropped out of high school and tried in vain to make a living as a truck driver, like his own father, but as an adult has been employed only episodically, in odd jobs like landscaping. David apologizes for not being able to tell us more about his father. "He's in prison," he explains, "and I can't ask him." David's parents separated when David was very little, and his mother moved out, so he can't tell us much about her, either, except to say that she lives in the Port Clinton area. "All her boyfriends have been nuts," he says. "I never really got to see my mom that much. She was never there."

David has bounced around a lot. He has grown up mostly in his father's custody, though his father has been in and out of prison. A steady stream of women flowed through his dad's life during David's childhood, often floating on drugs. David and his dad would live with David's paternal grandmother on the impoverished side of East Harbor Road for a while; then his dad would try to make it on his own, and another woman would come into his life. But eventually either his dad couldn't pay the rent, or he would start "partying" again, and they'd end up back with the grandmother. David has nine half-siblings, but no fixed address.

When David was ten or 11, his dad hooked up for several years with a woman whom David called his stepmother, although she was never actually married to his father. The stepmother, he says, was "crazy . . . drinking, pills, drugs," and now lives with another guy, with whom she has several other children. When she left, David says, his dad "went off the deep end" with drugs and women. The way adults moved in and out of his life without worrying about what happened to the kids left David feeling as though "nobody gave a shit" about him and his half-siblings.

David's father was recently sent to prison for a string of robberies. David can't visit him in prison, because he himself is on probation. He feels close to his father, the only adult who has been around all his life, but he worries that his father is unstable. "Sometimes he's mad at me," he says, "sometimes he's not. It's just if I catch him on a good day."

David's family life was obviously chaotic. He dealt with the stress by escaping with friends, staying away from home, and smoking marijuana. "I missed having a home," he says. "I know how close I want my own family to be, because of how close I wasn't." He adds, "I never really had around-the-table family dinners at all, so I never got to miss it."

Because of his dad's itinerant existence, David went to seven different elementary schools. School, he recalls, was always a problem. "I just let grades float until the end of the semester," he says, "and I passed every year. I've never been held back. In middle school I got into a fight with another kid, so they kicked me out and sent me to 'behavior school,'" which he hated. Finally, with assistance from a local teacher, in 12th grade he transferred to a "career-based intervention class" at a nearby high school, where he earned a diploma, mostly because he got school credit for working at Big Bopper's Diner. Immediately after graduation, the Big Bopper fired him.

David himself got into lots of trouble, in part because he started hanging out with the wrong kids. At age 13 he broke into a series of stores and was put under house arrest for five months. He could attend school, but otherwise he had to stay at home alone, where all he did was play video games. "It's all I had to do," he says. Out on probation, he got into further trouble by getting drunk and failing a drug test, which sent him back to juvie. He has essentially no support network. It was his pre-jail friends who got him in trouble in the first place, and the ones he met behind bars were no better. "If you make friends in jail," he says, "you usually go back to jail with them friends."

Since leaving school, David has had various temporary jobs—at fast food restaurants, in a plastics factory, and doing landscaping. He has a hard time getting a job because of his juvenile record, and he can't afford the "couple hundred dollars" in legal fees that it would cost to get the record expunged. He worked hard to qualify as foreman on the land-scaping job, but then lost that opportunity because he had points on his license for speeding.

Despite his troubles in school, David has clear educational aspira-tions. "I really want to get a higher education," he says. "I need one. It's hard to get a job without one anymore." But he has no idea how to get there. He can recall no helpful guidance counselor or teacher from his school years, and his parents are obviously useless. He notes bitterly that nobody at all in Port Clinton was willing to offer him help when he was younger. People in town knew what was going on in his family, he says, but no one cared enough to reach out to him. The fact that his father and mother "had a bad name in town," he believes, meant that towns-people were disinclined to treat him with any sympathy. In the most fundamental sense, David has had to fend for himself his entire life.

Unexpectedly, given his life experience, David feels great responsibil-ity for his diverse brood of younger half-siblings, because no competent adult is caring for them. "I'm the only one that can raise them," he says. David's sense of obligation to his half-siblings seems deep and sincere. "It's like everybody is looking at me to hold it together," he says, "and I feel a lot of pressure because of that." In fact, when we first met him in the park in 2012, he was affectionately watching over an eight-year-old half-brother. Earlier that day, he had been the only family member to attend the school Olympics in which his little brother had competed. In a conversation two years later, David reported that that same little brother was now himself caring for a still younger baby brother, born to the drug-addled stepmother.

In 2012 David's girlfriend became pregnant. "It wasn't planned," he says. "It just kind of happened." At that point, he was hoping that the birth of his child would bring his life together, but he admitted he wasn't sure if he could trust his girlfriend. Sadly, his instincts proved accurate: two years later she was living with a new partner (a drug addict, like her), and David shares custody of their daughter. He lives paycheck to paycheck, but says his daughter has provided him with a sense of purpose. "I love being a dad," he says. "She just looks at me like I'm the Almighty."

In 2012, we asked David if he ever felt like just giving up. "Yeah," he replied, "Sometimes I get that feeling that there's no point in it, but I bounce out of it. It kind of gets me down at times, but I try not to put my mind to it that much." By 2014, distraught by his girlfriend's betrayal and his dead-end job, he posted an update on Facebook. "I always end up at the losing end," he wrote. "I just want to feel whole again. I'll never get ahead! I've been trying so hard at everything in my life and still get no credit at all. Done . . . I'm FUCKING DONE!"

Comparing Port Clinton kids in the 1950s with Port Clinton kids today, the opportunity gap has widened dramatically, partly because affluent kids now enjoy more advantages than affluent kids then, but mostly because poor kids now are in much worse shape than their counterparts then. Frank's parents were relaxed about his indifferent performance at school, in contrast to Wendy's intensive parenting, from her "read, read, read, read" regime to her midnight hot-gluing of prom props. Frank's family encouraged him to hang out with kids from modest backgrounds, whereas Wendy hired limos for fancy birthday parties. Chelsea's neighborhood is exclusive, whereas Frank's wasn't. Chelsea dominated her high school's activities, whereas Frank definitely didn't. Chelsea and her mom are proud of Wendy's interventions at school on her kids' behalf, while Frank is appalled at the thought.

Compared to working-class kids in 1959, their counterparts today, like David, lead troubled, isolated, hopeless lives. Don, Libby, Cheryl, and Jesse all had stable, two-parent, loving families. David hardly has a family at all. Don's dad, despite working two jobs, came to every one of Don's games, and Libby's and Cheryl's moms were role models, while David's dad, mom, and stepmom are, at best, object lessons of failed lives. Libby learned manners, values, and loyalty at regular family dinners, but David has no idea what a family dinner would be like. All four of the 1950s working-class kids were encouraged by family or school or both to head for college, whereas David "floated" with virtually no guidance from anyone. Teachers, coaches, church elders, and even fur-clad matrons reached out to help Libby and Jesse and Cheryl and Don, while townspeople left David to fend for himself. Everyone in my parents' generation (from pool shark to pastor) thought of Don and Libby as "our kids," but surprisingly few adults in Port Clinton today are even aware of David's existence, and even fewer would think of him as one of "our kids."[16]

Port Clinton is just one small town among many, of course—but the rest of this book will show that its trajectory during the past five decades, and the divergent destinies of its children, are not unique. Port Clinton is *not* simply a Rust Belt story, for example, although it is that. Subsequent chapters will trace similar patterns in communities all over the country, from Bend, Oregon, to Atlanta, and from Orange County, California, to Philadelphia. But first, zooming out from our close focus on Port Clinton to a wide-angle view of contemporary American society, let's examine the principle of equality and what it actually means for Americans today.

Inequality in America: The Broader Picture

Contemporary discussion of inequality in America often conflates two related but distinct issues:

- **Equality of income and wealth.** The distribution of income and wealth among adults in today's America—framed by the Occupy movement as the 1 percent versus the 99 percent—has generated much partisan debate during the past several years. Historically, however, most Americans have not been greatly worried about that sort of inequality: we tend not to begrudge others their success or care how high the socioeconomic ladder is, assuming that everyone has an equal chance to climb it, given equal merit and energy.

- **Equality of opportunity and social mobility.** The prospects for the next generation—that is, whether young people from different backgrounds are, in fact, getting onto the ladder at about the same place and, given equal merit and energy, are equally likely to scale it—pose an altogether more momentous problem in our national culture. Beginning with the "all men are created equal" premise of our national independence, Americans of all parties have historically been very concerned about this issue.

These two types of equality are obviously related, because the distribution of income in one generation may affect the distribution of opportunity in the next generation—but they are not the same thing. The distribution of income and wealth among today's parents forms a crucial backdrop to our story, just as it does to the contrasting lives of Chelsea and David. However, this book will focus primarily on the distribution of opportunity among today's kids and will seek to answer this question: *Do youth today coming from different social and economic backgrounds in fact have roughly equal life chances, and has that changed in recent decades?*[17] The difference in starting points between Frank and Don in the 1950s, for example, seems dwarfed by the difference between Chelsea and David in the 2010s, but how far can we generalize those cases? I begin with an overview of aspiration, myth, and reality regarding inequality in both senses throughout the long course of American history.

Americans are today divided about how much (if at all) income and wealth should be redistributed, Robin Hood–like, from today's affluent to today's poor. More than two thirds of us (concentrated among Democrats, minorities, and the poor, but including majorities of people of all political persuasions and walks of life) favor a more equal distribution than obtains today. While large majorities favor pragmatic steps to limit inequality of condition, we are also philosophical conservatives, suspicious of the ability of government to redress inequality and convinced that responsibility for an individual's well-being rests chiefly with him or her.[18]

On the other hand, we are less divided about the desirability of upward mobility without regard to family origins. About 95 percent of us endorse the principle that "everyone in America should have equal opportunity to get ahead," a broad consensus that has hardly wavered since opinion surveys began more than a half century ago.[19] (The consensus is a bit shakier when the question is whether our society should do "whatever is necessary to make sure that everyone has an equal opportunity to succeed." Nine in ten Americans agree, but only 48 percent of the top quintile in terms of socioeconomic status agree *strongly*, as compared to 70 percent of the bottom quintile.[20]) About 90 percent of Americans of all political persuasions say they support more spending on public education to try to ensure that everyone gets a fair start in life. And if forced to choose, Americans at all income levels say by nearly three to one that it is "more important for this country . . . to ensure everyone has a fair chance of improving their economic standing [than] to reduce inequality in America."[21] As the former Federal Reserve chair Ben Bernanke has phrased it, "A bedrock American principle is the idea that all individuals should have the opportunity to succeed on the basis of their own effort, skill, and ingenuity."[22]

The roots of this primal commitment to equality of opportunity are deep and diverse. Ben Franklin's *Autobiography* laid down the quintessential "rags-to-riches" narrative of colonial America. The absence of a pre-existing feudal social structure—an important exception must be made for the antebellum slave-owning aristocracy—helped create and sustain an egalitarian political structure, marked especially by the rise of populist Jacksonian democracy of the 1830s. The vastness of the American frontier, with its virtually free land—free at least to the new settlers—made the ideal of upward mobility seem attainable. As Frederick Jackson Turner, the renowned historian of the frontier, put it, "The West was another name for opportunity."[23] Recurring spurts of evangelical religious fervor in America's Great Awakenings (like the abolitionist Second Great Awakening of the 1830s and the "Social Gospel" of the Progressive Era) provided morally freighted reinforcement for extension of the foundational national pledge that God had created each of us equal.

America's bounteous economy, finally, encouraged the hope that upward mobility was possible for all. The same 1950s boom that sustained Port Clinton's egalitarian culture led the historian David Potter in his 1954 best-seller *People of Plenty* to claim that American affluence had allowed more equality of opportunity "than any previous society or previous era of history had ever witnessed."[24] Even if the popular belief in equality of opportunity was exaggerated, he added, it had led Americans to believe that if we can't make it on our own, it's our own fault. Equality in America, Potter wrote, had come to mean not equality of outcome, as in Europe, but "in a major sense, parity in competition." That transatlantic contrast in outlook persists undiminished today.[25] Compared to our European peers, Americans remain more skeptical about redistributive policies and more emphatic about social mobility.

Although "the American Dream" is a surprisingly recent coinage (the term was first used in its modern sense in the 1930s), the cultural trope of Horatio Alger and the prospect of upward social mobility have very deep roots in our psyche. In 1843, *McGuffey's Reader*—in effect, our first national school textbook—told students, "The road to wealth, to honor, to usefulness, and happiness, is open to all, and all who will, may enter upon it with the almost certain prospect of success."[26]

Throughout the half century after World War II, roughly two thirds of Americans from all walks of life told pollsters that as a matter of fact, anyone who worked hard could get ahead.[27] In the twenty-first century, however, surveys have revealed a creeping pessimism about the chances for upward mobility for the next generation, and about whether hard work would really be rewarded. Nevertheless, on balance most Americans have believed (at least until recently) that equality of opportunity characterizes our society—that the American Dream, in other words, endures.[28]

Toward Two Americas?

So far we've surveyed Americans' beliefs about equality and mobility. But what about the facts? When it comes to class differences in America, what have been the trends, now and in the past?

Graphically, the ups and downs of inequality in America during the twentieth century trace a gigantic U, beginning and ending in two Gilded Ages, but with a long period of relative equality around mid-century. The economic historians Claudia Golden and Lawrence Katz have described the pattern as "a tale of two half-centuries."[29] As the century opened, economic inequality was high, but from about 1910 to about 1970 the distribution of income gradually became more equal. Two world wars and the Great Depression contributed to this flattening of the economic pyramid, but the equalizing trend continued during the three postwar decades (the egalitarian period during which my classmates and I grew up in Port Clinton). "From 1945 to 1975," the sociologist Douglas Massey has written, summarizing that era, "under structural arrangements implemented during the New Deal, poverty rates steadily fell, median incomes consistently rose, and inequality progressively dropped, as a rising economic tide lifted all boats."[30] In fact, during this period the dinghies actually rose slightly faster than the yachts, as income for the top fifth grew about 2.5 percent annually, while for the bottom fifth the rise was about 3 percent a year.

In the early 1970s, however, that decades-long equalizing trend began to reverse, slowly at first but then with accelerating harshness. Initially, the growing division appeared in the lower reaches of the income hierarchy, as the bottom dropped away from the middle and top, but in the 1980s the top began to pull away from everyone else, and in the first decades of the twenty-first century the very top began to pull away even from the top.[31] Even *within* each major racial/ethnic group, income inequality rose at the same substantial rate between 1967 and 2011, as richer whites, blacks, and Latinos pulled away from their poorer co-ethnics.[32] In the quarter century between 1979 and 2005, average after-tax income (adjusted for inflation) grew by $900 a year for the bottom fifth of American households, by $8,700 a year for the middle fifth, and by $745,000 a year for the top 1 percent of households.[33]

Income trends were especially divergent among men with different levels of education. "Between 1980 and 2012," reports economist David Autor, "real hourly earnings of full-time college-educated U.S. males rose anywhere from 20% to 56%, with the greatest gains among those with a postbaccalaureate degree. During the same period, real earnings of males with high school or lower educational levels declined substantially, falling by 22% among high school dropouts and 11% among high school graduates."[34]

Income inequality was momentarily reduced by the immediate impact of the Great Recession in 2008–2009, but in the ensuing years the trend toward increasing affluence at the very top, coupled with stagnation or worse for the rest of the society, resumed and even accelerated. From 2009 to 2012, the real incomes of the top 1 percent of American families rose 31 percent, while the real incomes of the bottom 99 percent barely budged (up less than half a percentage point).[35]

The causes of this breathtaking increase in inequality during the past three to four decades are much debated—globalization, technological change and the consequent increase in "returns to education," de-unionization, superstar compensation, changing social norms, and post-Reagan public policy—though the basic shift toward inequality occurred under both Republican and Democratic administrations. No serious observer doubts that the past 40 years have witnessed an almost unprecedented growth in inequality in America.[36] Ordinary Americans, too, have gradually become aware of rising inequality, though they underestimate the extent of the shift.

The growth of income inequality—especially the gap between the ultrarich and everyone else—has been widely discussed in the public square in recent years. This growing gap between rich and poor is reflected in many other measures of well-being, including wealth, happiness, and even life expectancy.

Since the 1980s, mortality has declined among college-educated white women but has actually increased among white women with less than a high school degree, largely because of growing differences in economic well-being. The sociologist Michael Hout reports that "the affluent were about as happy in 2012 as they were in the 1970s, but the poor were much less happy. Consequently, the gross income gap [in happiness] was about 30 percent bigger in 2012 than it was in the 1970s."[37]

Growing inequality in accumulated wealth is particularly marked, as shown in Figure 1.3. Even taking into account the losses of the Great Recession, the net worth of college-educated American households with children rose by 47 percent between 1989 and 2013, whereas among high school–educated households net worth actually *fell* by 17 percent during that quarter century. Parental wealth is especially important for social mobility, because it can provide informal insurance that allows kids to take more risks in search of more reward. For example, a child who can borrow living expenses from Mom and Dad can be more selective when looking for a job, whereas a child without a parent-provided life preserver has to grab the first job that comes along. Similarly, family wealth allows for big investments in college without requiring massive student debt that then cramps the choices open to a new graduate.

Figure 1.3: Growing wealth gap

By parental education, in constant (2013) dollars, 1989–2013

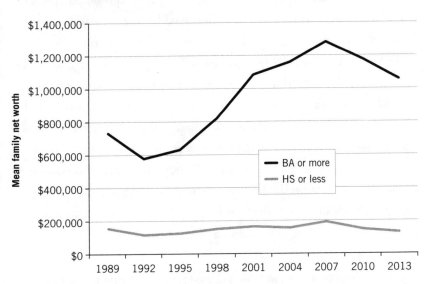

Source: Survey of Consumer Finance, Federal Reserve Bank, http://www.federalreserve.gov/econresdata /scf/scfindex.htm.

Less discussed than the growing gaps between affluent and impoverished Americans, but equally insidious, is the fact that the ballooning economic gap has been accompanied by growing de facto segregation of Americans along class lines.[38]

In Port Clinton of the 1950s, affluent kids and poor kids lived near one another, went to school together, played and prayed together, and even dated one another. These kids received different economic and cultural endowments from their parents, of course, because Port Clinton was not a commune. However, kids (and their parents) had acquaintances and even close friends across class lines. Nowadays, by contrast, fewer and fewer of us, in Port Clinton and elsewhere, are exposed in our daily lives to people outside our own socioeconomic niche. Three different dimensions of class segregation show just how pervasively American society has become divided along class lines during the past forty years.

NEIGHBORHOOD SEPARATION

Neighborhoods are important sites of growing class segregation. The sorting of households into distinct neighborhoods by income was significantly higher in 2010 than it was in 1970.[39] More and more families live either in uniformly affluent neighborhoods or in uniformly poor neighborhoods, as figure 1.4 shows, and fewer and fewer of us live in mixed or moderate income neighborhoods. This geographic polarization was made possible by the growth of suburbs and the expansion of the highway system, which allowed high-income families to move away from low-income neighbors in search of large lots, privacy, parks, and shopping malls. This class-based residential polarization has been accelerated by the growth of the income gap and (ironically) by changes in housing legislation that enabled more affluent minority families to move to the suburbs.

Figure 1.4: Families in high-, middle-, and low-income neighborhoods
Metropolitan areas with population <500,000, 1970–2009

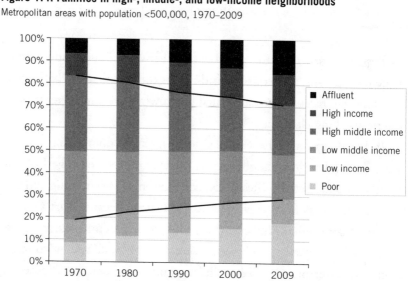

Source: Census Bureau data, as analyzed by Kendra Bischoff and Sean F. Reardon, "Residential Segregation by Income, 1970–2009," in *Diversity and Disparities: America Enters a New Century*, ed. John Logan (New York: Russell Sage Foundation, 2014).

So while race-based segregation has been slowly declining, class-based segregation has been increasing. In fact, the trend toward class segregation has been true *within* each major racial group, so affluent and impoverished black (or Latino) families are less likely to be neighbors now than they were 40 years ago.

Earlier in this chapter we mapped the increase of class-based segregation on either side of East Harbor Road in Port Clinton, and in subsequent chapters we shall see how exactly this same process—a kind of incipient class apartheid—has worked itself out in towns and cities across the country. It is a process that has powerful consequences for whom our children encounter in their daily lives—both in school and out, in terms of both peers and potential mentors, as we shall see in Chapter 5. Whether we are rich or poor, our kids are increasingly growing up with kids like them who have parents like us.

EDUCATIONAL SEGREGATION

Since the 1970s, increasing class-based residential segregation has been translated into de facto class-based school segregation. Schoolchildren from the top half of the income distribution increasingly attend private schools or live in better school districts. Even when poor and wealthier schoolchildren live in the same school district, they are increasingly likely to attend separate and unequal schools. And often within a single school, AP and other advanced courses tend to separate privileged from less privileged kids. Later on, kids from different class backgrounds are increasingly sorted into different colleges: for example, by 2004, kids from the top quarter of families in education and income were 17 times more likely to attend a highly selective college than kids in the bottom quarter.[40]

Once again, this educational segregation has consequences far beyond the classroom, in terms of friendship networks and other social resources. As we have already seen, in Port Clinton in the 1950s kids from all sorts of backgrounds attended the same classes, played on the same teams, and went to the same parties. Today, however, even though Chelsea and David live only a few miles apart, they are unlikely even to encounter each other. Educational segregation is so important that we will devote an entire chapter to it (Chapter 4).

MARRIAGE

People mostly tend to marry others like themselves, but the degree of intermarriage across various social boundaries changes over time. For two reasons, intermarriage rates are useful indicators of how strict boundaries are in social life. First, we mostly marry people that we've met. Therefore, the more permeable a boundary (for example, in neighborhoods or schools), the more likely that young people will meet mates on the other side. Second, a high intermarriage rate implies that interaction across that boundary will be more frequent in the future, at least within extended families. In short, high intermarriage rates today imply low social segregation yesterday, and still lower social segregation tomorrow. In recent decades, for example, increasing religious and racial intermarriage has reflected and reinforced the gradual lowering of religious and racial barriers throughout American society. What about intermarriage across class boundaries?

Trends in marriage across class lines throughout the twentieth century turn out to mirror almost precisely the Great U in income inequality.[41] During the first half of the century, marrying outside one's own social class became steadily more common. After mid-century, however, that trend reversed itself. In the second half of the century Americans increasingly married people with educational backgrounds similar to their own, with the most educated especially likely to marry one another.[42] In other words, as the gap between rich and poor narrowed in the first half of the twentieth century, more and more Romeos and Juliets jumped across, but as the economic and educational gulf has widened in more recent decades, fewer and fewer people are finding partners on the other side.

The decline in cross-class marriages has implications for the composition of extended families. Two generations ago, extended family gatherings might bring together small businessmen and manual workers, professors and construction workers, but the ripple effects of increasing endogamy (marrying within your own social class) ensure that one's kin networks today—and even more, tomorrow—are likely to be from the same class background as oneself, further reducing cross-class bridging. Fewer and fewer working-class kids will have rich uncles or well-educated aunts to help them ascend the ladder.

Ultimately, growing class segregation across neighborhoods, schools, marriages (and probably also civic associations, workplaces, and friendship circles[43]) means that rich Americans and poor Americans are living, learning, and raising children in increasingly separate and unequal worlds, removing the stepping-stones to upward mobility—college-going classmates or cousins or middle-class neighbors, who might take a working-class kid from the neighborhood under their wing. Moreover, class segregation means that members of the upper middle class are less likely to have firsthand knowledge of the lives of poor kids and thus are unable even to recognize the growing opportunity gap. One reason, in fact, for including life stories of young people in this book is to help reduce that perception gap—to help us all to see, in the words of Jacob Riis, a social reformer during the previous Gilded Age, "how the other half lives." [44]

EQUALITY OF OPPORTUNITY

To what extent has the American Dream of a fair start for everyone *in fact* been characteristic of American history? The answer to that question turns out to depend in part on the standard of comparison—the myth of perfectly open upward mobility, the reality of our own past, or the reality of similar countries. It also depends on the important distinction between *absolute* and *relative* upward mobility.

In a growing economy with rising educational levels, everyone could in principle do better than his or her parents in absolute terms, even if the relative standing of every family remained unchanged—if the children of college graduates got postgraduate degrees, for example, while the children of the illiterate graduated from elementary school. In such a world, a rising tide would lift all boats, even if no one ever moved from a dinghy to a yacht, so that relative mobility was zero.

Conversely, even if the economy as a whole were stagnant, in a system of perfect social mobility the more capable and ambitious children of lower-class parents on their way up would pass the ne'er-do-well scions of upper-class families on their way down. Such a world would have equality of opportunity, because where people ended up would not depend on where they started in life. So a society might have low absolute mobility but high relative mobility, or the reverse.

Over the grand sweep of history, relative mobility accounts for only a small portion of total mobility experienced by individuals across generations, whereas absolute (or structural) mobility accounts for most of it. During periods of high growth in income and education, or thinning out of manual occupations, many people from lower-class backgrounds will experience absolute upward mobility, regardless of changes in relative mobility.

In principle, of course, a society might have both high absolute mobility (a rising tide lifting all boats) and high relative mobility (dinghies doing even better than yachts). My classmates in Port Clinton in the fortunate 1950s and 1960s benefited from exactly that happy state of affairs, and scholars have identified the same pattern nationwide.[45] The underlying issue raised in this book is whether, by contrast, American youth now have the *worst* of both worlds—low absolute mobility and low relative mobility.

Most empirical studies of social mobility in America prior to the twentieth century focused on absolute upward mobility among white men, and used the national myth of perfect mobility as the standard of comparison. In other words, they asked how many upper-class men were strictly self-made—and the answer is "relatively few." In that sense, these earlier studies ended up debunking the national myth, because mobility seems never to have been as great as the rags-to-riches narrative implies.

On the other hand, careful statistical comparisons by historians suggest that economic growth and successive expansions of the educational system did allow significant absolute mobility, perhaps especially in the first half of the twentieth century.[46] In the decades after World War II, as I have said, absolute mobility (and to some extent even relative mobility) seems to have been unusually high, because economic growth and educational expansion allowed exceptional upward mobility.

The evidence now suggests, however, that absolute mobility has stalled since the 1970s, because both economic and educational advances have stalled.[47] Much recent public commentary asserts that relative social mobility in America has fallen in the past quarter century as well, though hard evidence for those claims is weaker.[48] In other words, Americans believe that income inequality has increased in recent years, and they are right about that. They aren't so sure that equality of opportunity (or upward mobility) has changed much, and so far they seem to be right about that, too, even if they overestimate the odds of moving from the bottom to the top. But—and this "but" is crucial for this book—*conventional indicators of social mobility are invariably three or four decades out of date.*

The conventional method of assessing mobility compares a son's (or daughter's) income or education *when they are in their 30s and 40s* with their parents' income or education *when their parents were in their 30s and 40s.* The rationale is that not until a given generation reaches early middle age do we know with confidence where they will end up on the socioeconomic ladder. However, that approach necessarily means that conventional measures of mobility are a "lagging indicator" of social change, since even the most recent conventional measures refer to a generation that was born 30 to 40 years ago. In assessing social mobility, therefore, policymakers and citizens who rely on the conventional method are like astronomers studying the stars: they have to contend with an information time lag, and can only see what has happened years or eons ago, not what is happening right now. David and Chelsea will not show up in statistical assessments of social mobility until the 2020s. Their childhood and adolescent experiences, compared with the experiences of my 1959 classmates, suggest that we've been veering further away from equality of opportunity for several decades—but if so, we won't detect that slowing of upward mobility in our conventional measurements for another decade or so. Similarly, if Alpha Centauri, our nearest stellar neighbor, exploded last night, we won't know about it for more than four years.

This book adopts a different approach, eschewing the conventional "rearview mirror" method and examining directly what has been happening to kids in the past three decades—the families into which they've been born, the parenting and schooling they've received, the communities within which they've been raised.[49] We know that those experiences will inevitably have a powerful effect on how well they do in life. Whatever changes we can detect in these areas will foreshadow changes in social mobility—which, distressingly, according to the evidence I describe in this book, seems poised to plunge in the years ahead, shattering the American Dream.

Conceptual Note

If this book were a sociological text, we would need to distinguish among different conceptions and indicators of social class, such as occupation, wealth, income, education, culture, social status, and self-identity, and we would have to worry about inconsistencies among these measures—a well-educated but poorly paid librarian, for example, or a barely literate billionaire.[50] For our purposes, however, and for the population as a whole, these various indicators are closely inter-correlated, and I know of no instances in which the core generalizations in this book depend entirely on the specific choice of indicator.

Education, and especially higher education, has become increasingly important for good jobs and higher incomes; in the language of economics, the "returns to education" have increased. While education and income are thus becoming more closely correlated, I generally prefer education as our indicator of social class, partly because income measures in most surveys are much "noisier" (error-prone or entirely missing) and because when both are available, education is typically the more powerful predictor of child-related outcomes. Here I follow the example of sociologist Douglas Massey, who operationalizes social class by "education, the most important resource in today's knowledge-based economy."[51] Another practical reason is that few of the long-term studies on which we are forced to rely have good measures of family income.

For consistency and simplicity, in this book I typically report class breakdowns either by education alone (college degree or more versus high school or less) or by a composite measure of socioeconomic status (based on income, education, and occupational status), depending on what indicators are available for a particular topic or survey. Roughly speaking, the educational attainment of Americans can be divided in thirds, with the top third college graduates, the bottom third no more than high-school-educated, and the middle third with some post-secondary education. So when I speak of kids from "upper-class" homes, I simply mean that at least one of their parents (usually both) graduated from college, and when I speak of kids from "lower-class" homes, I simply mean that neither of their parents went beyond high school. Other breakdowns would produce essentially the same patterns. For the sake of variety, in the text I often use the shorthand of "high-school-educated" or simply "poor" to refer to anyone who has no more than a high school education, and "college-educated" or simply "rich" for anyone with a college degree.

Chapter 2

FAMILIES

AT A PICTURESQUE TURNING OF THE DESCHUTES RIVER, AT THE eastern edge of Oregon's Cascade Mountains, where the arid scrub brush of the high desert gives way to Ponderosa pine, sits the town of Bend. For most of the twentieth century, Bend survived as a small logging town, set amidst scattered ranches. By the mid-1950s, when its population still barely topped 11,000, the logging industry began a long downward slide, ending with the closure of the town's last mill in 1994.[1]

In the 1970s, however, unlike many similar towns in the Northwest, Bend began to capitalize on the natural assets of its beautiful location and sunny weather to attract active vacationers and early retirees, especially from California.[2] Deschutes County, of which Bend is the county seat, became one of the fastest growing places in America: from 1970 to 2013, its population skyrocketed from 30,442 to 165,954. Construction and real estate accounted for nearly twice as many jobs in Deschutes County as elsewhere in Oregon. In the 1990s alone, Bend itself nearly tripled in population, from 20,469 to 52,029.[3]

With the tidal wave of newcomers came a substantial rise in per capita income and property values, along with all the familiar features of rapid development—traffic jams, a construction boom, and controversies about the advantages and disadvantages of "growth." Compared to many other boom towns, however, the classic cleavages between newcomers and old-timers, and between pro-growth and anti-growth advocates, were muted by the town's tradition of civic friendliness and by the cornucopia of new wealth.

Underneath the prosperous surface, however, a deeper social fault line opened. Longtime residents working in real estate and construction prospered, along with the affluent newcomers and the stockbrokers and financial consultants who set up shop to serve them. But unskilled laborers from the dying timber industry and the surrounding rural areas faced real poverty. Many could find jobs only in low-wage sectors like fast food restaurants or low-skill construction. Many others ended up jobless.[4] In fact, even though per capita income in the Bend statistical area grew by 54 percent in the 1990s, the number of residents living below the poverty line doubled, and the ratio of low earners to high earners rose from seven to one to nearly 12 to one.[5] The rising tide of prosperity in Bend definitely did not raise all boats.

Unlike many cities elsewhere in America, segregation in Bend is mostly economic, not racial. The town remains overwhelmingly white (91 percent) and not much affected by Hispanic immigration (only 8 percent Latino). Bend's poverty is concentrated on the east side of town. In 2008–2012, the child poverty rate in one census tract was 43 percent, more than ten times the rate in the upscale tract just across the river, on the west side of town.[6] (See Figure 2.1.)

Social service workers are acutely aware of poverty among the less skilled residents, but this persistent poverty in the midst of the boom is invisible to most upscale residents of Bend. In part, this invisibility is attributable to the growing segregation between the upscale gated communities in the hills on the west side of town, with their landscaped traffic circles, microbreweries, and public artwork; and the dreary, downscale east side desert, with its strip malls, pawn shops, and trailer parks.

Figure 2.1: Child poverty in Bend, Oregon (2008–2012)

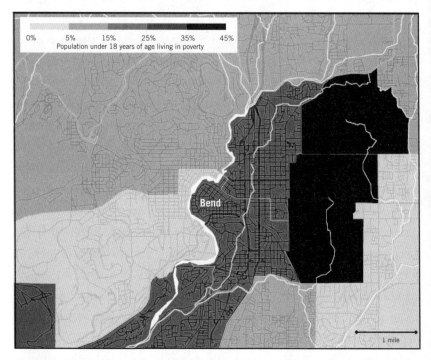

Source: ACS 2008–2012 (5-year estimates) data as compiled by Social Explorer, accessed through Harvard University Library.

One older newcomer muses about the implications of this segregation.

> When I grew up back East, rich people and poor people, or rich people and middle-class people, lived in the same neighborhood. Here you have your rich neighborhood, your middle-class neighborhood, and then there are less than middle-class neighborhoods. How that's gonna play out is difficult to see. It reminds me of when I go to Mexico and some of the houses have high walls with glass on top, and some have low walls but they have gates, and some of the houses have no walls at all.

Another resident reflects on the invisibility of economic distress in Bend:

> Many people have a stereotype of what it means to be poor. And it may be somebody they see on the street corner with a sign: "Will work for food." And what they don't think about is that person who's struggling every day. Could be the person who waited on us, took our bank deposit, works in retail, but who is barely above the poverty line.

These economic disparities are reflected in the families of young people in Bend and thus affect the futures of the kids. Kids raised on the east side and on the west side have radically different life chances. One important reason for this is that families on the two sides of town tend to be structured differently, a result of the economic disparities that have arisen in recent decades. These family differences produce very different starting points for rich and poor kids—as we learned by talking with two recent graduates of high schools in Bend who come from white families with deep roots in and around the city. Andrew, a loquacious and sunny-side-up college sophomore whose family lives in a sprawling home on a large lot in the hills on the west side of town, graduated from Summit High School. (Summit High School opened in 2001 and has a dropout rate of about 15 percent.) Kayla, wary and somber and adorned with a lip ring, lives about five miles from Andrew in a trailer on the east side of town and graduated from Marshall High School. (Marshall High School opened in 1948 and has a dropout rate of about 50 percent.)[7]

We open each of the two stories with flashbacks to their parents' lives growing up, drawing on interviews with both the parents and the kids, so that we can see how Andrew's and Kayla's very different family origins affect their prospects today.

Andrew and His Family

Andrew's father and mother, Earl and Patty (both 50-something), come from modest middle-class backgrounds in and around Bend. Earl's father was a crusty, hardworking small businessman in town, and he and his wife nurtured a close family, living in a small house on the east side of Bend. Earl was a self-described mediocre student in high school, earning Bs and Cs, but did well enough to head off to a four-year state college. At that point his parents' marriage failed, and then his father's business failed, but Earl (who had inherited his father's drive) put himself through school by selling life insurance part-time and taking out loans. Earl and Patty met when he was a senior and she was a sophomore, and within a month they were engaged. After he graduated, she dropped out of school in order to stay with him.

Earl is a hard-driven strategic planner, both in his business and in his family. "When we came out of college," he recalls, "we knew we wanted to have kids at a certain timeframe, so we could get a family started." Before taking this step, however, he and Patty, who is the sociable, level-headed member of the couple, planned to pay off their college loans and wedding bills, buy a home, and get on track financially. After a few years in Portland, where Earl worked as a stockbroker and Patty as a florist's assistant, they returned to Bend and founded what proved to be a remarkably successful construction business. Earl's business timing was perfect: the 1990s construction boom in Bend was about to take off, and within a few years they had passed all Earl's financial checkpoints.

Ten years after getting married, Earl, a self-described workaholic, had made his first $1 million, and he and Patty had paid off their loans and owned a new home "free and clear." Even before they'd had their first child, they had already started saving for college. They felt ready to start a family. On schedule, Andrew arrived, by which point the family was well on their way to serious wealth. A daughter, Lucy, followed. As Patty and Earl had planned from the outset, Patty stopped working once she started having kids, and she resolved to remain a stay-at-home mom until they were ready for college, after which she planned to return to finish her college degree (which she, in fact, did).

Earl feels parenthood changed him for the better. "It really brought us from a 'me' world to a world that was a unit," he says. "My business was such that everything revolved around me and my business. Then you have a kid, and all of a sudden you recognize that it's not all about you anymore. You start putting your energy into your kids. I mean, our generation has read every damn book you can read about being parents. Even more with this generation behind me, they've done all the homework for it." As part of that effort, Earl and Patty have committed themselves to making their marriage work. "You know," Earl says, "her parents divorced. My parents divorced. And our kids won't see us divorce."

Andrew confirms that he and his younger sister, Lucy, have been priorities for their parents. "My dad and my mom have always made sure that we eat dinner together," he says. "During the school year, when we are all busy, it's our only real time that all four of us could talk." Education, too, has been a priority. "Patty and I are on our kids about their education," Earl says. " 'Is your homework done?' We ask more questions in a week than my parents probably asked in four years through high school." Andrew (a solid B student in high school) backs up that account. Even though he's now in college, his parents still frequently check his grades, and he welcomes their concern.

Throughout high school, Andrew played soccer and ultimate Frisbee, but never as a zealous competitor. "It's hard for me to get really disappointed that we didn't win," he says. "I was just more into hang out and have fun." He focused instead on music, playing guitar with a group of close friends who eventually formed a successful band that continued into his college years. His parents furnished him with a guitar and six or seven years of lessons. Music, he says, remains his "number-one passion, next to firefighting."

Patty and Earl's affluence allows them unselfconsciously to help their kids in ways that are inconceivable to most families in Bend. Andrew attended a private school from pre-K through the eighth grade. "My parents wanted the best for me," he observes. Later, when Lucy fell in with what Andrew calls "a tough crowd" at Summit High, and was doing poorly, Andrew and his parents worried about her a lot—and intervened.

"We tried everything," Andrew recalls. "And finally she really connected with horseback riding and animals. So my dad jumped on it and built a barn out at our ranch and Lucy got a horse, and it was just a complete turnaround. She switched to Mountain View, the other high school here, which is well known for agriculture, and [suddenly] it's all hers. It's incredible. Last year she became a 4.2 student."

Patty and Earl honed their kids' work ethic and helped along the way, as Andrew proudly recounts. "I started working when I was 14 at the market right down the street from my house. My dad is pretty old-fashioned. So by 14 it was a big deal getting a job. And I wouldn't have wanted it any other way, honestly. It taught me work ethic. I went with one of my parents, I don't remember which, and I dressed up, went in, and asked for an application. I had always known them [the store owners] growing up, and I was really cool about it. So I took it home, filled out the application with my dad that night, put it all together, got all my references, and took that back and turned it in, and got the job there. It was probably a quarter mile from our house just down the hill, and my mom didn't like me walking by myself, so she usually would drive me, but it was close enough that I could get back and forth from home if I wanted to."

Andrew also fondly recalls how his parents helped him celebrate his birthdays at a cabin the family owns on the river north of Bend. "When I was younger," he says, "my dad helped me make it a tradition that every year I take my two best friends to the cabin for my birthday. And I haven't missed a year yet."

Andrew is now a sophomore at a nearby state university, where he hopes to get a business degree. Earl had expected that Andrew would join the flourishing family firm after graduating, but Andrew is more attracted to working as a firefighter. "I didn't want to look at blueprints for my life," he says. "I knew I loved this [firefighting]. So I met the chief when I came back after the first term, and I just told him that I wanted a job when I came out of school, and what do I need to do to line me up for the next four years to get it done?"

Earl was remarkably supportive when he discovered that Andrew did not plan to follow in his footsteps. When he learned that Andrew wanted to do a summer internship at the fire department, he gave Andrew the chief's phone number. (Earl and the chief were childhood friends.) Nevertheless, he insisted that Andrew make the call himself. Andrew got the internship, which was unpaid, and Earl paid him the equivalent of what he would have made working in the family business. Similarly, Andrew's parents gave him a pickup truck for high school graduation but required him to contribute toward it. "Their theory is for me to work and pay it off," Andrew says, "so that I can build credit and can learn paying off the truck. I like doing that, because I can manage my money, and I'm learning how to balance."

In ways that he probably doesn't even realize, Andrew's relaxed attitude toward his future has been molded by his comfortable upbringing. "I would rather live without all the big money and be happy. I can make good money doing this [firefighting]. It's a great life, you know. It's good money." On the other hand, he mentions casually that, like his parents, he may "do real estate on the side," and later, reflecting on his newfound interest at college in debate and public affairs, he allows that he might end up in politics. He confidently faces a future with many options.

Andrew is aware that he has benefited from his family's good fortune in many ways, both material and nonmaterial. Still, he seems unaware of the lives of hardship being led on the east side of town: "Bend is a small community and you don't see a whole lot of poverty." On the other hand, he says "I've never worried about money. My dad is very good at what he does. I always felt secure. I am sure lucky that I have a good situation." The family frequently travel together to Hawaii, San Francisco, the East Coast, and even occasionally Europe.

Andrew is very rooted in the Bend community. Life has taught him that his environment is stable and benevolent. He has lived in the same house with the same trustworthy neighbors and the same close friends since he was an infant. "There's nowhere I'd rather be than here at home," he says. "I know Bend like the back of my hand. The people are great. I just love the community life. I feel secure in Bend. For the most part, Bend is a community of really trusting people."

Not surprisingly, Andrew envisages a rewarding future that mirrors the life his parents have led. "The first thing that would be good for me," he says, "would be if I could build a home and have a family. Hopefully I will meet somebody that's like my best friend, and then give my kids close to the same as what I had. Ideally, if I could plan it perfectly, I want to get married at 25. And I would want to have a kid by the time I was 30. And I want to have two kids. I tell myself, if I could give them the same life that I have, that would be the way to go."

Perhaps the most striking feature about Andrew's view of life is the exceptional warmth he feels, even as a late adolescent, toward his family. "My friends love and trust my parents. They could talk to my parents more than they could talk to their parents. And I love that. I have no problem telling my parents something, because they are so understanding. I always feel bad for some of my friends who say 'I wish that my parents were as open, wish I could talk to my parents or they were understanding.' My dad always reminds me every day how much my mom and my dad love me," he says. "It's a good feeling, you know? Some of my friends give me a wisecrack like, 'Andrew's parents say they love him again!' But, it's like, yeah, that's how I want it."

Kayla and Her Family

Kayla's life has been very different from Andrew's, and the roots of that difference lie deep in the life histories of her parents, Darleen and Joe.

Life has disappointed Darleen in many ways, both materially and emotionally, leaving her looking older than her 45 years. She grew up in a calm and settled family, on an isolated ranch several hours outside of Bend, and she remains close to her aging mother. Like Earl, she describes her high school record as mediocre. After graduating, she worked as a retail clerk in a fast food restaurant and pumped gas, and at about 20, she got married and had two children. Her husband turned out to be abusive, however, and eventually she left him. He retained custody of the kids, perhaps because he had a steady job and she did not. Darleen left the marriage badly damaged, and all she will say about it today is that it was "a bad move."

After the split, Darleen got a job at Pizza Hut, where she struck up a casual relationship with her boss, Joe. Within two months, she was pregnant. "It didn't mean to happen," she says now. "It just did. It was planned and kind of not planned," she says. The result was Kayla.

Joe came from a background that was unusually deprived and tormented. Though seven years younger than Earl, he appears 10–15 years older. His father spent most of his life (before and after Joe was born) in the Texas State Penitentiary for bank robberies and assorted other crimes. Joe has had virtually no contact with him.

Joe's mother suffered from serious alcoholism throughout her adult life. After Joe was born, she had relationships with a number of other men, but they were always casual and temporary, so from an early age Joe was his mom's primary caregiver. "They wasn't really around," Joe says of the boyfriends. "They was always drinking, and basically I ended up taking care of her, rather than her taking care of me." She never remarried and remained without a regular job, living with Joe's ailing grandmother. Always worried about money, the family was constantly on the move throughout the rural West.

When Joe was eight, he was placed in a foster home, the first in a long series. He felt very much an outcast, but the last of those homes did provide him with the only stable parental figures in his life, Maddy and Pop. The few years he spent with them—wearing new clothes instead of hand-me-downs, celebrating his birthday, fishing in the nearby creek with Pop—represented the only time of contentment in his childhood.

The librarian in the local school taught him to read during her lunch break. Joe recalls Pop with nostalgia. "He taught me things that nobody else taught me," he says.

At 14, however, Joe left Maddy and Pop to resume caring for his mother. It was a mistake, he says, because "my mom wasn't ready for it. I'd wait at the bar from 9:00 p.m. to 2:30 a.m. so I could walk home with her." One night the police found her crawling in the street on her hands and knees, drunk, and called Joe to pick her up. "I loved her with everything I had," he says, "and I always tried to show her that, but it wasn't enough. I wished I'd stayed with Maddy and Pop."

Joe dropped out of school after the eighth grade. Living with his mother and caring for her as they bounced from town to town, he worked at various temporary jobs—yard work, chopping wood, "anything people would let me do." At the age of 18, he became involved with a young woman who soon announced that she was pregnant. Believing that he was the father and that he faced a choice between jail and marriage because she was underage, Joe felt compelled to marry her. She was, it turned out, heavily into drugs, and after their second child was born, Joe learned that she was in an incestuous, abusive relationship with her stepfather, and that the stepfather was actually the father of their first child. Concluding that he had been the victim of a marriage trap, Joe left her, although he continued to feel responsibility toward the two kids. Deeply depressed and lacking any economic prospects, he moved back in with his mother, now living with her latest boyfriend in a trailer outside of Redmond, just north of Bend, and found yet another impermanent job as a cook at Pizza Hut—where he met Darleen.

Joe and Darleen were both very fragile, economically and emotionally, when they met—low-wage refugees from disastrous first marriages. "We probably didn't know each other," Darleen recalls. Joe agrees: "We wasn't really that stable. I kept thinking 'Okay, we're just barely making ends meet now. Now we got a baby on the way.' And Darleen really wasn't ready to be a mom again, because she was still struggling with her own life, getting it back on track and figuring out who she was. So we really struggled when we had Kayla."

Desperately poor, the family lived hand-to-mouth in a trailer, surviving on Joe's transient, minimum wage jobs: first as an unskilled laborer working the graveyard shift at a local mill and then, when the mill eliminated that job, as a short-order cook and a gas station attendant. Through it all, Joe's budding relationship with his infant daughter kept him going. "It gave more meaning to life to me," he says, "because I had a reason to do everything I could. It gave me more hope. And I took care of her from then on."

Kayla grew up in a confusing web of five step-siblings—Kayla, the two children from Darleen's first marriage, and the two children from Joe's first marriage. This made for complex sibling relationships, as Kayla recalls. "We all got separate moms or separate dads. Bill and Clara: those are brother and sister from my mom. We've got the same mom. And then my brother Mathew, we have the same dad. And then Luke: he's kind of like a stepbrother, in a way. He is from my dad's first marriage. [Luke is actually the child of Joe's first wife and her stepfather.] They'd all come down for the summers and just hang out. We had a two-bedroom house, and my mom and dad had their room. I had to share a room with Clara, and the three boys slept downstairs. It worked for a while, and then everybody got on each other's nerves, and we'd start a big fight." Family dinners in this environment were a rarity. "We tried to get it like that," Darleen says, "but it wasn't always like that. You know, it took two parents. We would watch TV together."

Family finances in Kayla's youth were often strained to the breaking point. Kayla recalls wistfully her tenth birthday: "I couldn't have a cake or anything like that because we were struggling so bad. My dad said, 'We don't really have the money for it. We're going to do it in May or June.' I was like 'Oh, okay.' I was pretty sad about it, but I was like 'whatever.'"

After seven years of emotional and economic friction, Darleen fled the family with a new boyfriend, Charlie, whom she had met at work back at Pizza Hut ("my boss's boss," she laughingly explains). Charlie and Darleen led an itinerant life for a number of years, moving around the inland West and ending up homeless, with nowhere to stay but the bed of Charlie's Ford Ranger. For most of her youth, Kayla stayed with Joe, though for several years after puberty she wandered with Charlie and Darleen across the country, living in motels and, for a while, at what Joe calls "a Gothic" (perhaps some sort of commune) in Missouri.

Joe eventually married another woman (his third wife), who moved in with her three children from a previous marriage. The new arrangement did not work out well for Kayla, who didn't like her stepmother. "She'd treat her sons and daughter like royalty," she says, "and I was kind of like the peasant of them all." But Kayla didn't move in with Darleen and Charlie at this point, because they had no room for her in their trailer. Eventually, Joe's third marriage also dissolved. Joe—the one consistent, loving adult in Kayla's life—retained custody of her, even though he was desperately struggling to make ends meet.

Unsurprisingly, Darleen, Kayla, and Joe have very different perspectives on their relationships, but all agree on this fundamental fact: however difficult the marriage had been, Kayla was deeply scarred by her parents' divorce. Indeed, it was the seminal event in her life. It's useful to see that event from the perspective of each of the three.

Perhaps because Kayla was a not entirely intended product of a very traumatic period in Darleen's life, Darleen expresses an oddly detached and fatalistic perspective on her daughter's life throughout our interview, recounting Kayla's story less as a mother than as a bystander. "It don't do no good to worry about your children," she says. "Kids will do what they want." She does recognize, however, that her decision to leave the family hurt Kayla. "The split affected Kayla a lot," she says. "It was the hardest thing she went through." At the urging of a school social worker, Kayla began to see a professional counselor, but she soon stopped going, Kayla says, because she found it ineffective. Darleen agrees. "I think it just made her more depressed," she says. "So her dad and I were just there for her. Be there for her."

Joe remembers Darleen's role in Kayla's life during that time differently. "It was hard," he says, "because at that time her mom really didn't want to spend much time with her. So I ended up taking care of her. My biggest struggle was keeping her in school. From the seventh grade, she kept wanting to drop out of school, and I said, 'No, you ain't dropping out. You ain't making the mistakes I made.'"

Kayla, for her part, denies that her mother was "there for her" after the split. Her mom's departure, which was the most difficult experience of her life, left her with a lasting sense of abandonment that permeates her view of life. "That was pretty hard for me. I was pretty upset about it, pretty angry," she says. "I was like, 'Well, you know they're not getting along, but I'd like to have both of them growing up.' She'd leave the city, go to different states and everything, so I could see her only once in a great while."

Later we ask Kayla what it would mean for her to be a good mother to children of her own. "I think I would try to pay attention to them more than what my parents did," she replies. "I think a good parent would be somebody that's stable, that can actually be there for their kid and is actually old enough to be able to know right from wrong. . . . [My parents] could have waited a little bit longer [to have a child]."

Kayla hated school and had no outside activities during the years after the split. "She doesn't associate with the kids," a school social worker told Joe. "She just goes off by herself and sits." After school, Kayla retreated to her bedroom to read fantasy books and watch cartoons. In the mornings, she recalls, "I didn't want to get up at all." She was sent to a program for troubled adolescents at Marshall High School, and then to a Job Corps training program. She found the Job Corps program restrictive and isolating, however, and returned to Marshall, where administrators sympathetic to her plight allowed her to matriculate again, even though official policy discouraged that.

The administrators at Marshall offered Kayla much support. To Joe's surprise, a counselor arranged to pay for Kayla to get braces, to correct her embarrassingly crooked teeth, but made her promise not to miss any orthodontic appointments. "If you miss one," they told her, "you lose your braces." Later, a school librarian worked with her to identify a promising opportunity at the local community college and even helped her arrange financial aid.

During her months at the Job Corps program, Kayla acquired a boyfriend, and the two of them now live with Joe. Both Darleen and Joe are unhappy about the boyfriend. Darleen calls him "a worthless bum," and even Kayla seems uncertain about him. Like Joe and Kayla, he is unemployed, although he claims to be looking for a job. For now, all three are surviving on disability payments that Joe receives, and on Section 8 housing assistance. Compounding Kayla's problems, Joe now suffers from inoperable brain tumors, and Kayla has become his main caregiver. "He does weird stuff sometimes because of the tumors, like he'll kind of freak out for no reason, or he'll just sit there and talk to himself," she anguishes. "I worry about him a lot."

Kayla's hopes for the future, unlike Andrew's, are disconnected from any realistic plan of action in the here and now. "One of my biggest dreams," she says, "is to go all around the world and just study different things, like culinary things. Where I want to end up is probably in London. I heard it's really pretty there. I'm looking for a job, but it is hard, especially when you got no experience at all. People don't really want to take the time to train you or anything."

Kayla remains troubled psychologically, displaying classic symptoms of depression. At a fundamental level, her outlook is deeply skeptical and distrustful. Not unreasonably, given her life experiences, she finds the world unpredictable, intractable, and malign.

Kayla has a lot to worry about—her dad's illness, her finances, her uncertain college prospects, her boyfriend, her future. Essentially, she has no stable, trustworthy adults in her life. Confronted with the realities of her situation as she moves into adulthood, she has one great fear—"kind of having my life go downhill," she says, "everything kind of falling apart."

Interviewer: Do you feel like that might happen?

Kayla: Yeah, I feel like it.

Interviewer: What do you think will happen?

Kayla: Like, college isn't going to go through, or my grants ain't going to go through or . . . And then my dad getting sicker, where he just isn't really there anymore.

Interviewer: When you're feeling really overwhelmed, what do you do?

Kayla: I just kind of hang out on my own.

Interviewer: Have you ever had a time where you just felt like you couldn't make it?

Kayla: A lot actually.

Changing Family Structures in America

"Happy families are all alike; every unhappy family is unhappy in its own way," Leo Tolstoy claimed. Each of the scores of families whose lives we have explored in this research, however, seems distinctive—the fortunate as well as the forlorn. Relatively few American kids live like Andrew, in thoughtful, loving families that have attained extraordinary affluence. Only somewhat more live like Kayla, amidst the gloomy ruins of multiple broken families surviving at the edge of destitution. Neither is a "typical American family." Yet in many important respects their two families epitomize the ways in which American family life has been restructured along class lines over the last half century.[8]

Fifty years ago, most American families consisted of a breadwinner dad, a homemaker mom, and the kids: a stable, Ozzie-and-Harriet–style union. Divorce was uncommon, and births outside of marriage were rare in all social strata—4 percent overall in 1950, although the rate was slightly higher among the economically disadvantaged.[9] Although today this family structure is often considered "traditional," historians of the family have demonstrated that in fact it did not predominate in earlier eras of American history.[10]

Two social norms helped make the Ozzie-and-Harriet family possible: 1) a strongly patriarchal division of labor, coupled with widely shared prosperity that allowed most families to get by on one male income, and 2) a strong norm against out-of-wedlock births, so that premarital pregnancy was typically followed by "shotgun" marriage.[11] Most baby boomers, as a result, were raised by both biological parents.

In the 1970s, however, as the boomers themselves were coming of age, that family structure suddenly collapsed, in what demographers agree was the most dramatic change in family structure in American history. Premarital sex lost its stigma almost overnight; shotgun marriages sharply diminished, and then virtually disappeared; divorce became epidemic; and the number of kids living in single-parent families began a long, steady ascent.[12]

Those who have studied this change in family structure don't agree on exactly what caused it, but most agree that these factors contributed:

- Sex and marriage were delinked with the advent of the birth control pill.[13]
- The feminist revolution transformed gender and marital norms.
- Millions of women, in part freed from patriarchal norms, in part driven by economic necessity, and in part responding to new opportunities, headed off to work.
- The end of the long postwar boom began to reduce economic security for young working-class men.
- An individualist swing of the cultural pendulum produced more emphasis on "self-fulfillment."[14]

The collapse of the traditional family hit the black community earliest and hardest, in part because that community was already clustered at the bottom of the economic hierarchy. That led observers to frame the initial discussion of the phenomenon in racial terms, as Daniel Patrick Moynihan did in his controversial 1965 report, *The Negro Family: The Case for National Action*.[15] But it would turn out that white families were not immune to the changes, and with the benefit of hindsight it's clear that from about 1965 to 1980, American family life underwent a massive transformation.

During this period of seemingly anarchic change, it was possible to imagine that marriage and family were on their way to extinction. But the upheaval in family structure in the 1970s produced a different and unexpected outcome – a bifurcation into two very distinct family patterns. In the 1950s all social classes had largely followed the Ozzie-and-Harriet model, but the two family types that appeared after the 1970s were closely correlated with class. The result was a novel, two-tier pattern of family structure that is still with us today.[16]

In the college-educated, upper third of American society, a "neo-traditional" marriage pattern has emerged. It mirrors the 1950s family in many respects, except that both partners now typically work outside of the home, they delay marriage and childbearing until their careers are under way, and they divide domestic duties more evenly. The result is something like Ozzie-and-Harriet–except that Harriet is now a lawyer or a social worker, Ozzie spends more time with the kids, and on two incomes they can afford a few more luxuries. These neo-traditional marriages are more egalitarian in the gender division of labor, and they have become nearly as durable as the 1950s model, as divorce rates among this upper third have retreated from the peaks of the 1970s.[17] For the children of these families the news is good, as we shall see: the way they are being raised leads to many positive outcomes.[18]

In the high-school-educated, lower third of the population, by contrast, a new, more kaleidoscopic pattern began to emerge in which childbearing became increasingly disconnected from marriage, and sexual partnerships became less durable. In this model, dubbed "fragile families" by the sociologist Sara McLanahan and her collaborators, a child's parents may never have been married or even stably connected to each other.[19] Even if the parents were married at the time of the child's birth, that marriage was frail, as divorce rates in this social stratum continued to rise. Because both parents likely moved on to other partners, with whom they also had children, even family units with two adults often included step-parents and step-siblings. More common, of course, were single-parent families, when one parent jumped or got pushed off the marriage-go-round.[20]

Andrew's family and Kayla's family represent these two patterns almost perfectly. To be sure, Patty's role as Andrew's stay-at-home mom reflects a variant of the neo-traditional model, and Joe's role as the central adult in Kayla's life is atypical, since single fathers are much less common than single mothers. But it is not misleading to think of these two Bend families as representing the new two-tier family structure in America. Let's review the dimensions of this class-linked change nationwide— keeping in mind, of course, that the correlation between social class and family structure, although strong and growing stronger, is not perfect, since some poor families are traditional or neo-traditional in their structure and stability, and some rich families are kaleidoscopic.

MOTHER'S AGE AT BIRTH

College-educated mothers now typically delay childbearing and marriage until their late twenties or early thirties, about six years later, on average, than their counterparts a half century ago. High-school-educated mothers, by contrast, typically have their first children in their late teens or early twenties, slightly earlier than their counterparts in the 1960s, and ten years earlier than college-educated moms today. (See Figure 2.2.[21] This is the first in a series of "scissors charts" that will appear in this book, each showing a statistically significant divergence in trends between upper- and lower-class parents and children.) Delayed parenting helps kids, because older parents are generally better equipped to support their kids, both materially and emotionally. Andrew's parents recognized this and planned accordingly. Kayla's did not, as Joe, Darleen, and Kayla all now agree.

UNINTENDED BIRTHS

High-school-educated women don't aspire to have more children than college-educated women, but research shows that the former typically start having sex earlier, use contraception and abortion less often, and have more unintended or semi-intended pregnancies.[22] ("Planned and kind of not planned," as Darleen put it.) These class-linked differences are widening. According to the sociologist Kelly Musick and her colleagues, the most plausible explanations for this class discrepancy include the mother's ambivalence about pregnancy, the erosion of personal efficacy by low education and economic distress, and perhaps differential access or attitudes to abortion. Access to contraception doesn't seem to explain the pattern.[23]

Figure 2.2: Trends in median age of mothers at first birth, 1960–2010

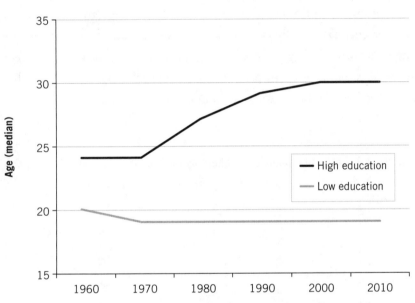

Source: IPUMS/ACS data, as reported by McLanahan and Jacobsen, "Diverging Destinies Revisited."

Whatever the reasons, children of less educated parents are increasingly entering the world as an unplanned surprise (complete or not, pleasant or not), while children of more educated parents are increasingly entering the world as a long-planned objective. That difference is very likely to affect the resources available for raising those kids, as it did in the contrasting cases of Andrew and Kayla.

NONMARITAL BIRTHS

Nonmarital births to college-educated women remain low (less than 10 percent) and have risen only slightly since the 1970s. Among high-school-educated women, however, they have risen sharply over the last 30 years and now make up more than half of all the births (about 65 percent in 2007) in this group. (See Figure 2.3.) The figure among high-school-educated blacks is higher (about 80 percent) but has not risen in more than 20 years, whereas during that same period it has nearly quadrupled among high-school-educated whites (now about 50 percent). The proportion of nonmarital births for black college graduates (about 25 percent) has actually fallen by a third over the last 20 years, while the figure for white college graduates has slipped from 3 percent to 2 percent over these same years. In other words, the racial gap within classes has narrowed, while the class gap within races has widened.

Figure 2.3: Births to unmarried mothers by education, 1977–2007

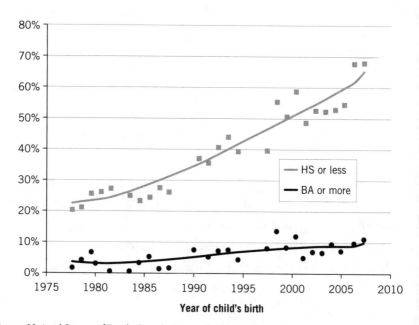

Source: National Surveys of Family Growth, Centers for Disease Control.

DIVORCE

The divorce rate in America, having more than doubled in the 1960s and 1970s, peaked around 1980 and then began to taper off. That broad national pattern, however, concealed another significant class divergence, for the divorce rate among college-educated Americans fell significantly after 1980, whereas it continued to rise among their high-school-educated counterparts, even as marriage itself was becoming less common in that stratum of society.[24] By 2000 the ratio of divorced to married people was nearly twice as great among high-school-educated Americans (roughly 24 per 100) as among college graduates (14 per 100), and by 2008–2010 the gap had grown further (roughly 28 per 100 to 14 per 100).[25] Once again, the families of Andrew and Kayla perfectly illustrate this sharpening contrast.

COHABITATION

At all levels of contemporary American society, cohabitation (an unmarried couple living together) has become common. But among younger Americans it rarely amounts to "marriage without a license." Although about two thirds of marriages nowadays follow a period of cohabitation, the average cohabitation in America lasts about 14 months and generally does not end in marriage.[26] Cohabitation patterns also increasingly differ according to class. The percentage of high-school-educated women who had ever cohabited doubled in the two decades after 1987, from about 35 percent to about 70 percent, while the percentage among college-educated women during that same period rose only from 31 percent to 47 percent.[27]

Among college-educated Americans, cohabiting couples seldom have children, but when pregnancy does occur, it tends to derive from a stable relationship, and a stable marriage is the likely outcome.[28] Among high-school-educated Americans, by contrast, cohabitation is generally not a way station to permanent partnership. Children are often born to cohabiting couples, but such cohabitation does not typically lead to marriage, nor do the partnerships generally last. Low-income men and women have children *while* searching for a long-term partner, not after they have found one. Nowadays, in short, most high-school-educated women cohabit; most college-educated women don't, and those who do, rarely have children.

To be sure, few of the nonmarital births in the lower third are the result of one-night stands. Most are to cohabiting couples who, like Joe and Darleen, are hopeful of making a go of it at the time their child is born. But most of these relationships will not survive for more than a few years. The shared desire to have a child usually fails to provide enough of a bond to persist through the trials of raising an infant amidst precarious work, fragile families, and dangerous neighborhoods. McLanahan and her colleagues found that five years after the birth of a child, more than two thirds of all women who were unmarried at the time of the birth (and about half of all who were cohabiting at the time of the birth) were no longer even romantically involved with the child's father.[29] The anticipated marriages are, in effect, "still-born," in the words of the demographer Frank Furstenberg.[30] What follows is often another round of cohabitation, conception, and dissolution, characterized by Kathryn Edin and Timothy J. Nelson as "a cycle of redemption and despair."[31] Indeed, most unmarried parents end up having children with other partners as well. This is exactly the tale told by Kayla's parents, Joe and Darleen.

MULTI-PARTNER FERTILITY

Demographers use the term *multi-partner fertility* to describe the emergence of the complex, impermanent structure characteristic of less educated American families today—"blended families," as family counselors describe them.[32] The "family" within which Kayla was raised, involving five temporary adult partnerships and eight step-siblings, and the "family" in which David (whom we met in Port Clinton) was raised, with uncounted adult couplings and nine step-siblings, in many ways typify this new pattern.

Many kids, especially from less affluent, less educated backgrounds, live without their fathers. Figure 2.4 portrays this aspect of the two-tier system, showing how many men of fathering age (15–44) have any biological children with whom they do not live, and of those nonresident fathers, how many have essentially no contact with their children. (In complex families, sometimes a father will engage intensively with offspring from one mother at the expense of his other offspring with other mothers.) Compared to college graduates, high-school-educated men are four times more likely to father children with whom they do not live, and only half as likely to visit those children.[33]

Figure 2.4: Less educated men are more likely to father nonresident children

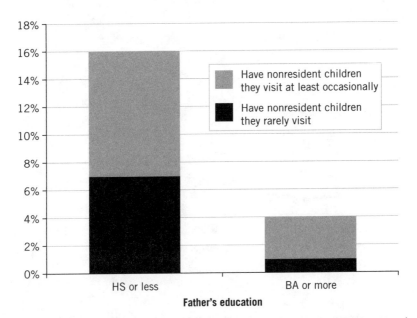

Source: National Survey of Family Growth, 2006–2010, men aged 15–44 (NCFMR FP12-02 and NCFMR FP12-08).

All these changes in family structure have produced a massive, class-biased decline in the number of children raised in two-parent families during the past half century or so. As Sara McLanahan and Christine Percheski summarize, "In 1960, only 6 percent of children in the United

States lived with a single parent. Today over half of all children are expected to spend some time in a single-parent family before reaching 18. . . . Children with mothers in the bottom educational quartile are almost twice as likely to live with a single mother at some point during childhood as children with a mother in the top quartile."[34] Figure 2.5 summarizes the growth of this remarkable gap.[35]

Figure 2.5: Children (aged 0–7) living in a single-parent family, by parental education

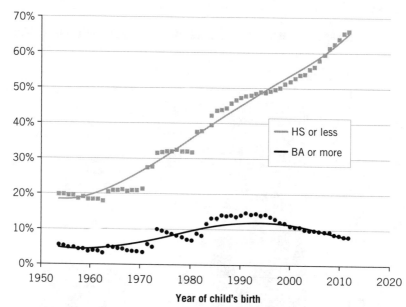

Year of child's birth

Source: IPUMS (Census 1970, 1980, 1990, 2000) and ACS 2001–2012.

Contrary to much popular commentary, these recent trends have little or nothing to do with an increase in teen pregnancy, which, in fact, has been steadily and sharply *declining* among all races for more than 20 years, with very little effect on rates of nonmarital births or child poverty or social mobility. The growth in unplanned pregnancies and nonmarital births that I have described is concentrated among women aged 25–34.[36] Of all unwed births in America nowadays, more than three quarters are to post-teen adults, and that share is growing.[37] "Children having children" is a significant problem, but it is *not* the central challenge facing the working-class family in America.

WOMEN'S EMPLOYMENT

After 1960, employment rates rose for all women, but the increase was faster and more substantial among college-educated women, so that in the era of two-tier families, college-educated mothers (70 percent) are more than twice as likely as high-school-educated moms (32 percent) to work outside the home.[38] (See Figure 2.6.) College-educated moms are also more likely to have a male breadwinner in the household. The result is a substantial class disparity in the financial resources available for childrearing. Other things being equal, working mothers today spend less time with the kids than stay-at-home moms today, but working mothers today spend as much time with the kids as stay-at-home moms did in the 1970s, because today's working mothers have cut back on other uses of their time.[39]

Figure 2.6: Trends in employment of mothers, 1960–2010

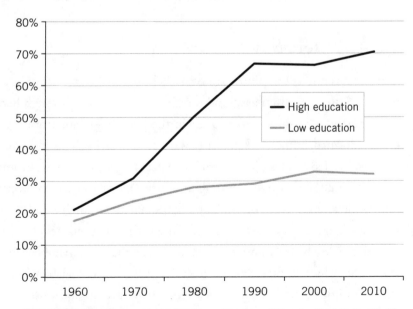

Source: IPUMS/ACS data, as reported by McLanahan and Jacobsen, "Diverging Destinies Revisited."

RACE AND CLASS

In the 1970s, the two-tier family structure was closely correlated with race, but since that time it has become increasingly associated with the parents' social class more than their race. The same two-tier, class-based pattern now appears among both blacks and whites. College-educated blacks are looking more like college-educated whites, and less educated whites are looking more like less educated blacks. The collapse of the working-class family, which began to happen to blacks in the 1960s, began to happen to whites in the 1980s and 1990s.[40]

Latino and Asian Americans account for an increasing fraction of American couples and children. Generally speaking, families in recent immigrant communities are much stronger by such conventional measures as marriage rates, nonmarital births, divorce, and two-parent families. This is true despite the lower educational and economic standing of most immigrant groups. In that sense, recent immigrants are the last exemplars of the "traditional" American marriage. On the other hand, some evidence suggests that second-generation immigrants are falling into the familiar two-tier pattern. In other words, this important exception to the class divide among American families may prove transitory.[41]

Why Two Tiers Now?

Marriage has not lost its allure. An overwhelming majority of Americans from all classes want to marry, and most expect to marry, although here, too, a class gap has begun to appear: in the late 1970s kids from high-school-educated homes (76 percent) were almost as likely as kids from college-educated homes (78 percent) to expect to get married in the long run, but by 2012 that figure among upper-tier kids had risen to 86 percent, while among lower-tier kids the figure remained unchanged.[42] On the other hand, scores of studies have found that married people of all educational levels are more satisfied with life than comparable single people. So why has the two-tier class divergence in actual behavior—which did not exist in nearly so clear-cut a way throughout most of the twentieth century—become so marked in the last 30 years or so?

Economics is certainly a very important part of the story. "The wages of men without college degrees have fallen since the early 1970s," the demographer Andrew J. Cherlin reports, "and the wages of women without college degrees have failed to grow."[43] The greatly reduced economic prospects experienced by poorer, less educated Americans over these four decades (greater job instability and declining relative earnings) have made it far more difficult for them to attain and sustain the traditional pattern of marriage. Unemployment, underemployment, and poor economic prospects discourage and undermine stable relationships—that is the nearly universal finding of many studies, both qualitative and quantitative.[44] A growing number of women in the lower portion of the economic hierarchy are reluctant to marry men who can offer little or no economic security. As in the case of Joe and Darleen, deep and chronic economic stress is an important cause of the impermanence among poor couples, even when they are married, causing them to become less reliable partners and parents.

As we saw in Chapter 1, economic hardship is an important precursor for the breakdown of the working-class family: divorce rates and nonmarital birth rates both skyrocketed in Port Clinton during the decade following the collapse of the local economy. And it was primarily the factory closings of the 1980s, not the cultural turmoil of the 1960s, that triggered this collapse. This was a national phenomenon, not limited to the Rust Belt.

Culture is another important part of the story, however. Gender and sexual norms have changed, in particular, as have the roles of less educated men and more educated women.[45] For poor men, the disappearance of the stigma against premarital sex and nonmarital birth, and the evaporation of the norm of shotgun marriages, broke the link between procreation and marriage. For educated women, the combination of birth control and greatly enhanced professional opportunity made delayed childbearing both more possible and more desirable.

The ethnographers Kathryn Edin and Maria Kefalas found that while poor women value marriage as much as affluent women, they also believe (just like their sisters higher up the economic hierarchy) that in order to be successful, marriage must be postponed until couples have achieved economic well-being.[46] The problem for poorer women is that economic well-being always seems out of reach. Motherhood, by contrast, is open to all women, married or not; it doesn't immediately require abundant resources, and it offers meaning to their lives. Like Darleen, they often believe that mothering basically involves "being there." On the basis of long-term ethnographic evidence from poor single mothers, both urban and rural, Linda Burton concludes that "moms in this context seek romance over marriage as a respite from their everyday poverty and uncertainty."[47]

Scholars debate the relative importance of "structural" (or economic) and "cultural" explanations for the emergence of the two-tier system. The most reasonable view is that both are important. Moreover, cause and effect are entangled here: poverty produces family instability, and family instability in turn produces poverty. A similar kind of mutual reinforcement occurs between affluence and stability. These complex causal dynamics and feedback loops are all plainly visible in the lives of Andrew's and Kayla's families.

One way of understanding this causal conundrum is to consider the impact of the Great Depression—the most massive economic dislocation in American history—on family formation and family life. Evidence from the Great Depression cuts both ways on the issue of economic versus cultural explanations. The Great Depression led to male joblessness and economic dislocation on a massive scale. As a consequence, the marriage rate fell, showing the perennial importance of economic stability in the marriage calculus. ("The boys have no jobs," one Chicago woman said. "I want a man with a job," said another.)[48] Moreover, according to a 1940 survey, 1.5 million married women were deserted by their husbands, and more than 200,000 vagrant children were said to be wandering the country as a result.[49] In a landmark study of the lives of 167 white children raised during the Great Depression, Glen Elder found that when fathers lost jobs and income, their ties with the family eroded, leading to a significant decline in the effectiveness of parental control. Eighty years (and several cultural revolutions) later, it's still true that hard times deter and destroy marriages.[50]

On the other hand, in the 1930s the birth rate also fell sharply, and between 1920 and 1940 unwed births remained consistently low.[51] In that era, men and women postponed procreation as well as matrimony. "No marriage license, no kids" was the cultural norm. Unlike today, desperately poor, jobless men in the 1930s did not have kids outside of marriage whom they then largely ignored. Today the role of father has become more voluntary, which means that, as Marcia Carlson and Paula England have put it, "only the most committed and financially stable men choose to embrace it."[52] This important cultural shift matters a good deal for the sorts of families within which poor kids today are raised.[53]

Could changes in public policy or political ideology have had the perverse effect of undermining the conventional two-parent family? The most commonly discussed possibility, by far, is that welfare benefits gave poor single women an incentive to have kids. Some careful studies have confirmed a modest, statistically significant effect of that sort. But the steady, accelerating increase in single-parent families over the last half century does not correspond to the ebb and flow of mothers on welfare. Welfare rolls increased in the late 1960s and early 1970s, declined gradually from 1972 to 1992, then declined more sharply throughout the 1990s. Moreover, since many mothers who experienced the collapse of the traditional family were not on welfare, the welfare system cannot have been the major cause. And the collapse continued apace even after welfare eligibility was tightened in 1996.[54]

"Family values" conservatives have sometimes argued that liberalism and secularism cause family disintegration. But unwed births and single-parent families are widely distributed across the country, and are concentrated neither in secular areas nor in "blue" states, which presumably have pursued more progressive policies. If anything, the opposite seems to be true: divorce and single-parent families are especially common in the Southeastern, heavily Republican, socially conservative Bible

Belt.[55] We can't make any inferences about causality from such simple correlations, but these patterns should caution us against assuming that the collapse of the working-class family (white or nonwhite) can be attributed to the decline of organized religion or to any political ideology. Changing personal values are an important part of the story, but only in conjunction with adverse economic trends, and ideology seems to have very little to do with it.

There was a set of policy choices in the 1980s that probably did contribute to family breakdown: the War on Drugs, "three strikes" sentencing, and the sharp increase in incarceration. Figure 2.7 shows the explosion of incarceration rates in the years after 1980, despite a decline in violent crime during that same period. That explosion was heavily concentrated among less educated young men, especially (but not only) young black men—a disproportionate number of whom, surprisingly, were young fathers.[56]

For both black children and white children, the risk of having a parent imprisoned by the time they reached 14 rose significantly between the birth cohort of 1978 (kids born in 1978) and the birth cohort of 1990, and that risk was concentrated among children whose parents were less educated. Children born in 1990 to high school dropouts were more than four times as likely to have a parent sent to prison as were children born that same year to college-educated parents. More than half of all black children born to less educated parents in 1990 experienced parental imprisonment.[57]

This period of exploding incarceration is precisely the period in which single-parent families became more and more common in the less educated, lower-income stratum of the population. Correlation does not prove causation, of course, but mass incarceration has certainly removed a very large number of young fathers from poor neighborhoods, and the effects of their absence, on white and nonwhite kids alike, are known to be traumatic, leaving long-lasting scars. They certainly did in David's life in Ohio and Joe's life in Oregon.

Paternal incarceration (independent of other facts about a child's background, like the parents' education and income and race) is a strong predictor of bad educational outcomes, like getting poor grades and dropping out of school. Indeed, the pernicious effects of incarceration "spill over" onto the classmates of kids whose dads are imprisoned, even if the dads of those classmates are *not* in prison. Although imprisonment and its effects on kids are much more common among racial minorities, the effects of imprisonment itself are fully as pernicious among white kids.[58] Having a dad in prison is, we shall see in the chapters ahead, one of the most common themes in the lives of poor kids.

Figure 2.7: U.S. imprisonment rate, 1925–2010

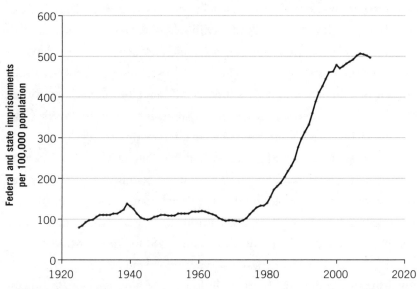

Source: *Sourcebook of Criminal Justice Statistics* (Maguire, n.d., Table 6.28.2010), http://www.albany.edu/sourcebook/pdf/t6282010.pdf.

Consequences of Two Tiers

Regardless of its causes, this two-tier family pattern has had an unmistakable effect on kids' lives. In the upper, college-educated third of American society, most kids today live with two parents, and such families nowadays typically have two incomes. In the lower, high-school-educated third, however, most kids live with at most one of their biological parents, and in fact, many live in a kaleidoscopic, multi-partner, or blended family, but rarely with more than one wage earner. Scores of studies have shown that many bad outcomes for kids are associated with the pattern now characteristic of the lower tier, whereas many good outcomes for kids are associated with the new pattern typical of the upper tier.[59] Contrast the stable parental support that enfolds Andrew and Chelsea with the dreadful chaos in which Kayla and David have grown up.

Children pay the cost of early childbearing and multi-partnered fertility in the form of diminished prospects for success in life. Children who grow up without their biological father perform worse on standardized tests, earn lower grades, and stay in school for fewer years, regardless of race and class.[60] They are also more likely to demonstrate behavioral problems such as shyness, aggression, and psychological problems such as increased anxiety and depression.[61] Children who spend part of their childhood in a single-mother home are also more likely to have sex earlier and to become young, single parents, re-creating the cycle.[62]

Children in divorced or remarried families face distinctive challenges, partly because their families' limited resources must be spread across more than one household, and partly because their parents' lingering grievances, and physical and emotional distance from one another, hamper effective communication and coordination. Multi-partner fertility is associated with less paternal involvement, less extended kin involvement, and more friction, jealousy, and competition, especially when there are children from different partnerships living in the same household, as we saw repeatedly in Kayla's life. All these problems are exacerbated when the various couples in a complex multi-partnered family were never married in the first place.[63]

Family breakup can often be better for the adults involved, of course, and sometimes even for their children, especially when the father is abusive, battling addiction, or frequently absent because of incarceration.

Moreover, many studies of family structure and kids' welfare are simply correlational, so we can't be sure whether the family fragility actually *caused* the bad outcomes. To some extent, the correlation between single parenting and bad outcomes may be spurious, reflecting a general syndrome of low income and family or personal disorganization. (So many things went wrong in Kayla's family, for example, that we cannot be sure that Joe and Darleen's divorce was the key factor, although all three of them see it that way.) But recent evidence strongly suggests that a causal relationship does exist.[64] As family specialist Isabel Sawhill says, "Generalizations are dangerous; many single parents are doing a terrific job under difficult circumstances. But on average, children from single-parent families do worse in school and in life."[65]

Given these handicaps, it is hardly surprising that recent research has suggested that the places in America where single-parent families are most common are the places where upward mobility is sluggish.[66] Of course, family structure is not an "uncaused first cause." It is entangled with a variety of factors, including race, residential segregation, community strength, and schooling. Since family fragmentation is, as we have seen, powerfully fostered by economic hardship, in one important sense family structure can be seen as merely an intervening variable between poverty in one generation and poverty in the next. Nevertheless, it is a prominent part of the picture. Though imperfect, the correlation is strong: more single parents means less upward mobility.

In the next chapter, we will turn to class differences in parenting practices, with a special focus on the latest evidence about how early practices affect child development. Increasingly, parents from different social classes are doing very different things *to* and *for* their kids, with massively consequential results.

Chapter 3

PARENTING

ATLANTA, SEEN FROM A DISTANCE, IS A SHINING EXAMPLE OF the rise of the New South, the jewel of the Sun Belt. Once the (fictitious) hometown of Rhett Butler and Scarlett O'Hara, Atlanta has been transformed into an affluent, sophisticated, and global metropolitan area, the ninth largest in the United States. Since 1970 no American metropolis has grown more rapidly. Atlanta has a strong, diversified, twenty-first-century economy, and is home to the headquarters of Coke, UPS, Home Depot, CNN, Delta Air Lines, and the U.S. Centers for Disease Control.

Affluent Atlanta is epitomized by Buckhead, a residential and commercial district of great wealth on the north side of town, where an urban core of high-rise condos, shopping districts, and restaurants is set amidst shady neighborhoods, golf courses, and million-dollar homes. The district is 95 percent white, with a median household income of roughly $150,000 and a child poverty rate of almost zero. It evokes contemporary Southern gentility, blending white pillars and lemonade with luxury office space and Jimmy Choo.

Just 15 minutes south along Peachtree Road, virtually in the shadows of Atlanta's downtown skyscrapers, lies one of the most drug- and crime-ridden ghettos in America—an area of boarded-up houses, barred windows, and concrete playgrounds, where idle men cluster on street corners. Here the population is 95 percent black, with a median household income of $15,000 and a child poverty rate of about 75 percent.

Throughout its history, Atlanta has been plagued by racial division.[1] By 1970, de jure segregation was gone, but white flight into the suburbs was well under way. Between 1960 and 1980, the white share of the central city's population plunged from 62 percent to 33 percent, while between 1960 and 2000 the fraction of the metro population living in Atlanta itself fell from 37 percent to 9 percent—the most centrifugal dispersion of any major metropolitan area in America. By 1970 the city had become the black center of a white doughnut, effectively maintaining de facto segregation in schools, housing, and much of social life.

By the early twenty-first century, Atlanta had the largest, most rapidly growing gap between rich and poor of any major American city.[2] That gap is heavily racial, of course, but within the black community itself, class and income differences have also grown. Atlanta has long had a strong, educated black upper class and middle class, and a rich black cultural heritage. Even under Jim Crow, a black elite emerged from the churches, universities, and black-owned businesses. During the Civil Rights movement, Atlanta's black politicians became among the most visible in America, and all of the city's mayors during the last 40 years have been black. Today the city is home to some of the largest black-owned firms in America, the largest concentration of black academics in the country, and (reportedly) the largest number of black millionaires.[3] Black commentators often refer to the city as the "Black Mecca."

Metro Atlanta's black population has grown dramatically in recent years. Between 2000 and 2010, the area received an influx of nearly half a million new black residents, by far the largest anywhere in the country. In 2008, metro Atlanta surpassed metro Chicago in total black population, and is now second only to New York City.[4] Of all black adults in greater Atlanta, 26 percent have a college degree, a higher figure (relative to other races in metro Atlanta) than in any of the other top ten metro areas. Many of the new, well-educated black Atlantans are, in fact, immigrants from the North, and an increasing number of them now live in mixed-race suburbs. The proportion of metro Atlanta blacks living in the city of Atlanta plunged from 79 percent in 1970 to 15 percent in 2010, as middle-class and working-class blacks fled the increasing dangers and desolation of the central city.[5] The more affluent of these new black suburbanites live in quiet, comfortable, mixed-race neighborhoods, while the less affluent live in suburbs with more than their share of bail bond billboards and pawn shops.

Those blacks who remain in Atlanta itself are desperately poor. Indeed, the racial concentration of poverty is greater in central Atlanta than in the central city of any other of the top ten metro areas in the country.[6] Large swaths of southern and western Atlanta itself are over 95 percent black, with child poverty rates ranging from 50 percent to 80 percent. Violent crime (concentrated in those areas) is rampant, with Atlanta consistently at or near the top of the central city ratings for the ten largest metro areas in America (first in 2005, third in 2008, second in 2009, second in 2012).

De facto racial segregation is more pervasive and intense than economic segregation in greater Atlanta, and skin color alone continues to affect residents' life chances. Nevertheless, the black community itself is increasingly polarized along economic lines.[7] The combination of continuing racial segregation and growing economic segregation has meant that the black upper class and middle class in Atlanta are increasingly separated both from their white counterparts and from poor blacks. Relatively speaking, Atlanta has more black college graduates *and* more concentrated black poverty than any of the other ten largest metropolitan areas in America. In that sense, metro Atlanta seems on its way to encompassing three cities, two of them prosperous and two of them black.

Greater Atlanta also has the second-lowest rate of intergenerational social mobility of all major American cities, just behind Charlotte,

North Carolina.[8] Racial disparities are certainly an important part of the story, but class disparities within each race are also important. We can open an interesting window on class differences in child development and parenting across America by meeting three black families from Atlanta, each representing a different slice of the socioeconomic hierarchy, and each illustrating a distinctive type of parental involvement and support for their children. Together, these three stories illustrate the interplay of economics, family structure, and parenting that affects the prospects of kids from different class backgrounds, whatever their racial background.

We'll first meet Desmond and his two younger siblings, the confident children of an upper-middle-class black family who moved about a decade ago from the Northeast to a comfortable, racially mixed suburb southwest of Atlanta.[9] A recent graduate of one of the South's best private universities, Desmond is on his way to a successful professional career, buoyed by the intensive, loving, conscientious support he has received from his parents, Carl and Simone.

We'll then move on to Michelle and Lauren, raised (along with two older brothers) in a series of mostly poor, mostly black suburbs by Stephanie, a tough-loving, hardworking single mom. As part of the 2000s exodus of middle- and working-class blacks fleeing the ghetto, Stephanie repeatedly moved her family further out of the city in search of better schools and safer neighborhoods.[10] Her approach to parenting is very different from Simone and Carl's and reflects the realities of her much less affluent circumstances.

Finally, we'll meet Elijah, an affable, soft-spoken, reflective young man who grew up largely unsupervised amidst extraordinary violence in the impoverished black ghettos of New Orleans and Atlanta.[11] In his preteen years, Elijah was mostly abandoned by his biological parents (neither of whom we were able to speak with), and his story allows us to appreciate how being socialized mostly by "the street" savagely constricts opportunity.

Simone, Carl, and Desmond

Simone, Carl, and their son Desmond greet us at the door to their sprawling home in a lovely suburban neighborhood of manicured lawns and large brick houses, three stylish cars parked in the driveway next to a basketball hoop. Simone, a teacher just returned from work, wears a tweed business suit, while Carl and Desmond lounge on the couch in tennis shirts and shorts. All three are strikingly fit, their words welcoming, their body language relaxed. (Desmond's two siblings are not at home during our visit.)

Simone grew up in an upwardly mobile, middle-class family in the New York City area. Her family started out in Harlem, moved through increasingly comfortable parts of the city, and finally crossed the river to a New Jersey suburb. Her father was recruited out of NYU to become a manager at Merrill Lynch; her mother was a medical secretary. "I don't think I ever really had a want for anything," Simone reflects. Her parents were happily married for more than 50 years and became what she describes as "amazing grandparents," part of a strong extended family. (Even in his 20s Desmond talks to his grandfather weekly, and his younger brother does so virtually every day.) Simone went to private and Catholic schools, and then attended the City University of New York, where she got a BA in industrial psychology.

Carl was born in Suriname to a black father and a Dutch mother, and as a youngster immigrated to New York. His father had worked for Alcoa, but like most immigrants, Carl says, his parents "had to start from scratch." In New York, his mother got a job at the U.N., while his father eventually built his own warehouse business. His parents were married for 33 years and then divorced amicably. Growing up in this family was "fantastic," Carl recalls. "Most everything [I have today] is because of my mom and dad," he says. The family always ate dinner together, with "pretty solid discussions" of school and news events, and they made religion an important part of their life. "We had a lot of friends that came to our home," he says, "and to them we were the perfect family. We were the only ones that had our mom and dad." Carl says that he went to "the worst high school in Brooklyn," but that his parents always expected him to go on to college. "I didn't really have much of a choice," he says. "'You have to go to college'—that was ingrained in us."

Simone and Carl met at CUNY. She was 20 and he was 21, and two years later they were married. She wanted a husband who was trustworthy and a reliable provider, and he was both. Before marrying, they talked to a mentor from church who encouraged them to wait five years before having children, and they took that advice to heart. Simone worked for nine years at a law firm in the city, moving swiftly up the ladder from receptionist to paralegal, but shortly after Desmond arrived, she became a stay-at-home mom.[12] "We were so blessed to have this beautiful little boy," she says. "It put things in perspective. You don't think about yourself so much."

At about the same time, Carl began work as an IT manager for a major Wall Street firm. Speaking of his career, he says modestly that "it's respectable. Work has always been a place where I've done well, definitely." He has always taken pride in his work and made a point of bringing his kids into the office. "Every couple of months," Desmond recalls, "my dad would take one of us to his job. He was always with the computer, showing me the ones and the zeroes. I'm fascinated. I don't know anything about it, and he was always telling me about it." These visits reflected Carl's priorities for his kids: "To help them to educate themselves to the best of their abilities," he says, "and surround themselves with people who are productive and not destructive."

Desmond recalls that education was a priority for his mom, too. "She used to give me these workbooks, like *Hooked on Phonics*," he says, "and I would sit at the table before dinner, or maybe after dinner, and do work." The emphasis his parents put on education made Desmond take for granted that he would continue his education after high school and become a professional. "I always thought that I was going to be a doctor, scientist, something like that," he says, "and I knew that college was the way to go to get to that point, so I always assumed that I was going to do it."

Simone brought Desmond up very purposefully. "I just always wanted my children to be ahead of the game," she says. "I didn't want anyone else raising my kids. We went to the 'Mommy and Me' class at the library. I tried to expose him to as much stuff as possible. There was a great hands-on museum by where we lived, and we would go. I was always arranging playgroups. When he got older, he did a sport every season. He played soccer all the way through high school. He played basketball. He took piano lessons. I even wanted him to do tap dancing, but my husband said no. I was very careful with what they ate. He wasn't allowed to eat the meat at McDonald's. They weren't allowed to drink soda. We were very strict about what went into their system."

Simone and Carl ensured that their kids were in good schools, and even comparison-shopped for kindergartens. During Desmond's early years, the family lived in northern New Jersey, just across the Hudson from Manhattan, but when Desmond was nine, they moved further downstate, to get Desmond into a better school system, even though it meant a grueling two-hour commute for Carl. "Not that our school system was bad," Simone says, "but I just didn't want him in the public schools [where we were living]."

Carl became increasingly annoyed that the long commute cut into his time with the kids, and after five years they decided to move to Atlanta. Simone recounts how they settled on the location of their new home. "I wanted Desmond to go to this local high school, because it's a really good school, and it's diverse. I didn't want him in an all-white school. I bought this house sight unseen, because all I cared about was the school. I figured if the high school was good, the feeder schools would be good."

Once her kids were in school, Simone explains, she committed herself to being more involved with their schoolwork than her own parents had been. "I would go to meetings at Desmond's school," she remembers, "and I would be able to tell them, 'Okay, this is where he's having a hard time, and this is what we need to work on.' I knew just as well as they did what was going on. In the summer, I put this workbook together, and one day it would be math, and the next day it would be reading. Every time was a learning lesson.

"They would have some cards with the presidents on them," she recalls, "and we would go to Florida sometimes, and I would have them do the flash cards in the car—I love flash cards. We would go somewhere [and I would ask], 'Why do you think we're going here?' We went to the Anne Frank house. We read the book before we went, so they would know who Anne Frank is. I read to them a book about a boy that grew up in a housing project and played basketball, totally different from how they grew up. I would read to them at night, the three of them."

Desmond recalls the same experiences with both annoyance and appreciation. "My mom would give us supplemental work and books to read in the summertime," he says. "We were in Florida and Universal Studios and sun outside, and I'm reading a book inside. It was the most atrocious time of my life. I had these math books, and every once in a while I'd look in the back to see the answers and pretend like I did some work. My mom would just watch me do it. Then she would say, 'You finished so quick, do the next page,' and I'm like, 'Why am I still doing work if I'm getting everything right?' She's like, 'Because I saw you cheating in the back.' My mom introduced me to *The Hardy Boys*, and I actually did like them. My dad was more practical. He would tell me to read the newspaper or look at the news every once in a while. Then he would ask, 'What did you learn?' 'Uh, I don't know, I can't remember.' [But] that's one thing that saved me from a lot of difficult times in school. Those were great times, man."

Today, Desmond loves reading. "It's weird," he says. "I never liked reading growing up. For some reason, I thought it was so difficult to find something that I was interested in reading. But now I do. Reading makes me feel smart."

Simone involved herself in her kids' school lives. Desmond's elementary school had a rule that once a child had left, he couldn't return, even if he had forgotten something. Desmond had a bad habit of forgetting his homework, so every afternoon Simone would show up at school and make him go through his book bag, to ensure he was bringing home everything he needed. After a couple of weeks, he learned to check himself. Simone also was an active volunteer in her kids' schools: she started the PTA at Desmond's kindergarten and became the PTO president of his elementary school.

Desmond recalls having a lot to say at family dinners when he was in elementary school. "I thought that everything that I noticed during the day was pretty important," he says. "I actually learned a lot from those conversations that we had at the dinner table." In general, Simone and Carl consider conversation and listening to be tools for educating their kids. "Spend that time with the kids," Simone says, explaining their philosophy. "Even if you don't feel like doing something, do it with them—just a little thing, like taking them to the grocery store with you. The kids remember that. Even when my daughter talks to me now about minor events in her life, I don't want to listen to all the stories, but I try to listen."

Carl echoes that sentiment and notes with pride how engaged he and Simone are with their children. "Nowadays," he says, "you must be involved with your kids more. When they struggle with their music lessons, find out why. Desmond [now 22] still calls every day, though he has [other obligations], so you have to let go a bit. But it is an extremely strong relationship. If I look at other people, the way they are with their kids, I'm just so thankful."

On issues of discipline and autonomy, Simone and Carl work together. "Always a team," says Simone. "If I wanted Desmond to do something or not to do something, we would always decide together—never that conflict where we're arguing in front of him." When problems arise, they try to be at once sensitive and firm. "As a parent," Carl says, "that's probably the most unpleasant thing, because you have to mix it with tough love. Often you have to drill it into him: 'This is what you need to do; this is what you have to do.' Sometimes that's when you pull that parental card and say, 'This is it.' Of course, as they get older there's less of that. So now if I see something, I'll say, 'You are doing that. Explain to me why you are doing that. Have you thought of this?'"

Simone has a nuanced and balanced approach to discipline. "I don't think I've ever necessarily punished Desmond," she says, "never had a privilege taken away or punished him, because I always felt like I want home to be somewhere where they look forward to coming. It's a sanctuary. Now, if you do something wrong, you're going to hear about it. But I don't think I ever have punished them or taken a privilege away. I've never said, 'No TV for a week.'"

Carl also always tried to foster a sense of autonomy in his kids. Even when he wants to encourage them in a particular direction, he limits his involvement. "Have them decide somehow on their own what they [want] to do," he says, describing his approach. "All I would do is expose them to as many things as possible." When Desmond was undecided about a medical career, rather than tell him what do to, Carl arranged for him to speak to some medical professionals and attend a six-week seminar.

Simone is warm, but she can also be tough and interventionist. An episode from Desmond's high school years in Georgia illustrates this facet of her parenting, as well as her ability to navigate tricky issues of race. While taking an economics exam, Desmond glanced at some index cards he had put on the floor. They were notes for his next class, but his teacher accused him of cheating. Desmond called his mom on his cell phone from school, and she immediately came to the classroom to ask what had happened. After discussing the situation with Desmond and Simone, the teacher agreed that he had misread it. "I can understand why you would think [that he was cheating]," Simone told him. "I would think the same thing. If you want to give him a zero on the test, because he should have been smarter than that, then I will back you 100 percent." The teacher declined the offer, calling Desmond "a good student." Desmond later complained to Simone that the teacher had been prejudiced. "No, he's not," she responded. "You have to use common sense. Why would you put cards there and be looking down? Put it in your binder under your desk. You have to be smart."

Religion has been a pervasive influence for Carl. He lists his life priorities as his spiritual life, his work, his family, and his exercise, in that order. Desmond, in turn, describes how religious community and religious beliefs have permeated his life. "We're a very spiritual family," he says, "and we pray before we eat. On Sunday, I didn't really pay attention unless it came to praying. After church on Sunday we would meet, and my dad would ask me, 'Desmond, what did you learn in church today?' And I said, 'About God,' and he was like, 'What else?' 'About Jesus.' And that's the end of the conversation. But when you come home, it starts to manifest a little bit differently, and you ask yourself, 'Why did you pray for that? Explain it a little bit more.' I got a really strong faith background, established myself individually in what I believe, and [asked myself] if I agree with everything that my parents have instilled.

"Most of my friends were involved in the church. When I was 12, I auditioned for a small group called the Joy Singers, and that's where I made some of my strongest friends. We sang every Wednesday night and Saturday night. We'd go to sing at youth camps and things like that. It made me confident in what I believed, made me open enough to talk about it should someone want to talk about it and confident in myself to hold it back if no one wanted to talk about it."

Simone also placed a strong emphasis on religion in raising her kids. "Desmond is a strong, Christian young man," she says. "I want him to be a godly man, in everything that means. I've told my boys that a girl that you date, that you're going to be 'involved with,' you may not want to be with her for a long term, but that's [going to be] someone's wife. So make sure you're very respectful. If you don't like her, don't mess around with her. My kids probably didn't know until they were in middle school that you could have kids when you're not married."

One telling illustration of the family's closeness emerged late in our conversation with Desmond, when he offhandedly raised an issue that his parents had not mentioned: that in the seventh grade he had developed diabetes. "It was a big deal," he says. "Changed the way we ate, changed our whole lifestyle. My whole family adapted with me, which was really helpful for me, because I definitely struggled. It's a battle every day. We started eating a lot more fish. We saved the ethnic dishes with sugar and fat for special occasions. My family really drew closer around that."

In many respects, Carl and Simone are like conscientious, educated parents anywhere. But race has been a daily factor in their lives—and their parenting. "I was raising black boys," she says, "and I'd always felt like black boys had it harder, so I always wanted them to be a step ahead. So I would say to Desmond, 'Honey, if you want an A, you can't get a 90 and expect you're going to get an A. You have to get a 95.'

"Incidents of racism do happen—not lots, but they do happen. Even though Desmond had a 4.0 average and was ranked eighth or ninth in his class, a college counselor suggested tech schools and two-year colleges. Another time Desmond asked a teacher for directions to his new chemistry class, and the teacher made some negative remarks. When I spoke to the school counselor, he said, 'Oh, yeah, I can see him saying that. He probably looked at Desmond and didn't realize that he was smart.'

"Society will look at a black boy . . ." She pauses and then begins again. "My middle son was home from college, and it was raining, he was going out, and he put his hood on. I said, 'Where you going with your hood on? Put a baseball hat on.' I'm very realistic: 'You're smart, you have everything going for you. If you have to work a little bit harder, oh, well.' "

Going away to college made Desmond reflect a lot on the importance of his family. "Freshman year was difficult for me," he says, "because I didn't really realize how much my family [mattered to me]. When I came home from my first day of classes, I just wanted to talk to my parents about the first day of school. I was like, 'Wow, I want to go home now.' The way my parents interact is what I try to mimic in myself, especially when they argue, or when they're discussing something that has happened on TV. Every time I have time to think to myself, I think about what they would do, how they would like me to act. Every once in a while I'll mess up, and it helps me grow a little bit better and learn a little bit more."

Toward the end of a subsequent conversation, Simone reflects on her life as a parent. "I really do have so much to be thankful for," she says, "but I will tell you that you never stop parenting." Just then Desmond, now interning with the Centers for Disease Control in Florida, calls her for advice about some missing car keys. Afterward, she points to her phone and says, "Proof perfect, right? You always are there for that support, that advice, that voice of reason. As a parent, it never ends."

Simone and Carl are nearly a continent away and a race apart from Earl and Patty in Bend and Chelsea's parents, Wendy and Dick, in Port Clinton. But all three couples belong to America's upper middle class, and their parenting styles are strikingly alike. In their intensive investments of time, money, and thoughtful care in raising their kids, the three families are much more similar to each other than they are to working- and lower-class families of their own race living a few miles away in their respective communities. We next turn to one of those working-class families in metro Atlanta.

Stephanie, Lauren, and Michelle

We meet Stephanie and her daughters in the dining room of their large tract home, located in a new development on the outskirts of Atlanta. The room has a generic, "model home" feel, complete with plastic flowers, but Stephanie fills it up with her big smile and her outgoing, maternal, good-humored personality. She wears the uniform of the hospitality business where she works as an office manager, her name stenciled above the pocket. Lauren (21), her older daughter, tall and graceful, projects a confident, elegant aura, and Michelle (19), her younger daughter, curvier than her sister, wears a pink velour sweat suit and restlessly checks her phone. (Stephanie's two sons no longer live at home.) Stephanie, self-conscious about her education, apologizes for her limited vocabulary. "I use a lot of wording, and [my daughters] will correct me. Even though I get mad, I like that." It quickly becomes clear, despite her apology, that she is a strong, reflective mother.

Stephanie grew up in Detroit, where her mother had fled after leaving Stephanie's abusive, alcoholic father, in Georgia. Her mother worked as an RN and "shacked," as Stephanie puts it, with Stephanie's stepfather, who worked on the line at Chrysler. Though they lived in a decent neighborhood, both her mother and her stepfather were alcoholics, and Stephanie fell in with a rough crowd from the projects. In junior high, she became a gang member and enjoyed getting into fights. "I sliced up a couple of people back in the day," she recalls. "I went to juvenile several times for being disobedient and fighting. If it's something I wanted, and they won't let me have it, I'd go and snatch it, or cut their hair. I don't know why I was bad. Sad to say that, but I was a bully."

As a result of her behavior, Stephanie was frequently suspended from school and suffered the consequences at home. "My parents would beat the hell out of me and make me read a book. I got a D in seventh or eighth grade and I really got a bad whupping. When I came home with two Es, a D, and two Cs, I was under punishment for a whole summer. No TV, no nothing."

When Stephanie wanted a ten-speed bike, her mother refused, because she was still under restriction. So Stephanie and her friends took matters into their own hands. "We went and stole it, come back and spray paint the bike in the color I wanted, and parked it in the alley," she says. "We didn't have to steal it, but we did. It was fun! Thank God my kids went the other way. As I got older, I made sure my kids had a better life."

Stephanie was 15 when her mother died. She moved in with an aunt in Detroit. "My aunt pushed me more than anybody," she recalls, "so that's why I respected her more." She continued to misbehave, however, and when she was in the 12th grade, she says, her aunt kicked her out for "being sassy, running off at the mouth, driving cars without a license, smoking pot." Moving to Atlanta, Stephanie got her GED in an adult education program and soon became pregnant with a son—"I was gambling," she says with a laugh. She married the father and would eventually have three more children with him: another son, and then Lauren and Michelle.

In retrospect, having her first child was the turning point in Stephanie's life. "When you have a baby," she says, "it makes you more responsible, because you got to take care of that kid and you got to take care of yourself. I wasn't thinking about a career path. I was just thinking about getting a dollar. I started getting focused when I got about 25. 'What you really want to do in life?' I started my goals off with my son. I wanted to make sure I was still going to the day care with them, so I would know who was teaching them, and then we just kept a roof over their head."

Given the uncertain economic prospects and uncertain loyalty of her husband, Stephanie arranged her life on the assumption that she alone was responsible for the economic security of her children. So her first priority was to find a job. She began working at Popeyes and then Hardy's Supermarket, but she wasn't earning enough to pay for gas and electricity, so she found a new job, at Zale's department store. One of her managers there spotted her customer-friendly, hardworking disposition and promoted her successively to cashier, department manager, and store manager. By the time Stephanie had had all of her children, she was working 40 hours a week and making what she considered "good money": about $35,000 a year, or twice the poverty level for a family the size of hers.

During those years, her husband began fooling around with another woman and then moved out—proving that Stephanie had been right to arrange her life on the assumption that she alone had to provide for her children. She eventually married again, to a forklift driver, and now says she has "a good marriage" with him. He has children of his own from a first marriage, however, and Stephanie and he have agreed that he is not responsible for her kids.

Fifteen years ago, Stephanie took a job with her current employer, where today she works as an office manager at a major branch. "I love customers," she says. Her sunny, outgoing disposition, coupled with her strong work ethic, has allowed her to build reasonable financial stability for her family. "If we wanted something, she always got it," Lauren says, "everything from laptops and iPads to clothes." (But "not designer stuff!" Stephanie insists.)

Michelle has similar memories about how her mother provided for her. "I did not worry with my mom, not at all. But my dad has so many children, you gotta get when you can, or he 'don't have it right now.' My mom said she never asked anybody to do anything for us, 'cause she'll do it. She did it by herself, and that's how she want us to be." She fondly remembers her 13th birthday, for example. "I got a bike," she says. "It was a nice day, and I was just riding around in the cul-de-sac. We had a little pool party and trampoline. It was nice." Michelle is very aware of her relative good fortune. Comparing her family with the fractured, destitute family of an acquaintance from the ghetto, she says, "I'm not saying we're rich, but compared to his family, we're rich."

She recognizes, too, just how hard Stephanie has worked to ensure a good life for her family. "My mother is my hero, my foundation," she says. "Everybody else is just there. She works every day. She worked herself up by herself. She still does it by herself, even if she has somebody by her side. She'll always say if he ever leaves, she can still pay her mortgage. My mom's husband's son had three children, and he done ran from all of them. Men will claim they're a man, but they run from their responsibility."

Lauren has learned a similar lesson. "You cannot trust people," she says. "You need to have your guard up at 100 percent every time, because you don't know who you're around and what they're capable of—family, everyone." Not surprisingly, Stephanie feels the same way. "I agree 100 percent," she says. "I learned in life that the only person you can confide in is yourself."

If Stephanie's first priority as mother was to provide for the material sustenance of her growing family, a close second was their physical safety. "When we was coming up," she says, referring to her own childhood, "you could walk the streets at night. But now walk the streets at night, you have pistol, a Uzi, or something." Their immediate neighborhoods were not so bad, but a few blocks away, she says, it was "getting rough." So Stephanie laid down the law for her kids. "You couldn't walk around at night," Lauren recalls. "We had to stay on our street."

"That's the rule," Stephanie explains. "You stay on our street so I could watch you. Our subdivision was a dead end, so if you came into the subdivision, the neighbors know you don't belong there. I sheltered my kids a lot in Fulton County [where they lived when the girls were preschoolers and the boys were in middle school]. I didn't want them around the roughnecks, so I sheltered them. But still one of my sons"—the younger of the two—"got out and then into the rough life." Stephanie refers to this son as her "challenge child—the most difficult one," and describes having to "call the police on him" when he lost his temper at home. How easily he slipped out of Stephanie's grasp and into the "rough life" (from which he has still not emerged 15 years later) is a reminder of the thin margin of safety for parents in Stephanie's situation.

Because she grew up in Detroit with a near-constant threat of physical violence, Stephanie has developed a tough love approach to mothering. "Were your parents warm parents?" we ask. "Lots of hugs or were they—" Astonished at our naïveté, Stephanie interrupts. "No, we don't do all that kissing and hugging," she says. "That's other races' stuff. I'm not kissing and hugging my kids. I love my kids to death, but I'm not a touchy-feely person, like the Beavers. In real life, that doesn't happen. You can't be mushy in Detroit. You can't be soft. You gotta be hard, really hard, because if you soft, people will bully you. If you go to Detroit, don't be soft. You gotta be hard. Be a thug!" Her stern admonition delivered, she relaxes, laughs, and adds, "That's how you got to be. I smile all day at work, but when it come down to my household, I'm strict."

Stephanie's approach to discipline, not surprisingly, is very different from Carl's and Simone's. All of her kids got "whuppings." A particularly unsettling illustration of her approach comes from Michelle's first weeks in preschool. When Michelle was left at school, Stephanie recalls, "she howled at the top of her lungs all day every day, for probably 30, 60 days straight." Eventually, Stephanie says, the school called the Division of

Family and Children Services, worried about mistreatment at home, but they investigated and found nothing. The five-year-old Michelle wanted to stay with her dad, who had just left the family, and Stephanie agreed. But after two weeks of whupping by her father, Stephanie continues, Michelle was still "hollering at the top of her lungs. So I say, 'This is going to have to stop.' Went to the school, called Michelle. She came out, took her in the bathroom, wore that ass out. She went to class and had no more problems." [13]

"And grew up to be a bully," Lauren softly adds.

As a hardworking single mother, Stephanie struggles to cope with demands on her time and energy, and this has affected her style of parenting in many ways. Parent-child conversations over dinner, for example, were uncommon. "We're not a sit-down-and-eat family," Stephanie says. "We didn't do that. You got to the table, you ate." "When it's time to eat," Lauren adds, "it's whoever wants to eat. It wasn't everybody sit at the table, like a party or something." "We ain't got time for all that talk-about-our-day stuff," Stephanie explains.

Exhausted from long hours of cheerfully helping difficult customers, Stephanie goes to bed early. Lauren confesses that this allowed her to get acquainted with vodka at night with her siblings. On the other hand, when Lauren was a star basketball player in high school, Stephanie rushed home from work to serve as unofficial "team mom."

Stephanie's concern about her children's education mirrors Simone's, although it is subject to different constraints. Stephanie twice moved away from the encroaching ghetto in search of better schools and safer neighborhoods. As Lauren says of the neighborhoods where she grew up, "they got better and better." Of course, those moves were enabled by Stephanie's hard-fought climb up the economic ladder.

Stephanie is unsure about whether she read to her children when they were young, but Lauren insists that she did. Stephanie knows that at least she got them library cards, "because," as she puts it, "a kid needs a book in the hand every day." In general, she is proud of her girls' education, although her measure of success differs from Carl's and Simone's or Wendy's and Dick's. ("They didn't skip school," she says.) As her economic situation has improved, she has felt able to offer her daughters an education at one of the nearby community colleges. Lauren has taken up her offer. Michelle tried it for a year but dropped out. "I'm not really a school person," she says.

Stephanie has developed a strong philosophy of parenting, based on her own experiences. "My mom was an alcoholic," she says, "and I wasn't choosing the same path. I go to work every day. I motivate my kids. I push my kids to go to college. I push them that if you need a shoulder to lean on, that's what I'm here for. I'm that support system.

"I try to do constructive criticism to get my children where they need to be. And you can only coach them. The coach take you to the field. He can only coach you to your bases. It's up to you to get that concept to where you need to go, first base, second base, and third base, and home. I try to show them in life that it's hard out here. Just because I make it easy for you, it's not easy. It's hard out here, so if you got children and you can't provide for them, don't make babies. And if you make babies, you got to take care of them.

"I'm not my children's friend! I'm the best of parents to my children. A parent don't need to be their kids' friend. They need to be their parents, so they can guide them in the right direction. Far as you calling me, 'Girlfriend, let me tell you what happened last night,' we don't do that here. You respect me as a parent, I'll respect you as my child. You need guidance. That's what I'm here for.

"Parenting is hard. It is so much work to have four children. You constantly on the move. You got to make sure they got that bath, got to make sure they got food, make sure they get on that school bus. They did good, though. I'm proud of them."

In terms of preparing her children for the twenty-first century, Stephanie's hard work and sacrifice have yielded mixed returns so far. Her older son (whom the girls call "everybody's golden boy") seems on the road to a decent life. He took courses from an online adult education school, and according to Stephanie, he is "doing real well, chasing that dollar." Her younger son (her "challenge child"), by contrast, was suspended from high school for an entire year, though he did eventually graduate and now works with his dad in a recycling center.

Lauren, Stephanie's older daughter, has mostly stayed on track. "I knew I was going to be straight," Lauren says, "unlike my siblings. I'm not ghetto." She turned down an athletic scholarship to play basketball at Kansas, despite strong urging from her coaches and her mother. "It was just getting too rigorous for me," she says. "I wanted to do something with juveniles." She will soon finish a degree at a nearby community college, but, unfortunately, funding for juvenile probation officers has been cut. The result, she says, is that she has to "go where the money is, which is with adults, which I did not want to do." She is dating a young man from the neighborhood, whom Stephanie calls "a good kid."

Stephanie calls Michelle another "challenge child." Michelle concedes that she hasn't been easy to raise. "I wasn't the worst child," she says, "but I wouldn't say I was a good child. I have my troubles in school. I had speech problems and a reading comprehension problem growing up. I just thought it was like a get-out-of-class thing—'Go to another class'—but now I realize it actually helped. I used to struggle with math and social studies. I got in trouble in middle school, because everybody else was acting out."

Despite her strong commitment to her kids, Stephanie is sometimes simply unable to help them over important hurdles. "I'll ask her for help [with homework]," Michelle says, "and she'll help me as much as she can, but she couldn't do it." Michelle struggled to pass the social studies test for high school graduation. "I had to take it six or seven times," she says. "It was very stressful, but I passed on my last try. My mom was supportive." "How?" we asked. "She would pray about it," Michelle says, "and talk to God."

Stephanie wasn't happy when Michelle dropped out of community college. "When I stopped going, it was a big deal with her." Michelle took a temp job but quickly quit, because, as she puts it, "I had to stand in one spot for ten hours, and my feet was hurting." She gave her mother a different explanation. "I just told her they didn't need me," she says.

Michelle now hopes to attend a local trade school and imagines herself working as a day care teacher. For now, she spends her days hanging out with a high school dropout from the inner city. Stephanie dislikes him. "He's a lazy bum," she says. "He came up in a rough environment. That type of life I shelter them from, see. And then for her to go into a relationship like that kind of mind-boggles me. That ain't the life I chose for her."

Given limited resources and a challenging environment, strong parental commitment and tough love is sometimes not enough.

Neither Stephanie nor her daughters believe that racial discrimination has limited their opportunities, perhaps because the barriers they encounter every day are more economic than racial. Michelle was once pulled over for an unpaid parking ticket and put in a holding cell for 45 minutes, but she resists the idea that racism was behind the cop's actions. "Maybe he just trying to meet his quota," she says. "But I don't think he was being racist. I don't think people are racist. I think black people have certain white people they don't like, and I think white people have some black people they don't like."

Lauren claims that racism was not a factor as she grew up. "Living in Georgia, you would expect that," she says. "But I never experienced racism, except by black people that's saying stuff about each other." She adds, "Out here [in the mostly rural, majority-white area where they now live], we never experienced it, because everybody got along with everybody. I've never seen racism, even in Clayton County."

Stephanie agrees with her daughters. "To me," she says, "it's not black people–white people. It's black people against black people. First time somebody do something, I don't care what color they are, they just use 'racism.' It's just a word that's out there that people use."

Stephanie claims she didn't even teach her kids to watch out for racism as they grew up. "I ain't got time for that," she says. "There's just too much energy disliking a different race. They did nothing to you."

Times have changed since Stephanie herself climbed the economic ladder. However admirably adapted it is to the environment in which she lives, her tough love parenting—privileging obedience over imagination, "whupping" over reasoning, and physical safety over verbal skills—is not so well adapted to the new economy as the "concerted cultivation" employed by Simone and Carl.[14] Nevertheless, Stephanie takes hard-earned satisfaction in what she has managed to do for her kids. "I think I have brought them to where they're at now—respectable. We have our ups and down, but respectable. And then I know that you have to go out there, either go to school or work for what you want in order to have it. Ain't nothing free in life. Nobody ever gave me anything in life. I said once I got to where I were now, I wasn't going back. I put God first, and everything else behind me could stay back, but God, my husband, my children. It's my path, and I hope that I did a good job with them."

Elijah

We encounter Elijah in a dingy shopping mall on the north side of Atlanta, during his lunch break from a job packing groceries. The shoppers and sales clerks around us are without exception black or Latino. Elijah is thin and small in stature, perhaps five foot seven, and wears baggy clothes that bulk his frame: jeans belted low around his upper thighs, a pair of Jordans on his feet. Elijah leans back in his seat, resting an elbow on a chair next to him. After some initial reluctance, he speaks calmly, his demeanor relaxed and comfortable. He gesticulates frequently, maintains eye contact, and is a talented raconteur. Despite describing traumatic and even incredible experiences, he speaks in a casual, objective tone, recounting facts rather than soliciting sympathy. At the end of the interview he tells us, "I kinda enjoyed talking about my life."

Elijah was born in 1991, in Nürnberg, Germany, where his parents were stationed with the U.S. Army. His mother had grown up in Georgia, his father in New Orleans. All Elijah remembers of his time with them is "a lot of abusive arguments." While he was only an infant, both parents became involved with other partners. "They couldn't live together for nothing," he says. By the time Elijah was three or four, his mother was back in Georgia with a new boyfriend, and Elijah had been left with his paternal grandparents in the deeply impoverished, mortally dangerous New Orleans projects. His recollections of his childhood, first in New Orleans and then in Atlanta, are surreal.

"They say my granddad got 36 kids," he says. "I heard strange noises in the bedroom when I was young, and I know he wasn't fighting. He came out in his underwear, and I said, 'Hey, Pa, what's that noise?' And he was like, 'Oh, that was me and your grandma. We were wrestling.' I didn't realize until I was 11 years old that my granddaddy was having sex with his girlfriend.

"I seen him get drunk and beat the mess outta my grandmother. I don't think no child should see that. I got beat by my granddaddy, but it was me being a knucklehead. I be up in the projects looking at my cousin smoking weed, selling it. I seen my granddaddy drunk naked one time. I was so disgusted I didn't go home for a week.

"I had a cousin named James. He was crazy. I seen him shoot at people, but I ain't never seen him kill nobody. And he be the one that taught me how to rob. When I first got up here [in Atlanta], I was robbing people. I was robbing them little Indians in my apartment, them little Muslims. I used to know how to go through the balcony and do the little key thing with the hanger to unlock the door. He taught me that, my cousin James. I don't know whether he dead or alive, 'cause when I left New Orleans he was serving 25 to life for first-degree murder.

"I was closer to him than to anybody, closer than my own daddy. When he tell me to go rob somebody for their money, and I give it to him, he give me like $50. He told me to go steal some shoes. I stoled it, and when somebody tried to come after me, he be shooting at them so they wouldn't try to catch me or take me to juvey. I'm just six or seven years old. I don't know no better. I'm like, 'That's what you gotta do. I'm in the 'hood.' That's what I'm good at. When you living in New Orleans you gotta be brave and be strong, and just stand on your own two feet. Don't let anybody try to punk you out."

Elijah's neighborhood in New Orleans was "real violent," he says. "If

I was hearing somebody get shot, I'm living right next door to the killer. Dead bodies all the time. People being kidnapped and raped and killed and murdered. Who wants to be around that? I'm seeing crackheads walking around the street, homeless, poverty. I hated it. I didn't like where I was from.

"I was ashamed of who I was, because I go to school and white folk used to pick on me. A lot of racism, too. The only people I used to get into a fight with [were] white people. Not black people. If I was fighting the black people, it was because of my cousin. My cousin told me to do it, and I do it. But I loved to fight back then. It the adrenaline you get, that 'hood mentality. So it was rough living. I hated it."

Elijah explains what he means by "'hood mentality": "Like, bullies used to come to school and take somebody for they lunch money: 'I want your lunch money.' With me, in New Orleans, I be like, 'I want all the money you got. I want your new shoes. I want your clothes. I want everything.' My cousin James can do it way better than me. He won't do it with his fists. He have a gun to your head and be like, 'Look, you don't give me this money, I'm gonna blast your head off.' I want him to do it, too. I never seen nobody in my family actually murder somebody. But I don't want him to do it."[15]

As a preschooler, Elijah became gradually inured to homicide. "When I was four years old," he says, "I seen this pretty little girl, rolling on her little scooter, die in the drive-by. Just out of nowhere. The next thing you know, I see her jump crazy with blood, shot through the forehead, nose, and all this right here [gesturing], bleeding all up on the mouth. And I'm shocked, I'm scared. I ain't never seen nothing like that before. It made me cry."

Later, Elijah heard a man in the alley get shot. "That scared the fool outta me," he says. "Every time my grandfather would take me to see a scary movie, it wouldn't scare me at all, because I seen worse. 'Go outside, I'll show you what's scary.'"

Finally, death came to his own doorstep. "I remember waking up one morning and going to look for my grandfather. I unlocked the front door, and I seen him standing over a dead body right outside of our doorstep. I ain't know what to say at first. I just ran to my room and went back to sleep."[16]

Elijah isn't sure where his parents were during his time in New Orleans. All he knows about his father in those years is that he left the Army and returned to the States. "Dad was a rolling stone," he says, "before he got saved." Elijah does not recall meeting his father until he was ten. "Shoot," Elijah says of that encounter, "it was good to see him for the first time." For those missing years, Elijah can provide only occasional glimpses of his father—serving time in prison, fathering children in Texas and Louisiana, and eventually becoming a street preacher south of Atlanta.

Meanwhile, his mother ended up back in Charleston, South Carolina, with her new boyfriend. When he was ten, Elijah was sent to live with them for a year. He found Charleston tame compared to New Orleans. "It wasn't too much action," he says, "because I used to the violence, the drugs, the shootings. So I would just come outside and wait for something to happen, and just get ready for some action."

After that year in South Carolina he returned to his paternal grandparents in New Orleans, where he would remain for several more years. During this period he saw his dad again. "This time he was in jail," he says, "and he told me why he was in jail. I liked to cry. It was hard holding it in, but I really had to hold it in, because he just looked me dead in my eyes and said, 'Everything gonna be all right.' And you know how fathers and sons are: I believe my dad, because when I'm around my dad, I feel I ain't got no worries. Everything is really gonna be all right."

When Elijah turned 13, his mother insisted that he move from New Orleans to Atlanta to help care for the year-old twins that she had had with her latest boyfriend—the result of "a little casual sex," Elijah says, "from what I hear." The boyfriend refused to care for them. "I didn't like this guy too well," Elijah says, "because, 'You up there having sex with my momma, got her pregnant, and now you can't take care of your kids, and I gotta be the one out here baby-sitting.' They were a handful, and

I ain't never dealt with kids before. So that would partially keep me away from the trouble that was on the street."

But only partially. Elijah did get into trouble during his first year in Atlanta—for arson. "I got locked up in juvie for some dumb junk," he says. "I did it, though: I ain't gonna lie. It was fun burning down that lady house [laughs]. I burnt down her house, because she called me a 'Negro.' I was like 'Okay, you . . .' I was young, wild, and crazy. I was ready, I was out there, I was real horrible then."

Within a week, Elijah's father got Elijah released, but then administered some justice of his own. "My dad came and put up a lot of money," he says, "and got me out and beat me senseless. That was the worst beating I probably ever went through [laughs]. I couldn't sit down for a good little week just getting beat like that. I was like, 'Oh man, I am never gonna burn nobody house again [laughs].'"

Elijah's mother and father both came down on him hard after the arson. "My mom and dad double-teamed me," he says, "and I didn't feel too good. She was fussing at me, and my dad was like, 'You actin' like the devil. You need to stop doing all this bad stuff.' And I'm like, 'Man, all right, I give up.' I go to school and stop skipping."

After school, Elijah would come home and watch TV. "I never had that many rules," he says, "because—I think it was the lack of discipline, because I didn't have my dad there physically. When I talked to him on the phone, he encouraged me, and ministered the Word of God to me, but my mother was just really going hard on me, verbally abusive to me, and I never kinda understood that.

"It's the same old, same old: 'Shut up talking to me. I don't wanna hear that crap.' Man, she is cussing at me, calling me just dumb and stupid. 'You gonna be just like your daddy—no job, living with your mother.' Don't get me wrong. My mom's not a terrible person. It's just the way she grew up, and that's how she got used to things. Her father is the reason why my mom is like the way she is."

Elijah offers another interpretation of his mother's punitive behavior. "At one time she had two jobs, and that's probably the reason why when my mom come home to me, she be frustrated. When you come home as a mother, and you see bills on the table, and you see the dishes ain't washed, and you see your son's room not cleaned up, and you see everything messy, I think that's why she's so angry. She angry at me a lot of times, and I can't blame her. But, at the same time, it's a limit that you speak to your child. When you cussing at your child all the time and just really going hammer, that really breaks . . . that really discourages your child."

Elijah describes 2006 (when he was 15, two years after the arson incident) as "the worst year of my life"—which is saying a lot. He's vague about why it was the worst year, but he calls it "a hellish point" between him and his mother. "My dad looked at me as like America's Most Wanted," he says. "My mom just looked at me as some nut that was born out of her stomach, and I'm going to my dad house and getting a whupping all the time."

Later, he reflects on how he would want to treat his own kids. "Tell 'em the right things," he says. "If my son gets rowdy and acts like a thug, like I used to do, and then starts robbing people, I just speak good words over his life. I mean, don't get me wrong: I'm gonna beat him, I'm gonna teach him what's right from wrong. But I'm gonna say good words over him. If you tell your child that he ain't gonna be nothin' but a low-down dirty-rat scoundrel, your child is gonna be a low-down dirty-rat scoundrel. You gotta believe that one day he's gonna be a fantastic person."

Elijah had a lot of trouble in school. He was expelled at least once for skipping class. He got "horrible" grades. Even just graduating sometimes seemed out of reach. "I felt really stupid," he says. "That graduation just ain't no joke. So I just set my mind on the book, so that I could get out of high school. And I didn't pass. I even went to summer school for it, and I still didn't pass. In total, I took the graduation test four times, and then I got it right."

Elijah graduated at age 19 and quickly slipped back into a life of drugs and drinking that eventually made his mother kick him out of the house. "I got high and drunk every night," he says, "chillin' out with the homies from midnight to eight in the morning. My momma couldn't tell me nothing. But after my little drug problem, and when I got kicked outta my momma house, it all came to sense. 'I'm 19 years old. I gotta stop doing this. I can't live my life like this.'"

Two years later, Elijah is still uncertain about the path forward. Since graduating, he's lived sometimes with his mother, occasionally with his father in south Georgia, and sometimes crashing with friends. "Last year," he says, "I got kicked out of my mom's house, so I went to live with one of my friends. He was on drugs, smoking weed and popping pills, going to the club and having sex. Man, that was crazy. I'm up there just losing my sanity. I don't know what to do, 'cause I'm like, 'Should I be a saint or a sinner, a loser or a winner?' And at that time I was trying to get my life together. So I left my job to go live with my dad. I was trying to do this church thing and believe in God. It ain't work, 'cause after five weeks with my dad, I went back doing the same thing. I started cussing, just thugging it out, being the old me. My mom and my dad try to pressure me into go into the Army, and I'm like, 'I don't wanna join no Army. That ain't me. You didn't do good in the Army.' My dad got lazy and quit the Army. Why do that?"

Elijah tried for a few months to make a living selling knives door-to-door—but doing the job successfully required contacts and a car, and he had neither.[17] "It was real new to me," he says, describing the work. "Shoot, I'm from the 'hood. I don't know anything about this. You gotta dress up every day, you had to be high-class to get that job. I coulda done good, but I didn't." Eventually, he returned to his job bagging groceries at Kroger's.

Elijah has disparate dreams about his future. In one of them he is an evangelical preacher, working in partnership with his dad. "We gonna have plenty of money," he says, explaining this dream. "I'm gonna have my own church, because my dad, he's a preacher and he like to teach the Word of God. We talk a lot about the Word of God. Just a real good father-and-son bonding."

Another future he envisions for himself is more secular and ultimately more compelling. "I'm a hip-hop head," he says, "so I wanna produce music. That's my dream. I wanna be a DJ. That's my dream right there, to have my own record label. I'm at a point now where I just don't care. I'm about to go ahead and save up some more money and get my own apartment and go to school. Nowadays I'm trying to get another job right now, and trying to fulfill that dream of being one of the greatest rappers of all time. I don't never normally tell nobody this, but all I do is write and listen to music. So that's what I see myself doing: being a rapper, living the high life."

After 21 violent, tumultuous years of life, Elijah is a self-sufficient survivor, though just barely. He still seems addicted to the adrenaline rush of violence that he first experienced as a six-year-old in New Orleans. "I just love beating up somebody," he says, "and making they nose bleed and just hurting them and just beating them on the ground." At the same time, he seems to recognize that he needs to keep his urge to be violent in check. "I try to keep it under control," he says, "because people think that weird and crazy. I don't want to go that route now, because I'm more mature now. I'm forever saying I don't live that life no more. I go to work, go to church and home. So God don't want me to beat nobody up no more. I'm pretty sure."

The troubles in Elijah's personal life obviously had roots in his parentless early childhood in New Orleans, but that turbulence accelerated with "the different transitions I had to go through, a lot of different experiences that I wasn't used to." On the other hand, he seems genuinely committed to improving his situation. As he puts it, "I ended [up] trying—becoming a champion of all my problems. Being a problem solver, and just believing that I can do everything."

He admits that he's still "going through a lot of personal issues" with his parents, but nevertheless he seems hopeful. "All I do is go to church," he says. "I have fun, chill with my friends, and just trying to be a good all-around American citizen."

• • •

The three families whose lives we have just glimpsed are obviously not representative. (Sadly, because of racial disparities in economic well-being and incarceration, Elijah's story is more typical of black youth than Desmond's story.) But the differences among these three families do help us understand the troubling class-based disparities in parenting that have emerged and grown in America in recent decades. These three families happen to be black, but the class disparities they demonstrate are at least as marked—and are growing at least as rapidly—among white families.

These changing patterns in parenting have great significance for children's prospects. I begin with a close focus on the latest scientific research on brain development in young children, which clarifies exactly what aspects of parenting help and hurt most in terms of a child's cognitive and socioemotional development. I then zoom back to a wide-angle view of class differences in parenting practices nationwide over the last several decades to explore how and why those class differences have grown, to the relative disadvantage of poor kids.

Child Development: What We Are Learning

Recent research has greatly expanded our understanding of how young children's early experiences and socioeconomic environment influence their neurobiological development, and how, in turn, early neurobiological development influences their later lives. These effects turn out to be powerful and long-lasting. "Virtually every aspect of early human development," write the authors of a landmark study by the National Academy of Sciences, "from the brain's evolving circuitry to the child's capacity for empathy, is affected by the environments and experiences that are encountered in a cumulative fashion, beginning in the prenatal period and extending throughout the early childhood years."[18] The bottom line: early life experiences get under your skin in a most powerful way.

The roots of many cognitive and behavioral differences that appear in middle childhood and adolescence are often already present by

18 months, and their origins, we now know, lie even earlier in the child's life. Neuroscience has shown that the child's brain is biologically primed to learn from experience, so that early environments powerfully affect the architecture of the developing brain. The most fundamental feature of that experience is interaction with responsive adults—typically, but not only, parents.

Healthy infant brain development requires connecting with caring, consistent adults. The key mechanism of this give-and-take learning is termed by specialists in child development "contingent reciprocity" (or more simply, "serve-and-return" interaction.)[19] Like serving in a game of tennis, the child sends out some signal (for example, by babbling), and when the adult responds (for example, by vocalizing back), detectable traces are left on the developing circuitry of the child's brain. Much of this learning is preverbal, of course. However, research has shown that the foundations of both mathematical and verbal skills are acquired in the earliest years more effectively through informal interaction with adults than through formal training.[20] This interaction is classically illustrated when a parent, while reading to a toddler, points at pictures and names them and the child is encouraged to respond.

Cognitive stimulation by parents is essential for optimal learning. Children who grow up with parents who listen and talk with them frequently (a practice that Simone and Carl followed regularly) develop more advanced language skills than kids whose parents rarely engage them in conversation (as happened with Stephanie, who explained, "We ain't got time for all that talk-about-our-day stuff"). The brain, in short, develops as a social organ, not an isolated computer.

Neuroscientists and developmental psychologists have identified an especially important set of brain-based skills that they call "executive functions," that is, the air traffic control activities that are manifest in concentration, impulse control, mental flexibility, and working memory. These functions, concentrated in the part of the brain called the prefrontal cortex, allow you to put this book down when your cell phone rings, make a mental note to pick up the kids after soccer, and then resume reading where you left off. Deficiencies in executive functions show up in such conditions as learning disabilities and ADHD.

Under normal circumstances, with supportive caregivers, executive functions develop especially rapidly between the ages of three and five. However, children who experience severe or chronic stress during that period—precisely when Elijah was living with his inattentive grandparents in the terrifying violence of the New Orleans projects, and when Stephanie deployed the only tool (whupping) she could think of to stop Michelle's howling—are more likely to have impaired executive functioning. This, in turn, leaves them less able to solve problems, cope with adversity, and organize their lives.

One important implication of this research is that skills acquired early in childhood are foundational and make later learning more efficient. Thus, experiences in those years are especially significant. Conversely, as the child ages, the brain becomes less able to change. One consequence of this fact is that early intervention is more powerful and cost-effective than intervention during adolescence.

Intellectual and socioemotional development are inextricably intertwined from an early age. Research has shown that so-called noncognitive skills (grit, social sensitivity, optimism, self-control, conscientiousness, emotional stability) are very important for life success. They can lead to greater physical health, school success, college enrollment, employment, and lifetime earnings, and can keep people out of trouble and out of prison. These skills are at least as important as cognitive skills in predicting such measures of success, and may be even more important in our postindustrial future than in the preindustrial and industrial past.[21]

So on the positive side of the ledger, the child's interaction with caring, responsive adults is an essential ingredient in successful development. On the other side of the ledger, neglect and stress, including what is now called "toxic stress," can impede successful development. Chronic neglect, in fact, is often associated with a wider range of developmental consequences than is overt physical abuse.[22] Beating kids is bad, but entirely ignoring them can be even worse.

Intuitively, we know that neglect is not good for a child, and abundant evidence from neuroscience helps explain why: neglect during early childhood reduces the frequency of serve-and-return interactions and produces deficits in brain development that are hard to repair. A landmark randomized study of Romanian orphans who were institutionalized at an early age found that extreme neglect produced severe deficits in IQ, mental health, social adjustment, and even brain architecture. Most of these impairments turned out to be reversible when children were placed in home settings before the age of two, but they were increasingly difficult to repair when placements occurred at later ages.[23]

The effects of toxic stress on brain development can be equally appalling. The stress response itself (that is, sharp increases in adrenaline, blood pressure, heart rate, glucose, and stress hormones) represents a highly effective defense mechanism, fashioned by evolution to help all animal species deal with immediate danger. Moderate stress buffered by supportive adults is not necessarily harmful, and may even be helpful, in that it can promote the development of coping skills. On the other hand, severe and chronic stress, especially if unbuffered by supportive adults, can disrupt the basic executive functions that govern how various parts of the brain work together to address challenges and solve problems. Consequently, children who experience toxic stress have trouble concentrating, controlling impulsive behavior, and following directions.

Extreme stress causes a cascade of biochemical and anatomical changes that impair brain development and change brain architecture at a basic level.[24] Stress caused by unstable and consistently unresponsive caregiving, physical or emotional abuse, parental substance abuse, and lack of affection can produce measurable physiological changes in the child that lead to lifelong difficulties in learning, behavior, and both physical and mental health, including depression, alcoholism, obesity, and heart disease.

Scientists have developed the Adverse Childhood Experiences Scale to measure the incidence of a selected list of events that can produce toxic stress.[25] (See Table 3.1.) Exposure to one or two such events in childhood is not typically associated with bad adult outcomes. However, as the number of negative experiences increases, the rates of lifelong adverse consequences escalate. Summarizing the results of many studies, the Nobel Prize–winning economist James Heckman writes, "Early adverse experiences correlate with poor adult health, high medical care costs, increased depression and suicide rates, alcoholism, drug use, poor job performance and social function, disability, and impaired performance of subsequent generations." [26]

Table 3.1: Adverse Childhood Experiences Scale

1. Household adult humiliated or threatened you physically
2. Household adult hit, slapped, or injured you
3. Adult sexually abused you
4. Felt no one in family loved or supported you
5. Parents separated/divorced
6. You lacked food or clothes or your parents were too drunk or high to care for you
7. Mother/stepmother was physically abused
8. Lived with an alcoholic or drug user
9. Household member depressed or suicidal
10. Household member imprisoned

As a child, Elijah experienced at least eight of these ten stressful events, so his very survival is extraordinary. To be sure, some kids (like Elijah) seem resilient even in the face of severe, chronic stress. Innate resilience can be overrated, however, because the wear and tear of chronic stress can have adverse physiological effects even on kids who seem to be beating the odds. [27] This is sometimes called the "John Henry effect," after the pile driver who hammered hard enough to beat a steam engine, but "worked so hard, it broke his heart; John Henry laid down his hammer and died." [28] Statistically speaking, Elijah is living on borrowed time.

Kids at any socioeconomic level can encounter such adverse

experiences, of course, but those who grow up in low-income, less educated families are at considerably greater risk. Even kids living at twice the poverty level (i.e., the level that Stephanie described as "good money") are two to five times more likely than their less impoverished peers to experience such trauma as parental death or imprisonment, physical abuse, neighborhood violence, and drugs or alcoholism in the family—all experiences that have been shown to have negative consequences, ranging from depression and heart disease to developmental delays and even suicide. As those experiences tend to cumulate, the overall impact can be very large.[29]

The toxic stress that undermines child development is itself typically a reflection of considerable stress in the lives of the parents—both severe (such as clinical depression) and the pile-up of daily hassles. Maternal stress during a child's first year is especially disruptive of infant-mother attachment and caregiving. And it's a vicious cycle: the results of childhood stress (for example, acting out or ADHD) often increase stress on parents, further worsening their parenting behavior.[30]

Biopsychiatrists at the Harvard Medical School have shown that mothers who frequently abuse their children even verbally can impair the circuitry of those kids' brains. "Young adults exposed to parental verbal abuse," the study reported, "had elevated symptoms of depression, anxiety, and dissociation."[31] This research confirms what we might call "Elijah's hypothesis": "When you cussing at your child all the time and just really going hammer, that really breaks—that really discourages your child."

On the other hand, a sensitive, responsive adult caregiver can minimize the effects of even significant stress on a child.[32] Laboratory studies have confirmed this in animals. McGill University neurobiologist Michael Meaney, for example, has demonstrated that newborn rat pups that had been licked and groomed frequently (which is the typical way in which mother rats nurture their newborns) display lower stress hormones, and grow up to be smarter, more curious, healthier, and better able to deal with stressful situations than newborn rats licked and groomed less frequently. Meaney and his colleagues then ingeniously demonstrated that the link between maternal behavior and pup behavior was not merely genetic. In a carefully designed study, they had genetically high lickers and groomers raise genetically vulnerable pups (that is, the offspring of mothers who were low lickers and groomers), and those pups grew up to behave more like their foster mothers than their biological ones: they were less prone to stress and flourished as adults.[33]

Providing physical and emotional security and comfort—hugging, for example—is the human equivalent of a mother rat's licking and grooming behavior and can make a great difference in children's lives. When Chelsea's parents in Port Clinton comforted her after the suicide of a close family friend, they were, in effect, "licking and grooming." Parents who have a warm, nurturing relationship with their children can help them to build resilience and buffer stresses that would otherwise be damaging.[34] Psychologist Byron Egeland found, for example, that among low-income mothers and children in Minneapolis, children who had been more warmly nurtured at age one did better in school than their less well nurtured peers and were less anxious and more socially competent years later.[35]

These early cognitive and socioemotional capacities (especially self-control and determination) in turn predict how well children do in school. A long-term randomized experimental study in Montreal shows that improving children's social skills (for example, taking turns and listening to others) and social trust as early as seven years old can powerfully enhance opportunity.[36] When kids and their parents are given a "dose" of sociability, in other words, the kids stay in school and out of jail, and do much better economically over the long run. Conversely, a childhood "dose" of social isolation and distrust, such as Elijah and Kayla received, significantly compromises their prospects.

The fundamental social significance of the neurobiological discoveries that I've just summarized is that healthy brain development in American children turns out to be closely correlated with parental education, income, and social class.[37] Consider some recent findings.

- Growing evidence indicates that children who grow up in poverty are at higher risk for elevated levels of cortisol, a frequently studied stress hormone. Poverty seems to contribute to a context of chaos that impinges on children's physiology.[38]
- A recent study found that the part of the brain responsible for emotional regulation was impaired in adults who had been exposed to the stresses of poverty as children years earlier.[39]
- Canadian researchers found differences in the brain waves of children from lower- and upper-class backgrounds that suggested the former had more difficulty in concentrating on a simple task, apparently because their brains had been trained to maintain constant surveillance of the environment for new threats.[40]
- Another recent study reported MRI evidence of slower brain growth and less gray matter in a small sample of young children living in poverty compared to children from more affluent backgrounds, though more research is needed before this finding can be generalized.[41]
- Kids from upper-income, well-educated homes benefit from richer verbal interaction because their parents have larger vocabularies and use more complex syntax.[42] In a landmark study, child development specialists followed 42 families in Kansas, carefully observing the families' daily verbal interactions one hour each month over three years. They estimated that by the time the children entered kindergarten, the children of the professional families had heard 19 million more words than the children of working-class parents, and 32 million more words than the children of parents on welfare.[43]
- According to one national study, 72 percent of middle-class children know the alphabet when starting school, as opposed to only 19 percent of poor children.[44]

In short, college-educated parents are more likely than high-school-educated parents to volley when their kids serve, and kids from more affluent homes are exposed to less toxic stress than kids raised in poverty. Moreover, class-based disparities in cognitive, emotional, and social capabilities emerge at very early ages and remain stable over the life course, which implies that, whatever the causal factors, those factors operate most strongly in the preschool years.[45] Of course, this does not mean that later interventions are useless, still less that the class-based disparities are God-given or predetermined, but it does suggest the importance of focusing on early childhood development.

Ironically, the new research findings tend to amplify class differences, at least in the short run, because well-educated parents are more likely to learn of them, directly or indirectly, and to put them to use in their own parenting.[46] As we'll see, a class-based gap in parenting styles has been growing significantly during recent decades. Simone and Stephanie both clearly love their children, but as their stories and the scientific research make clear, when it comes to parenting, love alone is not enough to guarantee positive outcomes.

Trends in Parenting

In the last 60 years, ideas about best practices in parenting have undergone two broad waves of change, in accord with the evolving views of developmental psychologists.[47] After World War II, the runaway bestseller *Baby and Child Care* by the famed pediatrician Dr. Benjamin Spock taught parents of the baby boom that children should be permitted to develop at their own pace, not pushed to meet the schedules and rules of adult life. Parents were encouraged to relax and enjoy their children. Beginning in the 1980s, and at an accelerating rate since the 1990s, however, the dominant ideas and social norms about good parenting have shifted from Spock's "permissive parenting" to a new model of "intensive parenting," in part because of the new insights into brain development that I have just described.

This newer ideal has reached all segments of society, through child-rearing manuals, family magazines, and experts on TV. Like previous changes in parenting philosophy, however, it has spread most rapidly and thoroughly among more educated parents. As Earl (our upper class dad from Bend) put it, "Our generation has read every damn book you can read about being parents. Even more with this generation behind me, they've done all the homework for it."

In the contemporary United States, parents seek to stimulate their children's cognitive and social skills from an early age, and as a result "good parenting" has become time-consuming and expensive. Especially among college-educated parents, "good mothers" are now expected to make immense investments in their children, and "good fathers" face more demanding expectations of involvement in family life and day-to-day child care.[48] Parents at all levels of society now aspire to intensive parenting, but, as we shall see, the less educated and less affluent among them have been less able to put those ideals into practice.[49]

The influential family ethnographer Annette Lareau has discerned two class-based models of parenting in American society today, which she calls concerted cultivation and natural growth.[50]

Concerted cultivation refers to the childrearing investments that middle-class parents deliberately make to foster their children's cognitive, social, and cultural skills, and, in turn, to further their children's success in life, particularly in school. When Simone briefed her kids on Anne Frank, made flash cards, gave Desmond *Hooked on Phonics*, or arranged playgroups, or when Carl took Desmond to work, discussed the news with him, or asked him what he had learned in Sunday School, they were engaged in concerted cultivation.

Natural growth leaves the child's development more to his or her own devices, with less scheduling and less engagement with schools. In this model, parents rely more on rules and discipline, less on close parental monitoring, encouragement, reasoning, and negotiation. Joe wanted to be a more engaged parent for Kayla as she drifted toward depression, but given the constraints he faced, as well as his own impoverished childhood, a natural growth strategy was the best he could manage. It's the parenting model still more characteristic of poorer families today, though it may be fading among them, too.

One broad class difference in parenting norms turns up in virtually all studies: well-educated parents aim to raise autonomous, independent, self-directed children with high self-esteem and the ability to make good choices, whereas less educated parents focus on discipline and obedience and conformity to pre-established rules. Figure 3.1 illustrates this sharp distinction. Parents with less than a high school education endorse obedience over self-reliance, 65 percent to 18 percent, whereas parents with a graduate education make exactly the opposite choice, 70 percent to 19 percent. Upper-class parents have more egalitarian relations with their children and are more likely to use reasoning and guilt for discipline, whereas lower-class parents are more likely to use physical punishment, like whupping.[51]

Figure 3.1: Parental education and parenting objectives

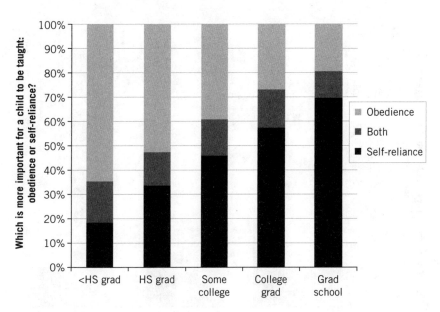

Source: Faith Matters national survey, 2006.

These class differences show up in parents' actual behavior, not just their avowed priorities. Simone can't recall ever punishing Desmond (not even "no TV for a week"). Carl likens a parent sometimes to a soccer referee ("That's when you pull that parental card and say, 'This is it'"), but as his kids got older, he preferred Socratic dialogue ("Explain to me why you are doing that. Have you thought of this?").

By contrast, Stephanie, whose parents "beat the hell" out of her, believes in very tough love ("You can't be soft. You gotta be hard, really hard"). Despite the undoubted fact that she "love[s her] kids to death," her first response to disobedience is a beating. Even Elijah—who was beaten unconscious by his father after the arson episode, who displays remarkable insight into the costs of abusive parenting, and who talks about the importance of "say[ing] good words" to children—doesn't display any doubts about how to handle a wayward son. ("Don't get me wrong: I'm gonna beat him. I'm gonna teach him what's right from wrong.")

Figure 3.2: Class differences in verbal parenting

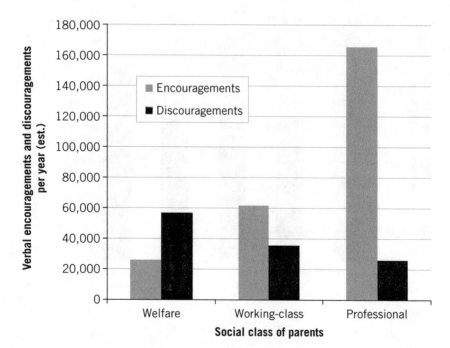

Source: Betty Hart and Todd R. Risley, *Meaningful Differences in the Everyday Experience of Young American Children* (Baltimore: Paul H. Brookes, 1995).

This class-based difference in positive and negative parenting also shows up in verbal interactions. A careful study of the daily verbal exchanges between parents and children found, as illustrated in Figure 3.2, that parents with professional degrees annually delivered about 166,000 encouragements and 26,000 discouragements, whereas working-class parents delivered 62,000 and 36,000, respectively, and parents on welfare delivered 26,000 and 57,000.[52]

Why is this class-based difference in parenting approaches—what we might term the "hug/spank ratio"—so stark and pervasive? An earlier generation of experts tended to attribute this difference to an ill-defined "working-class culture," but brain science has now shown that poor, less educated, more isolated parents are more restrictive, punitive, and harsher disciplinarians, in part because they themselves experience higher levels of chronic stress.[53] Elijah recognized this about his abusive mother: "When you come home as a mother, and you see bills on the table, and you see the dishes ain't washed, and you see your son's room not cleaned up, and you see everything messy, I think that's why she's so angry. . . . I can't blame her."

Harsh discipline is not just a function of "working-class culture" nor just a consequence of parental stress. It is often a sensible response to the differing environments in which upper- and lower-class families live. Well-off parents can use what the sociologist Frank Furstenberg and his colleagues call "promotive" strategies, nurturing their children's talents in comfortable settings that provide many opportunities and few dangers (like the one where Desmond and his family live). Impoverished parents, by contrast, use "preventive" strategies, aimed at keeping their children safe in rough neighborhoods where dangers far outnumber opportunities (like the ones where Stephanie raised her kids).[54] As Stephanie put it to us, "We don't do all that kissing and hugging. That's other races' stuff. . . . You can't be mushy in Detroit [or Atlanta]. . . . Be a thug!"

The evidence strongly suggests that the parenting style typical of affluent and educated parents, characterized by nurturance, affection, warmth, active involvement, and reasoned discipline—in short, more hugging and less spanking—leads to greater socioemotional competence among children. Elijah intuited this: "If you tell your child that he ain't gonna be nothin' but a low-down dirty-rat scoundrel, your child is gonna be a low-down dirty-rat scoundrel."

Class-based differences in parenting style are well established and powerfully consequential. The ubiquitous correlation between poverty and child development (both cognitive and socioemotional) is, in fact, largely explained by differences in parenting styles, including cognitive stimulation (such as frequency of reading) and social engagement (such as involvement in extracurricular activities, like those Simone encouraged her kids to join).[55] In particular, parental reading (controlling for many other factors, including maternal education, verbal ability, and warmth) fosters child development.[56] Child development specialists Jane Waldfogel and Elizabeth Washbrook have found that differences in parenting—especially maternal sensitivity and nurturance, but also provision of books, library visits, and the like—is the single most important factor explaining differences in school readiness between rich kids and poor kids, as measured by literacy, mathematics, and language test scores at age four.[57]

Have these class-based differences in parenting grown in recent years? Reliable indicators are hard to find, because persuasive measurement requires repeated, identical surveys over many years. But there is one exception: family dinners. And trends in family dining tell a revealing story.

Waldfogel has shown that (even after controlling for many other factors) family dining is a powerful predictor of how children will fare as they develop. "Youths who ate dinner with their parents at least five times a week," she writes, "did better across a range of outcomes: they were less likely to smoke, to drink, to have used marijuana, to have been in a serious fight, to have had sex . . . or to have been suspended from school, and they had higher grade point averages and were more likely to say they planned to go on to college."[58]

Among the folks we met in Bend and Atlanta, affluent families made regular dinner conversation between parents and children a priority. "My dad and my mom have always made sure that we eat dinner together," Andrew reported, adding, "it's our only real time that all four of us could talk." Desmond said, "I actually learned a lot from those conversations that we had at the dinner table." By contrast, the poorer families didn't—or couldn't—make eating together a priority. "We tried to," Darleen recalled, "but it wasn't always like that. . . . We would watch TV together." Stephanie and her daughter Lauren summed things up very simply. "We're not a sit-down-and-eat family," Stephanie said, and Lauren added, "When it's time to eat, it's whoever wants to eat. It wasn't everybody sit at the table, like a party or something."

From the mid-1970s to the early 1990s, as Figure 3.3 shows, family dinners became rarer in all social echelons, as families struggled to manage the new scheduling complexities of having two working parents. In the mid-1990s that steady waning of opportunities for family conversation was suddenly halted among college-educated parents, but it continued uninterrupted among high-school-educated families.[59] Single-parent families are less likely to have dinner as a family, but that doesn't account for much of the widening class gap, since the growth of the gap is actually concentrated among two-parent families. The result is another of the scissors charts that appear throughout this book—a growing gap in childhood experience between kids from well-educated, affluent backgrounds and kids from less educated, impoverished backgrounds.

Family dining is no panacea for child development, but it is one indicator of the subtle but powerful investments that parents make in their kids (or fail to make). What happened in the 1990s? It's hard to tell from these data, but a plausible interpretation is that better-educated parents were indirectly influenced by the growing recognition of the importance of serve-and-return interactions for child development—and devoted more time to making them possible, whereas less educated parents were slower to get the word or were leading such complicated lives that family dinners were not a realistic option.

Figure 3.3: Trends in family dinners, by parental education, 1978–2005

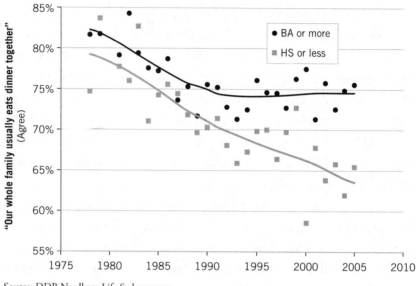

Source: DDB Needham Life Style surveys.

Parents from all social backgrounds nowadays invest both more money and more time in raising their kids than was true a generation ago. The increased parental investments are focused on experiences (especially enriched care for preschoolers) that foster cognitive and socioemotional development. However, college-educated parents have increased their investments of both money and time much more rapidly than less affluent parents—and not just at the dinner table, as we shall shortly see.

These increased investments in child development have come mostly at the expense of other aspects of home life (such as adult personal care, housekeeping, and consumer goods). Parents in all classes have been cutting back elsewhere to focus their resources on their kids, but because affluent, educated families have not only more money but also more time (because they typically split child care between two parents), they have been able to increase their investments much faster than poor parents (usually single moms). As a result, the class gap in investments in kids has become wider and wider.

To better understand what is happening, let's take a closer look at the ways in which parents from different classes devote money and time to their children.

MONEY

On average, parents from all socioeconomic strata have increased their spending on child care and education over the past five decades. But that spending, always somewhat unequal, has become steadily more unequal over the decades. (See Figure 3.4.) In fact, after the mid-1980s the very lowest income families began to spend less in absolute terms, mostly (but not entirely) because they had less to spend, while higher-income families continued to spend more, partly (but only partly) because they had more to spend. Between 1983 and 2007, spending per child by families in the top tenth of the income distribution increased by 75 percent in real dollars, compared to a drop of 22 percent in the bottom tenth. By 2007, the average child of parents in the top tenth of the economic hierarchy was the beneficiary of about $6,600 a year in enrichment spending: nine times the amount (about $750) spent annually on a child of parents in the bottom tenth of the income hierarchy.

The increase was concentrated in spending on private education and child care, but a class gap in spending is also visible for music lessons, summer camp, travel, school supplies, books, computers, extracurricular activities, recreation, and leisure. Moreover, even if income is held constant, disparities by parental education also appear to be high and growing. This means that children of affluent *and* educated parents (like Desmond and Andrew) have been getting a double dip, while children of poorer *and* less educated parents (like Michelle and Kayla) have been getting a double whammy.[60]

These differences in parental investment, in turn, are strong predictors of children's cognitive development.[61] In fact, the biggest increases in parental spending are concentrated in the preschool and college years: the two periods of development that we now know are especially important in determining upward mobility. Parents who can afford it are privately investing in these stages, providing their kids with great advantages in life—but as a society we have yet to invest adequately in those years, and instead devote most of our public resources to the K–12 years. (We shall explore class differences in schooling in the next chapter.)

Figure 3.4: Trends in spending on children per child, by household income, in constant (2008) dollars, 1972–2007

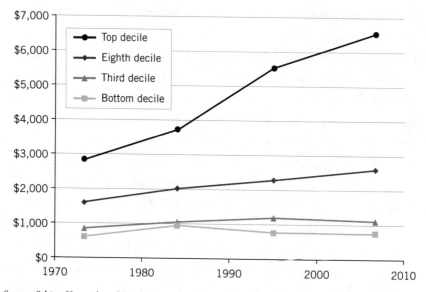

Source: Sabino Kornrich and Frank Furstenberg, "Investing in Children: Changes in Parental Spending on Children, 1972–2007," *Demography* 50 (2013): 1–23.

TIME

Parents at all educational and income levels are spending more time with their kids nowadays than their counterparts did a half century ago. However, as we saw above with money, the increase is much greater among college-educated parents than among high-school-educated parents. Moreover, the growing class gap is concentrated in "*Goodnight Moon* time": that is, time spent on developmental activities. (Researchers who study how parents allocate their time often distinguish between this *Goodnight Moon* time and the time spent on physical care of the child— "diaper time.") Finally, the class differences in time investment are concentrated during early childhood—precisely when, as we learned in the previous section of this chapter, time with parents matters most. Figure 3.5 shows trends in the time that parents from different educational backgrounds have spent on developmental care for infants aged 0–4.[62]

In the 1970s, there were virtually no class differences in how much time a child got with mom or dad. By 2013, however, the average infant or toddler of college-educated parents was getting half again as much *Goodnight Moon* time every day as the average infant or toddler of high-school-educated parents. That means they were getting nearly three quarters of an hour more of serve-and-return interaction every day.

Figure 3.5: Time spent by both parents in developmental child care, children aged 0–4, 1965–2013

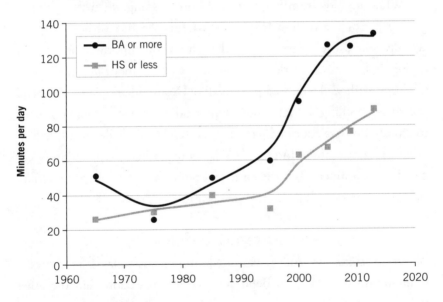

Source: Evrim Altintas, "Widening Education-Gap in Developmental Childcare Activities in the U.S.," *Journal of Marriage and Family* (forthcoming 2015).

College-educated moms are more likely to be working outside the home than less educated moms. This reduces the time they can spend with their kids—but this is mitigated by the fact that they are much more likely to have a partner who also spends time with the kids. More-over, even among married couples, college-educated parents engage more strongly in intensive parenting, with its emphasis on spending time with children and on dads sharing child care responsibilities. The higher incomes of married, college-educated parents need not come at the expense of time with the kids, whereas less educated single moms with jobs outside the home, like Stephanie, work hard merely to keep their heads above water, and this cuts into the time they can spend with their kids. So kids from affluent, educated homes get the best of both worlds—more monetary investment (because their parents can afford it) and more time investment (because their two parents are able to make it a priority)—whereas kids from lower-class homes get the worst of both worlds.

What are kids from less educated homes doing when they are not getting personal attention from their parents? Studies of how children actually spend their days suggest that the most important part of the answer is TV, just as Darleen said when we asked about family dinners. Children with well educated parents (like Desmond and Andrew) spend less time watching TV and more time reading and studying compared to children of less educated parents (like Kayla, Michelle, and Elijah).[63] With the spread of the Internet, TV is being gradually replaced by Web-based entertainment, but the basic fact remains: rich kids get more face time, while poor kids get more screen time.

NONPARENTAL CHILD CARE

About a third of college-educated moms nowadays are stay-at-home-moms, like Patty in Bend and Simone in Atlanta, but the other two thirds of them must (like many high-school-educated moms) find some sort of day care. Many studies have shown that better-educated working moms put their children in higher-quality day care, at least in part because they can afford it. In turn, higher-quality day care generally produces better results in terms of children's cognitive and noncognitive development, though some doubts remain about how strong that relationship is, and whether it tends to fade as the child progresses through school. Not surprisingly, good day care makes less difference to child development than good parenting—but, on average, children of more educated parents get more of both.[64]

This class gap, too, is growing, at least as it concerns access to professional and regulated day care centers for younger children. Over the last 15 years, better-educated mothers of kids aged 0–4 have shifted from informal to more professional day care arrangements for their children, whereas less educated working moms have come to rely more heavily on arrangements with relatives (especially grandparents) or no regular arrangements at all. To be sure, some day care centers provide less than top-quality care, and many grandparents provide excellent day care, but generally speaking, center-based care is higher-quality care. In short, more educated moms have upgraded their infant day care, while less educated moms typically have not.[65]

Class differences in child care for somewhat older children (aged 4–6) are even more substantial, with about 70 percent of college-educated moms using center-based, professional day care, compared to about 40 percent of high-school-educated moms. This class difference has been stable over recent years, even as class differences in day care for younger children have been growing. Well-educated parents have long invested more resources than less educated parents in high-quality day care for their 4–6-year-olds, but in recent years upper-class parents have extended that investment edge into an even younger stage of life (0–4)—precisely the stage that the latest brain science suggests is so critical developmentally.

These class gaps widen when we consider formal pre-K instruction. According to the National Institute for Early Education Research, "At age 4, enrollment in pre-K (public and private) is about 65 percent for the lowest 40 percent of families by income and 90 percent for the highest income quintile. At age 3, when state pre-K is rarely provided, enrollment is only about 40 percent for low-income and moderate-income families while it is 80 percent for the top income quintile."[66] In short, no matter what measure of parental investment in child development we use, kids from more educated, affluent homes have a substantial and even widening lead.

PARENTAL STRESS

The everyday hassles of parenting are stressful: cleaning up after the kids, managing multiple schedules, lack of privacy, and lack of time for self and partner. Moreover, parents also have to cope with the ordinary stresses of the rest of life, especially work. Everyday stress levels vary across families, of course, but a vast body of research links parental stress with less sensitive, less responsive parenting, and thus with bad outcomes for kids. Stressed parents are both harsher and less attentive parents.[67] Economic stress, in particular, disrupts family relations, fosters withdrawn and inconsistent parenting, and directly increases chronic stress among children.

All of the life stories in this book illustrate this linkage from economic hardship to stressed parenting to bad outcomes for kids. The Great Recession created exceptional stresses, but as Figure 3.6 shows, the class gap in economic stress on parents had been growing steadily for the previous three decades, with serious consequences for parenting. (Here financial worries are measured by an index of responses to a series of questions about family income and debt.[68]) As Laura Bush once observed in a 2007 White House discussion of the growing class gaps among American kids, "If you don't know how long you're going to keep your job, or how long you're going to keep your house, you have less energy to invest in the kids."[69]

The first lady's comments anticipated arguments that the behavioral economists Sendhil Mullainathan and Eldar Shafir made in their 2013 book, *Scarcity*. Under conditions of scarcity, they write, the brain's ability to grasp, manage, and solve problems falters, like a computer slowed down by too many open apps, leaving us less efficient and less effective than we would be under conditions of abundance. What we usually understand as an impoverished parent's lack of skills, care, patience, tolerance, attention, and dedication can actually be attributed to the fact that the parent's mind is functioning under a heavy load. "Good parenting," they write, "requires bandwidth. It requires complex decisions and sacrifice. Children need to be motivated to do things they dislike, appointments have to be kept, activities planned, teachers met and their feedback processed, tutoring or extra help provided or procured and then monitored. This is hard for anyone, whatever his resources. It is doubly hard when your bandwidth is reduced."[70]

Figure 3.6: Growing class gap in parental financial worries, 1975–2005

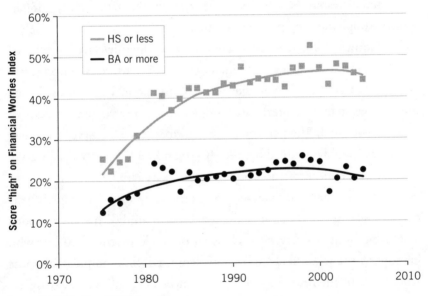

Source: DDB Needham Life Style surveys.

The investment gaps that we discussed above (time, money) tend most noticeably to affect cognitive development. Stress gaps, on the other hand, seem particularly important for children's socioemotional development, including mental health.[71] To make matters worse, single parents are more likely to experience stresses of the sort I have described even when education and income are held constant, and thus tend to be less able to offer nurturing, supportive parenting to their kids.[72] The widening economic cleavage in America exacerbates the parenting gap both directly and indirectly (via the effects on family structure we discussed in Chapter 2).

GRANDPARENTING

Grandparents today are often more important in their grandchildren's lives than their counterparts were a half century ago, because grandparents are healthier and wealthier than they used to be.[73] This trend plays out very differently in upper-tier and lower-tier families, however. Generally speaking, lower-tier grandparents mostly donate time, replacing parental resources, whereas upper-tier grandparents mostly donate money, supplementing parental resources.

Nationwide, 4 percent of all children are primarily cared for by their grandparents, as happened in Elijah's case. This pattern is concentrated among the children of younger, unmarried, poor, less educated, and unemployed parents, and these grandparents themselves tend to be poor and less educated. The percentage of grandparents who serve as primary caregivers roughly doubled between 1970 and 1997, with virtually all of that increase concentrated in poor and minority families.

Such full-time grandparents are increasingly forced to replace parents because of the collapse of the lower-class family. This has provided a valuable human safety net—children of single parents who live with grandparents are less likely to become depressed, for example, than those who don't. In the next chapter we shall meet Lola and Sofia, two sisters from Orange County, who are lucky that their maternal grandparents took them in when their drug-addicted mother died. But replacement grandparenting typically does little more than replace younger, poor, less educated (and now often missing) caregivers with older, poor, less educated caregivers—not much of a gain for the kids. (The kids are obviously better off with care from grandparents than with no care at all, but they are not better off than if their own parents were able to care for them.) Elijah's plight illustrates this situation. Replacement grandparenting is more common among nonwhites, but it is rising more rapidly among poor whites. In upper-tier families, by contrast, replacement grandparenting is infrequent and not rising, because the number of fractured families in that tier is relatively low and declining.

Upper-tier grandparents today are more affluent than their counterparts a generation ago. This means they are increasingly able to supplement (not simply replace) the financial resources that their grandchildren are already getting from their parents. Upper-tier kids are thus more likely than lower-tier kids to get financial assistance from their grandparents, even though they are less likely to need it. In short, taking grandparenting into account magnifies the growing youth class gaps.

I close with three cautions.

First, in recent years we've heard much talk of excessive parenting under labels like "helicopter parents" and "overparenting."[74] No doubt one can find occasional illustrations of that phenomenon, which irritates both the kids and bystanders. It is misleading, however, to assume a false equivalency between excessive and inadequate parenting. There is no credible evidence that excessive parenting produces anything approaching the abundant ills associated with inadequate parenting. Moreover, if there is a problem of excessive parenting, the solution lies in the hands of parents themselves, but that is much less true of the problem of inadequate parenting.

Second, although the research summarized here has established robust correlations between parental social class (especially education) and parenting practices, and between parenting practices and child outcomes, relatively few of these studies prove beyond all doubt that the correlations are causal. The studies that I have cited have all used careful statistical controls to try to exclude spurious correlation, but they have not typically used random-assignment experimental design. In short, the evidence is generally "state of the art," but the state of the art in this field is not perfect. This deficiency does not represent scientific carelessness. It would not be easy to get authorization for studies that randomly assigned children to parents, as scientists can do with rat pups.

Third, class-based differences in parenting are not the only factor handicapping children born to poorer, less educated parents. Material deprivation—poor nutrition, inadequate health care, exposure to environmental risks like lead paint—can have powerful long-term effects on children's intellectual and emotional development.[75] Conversely, several high-quality experimental studies have shown that simply giving poor families money can improve the academic and social performance of their kids—money matters.[76] Even ideal parenting cannot compensate for all the ill effects of poverty on children, and even incompetent parenting cannot nullify all the advantages conferred by parental affluence and education.

That said, the best scientific evidence confirms that the patterns of parenting illustrated by our three Atlanta families represent broad trends across America. The disadvantages facing poor kids begin early and run deep, and are firmly established before the kids get to school—which is the subject of the next chapter.

Chapter 4

SCHOOLING

FOR DECADES, ORANGE COUNTY, CALIFORNIA—HOME TO Richard Nixon, Disneyland, Botox, and *The Real Housewives of Orange County*—connoted wealthy, white, conservative suburbia. Picture-perfect cities lined the coast and multimillion-dollar beach homes glittered in the famously year-round sunshine. Sandwiched between Los Angeles County to the north and San Diego County to the south, it was the epicenter of escapist luxury and trophy wives on raw-food diets.

That image has, however, been gradually altered by large-scale demographic changes over the last 40 years. Since 1970 the population of Orange County has more than doubled to over 3 million people. The county is now the sixth most populous in the country and, in absolute numbers, the sixth most rapidly growing. Immigration explains much of that growth, prompting one observer to call Orange County "the Ellis Island of the twenty-first century."[1] By 2013, 46 percent of the county's population spoke a language other than English at home.[2] Latino immigrants today make up more than a third of the population (up from only

15 percent in 1980) and account for nearly half of the county's K–12 students.

Orange County includes 34 incorporated cities, many of them worlds apart. As one local demographer puts it, "You have areas of poverty and areas of great affluence and less of a middle."[3] Laguna Beach, for example, is 91 percent non-Hispanic white, with a per capita income of $84,000, whereas Santa Ana, the county seat, just 20 miles away, is 95 percent Hispanic (50 percent foreign-born), with a per capita income of $17,000.

Most Latinos in Orange County live in the impoverished cities of the inland valleys of the northern half of the county, among them Santa Ana. A 2004 report by the Nelson A. Rockefeller Institute of Government identified Santa Ana as the Most Troubled City in America because of its high unemployment, high poverty rate, undereducated population, and crowded housing. Latinos in Orange County are more likely to live not only in poverty but also amidst street violence and gang activity. Santa Ana alone is home to 29 street gangs.[4]

However, many upwardly mobile middle-class Latinos (mostly second- or third-generation descendants of immigrants) are moving rapidly from impoverished Latino areas in Los Angeles and Orange County into formerly white Orange County communities. Between 1990 and 2010, the percentage of Latino residents in each of the county's predominantly white, affluent cities increased. In north Fullerton, the home of Cal State Fullerton, where the median household income was roughly $100,000 in 2012, the percentage of Latinos more than doubled from about 10 percent to 25 percent. Though Fullerton is far from the most opulent part of Orange County, the draw for these Latinos is clear: high-quality schools, a thriving economy, and increasingly rich cultural pluralism.

The net result of these demographic transitions is that economic inequality *within* the Latino community in Orange County has grown significantly during the past four decades, just as it has *within* the black community in Atlanta. The percentage of Latino families living on less than $25,000 a year (in inflation-adjusted dollars) nearly doubled between 1970 and 2010, from 13 percent to 25 percent, at the same time that the percentage living on more than $100,000 a year rose from 12 percent to 17 percent. In short, Orange County is now home to more impoverished Latinos *and* more affluent Latinos.[5]

This inequality is also reflected in Orange County schools. Consider two high schools that "input" measures (see Table 4.1) suggest are surprisingly similar: Troy High School in Fullerton and Santa Ana High School. Spending per pupil at the two schools is comparable, for example, as are the student-teacher ratios, the number of guidance counselors, and two standard measures of teacher quality: formal education and experience. Troy offers a richer menu of extracurricular activities than Santa Ana, but, as we shall see, private fund-raising explains that difference, not unequal investment by the school districts. On the measures most obviously controlled by school systems—spending, teacher quantity and quality, and counseling—the two schools seem broadly similar.

What is decidedly *not* similar about these two schools, however, are their student populations, as measured by poverty rates, ethnic backgrounds, English proficiency, and even physical fitness. Santa Ana students are overwhelmingly poor and Latino and heavily Spanish-speaking, whereas Troy students come from ethnically diverse, economically upscale backgrounds. More striking still are the contrasts in the "output" measures of the two schools—graduation rates, statewide academic and SAT test scores, truancy and suspension rates. Students at Santa Ana are four times more likely than students at Troy to drop out, roughly ten times more likely to be truant or suspended, and only one third as likely to take the SAT. If they do take the SAT, on average they score in the bottom quartile nationwide, whereas the average SAT taker at Troy scores in the top 10–15 percent.

In this chapter, we will meet children from two Mexican American families with firsthand experience of these two schools: Isabella and her parents, Clara and Ricardo, who live in north Fullerton, just a few blocks from Troy High; and Lola and Sofia, two sisters who were raised by their grandparents in central Santa Ana, just a few blocks from Santa Ana High.[6] Their stories reveal a great deal about how the crosscurrents of family, economics, ethnicity, and schools influence kids' opportunities.

Table 4.1: Characteristics of Troy and Santa Ana High Schools, 2012

	City	Troy High School, Fullerton	Santa Ana High School, Santa Ana
School Resources	Student body size	2565	3229
	Spending per pupil	$10,326	$9,928
	Teachers' average years of service	14.9	15.0
	Teachers with master's degree	69%	59%
	Student-teacher ratio	26:1	27:1
	Guidance counselors	5	7
	Sports/arts/language extracurricular activities	34	16
Student Community	Students eligible for free/reduced price lunch (based on family poverty)	14%	84%
	Latino ethnicity	23%	98%
	Limited English proficiency	4%	47%
	Passed 6/6 fitness tests	70%	32%
Outcomes	Graduation rate	93%	73%
	California state Academic Performance Index (API) (out of 1,000)	927	650
	API compared to all California high schools	Top 10%	Bottom 20%
	Students who take SATs	65%	20%
	Average SAT	1917	1285
	Truancy rate	2%	33%
	Suspensions per 100 students	3	22
	Overall ranking among all 67 Orange County high schools[7]	3	64

Clara, Ricardo, and Isabella

Clara and Ricardo, both in their 50s, grew up in the 1970s in an impoverished Hispanic ghetto in South Central Los Angeles. By the 1990s they had become successful professionals, and in search of safe neighborhoods and stellar schools they moved to Fullerton with their growing family (Michael, now 27; Isabella, now 20; and Gabriel, now 15). Today they live in a large ranch-style house on a peaceful cul-de-sac and are well integrated into the Orange County middle class. To reach the house, we drive up into the hills, past palm trees, upscale shopping plazas, and Spanish colonial–style homes. It's a mostly upper-middle-class Anglo neighborhood, and the Latinos who live here tend to be even more affluent than their white neighbors.[8] "People here are friendly and trusting," Isabella will later tell us, "because it's a safe area."

We meet in the comfortable living room, facing glass doors opening onto a patio, a serene blue pool, and a colorful garden. Pictures of Isabella in dance costumes accent a grand piano. The adjacent dining room provides a calm space for conversation and homework, an environment that served as a refuge from Troy High School, which all three children attended and where, Clara reports, you can feel quivers of anxiety, as kids compete for the highest SAT scores and spots at Harvard, Stanford, and NYU. Her kids have had a very different experience growing up here than Clara and Ricardo had growing up a generation ago in South Central LA.

Clara and her twin brother, Francisco, were born and raised in a small Mexican village. Their father had come to California on his own as a bracero railway worker during World War II, and when Clara and Francisco were eight, he brought his entire family (the twins, their mother, and two older siblings) as legal immigrants to Los Angeles. Because family resources were scant, they settled first in Watts, a poverty-stricken, gang-ridden, mostly black neighborhood. As light-skinned Hispanics they stood out, and Clara has vivid memories of being chased home by black kids from school through a darkened freeway underpass.

That said, she also recalls that she and her brother were occasionally shepherded home by friendly black teachers. Seeking greater safety, the family moved around South Central and southeastern Los Angeles, always in poor, mostly Latino neighborhoods. "We grew up in a community where it was low-income, lots of drugs," Clara says, adding that many of her classmates in junior high and high school were "fried" from habitually sniffing glue.

Latino gangs—whom Clara calls "cockroaches"—dominated the schools that she and her brother attended.

> We witnessed the initiation of [would-be] gang members, where they get beat up badly by the gang members. The word is "courted." You get courted into the gang, and they time it for two to three minutes, and you're not supposed to fight back. If you fall down, they'll hurt you more, so it shows that you're tough if you're up, bloodied and bruised, both girls and boys. Back then it was just fistfights and maybe bats from time to time. Nowadays to get initiated into these gangs, they shoot people in the community, even innocent bystanders. I am ashamed of it as part of our culture.

Now a pediatric social worker, Clara has well-formed ideas about why gang culture took hold in the schools she attended. "I think it comes from the lack of family cohesion," she says, "Many families in the community were dysfunctional."

Clara's parents, neither of whom had gone beyond the third or fourth grade in Mexico, gave their kids lots of support and modeled a strong work ethic. They stressed the importance of doing well in school, and even though they had no idea what college was, they encouraged Clara and Francisco to become professionals. The children were sheltered from financial stress. Clara recalls that their father did occasionally take them to pick strawberries on weekends to help make ends meet, but even so she did not think of her family as poor. Her older siblings were politically and culturally sophisticated, and she grew up going to foreign films, discussing literature, and, she says, "listening to Bob Dylan and Joan Baez."

Clara and her brother Francisco attended schools in LA that she describes as "very tough," but the two were outstanding students and received strong, even loving support from their teachers, both black and white. In fact, recognizing that Clara and Francisco came from a disadvantaged background, on weekends their teachers sometimes took them with their own families to Disneyland and Knott's Berry Farm. "They were our role models and our mentors," Clara says. "We said, 'We're going to do well academically, and we're going to challenge ourselves, because we need to get out of the neighborhood.'"

Both Clara and Francisco found conscientious, caring counselor-mentors at school who helped them get scholarship aid for college—and, in Clara's case, a graduate degree.[9] Today both have become successful Orange County professionals—Clara as a social worker and Francisco as a financial advisor. "I wanted to make a difference in my community," Clara says, explaining her choice of profession, "hoping that fewer kids were going into gangs and drugs."

Clara and Francisco's story provides a classic example of upward mobility among second-generation immigrants. "We're pretty Mexican at home," Clara says of their assimilation, "but at work we're totally Americanized." Both have made a point of taking their children back to see the still grim neighborhood where they grew up. "In just one generation you can make that leap," Francisco admonished his kids, "but in one generation you can make the leap back."

After graduating from a major local university, suffering through an unsuccessful first marriage, and supporting herself for several years as a single mom (of Michael), Clara met Ricardo at their tenth high school reunion. They married, and in the years that followed had two more children, Isabella and Gabriel. During those early years of their marriage, Clara created a rapidly growing social work program at a local hospital, and then moved into a successful private psychotherapy partnership, while Ricardo, for his part, became a successful architect and then took on the role of project manager at a major nonprofit.

As Isabella reached school age, Clara and Ricardo moved to Fullerton in search of better, safer schools. Clara explains:

In LA most middle-class or professional Hispanics move to areas where they have better schools, because most of us grew up in the inner city, and so we were familiar with what [our children] would be exposed to—gangs and violence and probably lower-level education, unfortunately, where the teachers are basically managing the students. We knew exactly what we wanted for our kids. We wanted them to compete with the kids that go to Ivy League schools. So for us it's education, education, education for our children.

She goes on to describe how they ended up in their current neighborhood:

We specifically chose to live here so that they could go to Troy High School. My husband and I checked the high schools and their SAT scores. We also checked for their standardized testing at the elementary level, and we wanted to make sure that the elementary teachers were well trained and very highly motivated.

Even at the preschools, I interviewed all the teachers, because it's not cheap. If you go to private here, it's $700 to $900 a month. I wanted to know what their educational background was, and how they handled children that they needed to discipline appropriately, and that it was all pro–social skills and how they managed their classroom. I wanted to make sure that the preschools were clean and had enough staff per ratio for the children at all times. And the composition of the children and the families was important to me. I wanted [my kids] to really develop their language skills.

When Isabella entered kindergarten, Clara discovered that her teacher was in her first year of teaching and "not very organized," so she resolved to help. "What can we do as parents," she asked the teacher, "to make you succeed as a teacher for my daughter?" Soon she decided to get involved in the classroom herself. At least once a week that year, she hired a baby-sitter for Gabriel, so that she could volunteer in the class. She committed herself to the school, she says, because it offered a Gifted and Talented Education (GATE) program, which she hoped her kids would enter (as eventually they did). She also got to know the ladies from the school office. "If I ever call and ask about my daughter," she says, explaining her tactics, "they know who I am."

Clara rivals Wendy (in Port Clinton) and Simone (in Atlanta) in the depth of her commitment to raising her kids. During the years they were in school, she worked only part-time, because her priority—"my greatest challenge, my greatest accomplishment, my legacy"—was doing everything she could for her kids. Even before kindergarten, she and Ricardo spent a lot of time reading to their kids. "By the time they were in kindergarten," she says, "they were reading Dr. Seuss, and could count to 100 and write their names." The family always had dinner together.

During the summer Clara got math and reading workbooks for her kids, and took them to classes at UC Irvine and Cal State Fullerton. "That's also why we moved here," she says, "because the university was next to us, and I knew they offered courses for their age group. I did whatever it took to make sure that my kids were ahead a year. All three kids have always tested at least a grade or two above."

Troy High School

Isabella and her brothers all attended Troy High School, just down the hill from their home. Troy is a public magnet school, and by most academic measures is exceptional—in 2013 *Newsweek* ranked it as the 47th best high school in America. Kids from outside the district have to take a highly competitive entrance exam, and according to Clara only about 400 students are selected from among several thousand applicants each year. Troy offers a highly demanding science-and-technology track (dubbed Troy Tech) and an almost equally demanding International Baccalaureate curriculum, along with dozens of Advanced Placement courses. The school is a perennial winner of such national competitions as the Science Olympiad and academic decathlons, and its computer science curriculum is said to be among the best in the world. Ninety-nine percent of its graduates go on to college, 76 percent to four-year institutions, and 23 percent to community colleges. The student body is racially diverse, with 46 percent Asian American, 24 percent non-Hispanic white, 23 percent Latino, and 6 percent black and mixed-race minorities, though it is much less diverse in terms of its students' socio-economic backgrounds (as we saw in Table 4.1).

Isabella is full of enthusiasm for the school. "All the teachers are really great," she says, "and they're always there to help." Kira, a class-mate of hers with whom we also spoke, adds depth to this portrait of caring teachers. During her freshman year her English teacher learned that Kira's father had recently died, and reached out to her. "She talked to me about it," she says, "and said, 'If you ever need anyone, let me know.' I could just go into her classroom during lunch and talk it out with her. I still talk to her."

The quality of the students and curriculum at Troy virtually ensured that the academic atmosphere was highly competitive. Clara reports that in her elder son's graduating class, 15 students got 2400 on their SATs—that is, perfect scores. Isabella emphasizes that Troy is a pressure-cooker for the students.

> Some of my friends began practicing for the SAT in our freshman year. People would get 2200, and half would say, "I have to go back and take it again." Everybody is friends and everything, but some-times you can feel it. The only bad thing about that is that it's almost like a double-edged sword that you have to be in the top 10–12 per-cent. Getting Bs was considered failing.
>
> I went back this August to speak in an old class of mine to se-niors about college applications, and being back in that environment I could actually feel it this time. When you're in it, you don't really think about it, but coming back I could really feel like the pressure that they had on themselves. You're in a bubble at Troy.

Even extracurricular participation was highly competitive. Isabella, an excellent writer, learned this when she applied to work on the student newspaper. "They interview applicants in freshman year," she says, "and when I interviewed, I wasn't ready for it. Fifty people had interviewed, and they were only going to accept two. It's very prestigious, because those kids go into journalism at Berkeley, Stanford, all the top schools."

Stereotypically, competition at Orange County high schools is about nice clothes and fancy cars, but at Troy, Isabella insists, "it didn't feel like that. It was mostly stress from academics. I guess at other schools if somebody called you a 'nerd,' it was an insult, but it just wasn't at Troy. You wanted to do better than . . . I don't want to say better than other people [laughs], but as well as."

Where the competitive pressure at Troy comes from is an interesting question. Isabella says her parents didn't pressure her and her siblings. "They always wanted to make sure that we did the best that we could do," she says. "And if maybe I didn't get the best grade [they would say], 'Well, you tried your best. Just do better next time.'" On the other hand, as she and her mother explain, pressure from other parents on their kids tends to spread across the school.

"Tiger Moms!" is how Clara succinctly sums up her fellow mothers. "[When] kids would not do as well as they had wanted to do on a test," Isabella explains, "they wouldn't want to go home, because their parents would be waiting there to say, 'Okay, let me see your score. What's wrong? Why did you not do as well on this one?'" She adds, "A lot of people have got pressure on them from home to do really well to get into top schools. And sometimes they just put it on themselves, that pressure to want to do well, especially when you're competing with other people who are doing really well, too. It sets the bar high."

The result, Isabella says, is that "everyone is constantly stressed." She and her classmate Kira independently describe their typical school day in virtually identical terms: arrival at school 7:00 a.m., classes and then sports or other extracurriculars until 4:00 or 5:00 p.m., followed by four to six hours of homework after dinner, which left only five to six hours a night for sleep. "It was not a competition," Isabella says about the sleep, "but we'd say, 'Oh, I only got six hours.' 'Oh, well, I only got four hours!'" "I did more all-nighters in high school than I have in college," Kira says. "You're in robot mode, and you can't enjoy anything that way."

Clara and Ricardo helped out as much as they could with homework. "My husband is the one that does the math homework," Clara says. "All through high school, if they needed anything with writing, he would review their essays or their math. I did the easy stuff when they were in elementary, but once it got to higher math, he took over." But they also urged their kids to avoid overreaching, as in the case of one math class that Isabella took during her freshman year. "My husband and I went to the open house," Clara says, "we looked at her book, and we didn't understand it, and my husband says, 'Drop it.' It looked like Chinese to us. We couldn't help her. She hated the class, and I thought, *Why are we going to set her up to fail?* So we said, 'Drop it.' And she dropped the class."

Like many other Troy parents, Clara ensured that her kids took full advantage of the array of extracurricular activities available at school and in the wider community. "Soccer, baseball, Girl Scouts, art, piano, dance," she said, listing some of the activities to which she regularly drove her kids, in addition to driving them to school every day and bringing them lunch at school once a week. "I got three speeding tickets in 18 months, going everywhere!"

Troy High offers more than 100 different extracurricular clubs, each with its own advisor and at least ten active members—and that doesn't include athletics. Among the possibilities: Amnesty International, the Anime Club, the Archery Club, the Chess Club, the Coptic Club, the Drama Club, the Gay-Straight Alliance, the iStocks Investment Club, the Live Poets Society, the Math Club, the Muslim Club, the Polynesian Club, Serve A Soldier, World Vision, and Young Americans for Freedom. Each year, Troy produces all sorts of championship teams and ensembles, too, in band, basketball, chorus, cross-country, swimming, tennis, water polo, wrestling, and xylophone. "Even our dance team goes to nationals every year," Clara says proudly.

Running was Isabella's favorite extracurricular activity. "I just love the team and the coaches, because school was always so stressful," she says, "it was always real nice after school to have that break for exercise, and just to breathe." She mentions in passing that she was co-captain of the cross-country team and wrote the script for her class's video yearbook.

Troy is able to mount such an astonishingly wide range of extracurricular activities because of very active fund-raising among parents and community members. Many activities have an associated booster group. Clara explains that like other parents, they regularly donate money to the schools. "That's how they get laptop computers for all the kids in the tech program, and even in the elementary schools," Clara says. "The parents want their children to be well prepared technically. My girlfriend Samantha easily donates $1,000 a year to her elementary school, because she thinks it's cheaper—her daughter was at a private school, and it's $12,000 to $15,000 a year. So for her to donate $1,000 is nothing."

On top of all of this, the kids at Troy (and their parents) invest lots of time and energy in SAT preparation. Three times a week, for example, Isabella had to fit three-hour prep sessions into her schedule, plus a one-time "practice SAT day." Kira also attended an SAT prep summer program at the high school. "I just felt like I needed a little bit more help to feel more confident, she says. Adding, "In our junior year there were a few people who started bringing their books to study for the SAT in the five minutes between classes. It went a little overboard [laughs]."

Because they always have so much to do, Clara complains, the kids at Troy "hardly socialize," and may attend only one or two dances a year. Isabella agrees. "A lot of people didn't really have lives outside of school," she says. As she reflects on her kids' high school experience, you can almost hear Clara the ambitious mother and Clara the child counselor arguing with one another. "It's a lot of pressure for them. It's the one thing my husband and I don't like about this school. Academically, you have to [work hard] to get into top schools, unfortunately, [but] they're taking the fun out of it."

Isabella reflects the same ambivalence: "High school was really stressful, really terrible," she says. "But it was a really good education, and it really prepared me for college. I've never really done well in math, and I'm doing really well now." Despite struggling with advanced math at Troy, as a college sophomore she's tutoring seven college freshmen in pre-calculus.

When the time came, Clara and Ricardo actively helped their kids with their college applications. "Some of these essays from USC and Penn and NYU were difficult," Clara says. "You have to be very mature to answer some of those questions. Ricardo is a very good writer, and he's the one I give a lot of the credit to. I think he helped you [Isabella] and Michael maneuver the application process. And with Michael, I submitted his application to several friends of mine—they were professors and one was a university dean—just so I could get their feedback. We were new, and I wanted to make sure Michael would get accepted to the schools that he was applying to, because it is so competitive."

Both Michael and Isabella got into virtually all the colleges to which they applied. Michael graduated from an Ivy League institution, but by the time Isabella was ready for college, Clara and Ricardo, like many middle-class parents, had been hit by the Great Recession and worried about paying for college. So they encouraged Isabella to choose a local university, well known for its writing program, and in the end she decided to go there instead of the much more expensive, top-flight Eastern university that she preferred. Knowing that she will graduate without debt and thus have the option of graduate school, Isabella and her parents are confident that they have made a smart decision about her future.

Lola and Sofia

In off-peak traffic it's a 15-minute straight shot down the Orange Freeway from the pleasant hills around Troy High School to the neighborhoods of two-bedroom bungalows in the flats around Santa Ana High

School. In the early afternoon sun the area seems peaceable enough. Only the locksmith shops, storefronts like Bad Boy Bail Bonds, the sheriff's forensic lab, and the chain link fences around each house hint that we've entered the most dangerous urban battlefield in Orange County.[10] On the porch of one bungalow we are greeted by two sisters, Lola (29), looking pale and tired, and Sofia (21), tall and thin, with plastic-rimmed glasses. Sofia is pretty, but shy, while Lola offers maternal encouragement to her.

The house itself belongs to their step-grandfather—he has moved to a neighboring town, but has allowed the girls to stay here and helps out with the bills. They describe the older neighbors as friendly and their specific block as still "basically family," with several generations crowded together in each house. But the larger neighborhood has changed dramatically in recent years from stable working-class Latinos, like their step-grandfather (now retired but for many years a school janitor), to younger people heavily involved in drugs and gangs.

Beyond this relatively peaceful block, the wider neighborhood is cleaved by invisible, deadly borders into the territories of rival cholo gangs. Lola begins to sketch a map for us:

The gang on this street is the 6th Street gang, even though this is 4th Street. (They really don't know how to count, so you know how well educated they are!) Then there's another 6th Street gang that is really on 6th Street, but they're not friends with the gang here. Then there's a gang on 7th Street, which are friends with 6th. Then this whole section across Bristol over to Fairview, from 1st to 17th, that's another gang.

You don't really see them, but you know they're around. They're really dangerous. They think "this is our 'hood," so whenever someone walks by they're like, "Where you from?" Yesterday we were in another neighborhood, which was scary. We know who the gang members are around here. When you go into another neighborhood, they don't know you, so they eye you down.

They had gone to that other neighborhood to attend a vigil for a relative who had been shot to death the previous evening.

Sofia: His best friend shot him in the head twice—his friend that he grew up with.

Lola: He had joined a gang at a young age. Then he had a son, he grew up, and he tried to do better, and his friends seen him do better.

Sofia: Exactly, so they rejected him and decided to kill him.

Lola: When it got dark, the gang showed up for the vigil. So we had to be careful because they don't know who we are, and they could have shot us. One of them did have a gun, so we had to be careful what we said and what we did. We didn't know what was happening, so we had to walk out of the area fast.

The sisters draw a simple moral: You can't trust anyone, even your best friends.

The girls' neighborhood was not always so dangerous. From a very young age the two sisters were raised by their grandmother and step-grandfather (whom they know as "Grandpa"). Both grandparents had been born in the United States, but neither had graduated from high school. They provided the girls with a loving, stable home at a time when the neighborhood was still a good place to grow up. "We had the normal suburban life," Lola recalls. "It wasn't all about gangs and stuff. My grandma would let us go to the parks and play, and we all had bikes and a swing set. Everything that a little white kid would have, basically. So we had a childhood."

The sisters were very close to their grandparents and remain close to their step-grandfather. Family dinners were regular. Their grandmother "made sure I had braces," recalls Lola. Their step-grandfather rearranged his work schedule so he could pick them up from school, and he helped Sofia with her math homework. Both grandparents encouraged them to do well in school.

Sofia: My grandmother would say "You should do good in school!
    Did you do your homework?"
Lola: They would sit with us and check our homework.
Sofia: Reward us if we got B+'s or whatever—go the movies or to
    the mall.

Although the family wasn't affluent, their step-grandfather made enough money, Lola says, that "we never ever went without anything." The family always celebrated birthdays and went to the beach, to Sea-World, and to Disneyland three times a year. Lola recalls that their grandparents were "really, really strict," and raised the girls to have good manners and respect others.

Sofia: She was a tough grandmother.
Lola: If she wasn't the way that she was with us, I think we'd be one
    of those ghetto people outside.
Sofia: Exactly!
Interviewer: Did your grandparents talk to you about the kind of
    person they wanted you to be?
Lola: They never really talked to us about that. They just made us
    into that person.

Catastrophically, "everything changed once my grandma died," says Lola. Their step-grandfather continued to provide for the girls, but Lola (then 14) had to become a surrogate mother to Sofia (six). Five years later he moved out of the house, though he continued to support the girls financially. Lola explains, "I was 19 when he moved out. It was hard! My sister was in fifth grade, so it was hard learning how to cook and wash when I never had to do that stuff. I didn't have a choice. We really only had each other and my grandpa."

Lola had hoped to attend a better high school some distance away, but because of her unexpected childrearing responsibilities, she had to attend nearby Santa Ana High. Even there, "I wasn't really allowed to do stuff, 'cause I had to take care of her, because my grandpa worked. I had to grow up really fast." Eventually, Lola dropped out of Santa Ana, but she continued to care for Sofia, as these two young women faced the world together bereft of adult guidance.

Behind the story of their grandparents' loving custody lies a darker reality. They had different birth fathers, both drug addicts, and their birth mother was a gang member—in fact, one of the first female gang members in Santa Ana. After leaving the gang, she became a heroin addict and a prostitute. They have an older half-sister, who was raised in foster homes and has never been part of their lives. "Her dad was the one that got my mom into drugs and prostituting," says Lola.

Sofia has virtually no memory of her mother. Lola has somewhat fuller memories, but they're not good. "My mom was in prison most of my life," she says. "I just have memories of my mom being a heroin addict." Like many others of her generation, Lola and Sofia say, their mother "chose the streets." The girls' grandmother eventually called the cops on her daughter, feeling, Lola says, that "she needed to learn." As a result, their mother was imprisoned, and their grandmother took them in. When the girls were ten and two, their mother was released, but she died not long afterward (perhaps from AIDS, though the girls don't say so).

Years later Lola learned from police records about an earlier arrest. "The day after my ninth birthday, she was arrested down the street from here for prostitution. And she never came to see me. She was so close, [but] she chose prostitution and drugs over me."

Sofia has no idea who her father was. Lola's dad lives in Fullerton, but she despises him. "Gang member crackhead!" she spits out, when asked what he does for a living. "He's a douche. He called me a whore last time I saw him because I didn't want to hug him."

Ironically, their parents' status as gang members in Santa Ana continues to protect the girls to some extent from gang harassment. "We were never pressured into doing it [joining a gang] because of who our family was." The example of their mother has taught them never to do drugs or alcohol.

Santa Ana Schools

For Lola and Sofia, education was initially a rewarding experience. Their grandmother arranged for each of them to attend Head Start, and both girls have fond memories of elementary school. "It was really fun," Lola recalls. "I liked my first-grade teacher, Mrs. Garcia. She was really nice and caring. She was cool." Sofia recalls her experiences the same way. "The teachers actually cared," she says. "The schools I went to were good. I really did like school, to be honest with you." Sofia seems to have been a precocious student—smart, motivated, and selected for a gifted-and-talented program. "She was a weirdo," Lola says, teasing her. "She liked reading the dictionary." "I did," Sofia admits. "I enjoyed reading the dictionary. It was cool."

Lola says that Santa Ana High was "a total different story," compared to their previous schools. The girls observe that the Santa Ana High School buildings are not so bad, though they are ringed by a high chain link fence, "Keep Out" signs decorated with gang graffiti, and lurking police cars. It's the social environment, not the physical plant, that makes Santa Ana High a very different place from Troy High.

Sofia: Going to school every day was very scary. There were kids with guns in the school.

Lola: She [Sofia] was going there when someone was actually murdered.

Sofia: Right across the street. The kid who got murdered was just standing there, and these gangsters came up to him and asked him "Where you from?" He didn't say anything, so they just shot him and left him there.

Lola: There's still bullet holes in the signs.

Sofia: The kids will literally spit in the teachers' faces, start fights, try to kill them. A girl threatened to 1-8-7 me. ["1-8-7" is gangsta slang for "murder."]

Lola: The worst one for me was a guy in class that was a gang member, a druggie. One day out of nowhere he was sitting behind me, and he grabbed my hair and pulled me back and said that he would kill me if I didn't give him my money. And then he let me go and just laughed. But he would always talk about how he had a gun in his locker. I don't know how true that was.

Sofia: I felt scared a lot of times when guys in the class would give each other dirty looks and try to be big and bad and start fights. Girls too. They're so bad, fighting with each other for no reason.

"What was your typical day like?" we ask. Both girls respond immediately, finishing one another's sentences.

Seeing lots of fights, people throwing stuff in class, being very disrespectful to the teachers. Kids would tell them off, start arguments, be really rude. It was nasty. Kids took Ecstasy and drank [vodka-]spiked Gatorade in class all the time.

Under these conditions, it is perhaps not surprising that the teachers and administrators seemed to the girls apathetic and unhelpful. Classroom instruction and learning were not priorities. "What were academics like in your school?" we ask.

Lola: There wasn't any.
Sofia: [Laughing] What's "academics"?
Lola: In junior high, when all the stuff was good, the teachers actually cared.
Sofia: In high school teachers don't care.
Lola: The teachers would even say out loud that they get paid to be there.
Sofia: Just to be there. Just to baby-sit.
Lola: Yeah, that they're there just to baby-sit, that they don't care if we learn or not.[11]

Sofia says that a teacher once allowed her to skip a Saturday detention for talking during class so that she could baby-sit his child. Lola remembers a different kind of negligence. The school, wrongly assuming that Sofia spoke Spanish because she is ethnically Latina, assigned her to a class for native Spanish-speaking students. For an entire year she couldn't follow anything—the classwork, the reading, the homework, or the tests—and simply sat looking out the window. When Lola went to school to point out the mistake, they said that they couldn't change Sofia's placement, and that she would have to stay in that class, but they offered her an additional catch-up class—which met at 6:00 a.m.

Later, acting in effect as Sofia's guardian, Lola asked a math teacher about Sofia's performance in class and suggested that he might give her extra work to do, so she could catch up. His response, she says, was that Sofia was "pathetic," and that he wouldn't give her any extra work "because she wasn't going to do it anyway." Even the school counselors didn't seem to care. "They were there," Lola says, "but they were not there. Her counselor never wanted to help her."

Honors students were a separate, mysterious caste at Santa Ana High from the girls' point of view. "The smart kids stay to themselves," Lola says. "The ones in honors actually get the good teachers." Lacking help from counselors or parents or simply adult savvy, they have no idea how honors students are selected. When pressed to explain, Lola can only respond, "If you're smart"—and then observes that even being smart didn't help Sofia get into honors classes. "The thing is," she says, "in junior high and elementary school, she was really smart. She was a good student, and then once high school hit, it was a total different story." Taking the SATs, too, was something only for the honors students. "Only the smart kids knew about that," Lola says. "The only reason I knew about that was because some of my friends were doing it. Other than that, nobody talked about it."

While at Santa Ana, neither Lola nor Sofia ever participated in any extracurricular or other organized activities. Lola tried joining a reading club, but the teacher in charge refused to allow her in, saying her reading level wasn't good enough. Sofia wanted to play on the volleyball team, but was refused, because she was not an A or B student.

When Sofia fell behind at Santa Ana, she sought help in vain from her teachers and counselors. "You guys are no help. Literally no help. Why do you guys have me in here?" she protested. Sofia's step-grandfather was so angry with the school administrators (and perhaps intimidated by them) that Lola tried to intervene. (He tells us that when he was growing up here in the 1950s, all the parents were involved in the schools, but now they are completely uninterested. "They would rather let others do it, but then no one gets involved.") She asked to have her sister transferred to continuation school, an alternative program for kids who are not making adequate progress in a regular high school. The school refused. "They said they couldn't do anything about it," Lola says. "They basically just wanted her money, since a school gets paid for each student. They didn't care that she was going to fail."

The sisters appealed to the school district, however—and prevailed. Sofia entered the continuation program in her junior year, and it served her well. The girls explain that typically "the kids at the continuation school are the kids that the schools don't want—the ones that have ankle bracelets—and most of them don't want to be there." Sofia, however, "was one of the lucky ones that actually did the work."

Sofia did most of her studying at home, though she checked in at the school once or twice a week. In essence, she pursued a kind of guided independent study, and succeeded at it because she no longer had the distractions and bullying she had encountered at Santa Ana High, and because the staff of the continuation school turned out to be surprisingly conscientious. "Her teacher was amazing," Lola says. "She actually took her time and helped her out." Sofia seconds that. "Yeah, dude, she was awesome," she says. "And they gave me books and packets." Not only that, when Sofia encountered difficulties in math, the school arranged for her to be tutored. Lola was shocked: "They actually supplied the tutor."

Even with minimal structure Sofia flourished in this new setting. With encouragement from the continuation staff and no doubt helped by her native wit and motivation, she passed the "KC" [that is, the CAHSEE, or California High School Exit Examination]. A college counselor at the continuation school then helped her to enroll in a local community college, and, miraculously, Sofia found financial support. For some years the sisters had volunteered at a hospital with AIDS patients. According to the sisters, one of the major donors to the program heard about Sofia's story and offered to pay for her community college and books, removing all financial barriers to her postsecondary education.

Sofia is getting decent grades in community college and wants to become a teacher. But this story does not yet have a fairy-tale ending. Lola and Sofia are navigating the educational system on their own, without any steady guidance from the schools or support from their family. Without the institutional savvy that kids from more comfortable backgrounds have, things can seem very opaque to them. Sofia is confused, for example, about whether her college has a teacher-training program, or even whether it operates with a two-year or four-year curriculum. Lola reports that Sofia's school is overenrolled, which means she has been unable to register for the classes that she needs and is enrolled in a single class that she doesn't need. She is filling her time by working the counter at Hot-Dog-on-a-Stick, still hoping that somehow she will eventually make it through community college.

That's more than Lola hopes for herself. Worn down and performing badly because of the demands of raising Sofia, she dropped out of Santa Ana High just before the end of her junior year. She made that decision after a teacher advised her that she could get a GED through a community college—but that advice proved wrong. Eventually, she did get the degree, but the whole experience so soured her on education that she gave up on going to college. She now has a job that she hates, at a cheap chain clothing store, and is investing her hopes in Sofia. "I want her to be better than my family," she says. "No one's done anything."

Sofia shares that feeling. "Yeah," she says, "no one's done anything in our family. We have no people going in the Marines; we have no people going to the Army. We have no people graduated from university; no people becoming doctors or cops or anything. They're all losers."

Sofia wants to rise above that. When asked what she wants to do, she has a simple answer. "Make something out of myself," she says. "Yeah."

Clara and the Other Latino Orange County

Because Clara is professionally involved with low-income Latino kids from Santa Ana, she has an unusual perspective on the differences between her own children's educational experience and the experience of kids in Santa Ana. Let her summarize the contrast.

> If you go to downtown Santa Ana, the mostly Hispanic, low-income areas, they don't have the resources. A lot of these kids come from homes where they're monolingual Spanish, and the parents probably have fourth- or fifth-grade level education, if that. There's a small percentage of those students whose parents are not educated—like my husband and I were with our own parents—and do make it, but it's too small of a percentage, so small! But 70, 80 percent don't make it. They end up going to the military or trade schools, or they end up in junior colleges. And then they drop out because they get discouraged, because they need the money to be able to survive.
>
> [Comparing parental contributions to the schools], you find out where the discrepancy is, unfortunately, because financially in Santa Ana those parents are working just to pay their rent and their utilities. They really can't afford to donate money. They don't have the same opportunities that we did. They can't find jobs, and they live very badly. They share rooms, a house with three or four families.
>
> The teachers in these areas are basically managing the students because of their behavior, versus [working on] academics. These children are disruptive in class, they're truant, and they're on drugs, or there's violence. So yeah, academics? Are you kidding me? They'd rather go get high.
>
> It's a challenge for the teachers, because a lot of these students are not adequately prepared for high school. They are reading at the third- or fourth-grade level, and [yet] they get passed on to high

school, so they lack the studying and organizational skills and the commitment and the sense of ownership of responsibility to do well academically. I don't think it's just the students. It's a combination of things. The parents don't speak English, so they can't help the kids with their homework.

It's very tough for those kids, because the counselors fail to catch kids who are struggling. I asked a vice principal who's a client of mine, "Why are you promoting these kids who failed several classes? You're setting them up to fail, and of course, they're going to drop out. Who would want to go to school, if you're failing your classes and you don't feel you're adequate?" Of course, their self-esteem is going to be lowered, and that's when they get depressed, because they don't feel socially accepted or academically accepted. These are the kids that fall behind, and they go to continuation school.

They [the school counselors] probably get them in [to continuation school] to be able to say that they finished school. But these students are by far remedial students. They are probably not below average in terms of IQ. I think it's just for environmental reasons and economic reasons that these children are falling through the cracks. These kids are going to do poorly in their whole life, not just academically.

Though Clara herself is a Latina "Tiger Mom," deeply committed to enhancing her own children's opportunities, she is also sensitive to the plight of a very different category of Latino young people in Orange County, those from poor homes and dangerous neighborhoods. Unlike many affluent Americans today, but like affluent Americans a half century ago, she thinks of kids from places like Santa Ana as "our kids."

Troy and Santa Ana represent to some extent the extremes of American high schools, not the average.[12] The stark comparison between them heightens our awareness of the many contrasting features of schools in rich and poor communities today, but we can get a more accurate sense of how different such schools really are across America by examining systematic, nationwide evidence.

Schools: Whom You Go to School with Matters

The central question of this chapter is this: Do schools in America today tend to *widen* the growing gaps between have and have-not kids, do they *reduce* those gaps, or do they have little effect either way? Isabella and Sofia obviously came from very different family backgrounds and went to very different schools, but did the schools magnify or diminish the differences in where they are now? More subtly, if schools are somehow implicated in class divergence, are they *causes* of class divergence or merely *sites* of class divergence? What can the myriad empirical studies of schooling in contemporary America teach us about the various ways in which schools might perpetuate, narrow, or exacerbate class differences? Answering such questions turns out to be tricky but ultimately revealing.

The American public educational system was created to give all kids, regardless of their family origins, a chance to improve their lot in life. The system has been substantially expanded and transformed three times during the past two centuries, and each time a core objective was leveling the playing field.

- The Common School movement of the 1840s and 1850s eventually led to near-universal free public elementary education. "Education, beyond all other devices of human origin, is a great equalizer of the conditions of men," proclaimed Horace Mann, the first great educational reformer in America and the father of the Common School movement.[13]

- The comprehensive High School movement, from 1910 to 1940, eventually led to near-universal public secondary education. Economists Claudia Goldin and Lawrence Katz, leading analysts of this development, characterize it as the seminal force behind both economic growth and socioeconomic equality in America during the twentieth century.[14]

- The Land-Grant College movement, beginning with the Morrill Acts of 1862 and 1890, followed by the G.I. Bill during the

1940s and 1950s, provided the basis for mass higher education in America. The purpose of the Morrill Acts is often described as "the democratization of higher education"; and the provision of essentially free postsecondary education to nearly 8 million veterans of World War II and the Korean War under the G.I. Bill, most of them draftees from all socioeconomic backgrounds, massively expanded access to colleges and universities.[15]

These movements had other goals beyond equal opportunity (notably, improving the nation's economic productivity and undergirding democratic citizenship).[16] Moreover, despite their egalitarian claims these pre–Civil Rights era reforms largely excluded African Americans. That said, most of these educational reformers would have been disappointed if schools did not tend to narrow class gaps among the students, and virtually all would have been appalled if schools actually widened those gaps.

On the other hand, the experiences of Isabella, Lola, and Sofia seem to belie such egalitarian aspirations. So what does the available evidence tell us about social class and schools in America today?

Let's begin with test scores and K–12 education. In a landmark study, the Stanford sociologist Sean Reardon demonstrated a widening class gap in both math and reading test scores among American kids in recent decades. Indeed, Reardon's charts mirror the scissors graphs of other measures that animate the pages of this book. He summarizes his key finding succinctly: "The achievement gap between children from high- and low-income families is roughly 30–40 percent larger among children born in 2001 than among those born twenty-five years earlier."[17]

That gap corresponds, roughly speaking, to the high-income kids getting several more years of schooling than their low-income counterparts. Moreover, this class gap has been growing *within* each racial group, while the gaps *between* racial groups have been narrowing (the same pattern we discovered earlier in this inquiry for other measures, among them nonmarital births). By the opening of the twenty-first century, the class gap among students entering kindergarten was two to three times greater than the racial gap.

Reardon's distressing discovery jibes almost perfectly with much other research on class trends in child development, including non-cognitive measures. His finding is of fundamental importance, because academic achievement, as measured by test scores, is a dominant contributor to class disparities in later outcomes, such as college graduation, incarceration, and adult earnings.[18] Strikingly, Reardon's analysis also suggests that schools themselves aren't creating the opportunity gap: the gap is already large by the time children enter kindergarten and, he reports, does not grow appreciably as children progress through school. Reviewing the evidence, James Heckman writes, "The gaps in cognitive achievement by level of maternal education that we observe at age eighteen—powerful predictors of who goes to college and who does not—are mostly present at age six, when children enter school. Schooling—unequal as it is in America—plays only a minor role in alleviating or creating test score gaps."[19]

Other findings strengthen the view that schools themselves do not do much to exacerbate the opportunity gap. Among elementary-age children, for example, test score gaps expand faster during the summer, while kids are out of school, and then stabilize when the kids go back to school in the fall. Although school quality and resources are unequal between top and bottom socioeconomic schools, once we account for nonschool factors (such as family structure, economic insecurity, parental engagement, and even TV watching), school quality and school resources themselves seem to contribute relatively little to class gaps in test scores and other measures of cognitive and socioemotional skills.[20]

Our stories from Bend, Atlanta, and Orange County included frequent examples of school officials reaching out to help poor kids and level the playing field. Recall Joe's elementary school teacher, who used her lunch break to teach him to read; Clara's and Francisco's teachers who took the twins to Disneyland and Knott's Berry Farm; the counselor in Kayla's school who unexpectedly arranged for her braces, and the school librarian who helped her get financial aid; Michelle's special educators, who spotted and helped her to surmount her learning disabilities; Lola's first-grade teacher, Mrs. Garcia, simultaneously "caring" and "cool," and the "awesome" staff of her continuation school, who enabled her to get through high school and into college. On the other hand, few of the staff at Santa Ana High seemed to reach out to help poor kids.

Virtually all this evidence—quantitative and qualitative—might seem to exonerate schools from any responsibility for the widening class gap, and suggests that schools might be helping to level the playing field, just as America's educational reformers have hoped. But—and it is a big "but"—there's no denying that rich and poor kids in this country attend vastly different schools nowadays, which seems hard to square with the notion that schools are innocent bystanders in the growing youth class gap. Our comparison of Troy High School and Santa Ana High School illustrates this kind of class-based segregation all too vividly. And it matters greatly: quantitative studies have consistently found exceptionally wide differences in academic outcomes between schools attended by affluent kids and schools attended by their impoverished counterparts.

So what's going on?

A first, fundamental fact is residential sorting. As we have seen in Port Clinton, Bend, Atlanta, and Orange County, rich and poor Americans are increasingly living in separate neighborhoods.[21] Although not all kids attend schools based on their parents' residence, most still do. Thus, residential sorting by income over the last 30 to 40 years has shunted high-income and low-income students into separate schools.[22]

Ironically, school quality itself may help explain the increased residential segregation, because most parents now pay close attention to it when deciding where to live. This is true even of parents who have only modest educations themselves, as we saw in the case of Stephanie, our working-class mom in Atlanta. However, well-educated parents of all ethnic backgrounds now go to extraordinary efforts to identify the best schools for their kids and to move into those districts, as the stories of Simone in Atlanta and Clara in Orange County reveal. Both Simone and Clara started comparison shopping for schools when their kids were preschoolers, and both chose their current homes specifically so that their kids could attend high-quality high schools.

Upper-class parents generally have better information about school quality than lower-class parents[23] and are better able to afford homes in the right neighborhoods. Jonathan Rothwell of the Brookings Institution found that houses near a high-scoring public school cost more than $200,000 more than comparable houses near low-scoring schools.[24] Other research suggests that when people bid up prices for houses in good school districts, they are really bidding for a district with many affluent, well-educated parents, rather than for the best teacher quality, class size, or per-pupil spending, implying that parents believe that parental inputs are more important than school inputs in determining school quality.[25] (When my family moved to the Boston area years ago and sought a community with good schools, my wife used the "braces test"—how many kids in town were wearing braces? It was a reasonable proxy for parenting and income and thus for school quality.) This process clusters advantaged kids with other advantaged kids in one set of schools, like Troy High, and poor kids with other poor kids in another set of schools, like Santa Ana High.

Admirable though it may be for other reasons, "school choice" has had at most a slight impact on the class gap. It does allow an increasing proportion of students (roughly 15 percent) to attend schools chosen by their parents, rather than schools based on their residence. But especially among lower-income families, the choices parents make are often not well informed and are constrained by transportation and child care problems.[26] School choice would not likely have made much difference for the lower-class children we've focused on in this book, for example, because they lacked savvy parents to help them make better choices.

Regardless of their own family background, kids do better in schools where the other kids come from affluent, educated homes. This pattern appears to be nearly universal across the developed world.[27] "The social composition of the student body is more highly related to achievement, independent of the student's own social background, than is any other school factor," James Coleman, the first researcher to demonstrate this powerful fact, has written. This generalization applies not only to test scores, graduation, college enrollment, and so forth, but also to adult incomes, even holding constant the effects of a child's own family background and test scores.

That poor kids achieve more in high-income schools is described by Gary Orfield and Susan Eaton as "one of the most consistent findings in research on education." In a few studies, in fact, the correlation of a student's high school learning with her *classmates'* family backgrounds is greater than the correlation with her *own* family background.[28]

Try this mental experiment: Suppose that Sofia (with her "gifted and talented" designation and her precocious dictionary reading) had magically been transferred to Troy High School, while Isabella had been malevolently assigned to a high school like Santa Ana. It's hard to imagine that their respective achievements would remain unaffected. Indeed, Clara and Ricardo, you'll recall, performed exactly that mental experiment when deciding to move from their old neighborhood in LA to Fullerton. But why does the socioeconomic composition of a school seem to have such a powerful impact on its students?[29]

The first explanation that occurs to many people, experts and ordinary citizens alike, is school finance: that is, that schools in affluent areas, funded largely by local property taxes, can afford more and better teachers, administrators, programs, and physical plant. In fact, however, school finance is probably not a major contributor to the growth of the class gap. Most researchers have found, for example, that school finances (including spending per pupil, and teacher salaries) are not significant predictors of school performance.[30] In the past three decades, moreover, as the class gaps have rapidly widened, local property taxes in many states have funded a smaller and smaller fraction of school budgets, in part because court decisions in those states have mandated equalization of spending across school districts.

Teacher salaries are slightly higher in schools serving affluent students, but that pattern probably reflects a tendency for teachers with more seniority to migrate away from high-poverty, high-minority schools for nonmonetary reasons.[31] Moreover, the ratios of teachers and guidance counselors to students are, if anything, more favorable in high-poverty schools.[32] In this respect, the comparison of Troy and Santa Ana high schools in Table 4.1 accurately reflects the national pattern: differences in the factors under administrative control seem too small to account for the massive differences in student outcomes.

To be sure, hiring more and better teachers at higher salaries to teach in high-poverty schools would be a very good way to narrow class disparities. The challenges facing teachers and staff in high-poverty schools—indiscipline, language difficulties, inadequate academic preparation, and the myriad problems kids bring in from outside school, all illustrated at Santa Ana—are so great that more investment is required to level the playing field for the kids. Nevertheless, there is little evidence that the growing performance gap between low-income schools and high-income schools can be attributed to bias in the allocation of public resources.

More plausible suspects in our mystery are the things that students collectively bring with them to school, ranging from (on the positive side of the ledger) academic encouragement at home and private funding for "extras" to (on the negative side) crime, drugs, and disorder. These are the very factors that jump out from our paired portraits of Santa Ana and Troy.[33] Whom you go to school with matters a lot.

First, kids from affluent, educated homes bring their parents with them to school. Virtually all studies show that affluent, more educated parents are more likely than poor, less educated parents to involve themselves at their kids' schools. Our stories vividly illustrate this fact. "We ask more questions in a week than my parents probably asked in four years through high school," Earl said; Simone was a perennial PTA leader in both New Jersey and Atlanta; and Clara not only volunteered in class but also made a point of getting to know the school office staff. Our less affluent parents also tried to engage with their kids' schools, but their efforts were hampered by work obligations (Stephanie, in Atlanta), by cultural barriers (Lola's step-grandfather, in Santa Ana), and by their own educational limits (Joe, in Bend). In most cases the growing class gap in parental engagement is due less to lack of motivation than to economic and cultural obstacles, though Lola's step-grandfather suggests that less affluent parents have become more apathetic in recent years. Nevertheless, compared to low-income schools, schools in affluent areas are characterized by greater engagement and support from parents.

This fact has all sorts of consequences. Many studies have shown that parental engagement—everything from asking about homework to attending PTA meetings—is associated with higher academic performance, better socioemotional skills, and other facets of student behavior, such as less use of drugs and alcohol. As educational researchers Anne Henderson and Nancy Berla have put it, summarizing the trends in such studies, "When parents are involved at school, their children go further in school, and the schools they go to are better."[34]

Moving from correlation to causal certainty is more complicated. Parents who frequent school are also likely to have read to their children as infants, so is it the school visits or the reading that really mattered? Or is the causal arrow perhaps reversed, running from student performance to parental engagement? (Visiting school is a more attractive way to spend an evening if the teachers are likely to say nice things about your kids.) Questions about causality are not easy to answer definitively without controlled experiments, but most researchers are persuaded that parental engagement with schools encourages higher performance, especially among socioeconomically disadvantaged youth.

Kids from affluent homes also bring their parents' affluence to school. Anecdotally, "para–school funding" (parental and community fund-raising) provides a stark contrast between upscale and downscale schools. Such funding, we saw, allows for a richer menu of extras at Troy High than at Santa Ana High. At a more extreme level, on the Upper West Side of Manhattan, PTAs at several public schools raise nearly

$1 million annually to support school activities, earning the schools the label "public privates," and in Hillsborough, California, the annual take from the parent-funded foundation is $3.45 million, which supplements the school budget by 17 percent. Nationwide evidence to document these patterns is lacking so far, but the examples are striking.[35]

Parents in upscale communities also demand a more academically rigorous curriculum, which in turn helps produce more learning, fewer dropouts, and more college entrants.[36] For example, Figure 4.1, based on a 2011 survey of most public high schools in America, shows that low-poverty schools (roughly speaking, the top quartile of schools, in terms of parental income) offer three times as many AP classes as their high-poverty counterparts.[37] Once again, we can see the national pattern mirrored in the contrast between Santa Ana and Troy: all the kids at Troy are nerds, Clara told us, whereas the only thing Sofia had to say about academics at Santa Ana was to snicker, "What's academics?"

Figure 4.1: High-poverty high schools offer fewer Advanced Placement classes

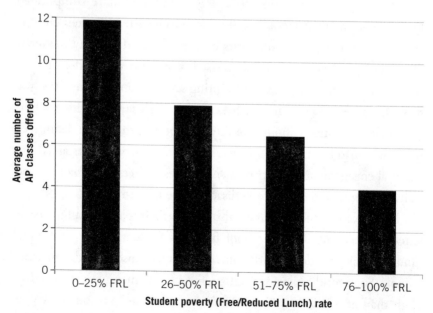

Source: Civil Rights Data Collection, U.S. Department of Education, 2009–10 school year.

Peer pressure, too, plays a powerful role in fostering high academic performance. The influence of peers, which tends to peak at ages 15–18, has been shown on teens' academic achievement, educational aspirations, college going, misbehavior, drug use, truancy, and depression, as well as consumer behavior. As peers transmit social norms, educational values, and even academic skills, peers at high-income schools thus serve as educational catalysts for one another. High standards and aspirations tend to be contagious—as do low standards and aspirations.[38] Peer pressure helps explain the correlation between a school's socioeconomic composition and student performance.[39]

But where do the affluent kids' standards and aspirations come from? Isabella gave us a clear answer—the parents. "[My parents] didn't try to put a lot of pressure on me, [but] a lot of people have got pressure on them from home. . . . [When] kids would not do as well as they had wanted to do on a test, they wouldn't want to go home, because their parents would be waiting there to say, 'Okay, let me see your score. What's wrong?'"

The net result in a school with lots of kids from well-educated, academically ambitious homes is that peer pressure—what Isabella and her classmates experience as "stress" and "competition"—amplifies the collective effects of the achievement motivation from their homes. Conversely, in a school like Santa Ana the peer environment dampens whatever academic aspirations any individual student might bring from home.

So, on average, what kids from affluent homes and neighborhoods bring to school tends to encourage higher achievement among all students at those schools. But the opposite is also true: the disorder and violence that kids from impoverished homes and neighborhoods tend to bring to their schools discourages achievement for all students at those schools. This is what we saw happening at Santa Ana High, with students whispering threats of mayhem in the classroom, and teachers confining themselves to baby-sitting.

High-poverty schools are characterized by higher rates of delinquency, truancy, disorder, and transience than low-poverty schools, and lower rates of English proficiency, because all of those characteristics are concentrated in poor communities.[40] As we witnessed in Santa Ana High, all those characteristics adversely affect *all* the students in such schools, whether or not they personally are delinquent, truant, disorderly, transient, or non-English-speaking. One careful study, for example, found that the presence in a classroom of kids who had been exposed to domestic violence reduced *other* kids' achievement, especially in high-poverty schools.[41]

Here, too, the class gap seems to have grown in recent years, yet again creating the familiar scissors effect. Between 1995 and 2005, victimizations at school declined by nearly 60 percent in suburban schools but by only 43 percent in urban schools. Not surprisingly, too, graduation rates are much lower in high schools with more crime-prone students, because of their impact on class climate and on teacher commitment. "Despite aggregate declines in school crime and fear," criminologists David Kirk and Robert Sampson conclude, "inequality by race and social class in educational experiences has likely increased because declines have been relatively more concentrated in suburban and private schools."[42]

Gangs, largely an urban phenomenon, contribute significantly to school crime and fear. Roughly one quarter of urban students report a gang presence at their high schools, and about one quarter of urban schools report 20 or more violent incidents annually.[43] Most of those incidents are not reported to police, but, as Figure 4.2 shows, suspensions are two and a half times more common in high-poverty high schools than in low-poverty high schools. We saw an extreme version of this disparity when (in Table 4.1) we compared the rates of suspension at Troy High and Santa Ana High. An even greater concentration of disciplinary problems in high-poverty schools is found among elementary and middle schools, though suspensions are rarer in the earlier grades.[44]

The result of this concatenation of disadvantage, other researchers have found, is that "high-poverty classrooms have four times the concentrations of academic, attention, and behavioral problems as low-poverty classrooms."[45] This is, of course, precisely the school climate that Sofia and Lola described for us in such harrowing detail: a climate that disrupts class management, student learning, and teacher morale, and lowers the odds that teachers with other options will choose to work or stay in such schools.

Figure 4.2: High-poverty high schools have more disciplinary problems

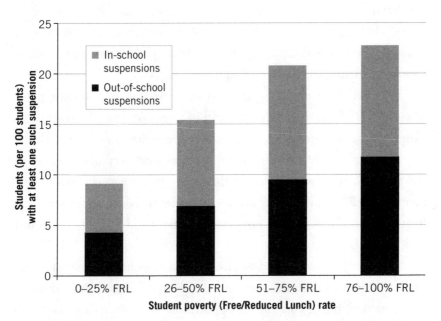

Source: Civil Rights Data Collection, U.S. Department of Education, 2009–10 school year.

A recent study of California high school teachers' daily classroom routines made vivid just how different the learning environments are in high-poverty and low-poverty schools.[46] Stressful conditions from outside school are much more likely to intrude into the classroom in high-poverty schools. Every one of ten such "stressors" is two or three times more common in high-poverty schools than in their low-poverty counterparts—student hunger, unstable housing, and economic problems; lack of medical and dental care; caring for family members and other family and immigration issues; community violence and safety concerns. One consequence is that even though the nominal number of instructional hours doesn't differ between high-poverty and low-poverty schools, over the course of the average week teachers in high-poverty schools spend roughly three and one half fewer hours in actual instruction, and over the course of the academic year high-poverty schools lose almost two weeks more to teacher absences, emergency lockdowns, and other challenges concentrated in such schools. Formally, high-poverty and low-poverty schools may be given the same resources, but the ecological challenges facing the former render them much less effective in providing quality instruction to their students, precisely as we saw when comparing Santa Ana and Troy High Schools.

Sofia and Lola describe the classroom atmosphere from the point of view of students, but they also offer glimpses of what the teachers at Santa Ana have to confront. "There were kids with guns in the school, lots of fights, people throwing stuff in class, being very disrespectful to the teachers. Kids would spit in their faces, tell them off, start arguments, be really rude. It was nasty." We were unable to speak with any Santa Ana staff, but we can imagine what the world of Santa Ana must look like to them.

Suppose that you were a bright, optimistic young teacher showing up each day to work in this war zone. Idealism might carry you through a year or two, but if you had an opportunity to move to a school with less mayhem and more students eager to learn, you'd jump at the chance. So faculty turnover would be higher, with more rookie teachers every year. Moreover, many of the teachers who remained would be timeservers: inured to turmoil, content to baby-sit, "paid to be there," cynical even about helping well-meaning students, dismissing them as "pathetic," lazily assuming that all Latinos speak Spanish.

Sadly, national data precisely confirm this picture. Better teachers, who can have a substantial effect on student success in later life, are disproportionately found in upper-income, high-performance schools, whereas more transient, less capable teachers are disproportionately found in lower-income, low-performance schools. This pattern is probably due less to district assignment of teachers and more to teacher flight. In short, poor teacher morale and higher turnover in low-income schools, driven by a climate of disorder and even danger, helps explain why low-income schools produce lower-achieving students, whatever the students' own background and ability.[47]

Two other factors have sometimes been proposed as explanations for the growing class gap in American schools, but the evidence suggests that they play only minor roles, if any.

The first is tracking: the practice of separating students into college-prep and non-college-prep tracks, which for decades was common and tended to provide a modest edge to kids from more educated homes. During the period in which the opportunity gap has widened, however, access to the college-prep track among kids from less privileged backgrounds has increased. Tracking continues to provide a slight advantage to upper-class kids, but it can't account for the substantial increase in the overall opportunity gap.[48] (To be sure, as Figure 4.1 shows, schools serving poor students offer fewer AP courses, with important consequences for the educational opportunities in such schools.)

Private schools are a second factor that is probably not so important a contributor to the growing opportunity gap as many people think. During the past several decades, the percentage of high school students in private schools has dropped from just over 10 percent to just under 8 percent. Kids from college-educated homes are somewhat more likely (roughly 10 percent) to attend religious or nonsectarian private schools, or to be home-schooled, than kids from high-school-educated homes (roughly 5 percent), but that gap has not changed. Private schools may give a modest edge to affluent students, but that edge has apparently not grown during the years in which the opportunity and achievement gaps have widened sharply.[49]

Extracurricular Activities

School-based extracurricular activities emerged roughly a century ago, as part of the same wave of progressive educational reform that produced the High School movement. The idea was to use extracurriculars to diffuse among all classes what we now call "soft skills"—strong work habits, self-discipline, teamwork, leadership, and a sense of civic engagement. But if we look at participation in extracurricular activities today—in everything from football to band to French club to the student newspaper—we can see yet another dimension of the growing class disparity in America's educational system.

Involvement in extracurricular activities has been shown repeatedly to have measurably favorable consequences. Consciously or unconsciously, affluent, more educated parents understand this, and as we saw earlier, they are increasingly investing substantial time and money in supporting their kids' involvement in extracurricular activities. It's why, in Bend, Earl bought his daughter Lucy a horse and built a barn for it; and why, in Atlanta, Desmond's mother, Simone, insisted that each of her sons do a sport every season; and why, in Orange County, Isabella's mother, Clara, paid those speeding tickets to ensure that her kids were extensively involved in extracurriculars. They had time and money that the poorer kids' families lacked, and they invested those resources in helping their children acquire valuable soft skills through extracurricular activities.

Consistent involvement in extracurricular activities is strongly associated with a variety of positive outcomes during the school years and beyond—even after controlling for family background, cognitive skills, and many other potentially confounding variables. These positive outcomes include higher grade-point averages, lower dropout rates, lower truancy, better work habits, higher educational aspirations, lower delinquency rates, greater self-esteem, more psychological resilience, less risky behavior, more civic engagement (like voting and volunteering), and higher future wages and occupational attainment.[50] One carefully controlled study, for example, showed that kids consistently involved in extracurricular activities were 70 percent more likely to go to college than kids who were only episodically involved—and roughly 400 percent more likely than kids who were not at all involved.[51] Another study, which has a special relevance to the students we met in Orange County, found that involvement in extracurricular activities among low-income Latino students (all too rare, as the experiences of Lola and Sofia illustrate) predicts school achievement.[52]

Leadership in extracurricular activities appears to have even more intense effects: one study found that club and team leaders are more likely to command higher salaries in managerial positions later in life.[53] And an intriguing study of students who attended high school in Cleveland, Ohio, in the 1940s even found neurological effects a half century later: students who had participated in extracurricular activities were substantially less likely than those who hadn't to suffer from dementia at the turn of the century, even after adjusting for differences in IQ and educational attainment.[54] The only negative finding that emerges from the dozens of studies that have been done on the correlates of extracurricular activities is not startling: among young men, participation in sports is often correlated with excessive drinking (but not drug use). Nevertheless, among both men and women, the extracurricular activity most consistently associated with high academic achievement is sports. Jocks turn out to be brainy, too.

To be sure, few of these studies were true experiments, randomly assigning some kids to participate and excluding others, so we cannot entirely rule out the possibility that the robust correlation between extracurricular involvement and life success might be due, at least in part, to some unmeasured variable, like innate energy level. On the other hand, a number of studies measure change over time in the same individual, which should eliminate the effects of any enduring personality trait. One clever study found strong effects on college attendance and labor market outcomes after Title IX widened girls' participation in sports, a kind of natural experiment; another study used comparison of siblings to tease out the causal effects of extracurricular involvement on later earnings; and several experimental studies have confirmed the effects of programs akin to conventional extracurricular activities.[55]

So why do extracurricular activities have such broad implications for a child's future? Many suggestions have been offered: the effects on self-confidence, time use (the "idle hands" theory), positive peer effects, and so on. One important advantage that we shall explore in the next chapter is exposure to caring adults outside the family: coaches and other adult supervisors often serve as valuable mentors, as we saw with Jesse's football coach in Port Clinton and Isabella's track coaches.[56]

But the biggest benefit of extracurricular participation seems to be what the educational reformers who invented this practice hoped it would be: soft skills and character. Presumably it was character, not military skills, that the Duke of Wellington had in mind when he famously exclaimed upon revisiting the playing fields of Eton, "It is here that the battle of Waterloo was won!" Noncognitive skills and habits such as grit, teamwork, leadership, and sociability are unmistakably developed among participants in extracurricular activities.

Many researchers believe that soft skills and extracurricular participation are as important as hard skills and formal schooling in explaining educational attainment and earnings ten years later, even controlling for family background. That's because employers increasingly value noncognitive traits, such as work habits and ability to work with others. These noncognitive traits may be even more important for students from more disadvantaged family backgrounds.[57]

To sum things up: extracurricular participation matters for upward mobility. It is thus distressing to learn that every study confirms a substantial class gap in extracurricular participation, especially when it comes to sustained involvement across different types of activity. Poor kids are three times as likely as their nonpoor classmates to participate in *neither* sports *nor* clubs (30 percent to 10 percent), and half as likely to participate in *both* sports *and* clubs (22 percent to 44 percent).[58]

Even more distressing is the fact that extracurricular participation rates in recent decades display the familiar scissors gap. One study found that during the past 15 years, activity levels in out-of-school clubs and organizations rose among affluent youth and fell among poor youth. From 1997 to 2012, the "extracurricular gap" between poor kids and nonpoor kids aged 6–11 nearly doubled, from 15 to 27 percentage points, while the comparable gap among kids aged 12–17 rose from 19 to 29 percentage points.[59]

Figure 4.3: Growing class gap in participation in school-based extracurriculars, 1972–2002

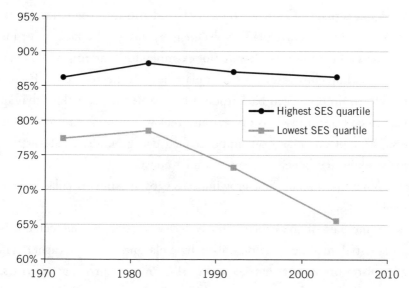

Sources: National Longitudinal Study of 1972, High School and Beyond (1980), National Education Longitudinal Study of 1988, Education Longitudinal Study of 2002.

Figure 4.3 draws on national high school surveys in recent years to illustrate the growing gap for extracurricular activities. Similar gaps have opened up for private music, dance, and art lessons, and for leadership positions on athletic teams. Seniors from affluent backgrounds have served as team captains more than twice as often as classmates from poorer backgrounds, a gap that has nearly doubled during the past several decades. This same basic scissors pattern applies to virtually every type of extracurricular activity, viewed separately. The principal exception is student government, where the gap has closed downward, as rich kids have dropped out even more rapidly than poor kids—a convergent disappearance of practice in self-government that is unfortunate for our democracy.[60]

These charts confirm nationally the class patterns that emerged clearly from our case studies. Recall Andrew's active (if laid-back) membership of the school soccer team, as well as his six years of guitar lessons; Desmond's year-round involvement in school sports, as well as his years of piano lessons; and Isabella's intense involvement in athletics, dance, and piano. Compare those rich and fruitful experiences to the total lack of extracurricular involvement by any of the kids we've met from less affluent homes, despite (for example) futile attempts by Lola to join a reading club and by Sofia to play on the volleyball team. Each of the kids from privileged backgrounds has learned the soft skills that appeal to college admissions officers and that will impress future employers. None of our kids from impoverished backgrounds, whatever their native skills, has benefited from a similar boost.

What can explain these growing class gaps in extracurricular involvement?

Some part of the explanation is perhaps active discouragement by school staff members, as described by Lola and Sofia. "Teachers and administrators serve as gatekeepers to slots in extracurricular activities," writes educational commentator Ralph McNeal, "recruiting students they perceive to be talented while restricting others who are disqualified by academic standards."[61] Lack of transportation might also be a factor. More important in the aggregate, however, is the constricted menu of extracurricular opportunities available in high-poverty schools.

For example, Figure 4.4 shows that across America high schools with affluent students offer twice as many team sports as high-poverty schools.[62] Other studies suggest that this extracurricular gap between affluent and impoverished schools is at least as great for nonsports activities like French club and orchestra. These differences in extracurricular offerings, in turn, turn out to be an important part of the explanation for the lower academic performance of high-poverty schools.[63]

Figure 4.4: High-poverty high schools offer fewer team sports

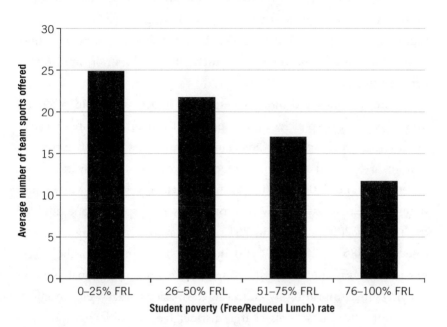

Source: Civil Rights Data Collection, U.S. Department of Education (2009–10 school year).

Fifty years ago, offering opportunities for all kids to take part in extracurricular activities was recognized as an important part of a public school's responsibilities to its students, their parents, and the wider community. No one talked then about soft skills, but voters and school administrators understood that football, chorus, and the debate club taught valuable lessons that should be open to all kids, regardless of their family background. Recall the rich array of extracurricular activities pursued by poor kids in Port Clinton High School in the 1950s.

In our new era of budget belt-tightening, high-stakes testing, and academic "core competencies," however, school boards everywhere have decided that extracurricular activities and soft skills are "frills." Affluent and impoverished school districts alike have felt this pressure, but given their different constituencies, they have followed different paths. Some poorer districts have simply cut back on extracurricular offerings, as reflected in Figure 4.4. Affluent districts instead have kept (and even expanded) their offerings by drawing on private resources. One such source, as we have seen, is para–school funding by parents and community members. While that approach obviously favors affluent school districts, at least within the schools themselves it does not discriminate between rich and poor students.

More insidious and more widespread has been the rapid proliferation of pay-to-play policies now imposed on students in more than half of American high schools. One nationwide survey in 2010 estimated that team fees and other costs of extracurricular sports averaged between $300 and $400 per student. An annual survey of six Midwestern states found that pay-to-play fees for high school sports alone doubled from $75 in 2007 to $150 in 2012, while average marching band fees rose from $85 in 2010 to $100 in 2013. Even in California, where pay-to-play was found by the courts to be unconstitutional, schools circumvented the ruling by collecting "donations" that were, in effect, mandatory.[64] Some schools charge distinct fees for different sports; in Painesville, Ohio, cross-country costs $521, football $783, and tennis $933![65] In addition, equipment costs (formerly borne by the school, but now typically borne by parents) amount to roughly $350 per year.[66]

Firm nationwide numbers are still unavailable, but a reasonable estimate nowadays for the total costs of extracurricular participation might be $400 per student per activity per year, or roughly $1,600 for two kids in a family participating in two activities each year. For parents in the top quintile of the national income distribution that would amount to about 1–2 percent of their annual income, but for a household in the bottom quintile, the same cost would amount to nearly 10 percent (or more) of their annual income. Given these numbers, the surprise is that any poor kids at all take part in extracurricular activities.

Schools often counter that they waive fees for poor kids, but given the inevitable stigma attached to the waiver, it is hardly surprising that in 2012, while 60 percent of all kids nationwide who played school sports faced a pay-to-play fee, only 6 percent received a waiver. Prior to the institution of fees, roughly half of all kids, whether from affluent or less affluent backgrounds, were playing sports, but when fees were introduced, *one in every three* sports-playing kids from homes with annual incomes of $60,000 or less—the national median is about $62,000, so many of these kids come from solidly middle-class homes—dropped out because of the increased cost, as compared to *one in ten* kids from families with incomes over $60,000. Within a few decades America's public schools have thrust the burden of extracurricular activity (and the resulting soft skills benefits) onto the family, reversing nearly a century of settled educational policy, with predictable results in terms of equality of access.

Yet even in today's America the provision of extracurricular opportunities through public schools remains less discriminatory than wholly private provision—piano lessons, club soccer, and the like. Children in low-income families are even less likely to participate in organized nonschool activities, such as after-school programs, athletic teams, music lessons, and scouts, than they are in school-based activities. Among these nonschool programs, moreover, researchers have found greater class disparities in participation in expensive activities like sports or music lessons than in low-cost programs run by churches or community organizations.[67] So by providing some working-class kids with activities to which they would otherwise have no access, schools still exert a modest leveling effect on extracurricular participation.

Are school-year jobs another contributor to the growing opportunity gap?[68] Here experts caution us not to confuse part-time jobs and virtually full-time jobs. Part-time jobs typically have positive benefits in terms of preparation for adult life, and such jobs were in past decades more common among relatively affluent teens. By contrast, virtually full-time jobs have fewer (if any) beneficial long-term consequences and may well interfere with extracurricular activities. The past 40 years have seen a steady decline in school-year employment of all sorts among kids from all backgrounds, although that decline has been slightly faster among more affluent kids, which has thus slightly closed the class gap. Work, therefore, can't be a major reason for the growing extracurricular gap. Budget cutting and the shifting priorities of American schools are probably the main reasons that extracurricular opportunities (and the soft skills they inculcate) are increasingly the preserve of more affluent young people.

So let's return to the core question in this chapter: Do K–12 schools make the opportunity gap better or make it worse?

The answer is this: the gap is created more by what happens to kids before they get to school, by things that happen outside of school, and by what kids bring (or don't bring) with them to school—some bringing resources and others bringing challenges—than by what schools do to them.[69] The American public school today is as a kind of echo chamber in which the advantages or disadvantages that children bring with them to school have effects on other kids. The growing class segregation of our neighborhoods and thus of our schools means that middle-class kids like Isabella hear mostly encouraging and beneficial echoes at school, whereas lower-class kids like Lola and Sofia hear mostly discouraging and harmful echoes.

What this means is that schools as *sites* probably widen the class gap. We've seen evidence that schools as *organizations* sometimes modestly contribute to leveling the playing field. For more than a century, school-related extracurricular activities have narrowed the opportunity gap, by providing important opportunities for kids from low-income backgrounds to build the soft skills that are increasingly important for economic and professional success. On the other hand, compared to Port Clinton in the 1950s (when my trombone, trombone lessons, and football coaching and equipment were all provided free of charge by the high school), recent decisions by school boards to withdraw from that historic responsibility are widening the class gap.

The fact that schools as organizations today have a mixed and modest impact on the opportunity gap does not mean that reforms in schools might not be an important part of the solution to the gap. On the contrary, even if schools didn't cause the growing opportunity gap—and there's little evidence that they have—they might well be a prime place to fix it. Americans concerned about the opportunity gap must not make the all too common mistake of blaming schools for the problem. Instead, we should work with schools to narrow the gap. School is, after all, where the kids are. As I discuss in the final chapter, promising reforms that might raise the performance of schools serving low-income students can be found across the country, raising the prospect that schools, though not a big part of the problem, might be a big part of the solution.[70]

Trends in Educational Attainment

Because education has long been the dominant pathway for upward mobility in America, trends in educational attainment—finishing high school, attending college, and completing college—are a crucial metric for how we are doing, and especially how we are likely to do in the future, as today's students join the workforce. If high school and college are important rungs on the ladder of opportunity between the childhood foundation provided by family and the rewards of adult life, how have kids from various class backgrounds been doing as they climb those rungs in recent years? In each case, it turns out, there is good news and bad news.

HIGH SCHOOL

Throughout most of the twentieth century the fraction of American young people who graduated from high school rose steadily, from 6 percent at the beginning of the century to 80 percent in 1970, the fruits of the High School movement I described earlier.[71] If we include the GED (the national high school equivalency test), that increase continued in the last three decades of the century. Moreover, the earlier class gap in high school diplomas (including GEDs) tended to close in those decades, as kids from less privileged backgrounds caught up. Even though a gap remains—virtually all kids from the top quartile of socio-economic status nowadays graduate from high school, whereas more than a quarter of kids from the bottom quartile don't—so far the news about trends seems encouraging.

But a closer look at the trends suggests some bad news, too.

First, most of the apparent improvement among kids from less privi-leged backgrounds in the years after 1970 was attributable to a rapid increase in GED credentials. In fact, by 2011 the GED accounted for 12 percent of all high school credentials issued, and a disproportionate number of those GEDs were issued to kids from poorer backgrounds, like Lola. Furthermore, much recent research has confirmed that the GED does not have the same value as a regular high school degree, either in terms of continuing on to college or in the labor market. In-deed, some research suggests that the GED adds very little compared to dropping out of high school and getting no degree at all. Many GED recipients say that their ultimate objective is to get a college degree, but only a tiny fraction ever do. In that sense, the closing of the class gap in terms of high school graduation during the past several decades is mostly an illusion.[72]

Second, although the value of a regular high school degree (not counting GEDs) relative to simply dropping out has remained more or less constant over these years, the value of a high school degree relative to a college degree has declined sharply, because the "college premium" has grown rapidly. In terms of average wages, a college degree was worth 50 percent more than a regular high school degree in 1980, but by 2008 the college degree was worth 95 percent more.[73] In that sense, the edu-cational gains of kids from poor backgrounds have been doubly illusory. They've been struggling to catch up on a down escalator.

COLLEGE

During recent decades, college preparedness (in terms of academic achievement) and college entry have risen for students from all socioeconomic backgrounds. However, a substantial class gap in college enrollment persists, though whether that gap has remained constant or increased is unclear.[74] The economists Martha Bailey and Susan Dynarski compared kids who would have entered college around 1980 with their counterparts about 20 years later. In the earlier cohort, 58 percent of kids from the most affluent quintile of the income distribution entered college, compared to 19 percent of kids from the poorest quintile. By the end of the century, those figures were 80 percent and 29 percent, respectively.

While college going for poorer kids grew faster, because the richer kids began at a much higher level of college entrance, the absolute gap between the two groups expanded from 39 percentage points to 51 percentage points. A detailed examination of this growing gap identifies many of the same causal factors that we have already discussed— academic preparation in elementary and high school, family and peer support—and others that we shall explore in the next chapter, especially support from mentors and the wider community.[75]

But even if we count these changes in advancement to postsecondary education as good news, we must note some bad news.

First, growing access by poor kids to college does not mean growing access to selective colleges and universities. Increasingly, poor kids who go on to college are concentrated in community colleges—14 percent of poor kids in college in 1972 were in community colleges, compared to 32 percent in 2004. Community colleges can play a valuable role as a ladder out of poverty, of course. They represent hope for disadvantaged kids, as they do for Kayla in Bend, Michelle and Lauren in Atlanta, and Sofia in Orange County. In the concluding chapter we shall consider the contribution that community colleges might make to narrowing the opportunity gap.

On the other hand, for most kids, community colleges are not really a rung on a taller ladder, but the end of the line, educationally speaking. When students enter a community college, 81 percent say they plan to get a four-year degree, but only 12 percent actually do.[76] So counting a community college as equivalent to a four-year institution (which our "good news" on college entry did) is misleading.

In terms of entry into more selective institutions, which for better or worse offer the best prospects for success in America, the class gap has actually widened in recent years. The fraction of kids from the bottom quartile of the income distribution who ended up at a selective college or university rose from 4 percent in 1972 to 5 percent three decades later, but for kids from the top quartile, the equivalent figures were 26 percent and 36 percent. By 2004, in the nation's "most competitive" colleges and universities—such as Emory, West Point, Boston College, and USC— kids from the top quartile of the socioeconomic scale outnumbered kids from the bottom quartile by about 14 to one.[77] Just as with high school degrees, even though young people from less privileged backgrounds are doing somewhat better now than kids from similar backgrounds did several decades ago, kids from privileged backgrounds are lengthening their lead.

That's bad enough, but there's worse news: much of the recent growth in enrollment in postsecondary institutions by low-income students has been concentrated in the rapidly expanding for-profit sector, in such institutions as the University of Phoenix and Kaplan. In 2013 this sector attracted 13 percent of all full-time undergraduates, compared to 2 percent in 1991. These students are disproportionately from low-income backgrounds (as well as older and ethnic minorities). Giving a leg up to such students could narrow the opportunity gap, and indeed Stephanie's "golden" son in Atlanta exemplifies that possibility. But for-profit institutions are twice as expensive for students as public universities—and have much worse records in terms of graduation rates, employment rates, and earnings. Not surprisingly, therefore, students at for-profit institutions have much higher debt burdens (especially government-backed loans) and much higher default rates. For-profit institutions have a better track record in shorter certificate courses, but including them in estimates of college enrollment exaggerates the gains among low-income students in recent years.[78]

The worst news of all, however, is this: enrolling in college is one thing, but getting a degree is quite another. The class gap in college completion, which was already substantial 30 to 40 years ago, has steadily expanded. This matters hugely, because completing college is much more important than entering college on all sorts of levels: socioeconomic success, physical and mental health, longevity, life satisfaction, and more. Figure 4.5 estimates the big picture over the past 40 years.[79] On the measure of postsecondary education that matters most—graduating from college—kids from affluent backgrounds are pulling further and further ahead, yet one more of our dispiriting scissors charts.

Figure 4.5: Growing gap in gaining a college degree, by family income, 1970–2011

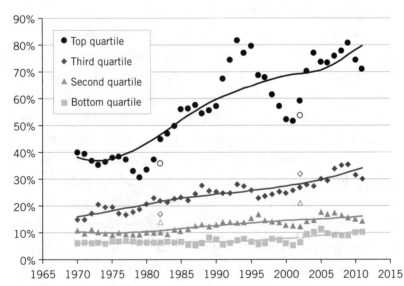

Source: "Family Income and Unequal Educational Opportunity," *Postsecondary Education Opportunity* 245 (November 2012).

In terms of the labor market, some college is better than no college at all. But because the biggest boost to economic success and social mobility comes from having a college degree, kids from upper-class backgrounds are once again widening their lead in the race that matters most. Kids from low-income backgrounds—like David, Kayla, Michelle, Lauren, Lola, and Sofia, to say nothing of Elijah—are working more or less diligently to improve their prospects in life, but no matter how talented and hardworking they are, at best they are improving their play at checkers, while upper-class kids are widening their lead at three-dimensional chess.

Summarizing the progress of rich kids and poor kids up the educational ladder in recent years, Figure 4.6 follows a single cohort of kids for a decade, from 2002 (when they were in the tenth grade) to 2012 (when most of them had climbed as far as they were likely to get).[80] The left-most pair of columns shows that most of the sophomore class of 2002 successfully received a high school diploma. That includes 92 percent of kids from the top quartile of the socioeconomic hierarchy, and 64 percent of kids from the bottom quartile.[81]

Figure 4.6 also shows that most of those who graduated from high school actually applied to college, though rich kids were much more likely to reach that rung (90 percent) than poor kids (59 percent). An even more serious winnowing took place as the kids actually crossed the threshold into college. Of all rich kids, 89 percent had enrolled in college within two years of high school graduation, compared to only 46 percent of all poor kids. And by the time this cohort actually reached the rung of college graduation, 58 percent of all rich kids had made it to the top, compared to only 12 percent of all poor kids. It was as if the poor kids had weights attached to their feet that grew heavier and heavier with each step up the ladder.

On the other hand, as we have seen throughout this chapter, it is important to distinguish between the *sites* of disparity and the *causes* of disparity. It would be too easy to assume that because family income so closely predicts college graduation, college costs must be the cause of class discrepancies. The fact that a given rung of the ladder (such as college graduation) is the site of a rapidly growing class gap does not imply that that rung itself caused the gap. In fact, all of the factors that we've discussed so far in this book—family structure, parenting, childhood development, peer groups, extracurricular opportunities—have contributed to the widening gap in college graduation rates in recent decades, along with the neighborhood and community influences that we shall discuss in the next chapter.[82] The burdens on the poor kids have been gathering weight since they were very young. Rising tuition costs and student debt are the final straw, not the main load.

Figure 4.6: Climbing the educational ladder (unevenly)
Of every 100 potential members of the class of 2004, roughly how many reached each rung?

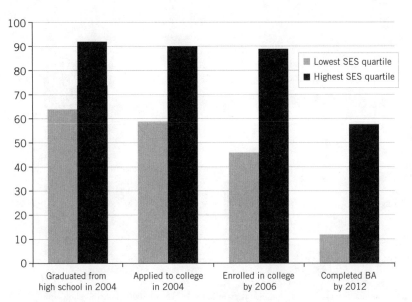

Source: Educational Longitudinal Study of 2002–2012, adjusted for prior dropouts.

Figure 4.7 brings this chapter to a close on a sobering note. As the twenty-first century opened, a family's socioeconomic status (SES) had become even more important than test scores in predicting which eighth graders would graduate from college.[83] A generation earlier, social class had played a smaller role, relative to academic ability, in predicting educational attainment.[84] Nowadays, high-scoring rich kids are very likely (74 percent) to graduate from college, while low-scoring poor kids almost never do (3 percent). Middling students are six times more

likely to graduate from college if they come from a more affluent family
(51 percent) than if they come from a less affluent family (8 percent).
Even more shocking, high-scoring poor kids are now slightly less likely
(29 percent) to get a college degree than low-scoring rich kids (30 percent). That last fact is particularly hard to square with the idea at the
heart of the American Dream: equality of opportunity.

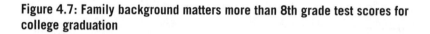

**Figure 4.7: Family background matters more than 8th grade test scores for
college graduation**

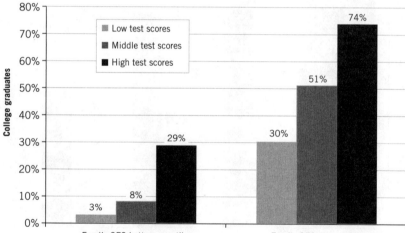

Source: National Education Longitudinal Study of 1988 (NELS:88/2000), Fourth Follow-up.

Chapter 5

COMMUNITY

THE PHILADELPHIA STORY, SET IN THE CITY'S WEALTHY MAIN Line suburbs in the midst of the Great Depression, and famously starring Katharine Hepburn, captured the social capers of the 1 percent of that era. Hepburn's character was modeled on the real-life Helen Hope Montgomery Scott, once described in *Vanity Fair* as "the unofficial queen of Philadelphia's WASP oligarchy."[1] The colossal manors of the Gilded Age, like her 800-acre Ardrossan Estate, have now mostly been replaced by winding, tree-shaded lanes along which can be found the fieldstone mansions of the new Philadelphia elites of finance, consulting, and "eds and meds" (universities and medical centers). Just as a century ago, bucolic Lower Merion Township and its neighboring towns remain home to some of America's most affluent, well-educated families.

Eleven miles to the east another classic of cinematic sociology, *Rocky*, was set in the gritty white working-class neighborhood of Kensington, close by the Delaware docks and the dying industries on which Philadelphia's prosperity had once been based. During the late nineteenth and early twentieth centuries Irish and Italian and Polish immigrants had worked in mills, tanneries, shipyards, and packing plants and had crowded into nearly identical, tightly packed two-story row houses. For generations, families remained in the same neighborhoods and attended the same Catholic churches and schools. By 1970, however, the factories and their neighborhoods had begun a long descent, and the city lost over a quarter of a million jobs between 1970 and 2000. Close-knit communities where housewives once proudly swept the front steps daily gave way to abandoned factories, open-air drug markets, and acres of crime-infested empty lots. As poor blacks moved ever closer to the white ethnic enclaves, racial tensions in the area erupted, symbolized by the brutal battles between Rocky Balboa and Apollo Creed.

Just as in the rest of America, inequality and class segregation within metropolitan Philadelphia have grown during recent decades. As late as 1980, median household income in Lower Merion Township was roughly double that in Kensington, but by 2010 the difference was four to one.[2] When the Social Science Research Council calculated the rate of "disconnected youth"—that is, people aged 16–24 who were neither working nor in school—in urban neighborhoods across America, the Kensington area was near the top of the national list (30 percent), whereas the Lower Merion Valley was near the very bottom (3 percent).[3] Kensington seemed a million miles from Lower Merion Township, not 11.

This chapter describes the community settings within which the growing opportunity gap is playing out across the country, and the contrasting social resources and neighborhood challenges that affect the fate of rich and poor kids. We begin by meeting two white families: one from Lower Merion Township and another from Kensington, each headed by a single mom struggling to raise a pair of daughters amidst family turmoil and dissolution, grappling with issues of drugs, teen sex, and trouble in school. As we shall see, both moms have tried hard to help their children, given their resources, and in some respects both have succeeded. However, we'll also see how the economic and social resources of the more educated, affluent family in the suburbs helped to buffer the kids from stress. Meanwhile, the Kensington neighborhood, once sustained by dense social networks that offered mutual support in modest economic circumstances, is now a source of problems, not solutions, for poor kids.

Marnie, Eleanor, and Madeline

Eleanor (19) and Madeline (18) have lived with their mother, Marnie (55), in Lower Merion Township virtually all their lives. When the girls were young, their parents stretched financially to buy the kid-friendly sidewalks, excellent schools (both public and private), and agreeable (if reserved) neighbors of Lower Merion. The area is rich in community institutions—from the Lower Merion Soccer Club, the Ardmore Community Center, the YMCA, and several active civic associations to numerous religious institutions catering to Jews, Presbyterians, Quakers, Catholics, Anglicans, Armenians, and evangelicals, all now complemented by a lively town presence on Twitter and Facebook.

Older residents say that the Main Line was once more diverse, with children of mailmen and longshoremen in local schools, but nowadays that's changed. "There's not a lot of diversity," Eleanor reports. "It's mostly upper-middle-class families [in] the Main Line bubble." Madeline, for her part, says that many kids at her high school "really buy into 'Ivy or Die': 'If I don't follow my parents' footsteps in making millions of dollars, then I will be a failure.'"

Marnie, the girls' mother, the daughter of a boom-and-bust movie producer, was raised in Beverly Hills and became the first person in her family to attend college. Her parents were alcoholic, and the family was dysfunctional (the parents married and divorced each other three times), which created a difficult home environment for Marnie, but Marnie herself was "super-brainy," as she puts it, at Beverly Hills High School, and graduated from a top Ivy college with straight As, majoring in economics. After a stint in theater management, she married, earned an MBA from Wharton, and joined a consulting firm.

The girls' father, Thad, got his BA from the same Ivy institution, followed by a graduate degree from another top university. For several years before and after the girls were born, he worked as a highly successful, well-paid entrepreneur, enabling the family to move to their large home in Lower Merion. Suddenly, however, when the girls were in middle school, Thad's business failed, and he fell into depression. After a year or two, Marnie ended the marriage. Since Thad was in no position to provide financial support, she recognized that she would be the sole breadwinner. Faced with this frightening prospect, Marnie made a momentous decision to become an independent consultant, aiming to earn enough to support her family in what one daughter calls "a very extravagant lifestyle," including private schools, horseback riding, and an extensive household staff. For better and worse, Marnie's decision to strike out on her own was a decisive turning point in all their lives.

Because of their mother's extremely long hours, well-remunerated professional skills, and frequent use of credit card debt, Eleanor and Madeline enjoyed a big house, piano lessons, summer sailing camp, costumed birthday parties, and (when they entered middle school) one of the best private schools in the area. The girls remember happy childhood years of hide-and-seek, lemonade stands, and stable friendships. "My mom is really a great, great mother," Eleanor says, "just in the sense that for most of her life she put me and my sister first. And she really worked hard and did everything for us to make sure that we had really great lives."

Their parents' divorce hit both daughters hard. "I really didn't see it coming," Eleanor says, adding that it "was probably the biggest event of my childhood." Initially, Marnie and Thad worked hard at co-parenting, hiring a marriage/divorce therapist to try to smooth the rough edges, and taking turns living at home with the girls. But these efforts did not work out, and Thad fled to the Mountain West "to heal."

Since Marnie's high-powered professional life (and the material support it provided) was all-consuming, she arranged for nannies, au pairs, and other household staff to be there when the girls got home from school, to drive them to activities, to prepare dinner, and so forth. "The staff raised us," Madeline interjects sarcastically. Later, Marnie smiles, philosophically. "They know that I'm a big part of what's been secure during this period. Someday maybe she'll look back on this with different eyes."

As her parents' marriage was falling apart, Eleanor decided to attend an elite boarding school for high school, in part because, as she puts it, "I didn't want to deal with the mess at home." Shortly after she left, Marnie learned from several other mothers that Eleanor and a group of girls in the area had previously taken advantage of Marnie's absence during the day to do drugs in her home. Shocked at her own naïveté, Marnie searched Eleanor's room and discovered an ounce of marijuana. She flew to the boarding school and "had it out" with Eleanor for six hours. "I told her my goal is for you to get through adolescence alive and not addicted and not messed up. I was an angel dancing on the head of a pin, and she wasn't about to jeopardize everything for us." Marnie cut off Eleanor's credit card, insisted that she wait to get her driver's license, and warned her that if she got in trouble with the law, "I am not the Main Line mom who will hire a fancy attorney to get you off." Tough love seemed to work in this case, because the problem did not recur.

At boarding school, Eleanor felt stress to achieve and to fit in, which meant being "rich, athletic, beautiful, smart—perfect." Severely depressed, she left the boarding school at the beginning of 11th grade and returned to the public high school back home. Eleanor herself suspected that she suffered from undiagnosed ADHD (Attention Deficit Hyperactivity Disorder), but not until she returned home did Marnie become aware of the problem.

Intensely supportive, Marnie sprang into action. She consulted specialists and through her contacts eventually found a psychiatrist who diagnosed the problem and prescribed effective medication, as well as consultants who could help Eleanor with learning strategies. Knowing that "ADHD kids need a quiet workspace," Marnie remodeled the third floor, giving Eleanor a bedroom, a tranquil, well-lit study, and an extra bedroom in case hers became cluttered and distracting. At the same time, sophisticated about the risk of kids being "labeled," Marnie carefully kept the ADHD diagnosis confidential. "We had constructed a road for this kid," she says, "and it was going to work. And it did."

Meanwhile, Madeline was encountering adolescent problems of another kind. During eighth grade, Marnie discovered that Madeline and her boyfriend, Sam, were close to becoming sexually active. Marnie and Sam's parents met over dinner, Marnie says, "to figure out what our common response was going to be." Marnie arranged for Madeline to have easy access to birth control. "I told her that I really didn't approve of her being sexually active this early, but I wanted to make sure that she was protected if she made that choice. And I told her that all four parents were going to work hard to make sure they never had an opportunity to be alone together. His mom and I had a texting relationship: 'I'm going to the grocery store. Please keep Sam at home until I get back.'"

Although Marnie and Thad tried to be mutually supportive when it came to their daughters, the girls themselves inevitably felt cross-pressures. In her sophomore year Madeline won her mother's approval to move out west to care for her dad. The year's escape from the Main Line bubble proved productive. For the first time in her life, Madeline was exposed to kids from humble backgrounds, and she was impressed by their values and hard work. "I had friends who were working in the cafeteria," she says, "so they could pay for lunch . . . just completely different from what everyone on the Main Line is so used to." Marnie, Thad, and Madeline all agree that it was a very good year for her.

However, Madeline also recognized that her schooling in the rural West was insufficiently demanding, so she returned home, enrolled in an elite private high school in Lower Merion Township, and persuaded her dad to move back to Philadelphia to live near her until she graduated. She also realized that she needed help with her writing, so with her mother's assistance, she arranged to take a writing course at the University of Pennsylvania. Madeline says her instructor has become an "extremely close" mentor, suggesting books for her to read and then discussing them with her and a few Penn students over dinner. "He's been absolutely life-changing for me," she concludes.

Marnie has encouraged this sort of support. "I've always believed that teens need to form attachments with safe adults who are not their parents," she says. And both girls have. While struggling with their parents' divorce, for example, they found mentors in the church that they regularly attended. Madeline describes "a really cool youth pastor whom I ended up seeing weekly for something like six months because my mom was worried about me, so she had me talk to him. He was never pushy about religion, but just would listen to me and my problems. It was almost a therapeutic relationship." Several of Madeline's friends' parents became role models for her as she matured, and many of her best friends remain the kids she met in church. When she moved out west, she met a friend of her dad's who happened to have a degree in counseling, and informally he also helped her cope with the transition.

Eleanor, too, had a number of supportive adults in her life besides her parents, including the youth pastor at their church and one of her father's female friends from graduate school with whom she went hiking out west every summer and could discuss family tensions. Both girls speak of close attachments to teachers and close, supportive friendships with peers, many of them dating back to grade school. Both also had professional tutors to help them prepare for the SAT exams. Madeline recognizes the importance of this broad network of supportive adults and peers. "I've been very lucky in my childhood to have all kinds of support systems when other support systems were failing or just not a right fit," she says. "I've been very lucky in finding cool adults all over the place and good friends as well."

Despite the turbulent rapids through which this family has passed, Marnie and her daughters seem now to be doing well. Eleanor is happily majoring in business at a major Midwestern university where she enjoys a strong network of middle-class friends who "are paying for school themselves and don't take opportunities for granted." Madeline is headed off to a prestigious Canadian university to study French and international development—mature, focused, and aiming for Yale Law School eventually. Marnie has happily remarried, and says that her girls, after some initial resistance, now love her new husband as "a second father."

Marnie is proud that she's been able to shepherd her daughters through adolescence to college success. "It was seriously nip and tuck," she says. "It was never *not* scary—but I managed. My family is like the submarine traveling through hazardous seas and having depth charges all around it—suicide attempts, bulimia, anorexia, running away, all one degree of separation away—and my daughters managed to come through all of this family turbulence."

Like air bags that inflate automatically to protect against unexpected crashes, financial, sociological, and institutional resources have cushioned Eleanor and Madeline when they encountered dangers.[4] They are only half aware of the protective role that their parents' extensive social networks have played, both within Lower Merion Township and well beyond the immediate neighborhood. As we shall see later, educated, affluent parents in America typically enjoy a wide range of what sociologists call "weak ties"—that is, casual acquaintances in disparate social niches (psychiatrists, professors, business executives, friends of the family, friends of friends), and Marnie's daughters clearly benefited from such connections. By contrast, people lower in the socioeconomic hierarchy lack such useful weak ties and instead rely heavily on family and neighbors for social support.

Molly, Lisa, and Amy

Molly (55) and her two daughters, Lisa (21) and Amy (18), along with Lisa's in-laws, have lived in the Kensington area for generations. We meet Molly and the girls in a 20-foot-wide, overcrowded row house where the family of Molly's current husband has lived for three generations.[5] Because both Molly and Lisa's mother-in-law, Diane (41), have always lived in this same area, our conversations with these two extended families offer an unusually detailed moving picture of how dramatically the neighborhood has been transformed during the past half century.

Kensington is today one of the most dangerous neighborhoods in one of America's most crime-ridden cities. But it was not always so. Molly and Diane both recall that when they were growing up, the area was so safe that on hot summer nights kids could sleep outside on rooftops, something no one would think of doing now. In that close-knit white ethnic working-class enclave, virtually everybody knew their neighbors by name, and together they kept the neighborhood safe and clean. Diane's grandfather was a cop in the neighborhood and knew all the kids and their parents personally. In fact, nearly everyone knew everyone else's kids, creating a pattern of communal childrearing. "Everybody looked out for each other," Diane reminisces. "If you got into trouble with the neighbor two blocks down, because your mother knew them, they would beat you, take you home, tell your parents, and your parents would beat you again." Molly adds, "You could not go down the street without [someone] saying, 'Molly, go back home,' or 'What are you up to?'"

The two mothers recall many organized, no-cost youth activities, including a local youth recreation club named (appropriately, in what was then an Irish neighborhood) the Leprechauns. Kids went skating at the local rink, hung out in the local parks and public pools, and—Molly recalls from her teenage years—drank beer at the secluded back of the park. The local Police Athletic League (PAL), along with fraternal organizations, sponsored team sports, and the city recreation department offered free jazz and tap dance classes. Even when Lisa and Amy were in elementary school, they were free to play outside, so long as they did not roam beyond the well-defined neighborhood borders.

Like the Main Line in those years, Kensington was also more diverse in class terms. "Factory workers, downtown [office workers], lawyers, you had every kind of worker on a block," Molly explains when we ask where the neighbors worked in those years. But just as longshoremen's children have long since disappeared from the Main Line, there are no more lawyers' kids in Kensington. Since the 1970s, Kensington's history is one of disappearing jobs, fracturing families, declining population, rising racial diversity, and above all, mounting crime and drugs.

Fear of crime is pervasive. Police no longer walk the beat, for fear of being shot. Three babies in the neighborhood have recently been hit by stray bullets, so Lisa is home-schooling her daughter. The residents' concern for neighborhood amenities has also collapsed. "No one stays involved in the neighborhood," Diane reports, and recalls how things used to be: "On the weekends, everybody had their brooms, and the city gave you the bags for the trash. Most people keep to themselves these days. No one gets involved if they see crime going on, or even kids spray-painting neighbors' homes."

Most of the rec centers and pools have closed, because the Parks and Recreation budget was the first to be cut in successive budget crunches. While the city budget has grown by about one third (in constant dollars) since 1970, spending on parks and recreation has fallen by more than 80 percent. Disinvestment has also shown up in dwindling public services like libraries. The Police Athletic League still exists, but nowadays participants have to pay to play.

Some longtime white residents blame the neighborhood's decline on the influx of nonwhites, though the neighborhood remains predominantly white. "It's so racist around here," Amy reports, "that they took the basketball courts off the park because black kids were coming around playing basketball with classmates from school." Clearly, economic stagnation and the disappearance of steady jobs in the neighborhood are also an important part of the story. But the women with whom we spoke blame the neighborhood deterioration primarily on drugs.

Marijuana, heroin, and meth arrived in the neighborhood in the 1990s. "It affected our family," Lisa says, "affected our neighbors, affected everyone, and it wasn't safe anymore. Everyone we knew got high. It didn't matter where you were, who you were." "Everyone" included Lisa's father, Amy's father, and both Amy and Lisa. Their next-door neighbor was a major drug dealer, and three different dealers on the block sold drugs to Lisa as a teenager.

"You could get high wherever, no matter what age you were," Lisa explains. "It just became our life. I don't know why. It just took over." Molly interjects, "I don't think it helped that my neighbor actually sat there and smoked right in front of everybody." And the situation has only deteriorated since then. "You can't walk down the street without being offered drugs," Molly adds. "Kensington Avenue [a few streets away] is the scariest avenue in the world. People get shot a lot. I hate to say this, but it's really, really *ghetto*."

Because of pervasive fear, Molly says, "you don't even know where people work now, because they don't ever come out of their houses. When we were younger, people would stop and say 'Hi.'" Lisa adds, "I try to smile and be friendly, but everyone is just grumpy." This is the pervasively paranoid social milieu within which Molly has raised Lisa and Amy, along with their two brothers. No wonder that both girls admonish us that "you can't trust anyone."

As a child, Molly (along with most of the residents of Kensington) was deeply involved in one of the many Catholic parishes. Indeed, as ethnographer Kathryn Edin and her colleagues have reported of this neighborhood, the Catholic Church and its ubiquitous parochial schools were the warp and weft of community here, and the weakening of those institutions has hastened neighborhood decline.[6] When Molly's father died and her mother was unable to support the family, the nine children in the family were sent to various foster homes. Molly herself was placed for six years in a Catholic Services orphanage that was closed down for child abuse shortly after she left, an experience that left her alienated from the Church, like Diane and many of their contemporaries.

When she finally returned home, just as the neighborhood's economic collapse was beginning, Molly often skipped school and became something of a wild child. "My mom was there but not there," she says, and she got no support from her family. School guidance counselors told her, she says, that she "was not going to end up being anything." She became pregnant in high school and dropped out in the 12th grade. The father of her child came from an alcoholic family next door, and her aunts and uncles urged her not to hook up with him, but she disregarded their advice and ended up having two children with him—Lisa and her older brother.

Molly's life story embodies the social and economic transformation of this neighborhood. Both she and Diane have warm childhood memories of a close-knit neighborhood, but their adult experiences of betrayal and abuse and dissolution parallel the neighborhood's degeneration, and Lisa and Amy have never really known anything better, as neighborhood solidarity has spiraled downward, and drugs and crime have ravaged the lives of the residents.

Molly's first husband ended up as an alcoholic and drug addict within a few years of their marriage, just as her family had feared. Molly left him and supported herself and her two kids for roughly a decade as a waitress and a construction worker. In her 30s she had two more kids—Amy and her younger brother—with a second man, who worked as a roofer. The girls say he was a good dad in the beginning, but he, too, got hooked on drugs, and Lisa and Molly kicked him out. He now is homeless, and the girls occasionally see him wandering the neighborhood.

To make matters even worse, Molly herself developed multiple sclerosis (MS), suffered a stroke, and ended up in a wheelchair. Her youngest son was diagnosed with autism around this time, too, so the family ended up with crushing medical bills and no insurance. Nearly destitute, they scraped by on various public welfare programs, though they found the welfare and tax bureaucracies inscrutable and unresponsive. Molly became seriously depressed and unavailable to her kids. Fortunately, at this point a Protestant church in the neighborhood stepped in to provide a lifeline.

The church offered an active program for youth in the neighborhood, including after-school tutoring and summer outings, and when Lisa was nine she started attending the church. When Amy's father was kicked out, and the family began to fall apart, Lisa says, "the church was our main support," physically protecting them from their drug-addled father and allowing them to sleep over at the church for respite. When Molly contracted MS, the church found the family a more accessible apartment near the church and built a ramp for her wheelchair, even though she was not a church member at the time. "We couldn't have made it without them," concludes Molly. Pastor Dan ("a big biker dude") and Angela, his wife (a youth pastor at the church), remain Lisa's closest confidants.

Lisa badly needed friends, because her life as a teenager was in shambles. Despite her involvement with the church, she was overtaken by the collapse of the neighborhood and of her family. Placed on probation because of her frequent truancy from school, she drank heavily and became addicted to the drugs that were by now omnipresent. Indeed, drugs were easily available in and around the church itself, because of the presence of recovering drug addicts. Lisa's special addiction was to "skittles," a derivative of cold medicine, but she also was impaired by "laced weed" that she got from their next-door neighbor.

Lisa became pregnant in the 12th grade, like her mother before her and like many of the girls at her school. The father of her child was a classmate who was also her pusher, and she refused to marry him. At this point her involvement in the church provided a kind of miracle. She and a boy (John) she had met at church fell in love, and although she was already seven months into her pregnancy, John asked her to marry him. "Because I love you," he told her, "I'm going to love this baby." (His mother, Diane, suggested that Lisa get an abortion, but Molly rejected that idea.) Four months later, they married.

Angela, the youth pastor, supported Lisa and John emotionally through this difficult period, though another pastor at the church forbade Lisa from coming to church during her pregnancy "because I was a bad influence on the other kids." Partly for that reason, but also because of theological differences, Lisa and John (along with pastors Angela and Dan) have recently switched to a rapidly growing evangelical church in the neighborhood. When living with John's alcoholic family became intolerable for Lisa and John, Angela helped Lisa find a new house, and the church helped John get a job at a Christian security firm. Although Lisa is worried that their current church, like their previous one, has become an enabling haven for neighborhood drug users, she concludes "I don't know where we would be without that church, honestly."

John graduated from a technical high school but dropped out of community college after deciding it wasn't for him. Lisa graduated from high school nine months pregnant and attended a for-profit technical school to get an associate degree as a pharmacy technician—but that led to no job and left her with a daunting $50,000 student debt. She is now taking an online course in early childhood education while home-schooling her daughter. Their marriage seems stable, but their neighborhood is very dangerous, and Lisa is "terrified" about her financial prospects.

Amy's story has distressing parallels to her sister's narrative, but begins and ends in a somewhat different place. In middle school she was a talented musician, admitted to an academic magnet school, and invited to join the Philadelphia Youth Orchestra. During adolescence, however, she became deeply ensnared in the same neighborhood traps of alcohol and drugs and unprotected sex. "I'd tell my mom I'm going to be at my friend's house around the corner," she says, "but I'd really be like two neighborhoods over, hanging out with boys and drinking." Because of Amy's involvement with drugs and rowdiness in school, Molly pulled her out to be home-schooled, but Amy cheated on an online examination and failed a grade. Eventually Molly allowed her to return to school, but three months after returning for tenth grade, Amy became pregnant, like virtually all of her friends. "All the girls that ever got in trouble with me and drank with me," she says, "every single one of them got pregnant."

Unexpectedly, Amy's pregnancy proved to be a positive turning point, because she transferred to a special high school for young parents, and counselors there helped her stay in school. In the new school she began to get straight As and was elected president of the student body. Her boyfriend (and the father of her son) is still hanging around, but she is not thinking of marriage. "Marriages just put you in debt," she says. "Why would I want to do that to myself?" Although she was admitted to several good state universities, she is planning to attend a liberal arts college upstate that has a special program for unmarried mothers. "Pregnancy changed my life," she says. "I wouldn't even be going to college if it wasn't for my son." Nevertheless, she worries about where the money for this hopeful future will come from, and she recently has tried raising funds on her Facebook page to help out.

Despite substance abuse and teen pregnancy, Lisa and Amy seem to have survived extreme family turbulence and neighborhood trauma. Churches played a significant role in their survival, as did (in Amy's case) the special public school program for teen moms. Their story powerfully illustrates the capacity of religious communities to help impoverished, troubled families, but evidence that we'll review later in this chapter is sobering: nationwide, poor kids are increasingly detached from religious institutions.

Molly tried to save her daughters from alcohol, drugs, and pregnancy, but she was unsuccessful, in part because their dads were destroyed by addiction, in part because of her own debilitating illness and depression, and in part because of the pervasive breakdown of the Kensington neighborhood. Recently Molly remarried, this time to a man she met at church, and the girls say that he is good for their mother. Neither daughter intended to get married or to have children, but both now say they love being mothers. However, quite reasonably, both are also fearful about their financial future.

In sum, both of our Philadelphia-area families seem to have attained a certain "happily ever after" equilibrium, but that equilibrium is much more precarious in Kensington than in Lower Merion. Marnie and Molly had very different capacities to protect their kids from the challenges of contemporary adolescence, and Marnie's daughters are much better positioned for success in life than Molly's. If it takes a village to raise a child, the prognosis for American children isn't good: in recent years, villages all over America, rich and poor, have deteriorated as we've shirked collective responsibility for our kids. And most Americans don't have the resources that Marnie did to replace collective provision with private provision.

Private provision in Marnie's case meant, in part, buying help for childrearing (household staff; therapists; writing instructors; SAT tutors; private schools; the remodeled suite to help Eleanor cope with ADHD), but it also meant using social networks (other cooperative parents in the neighborhood to minimize the risks of drugs and teen sex; professional networks that led to top-flight medical specialists; friends and colleagues to offer mentoring; and other "cool adults" to befriend the kids) that were unavailable to Molly and her daughters. With the partial exception of the churches, the neighborhood networks within which Molly, Lisa, and Amy found themselves were much more likely to transmit problems than solutions, and even the churches themselves, the last remaining community institutions, are vulnerable to adverse neighborhood influences.

Communities and Kids: Social Networks, Mentors, Neighborhoods, Churches

We Americans like to think of ourselves as "rugged individualists"—in the image of the lone cowboy riding toward the setting sun, opening the frontier. But at least as accurate a symbol of our national story is the wagon train, with its mutual aid among a community of pioneers. Throughout our history, a pendulum has slowly swung between the poles of individualism and community, both in our public philosophy and in our daily lives.[7] In the past half century we have witnessed, for better or worse, a giant swing toward the individualist (or libertarian) pole in our culture, society, and politics. At the same time, researchers have steadily piled up evidence of how important social context, social institutions, and social networks—in short, our communities—remain for our well-being and our kids' opportunities.

Social Networks

Social scientists often use the term *social capital* to describe social connectedness—that is, informal ties to family, friends, neighbors, and acquaintances; involvement in civic associations, religious institutions, athletic teams, volunteer activities; and so on. Social capital has repeatedly been shown to be a strong predictor of well-being both for individuals and for communities. Community bonds and social networks have powerful effects on health, happiness, educational success, economic success, public safety, and (especially) child welfare.[8] However, like financial capital and human capital, social capital is distributed unevenly, and, as we'll explore here, differences in social connections contribute to the youth opportunity gap.

Many studies have shown that better-educated Americans have wider and deeper social networks, both within their closest circle of family and friends and in the wider society.[9] By contrast, less educated Americans have sparser, more redundant social networks, concentrated within their own family. (By "redundant," I mean that their friends tend to know the same people they do, so that they lack the "friend of a friend" reach available to upper-class Americans.) In short, college-educated parents have both more close friends and more nodding acquaintances than less educated parents.

Figure 5.1 shows that both race and class matter for the density of "close" friendship—the sort of "strong ties" that can provide socioemotional and (in a pinch) material support.[10] Holding race constant, parents in the top fifth of the socioeconomic hierarchy report about 20–25 percent more close friends than parents in the bottom fifth. (Holding social class constant, white parents have 15–20 percent more close friends than nonwhite parents.) Contrary to romanticized images of close-knit communal life among the poor, lower-class Americans today, especially if they are nonwhite, tend to be socially isolated, even from their neighbors.

Figure 5.1: Educated, affluent white parents have more close friends

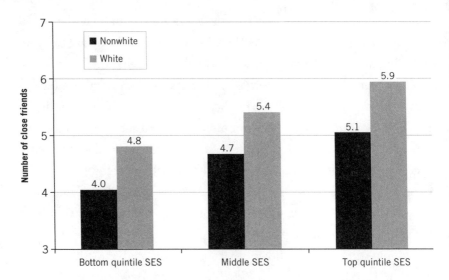

Source: Social Capital Community Benchmark Survey, 2000.

Perhaps more important, more educated Americans also have many more "weak ties," that is, connections to wider, more diverse networks. The reach and diversity of these social ties are especially valuable for social mobility and educational and economic advancement, because such ties allow educated, affluent parents and their children to tap a wealth of expertise and support that is simply inaccessible to parents and children who are less well off.[11]

As Figure 5.2 shows, college-educated parents are more likely to "know" all sorts of people. This weak-tie advantage is especially great when it comes to occupations that are most valuable for their kids' advancement—professors, teachers, lawyers, medical personnel, business leaders—but it is visible even among more traditional working-class connections, like police officers and neighbors. Only in knowing janitors, it appears, do less educated parents have an edge, and even there it's close![12]

We've already seen the consequences of this pattern in the lives of the families we've met.

- Andrew in Bend used his parents' weak ties with a store owner and the local fire chief when he went looking for jobs.
- Carl in Atlanta arranged for Desmond to speak to some "medical folks" to explore a career in medicine.
- Clara in Orange County sought advice on her son's college application from two friends who just happened to be a college professor and a dean.
- Marnie in Lower Merion used her personal networks to find a top ADHD consultant for Eleanor.

Figure 5.2: More educated parents have broader social networks

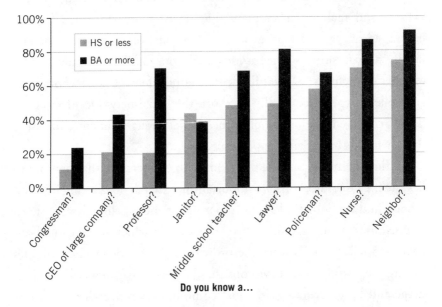

Do you know a...

Source: Pew Research Center, November 2010 survey.

Virtually none of our lower-class families had weak ties like this to help with jobs or college placement or health issues. (A notable exception was the church tie that got Lisa's husband, John, his job at a security firm.) On the contrary, lower-class parents' social ties are disproportionately concentrated within their own extended family (and perhaps a high school friend and a neighbor or two), who, because of their own location in the social hierarchy, are unlikely to expand the reach of the parents. Though more educated, affluent parents have a quantitative edge in the size of their personal networks, even more important is their qualitative edge, in terms of what their friends and acquaintances can do for them and their kids.

Upper-class parents enable their kids to form weak ties by exposing them more often to organized activities, professionals, and other adults. Working-class children, on the other hand, are more likely to interact regularly only with kin and neighborhood children, which limits their formation of valuable weak ties.[13] (When those working-class neighbors had good jobs and could refer friends to those jobs, those neighborhood ties were more valuable.) When adjusting to college, choosing college majors, and making career plans, kids from more affluent, educated homes engage a wider array of informal advisors—family members, faculty, and outsiders—whereas kids from poor families typically consult one or two members of their immediate family, few if any of whom have any college experience at all.[14] In short, the social networks of more affluent, educated families amplify their other assets in helping to assure that their kids have richer opportunities.

Affluent families provide their kids with connections that poor families can't. But connections are important not merely for getting into top schools and top jobs. At least as important as the pipeline from a prized internship to a corner office job are the ways in which social capital can protect privileged kids from the ordinary risks of adolescence. Studies during the past 40 years have consistently shown that, if anything, drug usage and binge drinking are more common among privileged teenagers than among their less affluent peers.[15] What is different, however, are the family and community "air bags" that deploy to minimize the negative consequences of drugs and other misadventures among rich kids. Marnie's ability to fend off the challenges of drug use for Eleanor was greatly strengthened by Marnie's ties to other mothers in the community, whereas Molly's pot-smoking, drug-pushing neighbors were the very source of her daughters' addictions. To be sure, social capital is not the only advantage that privileged kids have in confronting unexpected risks; it was financial capital, after all, that enabled Marnie to get top-quality professional help and to remodel Eleanor's study space to help her ameliorate ADHD.

Have class differences in social networks changed in recent years? Fifteen years ago, in *Bowling Alone*, I compiled evidence that revealed a steady withering of Americans' community bonds. Ten years later, an independent study (by scholars originally skeptical of my findings) reported that both kin and nonkin networks have shrunk in the past two decades, but that the decrease in nonkin networks was greater. In effect, they found, Americans' social networks are collapsing inward, and now consist of fewer, denser, more homogeneous, more familial (and less nonkin) ties.[16] Americans' disengagement and their retreat to relative social isolation, an even more recent study in this field concludes, "constitute a trend that, even if common to individuals of all classes, affects members of the lower classes disproportionately, ultimately reinforcing differences between social classes."[17] While hard evidence is still too limited for a final verdict, there is reason to believe that class differences in social ties—especially weak ties that are important for upward mobility—are not only great, but may be growing.

But what about the Internet? Does it help close the networking gap between rich kids and poor kids, does it widen that gap, or does it have no net effect? In principle, it could multiply weak ties—that's the purpose of LinkedIn, for example. However, since online and offline connections tend to be closely correlated,[18] simply multiplying online ties would not necessarily narrow the class gap if those online ties were (like "real life" ties) more readily available to more educated Americans. Is there a "digital divide"?

In the early years of the Internet, simple *access* was unequally distributed, as less educated Americans, especially nonwhites, were slower to gain access to the Web. More recently, however, this digital *access* divide has narrowed substantially, and indeed racial differences have virtually disappeared.[19] But having equal access to the Internet does not mean that everyone gains equal benefit from that access.

Sociologist Eszter Hargittai and her collaborators, experts on how the Internet is actually used, point out that "growth in basic user statistics does not necessarily mean that everybody is taking advantage of the medium in similar ways." Compared to their poorer counterparts, young people from upper-class backgrounds (and their parents) are more likely to use the Internet for jobs, education, political and social engagement, health, and news gathering, and less for entertainment or recreation. Affluent Americans use the Internet in ways that are mobility-enhancing, whereas poorer, less educated Americans typically use it in ways that are not.[20] (The same was true of books and the postal system; the point is that the Internet is not immune from that inequality in usage.)

After talking with scores of teenagers nationwide about how they use the Internet, the ethnographer Danah Boyd concluded that offline inequalities carry over online. "In a world where information is easily available," she writes, "strong personal networks and access to helpful people often matter more than access to the information itself. . . . Those whose networks are vetting information and providing context are more privileged in this information landscape than those whose friends and family have little experience doing such information work. . . . Just because teens can get access to a technology that can connect them to anyone anywhere does not mean that they have equal access to knowledge and opportunity."[21]

Kids from more educated homes learn more sophisticated digital-literacy skills—knowing how to search for information on the Internet and how to evaluate it—and have more social support in deploying those skills. Such children are using the Internet in ways that will help them reap the rewards of an increasingly digital economy and society. Even though lower-class kids are coming to have virtually equal physical access to the Internet, they lack the digital savvy to exploit that access in ways that enhance their opportunities. At least at this point in its evolution, the Internet seems more likely to widen the opportunity gap than to close it.[22]

Mentors and "Savvy"

As we have seen repeatedly, adults outside the family often play a critical role in helping a child develop his or her full potential:

- Cheryl, my black classmate in Port Clinton, was crucially supported in her college aspirations by the older white woman whose house she cleaned every week.
- Don, the working-class quarterback in my high school class, made it to college (about which his parents "didn't have a clue") with the support of his pastor.
- Andrew in Bend got detailed career guidance from his father's high school classmate, the fire chief.
- In Orange County, Clara was urged toward graduate school by a supportive college teacher, and a generation later her daughter Isabella entered an unexpected career because of her screenwriting instructor at Troy High School. Meanwhile, Isabella's classmate Kira survived the trauma of her father's death with consistent help from her English teacher.
- Madeline's writing instructor at Penn became a "life-changing" mentor, while Eleanor's father's female friend from graduate school became "the most important person in my life" (apart from her parents) during their long conversations on summer hikes.
- Youth pastors played critical roles as supportive mentors to all four of the Philadelphia young women, both in Lower Merion and in Kensington, during periods of family turmoil.

All these examples represent "informal mentoring"—natural relationships that spring up with teachers, pastors, coaches, family friends, and so forth. "Formal mentoring," by contrast, is the result of organized programs, like Big Brothers Big Sisters and My Brother's Keeper. Careful, independent evaluations have shown that formal mentoring can help at-risk kids to develop healthy relations with adults (including parents), and in turn to achieve significant gains in academic and psychosocial outcomes—school attendance, school performance, self-worth, and reduced substance abuse, for example—even with careful controls for potentially confounding variables. These measurable effects are strongest when the mentoring relationship is long-term, and strongest for at-risk kids. (Upper-class kids already have informal mentors in their lives, so adding a formal mentor does not add so much to their achievement.) Measurably, mentoring matters.[23]

Formal mentoring is much less common and less enduring than informal mentoring. In 2013 a nationwide survey of young people asked about both formal and informal mentoring. Sixty-two percent of kids of all ages reported some sort of informal (or "natural") mentoring, compared to 15 percent who reported any formal mentoring. Moreover, informal mentoring relationships lasted about 30 months on average, compared to roughly 18 months for formal mentoring.[24] So combining frequency and duration, American kids get about eight times as much informal as formal mentoring.

Those national averages, however, obscure substantial class differences in access to mentoring. Informal mentoring—exactly as in the instances I've just recalled from our contemporary case studies—is much more common among upper- and upper-middle-class kids than among lower-class kids. (Our case studies in Port Clinton hint that informal mentoring of poor kids was more common in the 1950s, but I know of no quantitative evidence to support that conclusion.) Figure 5.3 summarizes the pattern today, showing that kids from affluent, educated homes benefit from a much wider and deeper pool of informal mentors.

For virtually all the categories of informal mentors outside the family—teachers, family friends, religious and youth leaders, coaches—kids from affluent families are two to three times more likely to have such a mentor. Privileged children and their less privileged peers are equally likely to report mentoring by a member of their extended family, but family members of privileged kids tend to have more valuable expertise, so family mentors tend to have more impact on the educational achievements of the privileged kids.[25] All told, the informal mentoring received by privileged kids lasts longer and is more helpful (in the eyes of the kids themselves) than the informal mentoring that poor kids get. In short, affluent kids get substantially more and better informal mentoring.

Figure 5.3: Affluent kids have a wider range of informal mentors

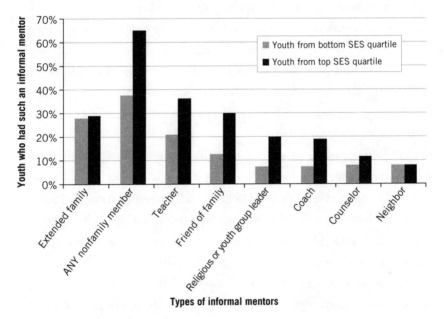

Source: The Mentoring Effect survey, 2013.

The informal mentoring gap is substantial in elementary school and steadily increases as children age through middle school and into high school, and as things stand now, formal mentoring barely begins to close the gap. In fact, the modest compensation from formal mentoring is concentrated in primary and middle school and disappears as kids age.[26] In high school, there is no difference at all in the incidence of formal mentoring (8 percent) between rich kids and poor kids. Thus, the total class gap in mentoring (informal plus formal) begins in elementary school and balloons just as the kids most need help outside their families.

In sum, nearly two thirds of affluent kids (64 percent) have some mentoring beyond their extended family, while nearly two thirds of poor kids (62 percent) do not.[27] And this stunning gap exists not because the poor kids don't want mentoring; in fact, they are nearly twice as likely as rich kids (38 percent to 22 percent) to say that at some point in their lives they wanted a mentor, but didn't have one. So mentoring contributes significantly to the opportunity gap.

One consequence of the mentoring gap is to exacerbate the *savvy gap* that we first noticed in the previous chapter. As we talked with scores of rich kids and poor kids across the country, one of the most striking differences was the stark contrast in their capacity to understand the institutions that stand astride the paths to opportunity and to make those institutions work for them.

Kids from more privileged backgrounds are savvier about how to climb the ladder of opportunity. The stories we heard from David in Port Clinton, Kayla in Bend, Michelle and Lauren in Atlanta, Lola and Sofia in Santa Ana, Lisa and Amy in Kensington, and the dozens of other disadvantaged 18- and 19-year-olds we met across the country are, however, replete with confusion and mystification. These kids are baffled about school practices, two- and four-year colleges, financial affairs, occupational opportunities, and even programs (both public and private) specifically designed to assist kids like them, such as educational loans. Their less educated parents' limited skills and experience explain part of this, but equally important is the fact that these kids lack the dense networks of informal mentors that surround their upper-class counterparts. One poignant example from our fieldwork arose when a working-class dad asked if he could bring along a younger daughter to our interview with his son, just so she could meet an actual college graduate. Any serious program to address the growing opportunity gap must address the savvy gap and therefore the mentoring gap.

Neighborhoods

As we observed in Chapter 1, class segregation across America has been growing for decades, so fewer affluent kids live in poor neighborhoods, and fewer poor kids live in rich neighborhoods. Lower Merion and Kensington perfectly illustrate that pattern. That simple fact poses a central question for this chapter: Does the character of the neighborhood where kids grow up have an effect on their future prospects, apart from their individual characteristics? Growing up in a poor family and going to school with poor kids both constrain opportunity, as we have seen in the previous three chapters. Here the question is whether growing up in a poor neighborhood imposes any additional handicaps. The answer is yes.

America's leading expert on neighborhoods, Robert Sampson, has shown that neighborhoods in America are deeply unequal and that that inequality has powerful effects on their residents. Pervasive neighborhood inequality, he writes, has consequences "across a wide range of how Americans experience life . . . crime, poverty, child health, public protest, the density of elite networks, civic engagement, teen births, altruism, perceived disorder, collective efficacy, [and] immigration." He concludes, "*What is truly American is not so much the individual but neighborhood inequality.*" [28]

These neighborhood effects seem to be most powerful during infancy and then again in late adolescence. [29] The longer kids live in a bad neighborhood, the worse the effects. These consequences are often compounded by multigenerational disadvantages: kids whose parents grew up in poor neighborhoods and are themselves still living in poor neighborhoods are doubly disadvantaged, because the parents bear scars from the neighborhood of their childhood. [30] This double disadvantage is illustrated in the lives of Molly and her daughters.

Neighborhood affluence and poverty have been shown repeatedly to influence many aspects of child and youth development, even after taking into account the characteristics of kids and their immediate families. Race also matters a lot in neighborhood effects, quite apart from social class, because of the nation's bitter history of racism, racial discrimination, and racial segregation, as illustrated in Kensington, but our primary focus here is on the powerful effects of class that affect kids of all races.

Affluent neighborhoods boost academic outcomes, largely because of the school effects discussed in the previous chapter, but also because other youth-serving institutions, like quality child care, libraries, parks, athletic leagues, and youth organizations, are more common there than in poor neighborhoods like Kensington. Well-developed social networks in a community provide an important resource for school leaders.[31] Conversely, many careful studies have documented that poor neighborhoods foster behavioral problems, poor mental and physical health, delinquency, crime, violence, and risky sexual behavior.[32] Most neighborhood studies have focused on cities, but recent research has shown depressingly similar effects in rural areas.[33]

Neighborhood poverty is bad for kids for many reasons, but probably the most important is that social cohesion and informal social control, based on cooperation among neighbors—what sociologists, following Sampson, term "collective efficacy"—are lower in poor neighborhoods like Kensington or Santa Ana or the Atlanta ghetto. In Sampson's words, "Collective efficacy among citizens is primarily about informally activated social control and shared expectations rooted in trust."[34]

The communal parenting that Diane and Molly recall from their youth was a vivid illustration of collective efficacy, while the failure of residents in Kensington nowadays to intervene to halt spray-painting of neighbors' homes is a stark illustration of its absence. Collective efficacy, reflected in trust in neighbors, is higher in richer, more educated neighborhoods, and that collective efficacy in turn helps all the young people in the neighborhood, regardless of their family resources. The evidence linking neighborhood collective efficacy and adolescent outcomes is pervasive and robust.

The close association of neighborhood trust and neighborhood poverty is illustrated in Figure 5.4.[35] Regardless of your own characteristics, if you live in an affluent neighborhood, you are much more likely to know and trust your neighbors. Both janitors and jurists are more likely to know and trust their neighbors if they live in more affluent neighborhoods. As we have seen, more poor kids are living in poor neighborhoods, while more rich kids are living in rich neighborhoods, so the benefits of collective efficacy and trust are increasingly concentrated on rich kids. In short, it does indeed take a village to raise a child, but poor kids in America are increasingly concentrated in derelict villages.

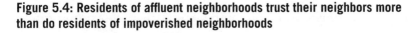

Figure 5.4: Residents of affluent neighborhoods trust their neighbors more than do residents of impoverished neighborhoods

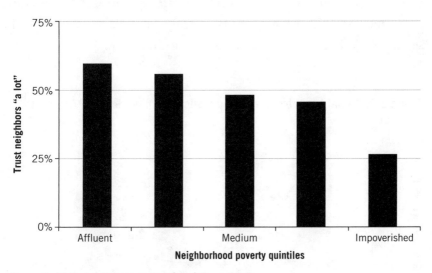

Source: Social Capital Community Benchmark Survey, 2000.

That poor kids are increasingly living in untrustworthy social environments is confirmed by trends in social trust among high school seniors over the past four decades, as measured by a question that asked kids to choose between two options: "Most people can be trusted" or "You can't be too careful in dealing with people." (This often used question taps feelings not merely about one's neighbors, but about one's experiences with other people in general.) Answers to this simple question have been shown to predict health, happiness, and other indicators of human thriving, perhaps because constant fear of one's social environment puts continuing stress on the human body. Around the world, social trust is almost always higher among haves than have-nots, and that pattern has long held true for American youth.[36]

Trust has fallen among youth of all social backgrounds during the past half century.[37] However, as Figure 5.5 shows, during the past several decades the long-standing class gap in social trust among American adolescents has significantly widened, producing yet another scissors chart. From the late 1970s to the early 2010s the fraction of 12th graders from more educated homes (the top third) who say that most people can be trusted fell by roughly a third, whereas the fraction of trusters from the least educated third of homes fell by roughly one half. Nearly six out of seven poor kids nowadays choose the distrustful option.

Figure 5.5: Social trust, by parents' education, 12th graders, 1976–2011

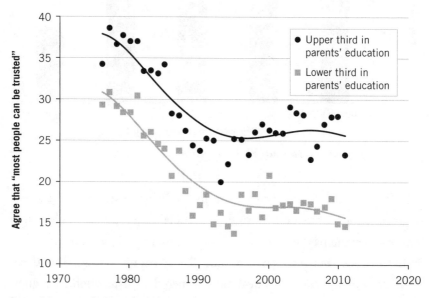

Source: Monitoring the Future annual surveys.

When we asked the kids we met across the country this same question, not one of the poor kids said that "most people can be trusted," and most reacted as though (given the lives they'd just been describing) the question answered itself. Life had taught them that "you can't be too careful." By contrast, almost all our richer kids said that (with some qualifications) they do trust other people. That comparison reflects not paranoia on the part of poor kids, but the malevolent social realities within which they live and the fact that people and institutions have so often failed them.

Trust was once high in both Lower Merion and in Kensington, but it is mostly gone in Kensington. When Eleanor in Lower Merion says that most people can be trusted, and when Molly in Kensington says, "You can't trust anyone in Philly, not even your loved ones," each is accurately reflecting the trustworthiness of her surroundings. Andrew was speaking of the upscale Bend he knows when he said, "Bend is a community of really trusting people," but that is not the uncaring Bend that Kayla knows. In a bitter Facebook posting, Mary Sue (an impoverished young woman we met in Port Clinton) expressed a common view among poor kids across the country: "Love gets you hurt; trust gets you killed."

Low trust and collective efficacy are not the only reasons that poor neighborhoods are bad for kids. Another important channel between neighborhood poverty and bad child outcomes is neighborhood crime, drugs, and violence, as we have witnessed in Atlanta, Santa Ana, and Kensington.[38] Partly for this reason, poor neighborhoods shape parenting in ways that are not good for children. As illustrated by the cases of Molly in Kensington and Elijah's mother in Atlanta, parents in poor neighborhoods are more likely to experience depression, stress, and illness, which in turn "are associated with less warm and consistent parenting."[39] To be sure, exactly what style of parenting is best may vary from neighborhood to neighborhood: as we've seen, parents in high-resource neighborhoods are more likely to nurture their children's talents by enrolling them in structured opportunities, while parents in low-resource communities are more likely to keep their children at home for safety's sake.[40] Living in poor neighborhoods remains almost always a high-risk factor for disorder, suboptimal parenting, and adverse child development.

Similarly, neighborhood poverty is known to have deleterious health effects. For example, obesity is systematically worse in poor neighborhoods.[41] Our own research shows yet another classic scissors chart in this domain.

Figure 5.6: Adolescent obesity, aged 12–18, by parents' education

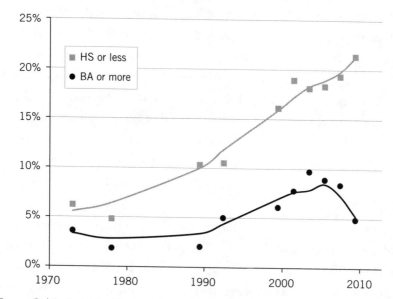

Source: Carl B. Frederick, Kaisa Snellman, and Robert D. Putnam, "Increasing Socioeconomic Disparities in Adolescent Obesity," *Proceedings of the National Academy of Sciences* 111 (January 2014): 1338–42.

In the 1990s, as shown in Figure 5.6, as the obesity epidemic raged across the country, obesity increased at similar rates for all adolescents, but in the past decade or so obesity has begun to diminish among kids from college-educated homes while continuing to expand among kids from high-school-educated homes. Thus, the class gap in adolescent obesity has widened significantly.

Why this growing gap? Part of the explanation is probably that public health messages were quicker to reach upper-class kids, precisely because those kids are embedded in much richer transmission networks for such messages. Conversely, the relative social isolation of poor kids leaves them more vulnerable to all sorts of threats. Neighborhood quality is another likely explanation for this growing gap, since the obesity disparity appears to be due primarily to disparities in physical activity, so differential access to outdoor activities and athletic amenities is a prime suspect. In fact, a controlled experiment called "Moving to Opportunity" found that randomly chosen poor families who were enabled to move to low-poverty neighborhoods experienced significant reductions in obesity and diabetes.[42]

The pervasive growth of neighborhood economic segregation goes back several decades, as we have noted, becoming visible soon after the rise in nationwide economic inequality in the 1970s. The onset and aftermath of the Great Recession in 2008 only accelerated these disparities. Given the manifold ways in which neighborhood economic differences affect the lives and opportunities open to young people, it is hardly surprising that neighborhood inequality across metropolitan areas is associated with less equality of opportunity.[43] Unlike in Port Clinton in the 1950s, where affluent Frank and impoverished Don lived only four blocks apart, when rich and poor live in separate neighborhoods, the benefits of neighborhood affluence are concentrated on rich kids and the costs of neighborhood poverty are concentrated on poor kids. The greater the inequality across neighborhoods, the lower the rate of upward social mobility and the greater the opportunity gap. This is a powerful illustration of how social context (even apart from families and schools) powerfully conditions our kids' chances of success in life.

Religious Community

Religious communities in America are important service providers for young people and the poor. Weekly churchgoers are two to three times more likely to volunteer to help the poor and young people than are nonchurchgoers, holding other things constant, and are much more likely to contribute financially to those causes. This religious edge appears for volunteering and giving through secular organizations, as well as for volunteering and giving through religious organizations. And the crucial ingredient seems not to be theology but rather involvement in a religious congregation.[44] In that sense, the role that churches played in palliating the impact of poverty on Molly and her family is not unusual.

In addition to philanthropy and good works, religious involvement among youth themselves is associated with a wide range of positive outcomes, both academic and nonacademic.[45] Compared to their unchurched peers, youth who are involved in a religious organization take tougher courses, get higher grades and test scores, and are less likely to drop out of high school. Controlling for many other characteristics of the child, her family, and her schooling, a child whose parents attend church regularly is 40 to 50 percent more likely to go on to college than a matched child of nonattenders.

Churchgoing kids have better relations with their parents and other adults, have more friendships with high-performing peers, are more involved in sports and other extracurricular activities, are less prone to substance abuse (drugs, alcohol, and smoking), risky behavior (like not wearing seat belts), and delinquency (shoplifting, misbehaving in school, and being suspended or expelled). As with mentoring, religious involvement—when it happens—makes a bigger difference in the lives of poor kids than rich kids, in part because affluent youth are more exposed to other positive influences.

Religious engagement has traditionally been less class-biased than virtually any other sort of community or extracurricular activity.[46] Nowadays, however, poor families are generally less involved in religious communities than affluent families, and this class gap, too, is growing. Throughout the ups and downs of American religiosity during the past several decades, religious observance has tended to rise faster, or fall more slowly, among better-educated Americans. Moreover, although black Americans in all social classes are more religiously observant than their white peers, the growing class gap in church attendance appears among blacks as well as whites.

The evangelical boom of the 1970s and 1980s was concentrated among the middle and upper middle classes. Since the late 1970s, weekly church attendance has been almost flat among middle-aged college-educated white adults (slipping from 30 percent to 27 percent, roughly speaking), but has dropped by about one third among their non-college-educated counterparts (from about 30–32 percent to about 20–22 percent), opening up a substantial class gap that did not exist at mid-century. If you listen carefully, hymns in American houses of worship are increasingly sung in upper-class accents.[47]

Not surprisingly, this same trend shows up among adolescents. Young people's church attendance has fallen nationwide in recent decades, but has fallen twice as fast among kids from the lower third of the socioeconomic hierarchy as among kids from the upper third. The now familiar scissors gap shown in Figure 5.7 testifies to the fact that the powerfully positive role that religion played in the childhoods of Lisa and Amy in Philadelphia is increasingly atypical of poor kids nationwide.

Figure 5.7: Church attendance by parents' education, 12th graders, 1976–2012

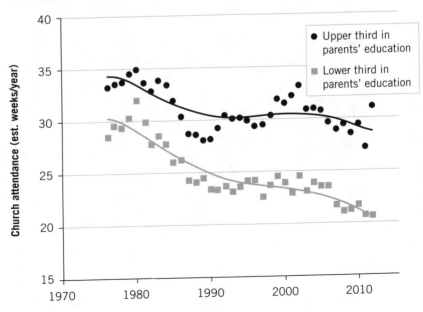

Source: Monitoring the Future annual surveys.

In this chapter we have seen that social networks, communities, and community institutions like churches can be powerful resources for child development and social mobility. But we have also seen that in today's America these resources have become less public and collective, forcing all parents to rely more heavily on private provision.[48] Affluent parents have an abundance of financial and social capital, so they have adapted more easily to the privatization of support for children. Caring for kids was once a more widely shared, collective responsibility, but that ethic has faded in recent decades. That narrowing of the effective scope of "our kids" has had dramatically different effects on privileged and impoverished children. Which leads to the questions we will ask in the next chapter: "So what?" and "What is to be done?"

Chapter 6

WHAT IS TO BE DONE?

THIS BOOK HAS PRESENTED A SERIES OF PORTRAITS OF THE contrasting lives of American young people from more and less privileged backgrounds, alongside more rigorous evidence that those personal portraits represent nationwide realities. We have examined the concentric circles of influence—families, schools, and communities—within which today's youth are growing up, and we have seen how in recent decades the challenges and opportunities facing rich and poor kids have grown more disparate.

This up-close-and-personal focus runs the risk that we miss the deeper connection between the opportunity gap and growing income inequality. From Port Clinton to Philadelphia, and from Bend to Atlanta to Orange County, economic disparities among the families have been an important part of each story. In every movement of this composition the deep, throbbing, ominous bass line has been the steady deterioration of the economic circumstances of lower-class families, especially compared to the expanding resources available to upper-class parents.

To be sure, the link from income inequality to opportunity inequality is not simple and instantaneous. As our cases illustrate, it took several decades for economic malaise to undermine family structures and community support; it took several decades for gaps in parenting and schooling to develop; and it will take decades more for the full impact of those divergent childhood influences to manifest themselves in adult lives. Moreover, this sad sequence started at different times in different parts of America. For example, this process began earlier and has progressed further in nonwhite communities, though it is now thoroughly under way in white communities, too.

These time lags of indefinite duration complicate our ability to draw a simple statistical correlation between inequality of income and inequality of opportunity. This methodological dilemma is not unlike the comparable problem of diagnosing global warming. Decades passed between the invention of the internal combustion engine and the changing chemistry of earth's upper atmosphere; decades more passed between that atmospheric change and glacial melting; and it will take years more before the sea floods Manhattan and Miami. Those long lags lead inevitably to debate among scientists about the pace and even the reality of systemic change. In both cases—global warming and the opportunity gap—causal links and future projections remain uncertain, but in both cases, if we wait for perfect clarity, it will be too late.

Is upward socioeconomic mobility poised to plunge? The factors for which we have found growing class gaps are precisely the same factors that the economist Raj Chetty and his colleagues have found to be associated with socioeconomic mobility across America today—family stability, residential segregation, school quality, community cohesion, and income inequality. That fact suggests (as this book argues) that those factors are leading indicators of trends in mobility. Chetty himself believes that the early returns from his research show no decline in socioeconomic mobility, but others (including me) are more doubtful that those early results will hold up when the full returns from the younger generation begin to arrive, about a decade from now.[1]

All sides in this debate agree on one thing, however: as income inequality expands, kids from more privileged backgrounds start and probably finish further and further ahead of their less privileged peers, even if the rate of socioeconomic mobility is unchanged. The economist Isabel Sawhill makes this point eloquently in *Getting Ahead or Losing Ground.* "As inequality has increased," she writes, "debate about the extent of mobility in American society has heightened. As income gaps have widened, the opportunity that children have to do better than their parents is increasingly important. . . . Whether they do so at a faster or slower rate than they did in the past is not a settled question. But since the rungs of the ladder are further apart than they used to be, the effects of family background on one's ultimate economic success are larger and may persist for a longer period of time."[2]

Perhaps unexpectedly, this is a book without upper-class villains. Virtually none of the upper-middle-class parents of our stories are idle scions of great wealth lounging comfortably on family fortunes. Quite the contrary, Earl and Patty and Carl and Clara and Ricardo and Marnie were each the first in their families to go to college.[3] Roughly half of them came from broken homes. Each has toiled exhaustingly to climb the ladder, and they have invested much time, money, and thought in raising their kids. Their own modest origins—though not destitute—were in some respects closer to the circumstances facing poor kids today than to the circumstances in which their own kids have grown up.

These parents were able to be upwardly mobile in part because the era of their youth was relatively favorable to upward mobility. Though it might seem natural to label them "self-made," in many unnoticed ways they benefited from family and community supports that are nowadays less readily available to kids from such modest backgrounds. They grew up in an era when public education and community support for kids from all backgrounds managed to boost a significant number of people up the ladder—in Bend, Beverly Hills, New York, Port Clinton, and even South Central LA. Those supportive institutions, public and private, no longer serve poorer kids so well. That is the point of this book.

But most readers of this book do not face the same plight, nor does its author, nor do our own biological kids. Because of growing class segregation in America, fewer and fewer successful people (and even fewer of our children) have much idea how the other half lives. So we are less empathetic than we should be to the plight of less privileged kids.

Before I began this research, I was like that. I've worked hard, I thought, to rise from a modest background in Port Clinton—much of the time heedless of how much my good fortune depended on family and community and public institutions in that more communitarian and egalitarian age. If I and my classmates could climb the ladder, I assumed, so could kids from modest backgrounds today. Having finished this research, I know better.

The absence of personal villains in our stories does not mean that no one is at fault. Many constraints on equal opportunity in America today, including many of the constraints apparent in our stories, are attributable to social policies that reflect collective decisions. Insofar as we have some responsibility for those collective decisions, we are implicated by our failure to address removable barriers to others' success.

But why should the opportunity gap matter for those of us on its lucky side? The answer is that the destiny of poor kids in America has broad implications for our economy, our democracy, and our values.

Unequal Opportunity and Economic Growth

Poor kids, through no fault of their own, are less prepared by their families, their schools, and their communities to develop their God-given talents as fully as rich kids. For economic productivity and growth, our country needs as much talent as we can find, and we certainly can't afford to waste it. The opportunity gap imposes on all of us both real costs and what economists term "opportunity costs."

In 1975 economist Arthur Okun famously formulated what he called "the Big Tradeoff" between equity and efficiency.[4] We could pursue policies that would enhance social equity—say, by redistributing income through the tax system—but only at the cost of economic productivity. It is sometimes forgotten that Okun himself argued that this ironclad tradeoff does *not* typically apply to the pursuit of equality of opportunity. In such cases, there is no such tradeoff, because investment in poor kids raises the rate of growth for everyone, at the same time leveling the playing field in favor of poor kids. That has been the core rationale for public education throughout U.S. history, and much empirical research confirms that premise.[5]

The costs of underinvesting in poor kids are even greater in an era of globalization, because of a "skills mismatch" between what low-skilled workers can do and what employers need in an age of rapid technological change. This leads, as the economists Claudia Goldin and Lawrence Katz put it, to the "decreased utilization of the less educated" and slower economic growth.[6] Our contemporary public debate recognizes this problem but assumes it is largely a "schools problem." On the contrary, we have seen that most of the challenges facing poor kids are not caused by schools. Drawing on an entirely independent stream of evidence, the economists Daron Acemoglu and David Autor reach the same conclusion: "The U.S. educational system cannot be the sole cause of the waning educational stature of the U.S."[7]

It is not easy to put hard numbers on the economic costs of the opportunity gap, but three independent studies, using diverse methods, have arrived at broadly comparable—and surprisingly large—estimates.

- Harry Holzer and his colleagues estimate the aggregate annual costs of child poverty to the U.S. economy. They conclude that "these costs total about $500 billion per year, or the equivalent of nearly 4 percent of gross domestic product (GDP). More specifically, we estimate that childhood poverty each year: (1) reduces productivity and economic output by an amount equal to 1.3 percent of GDP, (2) raises the costs of crime by 1.3 percent of GDP, and (3) raises health expenditures and reduces the value of health by 1.2 percent of GDP."[8]

- Clive Belfield and his colleagues focus on what they term "opportunity youth," that is, young people aged 16–24 who are neither in school nor at work, a group that largely overlaps with the kids from poor, less educated homes who are the focus of this book.[9] Belfield and his colleagues painstakingly estimate both the annual and lifetime costs imposed on taxpayers for each opportunity youth. They then do the same thing for the burdens imposed on society as a whole (for example, the private costs of crime or the costs of slower aggregate growth) for each opportunity youth. Their analysis is so comprehensive that it even recognizes the seeming "cost savings" to the educational system that we currently enjoy because these kids have dropped out. The total costs they itemize, as summarized in Table 6.1, are staggering.

Table 6.1: Economic Costs of "Opportunity Youth"
(Belfield et al., 2012)

	Taxpayer burden	Societal burden
Annual (per youth)	$13,900	$37,450
Adult lifetime (per youth)	$170,740	$529,030
Aggregate lifetime burden (in present value terms) from the current cohort of opportunity youth	$1.59 trillion	$4.75 trillion

Roughly two thirds of these costs reflect lost earnings, lower economic growth, and lower tax revenue, while less than 5 percent reflect the costs of "welfare" programs. Even if we harden our hearts and simply leave these poor kids to fend for themselves, we will still have to reckon with the lion's share of these costs, because these kids will not be contributing to the national economy.

- Finally, Katharine Bradbury and Robert K. Triest summarize previous studies that have shown that inequality of opportunity slows growth by keeping disadvantaged potential workers from developing their full capacity. Then, comparing the social mobility and growth rates of different metropolitan areas in America, they find that social mobility appears to speed economic growth beyond what would have been predicted on the basis of standard growth theory. If the Atlanta area (which has low intergenerational mobility) were to increase its mobility to match the rate of the Salt Lake City area (which has high intergenerational mobility), that would increase the 10-year growth rate of real per capita income in the Atlanta area by an estimated 11 percentage points. If the Memphis, Tennessee, area increased its rate of intergenerational mobility to match the rate of the Sioux City, Iowa, area, the estimated 10-year growth rate of real per capita income in Memphis would jump by an estimated 27 percentage points.[10]

Further research will no doubt refine these numbers, but the estimates are serious and thoughtful. Moreover, the estimates are surprisingly convergent on the key point: Writing off such a large fraction of our youth is an awfully expensive course of inaction.

Estimating the high costs of inaction does not tell us what actions to take to avoid those costs, nor what the costs of those remedial actions would be—though, to take a single example, the Nobel Laureate economist James Heckman has estimated that even expensive investments in early childhood education would yield real rates of return (approximately 6 to 10 percent) that outstrip long-term stock market returns.[11] Even acknowledging the back-of-the-envelope nature of these calculations, one can't help concluding that ignoring the plight of poor kids imposes a substantial economic burden on all of us. And ignoring it, of course, doesn't make it disappear.[12]

These statistical findings rhyme perfectly with the life stories we've examined in this book. For example, David in Port Clinton is a decent, hardworking kid—taking responsibility for his eight half-siblings as well as his own infant daughter, and trying to eke out a living in a succession of part-time, low-wage jobs. But he is held back by his juvenile criminal record, inadequate schooling, the malign influences of his family and community, and the limited economic options open to him. Rather than contributing to a revival of the Port Clinton economy, as he would like to, he's unintentionally imposing costs on the community's resources—both real costs and opportunity costs. Without some help from the rest of us, he is likely to do so for the rest of his life. Broadly speaking, the same is true of Kayla, Elijah and Michelle, Lola and Sofia, and Lisa and Amy. If we could begin to close the opportunity gap, these kids could become not a drag on our economy but contributors, as they wish to be.

To say that the Okun tradeoff is not inevitable does not mean that there is never such a tradeoff. We can easily imagine redistributive schemes that might entail unacceptable costs to social productivity. This is in the end a pragmatic issue: When does a particular effort to promote equality of opportunity entail unacceptable costs? A reasonable assessment is that America today has plenty of scope for simultaneously enhancing equality of opportunity and economic growth. But in order to achieve those results, we have to make significant investments now.

Unequal Opportunity and Democracy

The essence of democracy is equal influence on public decisions.[13] A representative democracy requires at least widespread, if not universal, voting and grassroots civic engagement. The more that other means of political influence, such as money, are powerful and unevenly distributed across citizens, the more important electoral and grassroots involvement becomes for ensuring some approximation to democracy.

That more educated and affluent citizens participate more actively in public affairs, and have more political knowledge and civic skills than their impoverished, ill-educated fellow citizens and are more likely to take part in virtually all forms of political and civic engagement, is one of the most robust findings of students of political behavior. So what are the implications of the growing opportunity gap for American democracy? Rich kids are more confident that they can influence government, and they are largely right about that.[14] Not surprisingly, poor kids are less likely to try.

The U.S. Census Bureau periodically asks a national sample of Americans about their civic involvement, including whether they have recently discussed politics, belonged to a voluntary organization, attended a public meeting, engaged in a boycott or "buycott," worked with others to fix a neighborhood problem, and contacted a public official. Figure 6.1 summarizes the frequency of such activities among young adults aged 20–25 in 2008 and 2010. More than twice as many high-school-educated youth are completely detached from virtually all forms of civic life, compared to college-educated youth, while more than twice as many college-educated youth engage in more than one of these activities.[15]

Figure 6.1: College-educated young people are more civically engaged

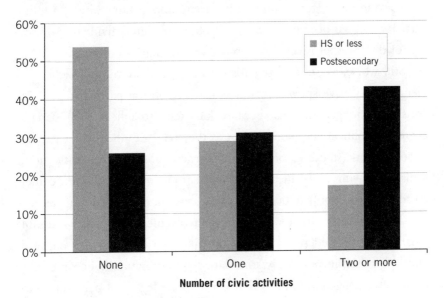

Source: Current Population Survey, 2008 and 2010.

Worse yet, on the single most fundamental form of democratic participation—voting—this yawning class gap among young people has widened in recent decades—yet another scissors gap. In recent national elections, college-educated youth have been two to three times more likely to vote than their peers who had not gotten beyond high school.[16]

Ironically, by many measures of civic engagement other than voting—from attending a public meeting to signing a petition—the class gap appears to have narrowed in recent years, but only because affluent kids are withdrawing from civic life even more rapidly than poor kids.[17] This downward convergence, which we also saw in student government participation in Chapter 4, might be comforting, except that it means that fewer and fewer of the next generation are involved at all— and despite the closing scissors, a substantial class gap remains.

High-quality national surveys of high school seniors confirm that kids from less educated homes are less knowledgeable about and interested in politics, less likely to trust the government, less likely to vote, and much less likely to be civically engaged in local affairs than their counterparts from college-educated homes. Moreover, these class differences are much larger among whites than among nonwhites.[18] Online participation has been growing rapidly, but the digital divide on political uses of the Internet is very great and shows no signs of diminishing.[19]

Still worse, as political scientists Kay Schlozman, Sidney Verba, and Henry Brady have shown, this class gap in political participation is increasingly intergenerational, because kids tend to inherit their parents' degree of political engagement, just as they tend to inherit their parents' socioeconomic standing. So across the generations, class disparities accumulate. "Having well-educated and affluent parents," they write, "confers an advantage not only in occupational success but also in political voice."[20]

Thus, the inheritance of political involvement represents a double whammy. Educated parents are more likely to be politically engaged, and kids raised in politically stimulating homes naturally become more politically engaged as adults. That is the direct legacy of parental political involvement. But in addition, kids from educated homes are much more likely to grow up to be educated adults themselves, and their greater education also favors their political engagement as adults, an indirect inheritance. Conversely, political engagement by kids from less privileged backgrounds is discouraged both by the absence of civic role models at home and by their own limited educational attainment.

This double whammy is, in turn, a double challenge to traditional U.S. ideals that we explored in Chapter 1—first, Americans generally believe that political inequality is worse than economic inequality, and second, we believe that inherited inequality is worse than inequality within a given generation. Inherited political inequality brings us uncomfortably close to the political regime against which the American Revolution was fought.

In our interviews, we found evidence of widespread and growing political estrangement among kids from all backgrounds—rich and poor. Virtually all Americans nowadays are unhappy about politics and government. But that's where the similarities end. The lower-class kids we met were unremittingly alienated from civic life, whereas most of their upper-class counterparts have been encouraged by parents, peers, and mentors to take part in politics. Consider several examples.

In Port Clinton, Chelsea's parents are active in the community and talk about politics a lot. "For the most part I align with them politically," she says, "but there's things that I'm still figuring out, because I can vote now. I'm going to be in the workforce and contributing to society, so I need to get more educated on what's happening."

On the other side of the tracks, David lives in a chaotic family situation with no role models at all for political or civic engagement, so our questions about those topics elicited a puzzled stare and a brief response, as though we had asked about Mozart or foxhunting.

Q: Do you ever vote?
A: Never voted.

Q: Do you know if your parents are involved in politics, or if they get involved in stuff?
A: I don't talk to them about it.

Across the country, in Bend, Andrew says that, like his parents, he is involved in community activities, and he plans to vote (though for a different party from his dad, he adds). Though hardly an activist at this stage in his life, he's become more interested in public issues through college debate and can imagine going into politics himself.

By contrast, politics is the furthest thing from Kayla's mind, preoccupied as she is with her grave personal problems.

Q: Are you involved in political stuff or community stuff?
A: Not really.

Q: Are you interested in watching the news?
A: It gets old after a while. Somebody shot somebody, or somebody robbed somebody. I'm not that interested.

Q: Are you excited about the election coming up? Do you think you'll vote?
A: Nah. I don't care.

Q: Do you have a party that you like?
A: They all kinda suck.

Q: Are your parents involved in politics at all?
A: Not really.

This contrast between upper-class engagement and lower-class estrangement, apparent both in statistical analyses and in conversations with young people, poses two fundamental risks to American democracy, one more obvious, the second more subtle.

First, as class differences in political voice are amplified, the political system becomes less representative of Americans' interests and values, in turn exacerbating political alienation. In fact, increasing evidence points in exactly this direction.[21] Money is becoming more important in

American politics today, so the absence of pressure from the ballot box enhances misrepresentation. "Elections have consequences," politicians like to say, but if you don't participate, the consequences of those elections are unlikely to be good for you. "If you are deprived of an equal voice in the government," wrote political scientist Robert Dahl, "the chances are quite high that your interests will not be given the same attention as the interests of those who do have a voice. If you have no voice, who will speak up for you?"[22]

A blue-ribbon task force of the American Political Science Association came to a similar conclusion a decade ago. "Today," the authors wrote, "the voices of American citizens are raised and heard unequally. The privileged participate more than others and are increasingly well organized to press their demands on government. Public officials, in turn, are much more responsive to the privileged than to average citizens and the least affluent. Citizens with lower or moderate incomes speak with a whisper that is lost on the ears of inattentive government officials, while the advantaged roar with a clarity and consistency that policy-makers readily hear and routinely follow."[23] In short, the opportunity gap undermines political equality and thus democratic legitimacy.

The growing political estrangement of American youth, especially those on the wrong side of the opportunity gap, poses a second, more subtle and more conjectural danger to democratic stability. It's a danger that would have been salient to observers such as the political theorist Hannah Arendt and the sociologist William Kornhauser, who after World War II were transfixed by the economic and political nightmares of 1930s and the rise of antidemocratic extremism.

An inert and atomized mass of alienated and estranged citizens, disconnected from social institutions, might under normal circumstances pose only a minimal threat to political stability, with any menace muted by the masses' very apathy. Government under such circumstances might not be very democratic, but at least it would be stable. But under severe economic or international pressures—such as the pressures that overwhelmed Europe and America in the 1930s—that "inert" mass might suddenly prove highly volatile and open to manipulation by anti-democratic demagogues at the ideological extremes.

Kornhauser argued in *The Politics of Mass Society* that the citizens most vulnerable to demagogic mass movements, such as Nazism, Fascism, Stalinism, or even McCarthyism here at home, were precisely those "who have the fewest opportunities to participate in the formal and informal life of the community."[24] Arendt made a similar argument in her classic *Origins of Totalitarianism*. "The chief characteristic of the mass man is not brutality and backwardness," she wrote, "but his isolation and lack of normal social relationships."[25] Without succumbing to political nightmares, we might ponder whether the bleak, socially estranged future facing poor kids in America today could have unanticipated political consequences tomorrow. So quite apart from the danger that the opportunity gap poses to American prosperity, it also undermines our democracy, and perhaps even our political stability.

Unequal Opportunity and Moral Obligation

So far we've focused on the economic and political consequences of the plight of disadvantaged kids in this country—those like David, Kayla, Elijah, Lola, and the others whose stories are told in this book. But there's a bedrock argument underneath that: to ignore these kids violates our deepest religious and moral values.

Virtually all religions share a profound commitment to caring for the have-nots. Proverbs 29:7 intones prophetically that "The righteous care about justice for the poor, but the wicked have no such concern." Jesus (Mark 10:21–25) admonished a religious rich man that he should give up everything to the poor, since "it is easier for a camel to go through the eye of a needle than for a rich man to enter the kingdom of God." Isaiah's angry God (Isaiah 3:15) thundered at Israel's elders and rulers, gathered to face his righteous wrath: "How dare you crush my people, grinding the faces of the poor into the dust?"

The most important service that Pope Francis has rendered to men and women of all faiths and of no faith at all is to remind us of our deep moral obligation to care for our neighbors and especially for poor kids. "Almost without being aware of it," he said in 2013, "we end up being incapable of feeling compassion at the outcry of the poor, weeping for other people's pain, and feeling a need to help them, as though all this were someone else's responsibility and not our own. . . . [When] we isolate [young people], we do them an injustice: young people belong to a family, a country, a culture, a faith . . . they really are the future of a people."[26]

The foundational documents of our national history, from the Declaration of Independence to the Gettysburg Address, have espoused the fundamental precept that all humans are of equal moral worth. For much of our national history we made silent, shameful exceptions to that principle for nonwhites and women. Virtually any moral theory of fairness and justice leads to that principle, however, and it is the anvil on which the hammers of the liberation movements of the last 100 years have wrought the expansion of equal rights. As Martin Luther King said at the 1963 March on Washington, "When the architects of our republic wrote the magnificent words of the Constitution and the Declaration of Independence, they were signing a promissory note to which every American was to fall heir."

As we saw in Chapter 1, 95 percent of us say that "everyone in America should have equal opportunity to get ahead"—a level of consensus that is virtually never reached in contentious contemporary America. The norm of equality of opportunity is complex in detail, especially because of the thorny issue of what exactly needs to be equalized. Philosophers debate whether or not genetic differences in intelligence or health or energy level could justify unequal opportunity, for example, or even whether the principle of equal opportunity means that we should try to redress bad luck.

These abstract debates seem to have implications for contemporary debate: If someone drops out of high school because they lack intelligence or grit, does that violate the principle of equality of opportunity?[27]

In some theoretical worlds we would need to address those complexities, *but not in real-world America today*. As this book has demonstrated, we are today so far from equality of opportunity, even for talented and energetic kids—so far from our own performance in the past—that there is little danger that we might apply the principle too stringently.

Even in our world, equality of opportunity needs to be weighed against other values, among them liberty and autonomy. It would be absurd (in the name of equality of opportunity) to prevent affluent parents from reading *Goodnight Moon* or to require couples to marry before having children. On the other hand, sometimes our principle of equal opportunity does trump other values: for example, we require parents to provide an adequate education for their kids, either through public schools or privately, on the principle that parental autonomy should not trump the child's right to basic education.

We're sometimes justified in blaming parents for how they've raised their kids. We might condemn Elijah's parents, or Kayla's or David's or Sofia's, for bad decisions—indeed, the kids themselves do! But to hold kids responsible for their parents' failings violates most Americans' moral sensibility.[28]

Equality of opportunity is not a simple guide to public action. However, we don't need to resolve those philosophical conundrums to recognize that the growing opportunity gap between rich kids and poor kids in America today is morally unacceptable. We don't have to believe in perfect equality of opportunity to agree that our religious ideals and our basic moral code demand more equality of opportunity than we have now.

What Is to Be Done?

What can we do—as individuals, as members of our communities, and as a country—to help poor kids begin to catch up with rich kids? As this book has outlined, this problem is not simple, and it does not have a simple solution. On the contrary, in our increasingly "red" versus "blue"

America, it is the ultimate "purple" problem, with many contributing factors. Some causes (like nonmarital births) are seen more clearly through "red" conservative lenses, while others (like growing income inequality) are accentuated by "blue" liberal lenses. Our civic leaders will need to reach across boundaries of party and ideology if we are to offer more opportunity to all our children. In addressing the opportunity gap, we must consider the full spectrum of potential solutions.

The pages that follow offer a menu of complementary approaches that have some collective promise of changing our current course.[29] It will take hard work to turn this set of suggestions into a comprehensive plan of action. Different mixes of policies may be needed in different settings—this is a vast, diverse country, so what could work in Port Clinton may well be different from what is needed in Atlanta or Orange County or Philadelphia or Bend. The top priorities for national policymakers will differ from the most effective approaches for civic or religious activists. The broad agenda for action that follows aims to stimulate reflection and action by all Americans.

My suggestions here are based on the best evidence currently available. This is fortunately an exciting area of rapid research, as both scholars and practitioners seek more imaginative solutions. We should look for cost-effectiveness, but given the scope of the opportunity gap, narrowing it will cost money. We must pursue a strategy of trial and error, learning from practical experience what works where. So my criterion is not whether any given proposal has already proven effective, but whether the best available evidence suggests that it has promise.

Fortunately, the American federal system is well designed for such a strategy, for it encourages us to try many ideas in many places and learn from each other. In previous historical periods we have successfully addressed comparably big problems this way. At the end of the nineteenth century in the midst of rapid urbanization, massive immigration, tumultuous social and economic and technological change, political strife, and high economic inequality, civic leaders from both parties across the country explored a vast variety of social, economic, and political reforms. Some failed and were discarded, but others proved unexpectedly effective. Those Progressive Era successes rapidly diffused across the country, and eventually federal legislation (and funding) extended reform nationwide. Change was both bottom-up and top-down. We must now emulate that period of successful innovation.

FAMILY STRUCTURE

In our polarized public debate an unexpected consensus has begun to crystalize across ideological lines that the collapse of the working-class family is a central contributor to the growing opportunity gap, as we saw in Chapter 2. Unfortunately, agreement has also begun to emerge that (apart perhaps from reversing the long decline in working-class incomes) direct, government-based approaches to solve this problem have so far shown very little promise.

"Marriage policy"—reducing the number of single-parent families by restoring the norm of traditional marriage—has been stressed by some conservative commentators.[30] Regardless of the merits of that objective, however, the hard fact is that well-meaning policy experiments to increase the rate of stable marriage have not worked. The welfare reforms of 1996 that ended "welfare as we know it" had very little effect on the steady decline of marriage among poorer, less educated Americans. The George W. Bush administration pursued an array of policy experiments designed to enhance marriage and marital stability and rigorously evaluated the results. Among them, the Building Strong Families initiative provided relationship skill training and other services to unmarried parents, while the Supporting Healthy Marriage program offered similar supports to married couples. Despite isolated hopeful signs, however, neither of these experiments offered much evidence that even well-designed, well-funded public programs can increase marriage rates or keep parents together. To be sure, religious communities can influence their members without involving government, so churches could strengthen support for marriage, parenting, and responsibility for children.[31] On the other hand, other than a reversal of long-established trends in private norms, or a strong and sustained economic revival concentrated on the working class, I see no clear path to reviving marriage rates among poor Americans.[32]

In the absence of a revival of marriage, could we reduce the number of single-parent families by reducing nonmarital birth rates? It is almost surely too late to reestablish the once strong link between sex and marriage, even if that were desirable. But could we delink sex from childbearing through more effective contraception? The economist Isabel Sawhill has argued for this approach.

> Too many young adults are sliding into relationships and having babies before they are ready to make commitments to each other and to their children that parenthood requires. Social norms that used to stigmatize unwed parenting now need to stigmatize unplanned parenting. New low-maintenance and long-acting forms of birth control make changing the default possible.[33]

Is contraception the answer?[34] Despite strong opposition on moral grounds from some religious leaders, nine out of ten Americans support birth control. By some estimates, 60 percent of all births to young, single women are unplanned, and low-income women don't aspire to have more children than more affluent women. We don't really understand this large discrepancy between what people say and what they actually do. Long-acting reversible contraceptives (LARCs), such as IUDs or implantable contraceptives, are about 20 times more effective than the pill at reducing the incidence of unplanned pregnancies among contraception-using women, but we don't know how many poor young women would, in fact, choose subsidized LARCs, since the empirical evidence so far comes from women who had already chosen to seek birth control.

Changing the norm from childbearing by default to childbearing by design might have a big effect on the opportunity gap. Social marketing like Iowa's "Avoid the Stork" campaign has shown some progress, and the dramatic drop in teen pregnancy over the last several decades gives some hope that social norms can change, although so far we have no firm evidence that this approach would reduce nonmarital childbearing among adult women, especially since, as we saw in Chapter 2, many of these births are "semi-intended."

So families headed by poor, less educated single moms are not likely to disappear soon. How can we help those families and especially their children? Money obviously matters. The backdrop to the problems facing poor families, poor schools, and poor communities is the stagnant economy that has seen virtually no real growth in decades for the less educated part of our population. The cause-effect linkage here is clear and profound. For example, changes in local economic conditions arising from plant closings in North Carolina had large measurable effects on children's reading and math scores, especially among older kids.[35] Sustained economic revival for low-paid workers would be as close to a magic bullet as I can imagine, not least because that might also delay childbearing and perhaps even encourage marriage among poorer men and women.

Simply providing relatively small amounts of additional cash to poor families can improve the achievements of their kids at school and put the children on a path toward higher lifetime income, especially if the added funds are concentrated on the child's earliest years. Carefully controlled policy experiments have shown the power of money during the preschool and elementary school years to narrow the opportunity gap, perhaps because of the effects of reduced family stress on early brain development.

An increase in family income by $3,000 during a child's first five years of life seems to be associated with an improvement on academic achievement tests equivalent to 20 SAT points and nearly 20 percent higher income later in life. As social policy expert Lane Kenworthy summarizes this research, "government cash transfers of just a few thousand dollars could give a significant lifelong boost to the children who need it most."[36] Getting such resources where they are most needed could be done in a variety of well-tested ways.[37]

- Expand the *Earned Income Tax Credit* (EITC), especially for families with young children. Originally conceived by conservative economist Milton Friedman and expanded by administrations of both parties during the last quarter century, this program is widely regarded as a reasonably efficient way of increasing the disposal income of poor parents who are working, and it has become one of the largest antipoverty programs in America (after food stamps and Medicaid). On the other hand, this program only helps the working poor, so it doesn't reach the poorest of poor kids.

- Expand the modest existing *child tax credit* (as advocated by Tea Party favorite Senator Mike Lee [R., Utah]), but make the credit fully refundable, so that it can benefit children in families too poor to owe any federal taxes at all, thus reaching the poorest kids.

- Protect long-standing antipoverty programs, like food stamps, housing vouchers, and child care support. These have not been enough to halt the widening opportunity gap, at least at current funding levels, but in the aggregate they are an important part of the safety net.

Any serious effort to deal with the family and community facets of the opportunity gap should include efforts to reduce incarceration for nonviolent crime and enhance rehabilitation.[38] Incarceration, especially paternal incarceration, was part of the story of virtually every poor kid we met in this study. Crime has fallen to near-record lows, while the massive increase in incarceration in recent decades has come at great expense both in terms of taxpayer dollars and in terms of impact on families and communities. This problem is now widely recognized across party lines, both in Washington and in state capitals around the country. Among policy changes that could eventually begin to narrow the opportunity gap are these:

- Reduce sentencing for nonviolent crime and use greater discretion in parole administration.

- Rehabilitate ex-prisoners, keeping in mind that the prison population is comprised of young men with very little education, poor job records, and frequent histories of mental illness and substance abuse.
- Redirect current funding for prisons to funding for job training, drug and medical treatment, and other rehabilitation services.

CHILD DEVELOPMENT AND PARENTING

In Chapter 3 we saw that childcare and parenting, especially in the earliest years of childhood, are important contributors to the opportunity gap. What ideas about solutions does that insight suggest? First, the best recent evidence is that on average the highest-quality child care, especially in the early years, comes from a child's own parents. Child development specialist Jane Waldfogel summarizes these findings: "Children do fare better on average if their mothers do not work full-time in the first year of life."[39] Thus, if we want to close the opportunity gap, we should allow parents more options for workplace flexibility and for parental leave (at least part-time) in the first year of life and avoid policies (now pursued by some states) that require welfare recipients to work during a newborn's first year. Virtually all other advanced countries provide much more support for parents (especially low-income parents) during their children's first year of life than we do.[40]

As children move into day care, research clearly shows, quality matters. Moreover, leaving aside care provided by parents, the research also shows that center-based care is generally better than informal arrangements with relatives, neighbors, or friends.[41] To be sure, quality varies greatly within each of these categories, and measuring quality itself is complicated and controversial. Yet access to high-quality, center-based day care is another dimension in which the class gap that we have seen so often in this book is widening—rising among kids from affluent homes, stagnant or falling among poor kids. So figuring out how to provide affordable, high-quality, center-based day care for low-income families should be high on the priority list for anyone who wants to narrow the opportunity gap. Among the most notable initiatives in this area are so-called Early Head Start programs and Educare, a comprehensive nationwide network of nonprofit day care centers subsidized by private philanthropists.[42]

Whatever day care kids have, we learned in Chapter 3 about the growing "parenting gap" between more educated and less educated families. Part of this gap is the direct consequence of material resources, but part of it is due to poor parenting skills among too many less educated parents. Teachers, social workers, and medical specialists on the front lines of the struggle to help poor kids—in poor neighborhoods that we visited in Oklahoma City, for example—stress the problems that the kids face at home and the need to provide "wraparound" family services, working one-on-one with the parents (typically single moms), especially via home visits.

Advice as simple as "read to your children every day" can be valuable, but even more powerful is professional "coaching" of poor parents. Examples of programs that have been shown to improve children's developmental outcomes include the Nurse-Family Partnership, HIPPY (Home Instruction for Parents of Preschool Youngsters), Child First, and (in the U.K.) the government's Troubled Families initiative. What these programs have in common is regular home visits by trained professionals to help families cope with health problems, childrearing, stress, and other family issues. Though costly, such programs have a favorable "rate of return."[43]

As we saw in Chapter 3, there is a growing consensus among child development specialists on the importance of preschool education. Yet in terms of enrollment in early childhood education the United States ranks 32nd among the 39 countries in the Organisation for Economic Co-operation and Development (OECD). On average, across these advanced countries, 70 percent of three-year-olds are enrolled, compared to 38 percent in the United States.[44] A few high-quality programs have been studied using the gold standard of program evaluation, with randomized controls and follow-up over decades. The classic studies of the initial Head Start program in the 1960s in Michigan and the Abecedarian Project in the 1970s in North Carolina showed remarkable effects: they boosted initial educational progress, reduced trouble with the law as the children became adults, and increased the participants' lifetime income.[45]

Subsequent studies of Head Start have not shown such substantial effects, leading some to question whether the cost-benefit ratio of early childhood education is quite so favorable. Specialists generally attribute the weaker apparent effects of the later programs to a) the general improvement in parenting across all segments of American society (which raises the bar for identifying the effects of special programs), b) the sometimes lower quality of the later programs, with less wraparound support, and c) an excessive focus on short-run test scores, whereas the most positive original results showed up later in the child's life in terms of socioemotional development and behavior, such as criminality, not just academic achievement. The quality of early childhood education programs (e.g., teacher training, duration, curriculum) varies widely, and higher-quality programs seem to have bigger effects, though measuring quality with precision has been a stumbling block.[46]

Nevertheless, one clear finding is that well-designed, center-based early childhood education is better than the alternatives, though it is also more costly. For example, the carefully studied, high-quality pre-K program offered in all public elementary schools in Boston has been proven highly effective, though expensive. Key ingredients of the Boston program, according to education specialists Greg Duncan and Richard Murnane, include a high-quality curriculum; well-paid, well-trained, well-coached teachers; and provisions for accountability. Duncan and Murnane conclude that "well-designed and well-implemented pre-K programs have the potential to be a vital component of a strategy to improve the life chances of children from low-income families."[47]

State funding for early childhood education has grown steadily in recent years, though as I noted, America still lags far behind other advanced countries in this domain. One notable statewide early childhood education initiative was begun in 1998 in Oklahoma, one of the reddest states in America. By 2012 the program was offered in 99 percent of Oklahoma school districts and enrolled 74 percent of all four-year-olds in the state. The Oklahoma program meets nine of the ten quality standards of the National Institute for Early Education Research, and in addition offers wraparound support and guidance for parents. Initial evaluations of the flagship program in Tulsa have shown remarkable student gains in reading, writing, and math skills.[48]

SCHOOLS

Chapter 4 showed that while rich kids and poor kids attend schools of very different quality, the resources and challenges that kids bring with them to school explain this contrast better than the policies that the schools pursue. Thus, the most promising approaches in this domain involve moving kids, money, and/or teachers to different schools.

We have seen throughout this book that growing residential segregation by social class is a key underlying cause of differences in kids' educational experiences. Residential segregation is deeply rooted in growing income inequality, in people's desire to live around people like themselves, and in the financial equity that middle-class Americans have embodied in their homes, so efforts to reduce class segregation are fiercely resisted. While some government policies are designed to reduce neighborhood inequality, other policies, such as exclusive zoning regulations and the home mortgage tax deduction, indirectly encourage residential segregation. But efforts to alter such policies, as well as school district boundaries and school siting, are objects of great political contention.

Publicly subsidized mixed-income housing is one potential solution that has been tried in various forms for the past several decades. Propinquity does not automatically produce "bridging social capital," that is, poor newcomers to a rich neighborhood are not automatically integrated into that neighborhood socially. Nevertheless, poor kids moved to better schools generally do better. One natural experiment in Mount Laurel, New Jersey, for example, showed that poor kids whose families were moved into a more affluent area achieved higher test scores and went further in school than comparable kids who were not moved, in part because their parents became more supportive of the kids' education. For example, 96 percent of the kids whose parents moved into the new neighborhood (and schools) graduated from high school, compared to 29 percent of the kids in the control group. Sociologist Douglas Massey, who followed the Mount Laurel experiment for many years, concluded that this case of mixed-income housing

> [doesn't] necessarily provide a model of mobility for all poor and disadvantaged families in the United States. Those mired in substance abuse, criminality, family violence, and household instability are not good candidates for affordable housing developments. . . . Affordable housing developments do constitute an appropriate intervention, however, for the millions of low- and moderate-income families who are trapped in distressed urban neighborhoods for lack of anywhere else to go, but who nonetheless plug away to do the best they can at school and work hoping for a chance to advance.[49]

An alternative to moving poor kids to better schools is to invest much more money in their existing schools so as to improve their quality. Most fundamentally, school systems need to put higher quality teachers in poor schools under conditions in which they can actually teach and not just keep order. As our comparison of two Orange County high schools illustrated in frightening detail, schools in impoverished areas face much bigger challenges. If we care about the opportunity gap, our aim must be not merely to equalize funding, but to more nearly equalize results, and that will require massively more compensatory funding. Equal numbers of guidance counselors, for example, cannot produce equal college readiness if the counselors in poor schools are tied up all day in disciplinary hearings. In 2012 only 17 states allocated more money per student to school districts with high poverty, while 16 states had the opposite—"regressive" school funding systems.[50] The 2013

Equity and Excellence Commission recommended to the U.S. secretary of education a multipronged strategy for equalizing our nation's K–12 schools through state and federal policy changes, including substantial new resources targeted at schools with high concentrations of poverty.[51]

One important objective of additional funding for poor schools is to recruit better-trained, more experienced, and more capable teachers. As we have seen, teacher flight from the challenges in such schools—violence and disorder, truancy, lower school readiness and English-language proficiency, less supportive home environments—means that students in these schools get a generally inferior education. Many teachers in poor schools today are doing a heroic job, driven by idealism, but in a market economy the most obvious way to attract more and better teachers to such demanding work is to improve the conditions of their employment. On an experimental basis, the federally funded Talent Transfer Initiative paid top urban teachers $20,000 extra over two years to teach in high-poverty, low-performing schools in ten large, diverse school districts. Almost nine out of ten teaching vacancies were filled by top teachers, most of whom remained even after the bonuses expired, and reading and math test scores in the affected schools were significantly boosted.[52]

Other elements in the national "school reform" agenda might also help narrow the opportunity gap.[53] Extending school hours to offer more extracurricular and enrichment opportunities has shown some promise.[54] Several charter schools, such as KIPP Schools and the Harlem Children's Zone Promise Academy (discussed below), have been shown to produce good results for poor kids. However, careful studies have concluded that charter schools are no panacea and generally do not narrow the class gap, in part because more educated parents are better able to manage the process of choosing a good school and transporting their kids to that school.[55]

Another broad approach to education as a means of narrowing the opportunity gap derives from the long tradition of educational reformers (dating back to the work of John Dewey in Chicago during the

Progressive Era) who emphasize links between schools and the community.[56] One strand in this approach puts social and health services in schools serving poor children. The Coalition for Community Schools concludes, "A community school is both a place and a set of partnerships between the school and other community resources. Its integrated focus on academics, health and social services, youth and community development and community engagement leads to improved student learning, stronger families and healthier communities."[57] Typically, community schools include youth activities at all hours and programs to engage parents and community members actively in the educational process, as well as to link children and families to social service and health agencies. Similar schools are found in many other countries, like the United Kingdom, where evaluations have been very positive, especially for kids and communities facing difficulties, even though the program is expensive. More limited evaluations of American community schools have so far been favorable.[58]

Another strand in the school-community approach involves community-based groups taking a more active role in creating neighborhood charter schools or organizing the community to press for better schools. The most renowned and thoroughly studied initiative of this sort is the Harlem Children's Zone, created by the charismatic educator/organizer Geoffrey Canada. Begun in 1970, HCZ includes early childhood programs, after-school tutoring and extracurricular offerings, family, community, and health programs; college encouragement; foster-care-prevention programs; and many others. The central academic investment is the charter school (HCZ Promise Academy). Rigorous evaluations have shown that the Promise Academy has made major progress in closing the racial gap in test scores with other public school students in New York.[59]

Yet another example of the benefits to schools from close ties to the wider community are Catholic schools. In a nationwide study—later confirmed and extended by Anthony Bryk and his colleagues—James Coleman found that (even with extensive controls for the sorts of kids who attend them) Catholic schools produced higher levels of achievement than public schools, especially for kids from poor backgrounds. Coleman, Bryk, and their colleagues attributed this strong performance to the social and moral community within which parochial schools are embedded. Cristo Rey schools, for example, are a well-regarded nationwide network of Catholic high schools that offer inner-city Latino children educational support and on-the-job training.[60]

America once had a vigorous system of vocational education, apprenticeship, and workforce training, both in and out of schools. Other countries, like Germany, still do, but over recent decades we have disinvested in such programs. Part of the reason is the rise of the "college for all" mantra, reflecting the belief that a college degree is the ticket to success in the contemporary economy. While it is true that the "college premium" is high, it is also true that (as we saw in Chapter 4), very few kids from disadvantaged backgrounds now obtain college degrees. Efforts to improve access and completion rates for poor kids in four-year institutions are worthwhile, and those efforts must begin well before college looms, since as we have seen, the challenges that poor kids face are daunting even before they enter elementary school.

Nonetheless, the "college for all" motto has tended to undercut public and private support for secondary and postsecondary education in vocational skills. A notable example of the potential for contemporary vocational education is provided by Career Academies, as described by author Don Peck: "Schools of 100 to 150 students, within larger high schools, offering a curriculum that mixes academic coursework with hands-on technical courses designed to build work skills. Some 2,500 career academies are already in operation nationwide. Students attend classes together and have the same guidance counselors; local employers partner with the academies and provide work experience while the students are still in school."[61] A controlled trial study found that earnings for academy participants were 17 percent higher per year than for nonacademy participants, and that career academy students earn postsecondary degrees at same rates as non-career-academy students.[62]

Specialists in this field cite other promising experiments, such as the Georgia Youth Apprenticeship Program and comparable programs in Wisconsin and South Carolina, as well as the nationwide YouthBuild network. But robust evaluations are rarer in this area than in conventional K–12 education. Research from other countries suggests that the benefits of expanded technical and vocational education could be quite high, both for the individual student and for the economy, but the United States spends (as a fraction of our economy) roughly one tenth as much on such programs as other countries.

Fears that such programs might lead to a class-based, two-tier educational system are not unrealistic. Any effort in this area would need to erase the stigma of voc ed or apprenticeships as second-class education, by integrating quality academics and by having much tighter partnerships of industry and postsecondary schools to develop and implement quality standards. Moreover, significant investment in student guidance would be required. Rigorous research is still needed to identify which programs are cost-effective and which are not. Nevertheless the choice facing young people like David and Kayla and Michelle and Lauren and Lola and Sofia and Lisa and Amy is not between serious training leading to a vocational certificate and four years of college leading to a highly paid career. It is between quality vocational training and no postsecondary education at all. Apprenticeship and vocational education is a promising area in which states and cities should experiment, especially with high-quality evaluation.[63]

Community colleges were founded initially in the Progressive Era, and greatly expanded during the 1960s and 1970s, to provide access to postsecondary education for students who, for whatever reason, could not begin at the university level. Community college advocates have long been divided on whether these institutions were primarily intended to provide an avenue to four-year institutions or an alternative for vocational education. In the 1960s three quarters of their students were in the "transfer" track, but by 1980 nearly three quarters were in the "terminal" track. By now, nearly half of all postsecondary students nationwide are in community college. While more than 80 percent of them aspire to a baccalaureate degree, only a small minority will ever achieve that goal.

The advantages of community college for nontraditional students are clear: mostly open enrollment, local access, part-time (so college can be combined with a job), and above all, low costs. The limits of this avenue are also clear: nearly two thirds of their students drop out before receiving any degree or transferring to a four-year institution. Community college is not nearly so remunerative as a four-year degree, but as in the lives of the poor kids we've met in this book, community college is more attractive than the only realistic alternative—simply ending their education after high school. On the other hand, only 40 percent of those who enroll in community college are the first in their family to attend college, and that group is even less likely to go on to a four-year institution, so community colleges are not very effective in getting low-income kids headed to a BA.

Community colleges are asked to do many things with meager funding, and in recent years that funding has been cut back, limiting financial aid, raising tuition, and reducing student services. Counseling and instructional quality is often uneven. All these deficiencies disproportionately affect low-income students. Nevertheless, the key issue in evaluating community college performance is "compared to what?" Proprietary schools (like the one from which Lisa got her useless associate degree in pharmacy technology) have a better completion rate for certificates than community colleges, but they cost three times as much, so their students graduate with much more debt than community college students ($50,000 in Lisa's case).

Despite their mixed record, community colleges have real promise as a means of narrowing the opportunity gap by providing poor kids with a realistic path upward. To serve that role, they need more funding, improved student support services, better connections to local job markets and to four-year institutions, and a lower dropout rate. The best community colleges in the country, such as Miami Dade College, have taken up this challenge with gusto. As two experts on community colleges, Arthur Cohen and Florence Brawer, conclude, "The community colleges' potential is greater than that of any other institution because their concern is with the people most in need of assistance. . . . If the community colleges succeed in moving even a slightly greater proportion of their clients toward what the dominant society regards as achievement, it is as though they changed the world." [64]

COMMUNITY

At the permeable boundary between schools and community are afterschool activities, mentors, and above all, extracurricular activities. As we discussed in Chapter 4, America invented extracurricular activities precisely to foster equal opportunity, and we know from dozens of research studies that this strategy works. Extracurricular activities provide a natural and effective way to provide mentoring and inculcate soft skills, and we already have a dense, nationwide network of coaches, instructors, advisors, and other adults who are trained to help kids. In short, Americans have already invented and deployed a near-perfect tool to address this problem—as close to a magic bullet as we are ever likely to find in the real world of social, and educational, and economic policy. Perversely, as the opportunity gap has widened, we have increasingly excluded poor students from participation in this time-tested system by instituting pay-to-play.

So if you are concerned about the issues discussed in this book, here is something you could do right now. Close this book, visit your school superintendent—better yet, take a friend with you—and ask if your district has a pay-to-play policy. Explain that waivers aren't worth the paper they're written on, because they force poor kids to wear a virtual yellow star, saying "I'm so poor my parents can't afford the regular fee." Explain that everyone in the school will be better off if anyone in the school can be on the team or in the band. Insist that pay-to-play be ended. And while you're there, ask if there are things you could do to help the local schools serve poor kids more effectively, both in the classroom and outside.

One important way to help is through mentoring programs. We saw in Chapter 5 that mentoring can make a measurable difference in kids' lives, but we also saw that formal mentoring programs have so far barely begun to close the enormous class gap in access to informal mentoring. Local mentoring programs exist in many communities across America, but poor kids themselves yearn for more adult mentoring. If such programs were dramatically expanded, it could make a real difference in narrowing the opportunity gap.

To be sure, serious mentoring requires serious training, careful quality control, and above all, stability.[65] The last thing that poor kids need is yet another unreliable, "drop-by" adult in their lives. Mentoring works best as the by-product of a connection that rests on some shared interest, like tennis or skateboarding or fishing.[66] To focus the national AmeriCorps volunteer program massively on mentoring for poor kids would be a sign of real national commitment to narrow the opportunity gap.

Support and mentoring from church leaders was of vital value to all four of our young women from the Philadelphia area. Nationwide, however, churches are just scratching the surface of their possible contribution. For example, the national youth survey of mentorship that we described in Chapter 5 found that (as seen by kids at risk) religious institutions were *not* a major source of mentoring, formal or informal. If America's religious communities were to become seized of the immorality of the opportunity gap, mentoring is one of the ways in which they could make an immediate impact.

Given the importance of neighborhood effects, as discussed in Chapter 5, neighborhood regeneration could make an important contribution to narrowing the opportunity gap. Such efforts are relevant both to school performance and to the lives of poor kids outside of school. Neighborhood redevelopment is hardly an unplowed field, since local, state, and national policymakers, as well as business and community leaders, have experimented with many revitalization strategies over the last half century. Broadly speaking, these strategies fall into two categories.

- Invest in poor neighborhoods. Many such efforts have been attempted since the 1970s, with mixed success.[67] For example, the New Hope program in Milwaukee in the 1990s offered wage and job supports to poor families in poor neighborhoods, successfully improving the parents' income and the kids' academic performance and behavior. Jobs-Plus programs in Baltimore, Chattanooga, Dayton, Los Angeles, and St. Paul reported similar positive results.[68] The key ingredient for programmatic success seems to be partnership between government, the private sector, and the local community.

- Move poor families to better neighborhoods. A number of closely evaluated programs of this sort have had mixed, modest, but generally positive results, especially on younger kids. There is some evidence that the results can be improved when combined with intensive counseling to support the families moving into new neighborhoods.[69]

We Can Diminish the Opportunity Gap

The opportunity gap dividing America's have and have-not kids is a complex problem that has grown gradually. That means that there is no simple, quick solution, but also that there are many places to start. Some things we can do quickly, like ending pay-to-play for extracurricular activities. Other bigger changes, like instituting nationwide early childhood education or restoring working-class wages, will take longer to implement, but we should start now. While seeking robust evidence of cost-effectiveness, we need a bias for action.

It took many decades for public high schools to become nearly universal in America, but the High School movement that made America a world leader in economic productivity and social mobility began in earnest in local communities across the nation a century ago. The essence of that reform was a willingness of better-off Americans to pay for schools that would mainly benefit other people's kids.

This is not the first time in our national history that widening socio-economic gaps have threatened our economy, our democracy, and our values. The specific responses we have pursued to successfully overcome these challenges and restore opportunity have varied in detail, but underlying them all was a commitment to invest in other people's children. And underlying that commitment was a deeper sense that those kids, too, were our kids.

Not all Americans have shared that sense of communal obligation. In his essay "Self-Reliance," Boston Brahmin Ralph Waldo Emerson once wrote, "Do not tell me, as a good man did to-day, of my obligation to put all poor men in good situations. Are they my poor? I tell thee, thou foolish philanthropist, that I grudge the dollar, the dime, the cent, I give to such men as do not belong to me and to whom I do not belong."[70] Emerson spoke eloquently for the individualist tradition in America.

The better part of two centuries later, speaking of the recent arrival of unaccompanied immigrant kids, Jay Ash, city manager and native of the gritty, working-class Boston suburb of Chelsea, drew on a more generous, communitarian tradition: "If our kids are in trouble—my kids, our kids, anyone's kids—we all have a responsibility to look after them."[71]

In today's America, not only is Ash right, but even those among us who think like Emerson should acknowledge our responsibility to these children. For America's poor kids do belong to us and we to them. They are our kids.

The Stories of Our Kids

JENNIFER M. SILVA AND ROBERT D. PUTNAM

Our Qualitative Research

Some of us learn from numbers, but more of us learn from stories. Since one central purpose of this book is to enlarge the number of educated Americans who appreciate "how the other half lives," we have given pride of place to the life stories of rich kids and poor kids. Much of this book consists of rigorous quantitative evidence of a robust and growing opportunity gap among American kids. But while the quantitative data can tell us *what* is happening to America's children and *why* we should be concerned, such data can't tell us much about the experiences of growing up in a world where fostering opportunity for kids is increasingly a private responsibility, where the sense of "our kids" has shriveled.

Quantitative data can't show us the *hows* of everyday life: how a single mother like Stephanie, raising children alone on modest wages, interacts with her kids when she's worried about keeping a roof over their heads and defending them from the danger of the streets; how a boy like David, bitter about being abandoned by his imprisoned dad and his alcoholic stepmother, struggles to be a good father in a community that constantly fails him; how even an upper-middle-class mother like Marnie faces daily anxiety about whether she is adequately preparing her children for a world of cutthroat jobs and fragile families.

In search of these hows, Jen Silva spent two years traveling across the United States interviewing young adults and their parents about "what it's like to grow up today." Her first stop was Bob Putnam's hometown of Port Clinton, Ohio. Bob remembered Port Clinton as a place where parents, shopkeepers, teachers, pastors, principals, and coaches offered advice, opportunity, and support to all kids—rich or poor, black or white. Interviews with a dozen of his classmates, along with a written survey of his entire class (discussed later), confirmed these memories. But the Port Clinton of the 1950s—with its shared prosperity, strong sense of community, and remarkably equal opportunity—was nowhere to be found when Jen visited in the spring of 2012. Instead, Jen sent back a tale of two Port Clintons (representing two Americas)—upper-middle-class kids growing up with college funds, traveling soccer teams, and caring godparents, while their working-class peers faced a deluge of unanticipated obstacles—abusive stepmothers, incarcerated fathers, unplanned pregnancies, and juvenile detention. Bob's initial shock at what had become of less affluent kids in his hometown in just half a century made us wonder if we had stumbled upon atypical working-class kids caught in Rust Belt circumstances far worse than the national average.

We extended our sample, adding Duluth, Minnesota; Philadelphia, Pennsylvania; Atlanta, Georgia; Birmingham, Alabama; Austin, Texas; Bend, Oregon; Orange County, California; and Waltham and Weston, Massachusetts, to our research sites. These sites represent various kinds of local economies and cultures across the United States, encompassing deindustrializing small towns in the Rust Belt (Port Clinton and Duluth), gentrifying tourist destinations (Bend), booming high-tech "miracle" cities (Austin), unevenly revitalizing urban centers (Philadelphia and Atlanta), and Birmingham, still coming to terms with the Civil Rights revolution. Orange County was chosen because of its reputation as the mecca of the extraordinarily wealthy, allowing us to explore the poor and working-class immigrant communities obscured by the "OC" mythology. Waltham and Weston, cheek-by-jowl suburbs of Boston with vast differences in household income, school quality, and housing prices, provided an opportunity to see how "two Americas" can exist on opposite sides of Route 128, "America's Technology Highway."

We spent the next two years and hundreds of hours talking with families in these research sites, interviewing 107 young adults and their parents. Jen conducted virtually all the interviews featured in this book, while Jasmin Sandelson, a talented graduate student in the Harvard Sociology Department, discovered Elijah in an Atlanta shopping mall. We chose to begin with young adults aged 18–22—kids just past high school and old enough to be contemplating college and future jobs. By focusing on early adulthood, a time when people leave the institutional settings of family and high school behind and begin to think seriously about how to build their own identities and lives, we got a glimpse into how these young adults were making sense of their childhoods and transitioning into their futures. We were also able to juxtapose their aspirations for their futures with the financial, social, and cultural obstacles that stood in their way.

We supplemented the interviews with young adults by talking to at least one of their parents. (Sometimes parent and child were interviewed together, but when possible, we interviewed them separately. In a few cases, the young adults were no longer in contact with either parent, so we lack that perspective.) Parents filled in the details of family finances, decisions about where to live and where to send the children to school, philosophies and practices of childrearing, and fears and anxieties about where their children would land. In reflecting on their own childhoods, parents also offered important insights into how growing up has changed over the last few decades, whether in terms of parenting, neighborhood and community closeness, or school practices.

This book is about growing class gaps, so we divided our interviewees into upper-middle-class respondents and working-class respondents. Since "social class" is an ambiguous and contentious term in American culture, we simply used parents' education as our indicator—four-year-college graduates (and their children) were classified as upper-middle-class, and parents who had not gone beyond high school (and their children) were classified as lower- or working-class. Among the ten upper-middle-class parents featured in this book, five have a college degree, four more have a graduate degree, and one returned to college after raising her kids. All of their children are either enrolled in college or have completed college. Among the thirteen working-class parents featured in the book, five have less than a high school diploma, four have high school diplomas, and an additional four are unknown (because they are no longer in their children's lives). None of our working-class kids have less than a high school diploma (or GED), and three have some college, though none has earned a degree.

In each city, we aimed ideally to pursue a "quartet" model: one working-class girl and her mother plus one upper-middle-class girl and her mother; or one working-class boy and his father plus one upper-middle-class boy and his father. (Sometimes local exigencies prevented us from following this quartet model perfectly, and in most sites we interviewed more than a single quartet.) We matched children with their same-sex parent in order to hold gender constant in our comparisons of how growing up has changed over time. For example, Wendy in Ohio recalls that her parents never expected her to achieve much in her career; her daughter, Chelsea, on the other hand, has been primed from an early age to be a lawyer. This approach allowed us to see how childrearing practices are converging by gender but diverging by social class.

To recruit families, we began by asking for referrals from local guidance counselors, school committee members, nonprofit organizations, and other knowledgeable community members. But we also did a lot of recruiting "on the ground"—driving from Walmarts to video gaming halls to fast food outlets, from colleges to auto body shops to temporary agencies to malls, seeking out young adults in the places they shop, work, study, and hang out. Other "fishing holes" for us included police and fire stations, factories, restaurants, community centers, recreation venues, and community, regional, state, and private colleges.

Participants were asked if they would be willing to "participate in a study about what it's like to grow up today." Only a handful of those whom we approached refused to participate, though several of the poorer kids declined to connect us with their parents because of deep, enduring estrangement between parent and child. We offered all recruits fifty dollars in exchange for their time. How they used this money was telling: upper-middle-class parents often refused the payment and upper-middle-class kids joked about beer money, but working-class respondents used it to pay for immediate, dire needs. A religious family in Orange County viewed us literally as "a gift from God," because they hadn't known how they were going to pay for both gas and lunch that day. Lola, also in Orange County, put the money toward the funeral of a family member who had just been killed in a gang shooting.

Often the recruitment process taught us a great deal about their daily lives. For example, when we approached Stephanie at her service job in Atlanta and told her we would offer her daughters $50 to participate in a study, she immediately called her daughter Michelle to insist that Michelle not leave the house without speaking to Jen—a sign of how desperately Michelle, out of work and out of school, needed money for gas and food. And when Bill, a Bend firefighter, met Jen at a local fried fish restaurant with his entire family in tow, explaining "We wanted both kids to see someone who had graduated from college and was doing something with her life," we realized in a visceral way how bewildered some working-class families feel when they try to guide their children into a baffling future.

During the interviews we began our structured set of topics to be covered with the family's economic situation, including where they lived, whether they owned or rented their home, whether they had enough money to pay their bills, whether they had health insurance and retirement plans, and if they could tell us about times when they felt that money was tight. We next asked about family structure, parenting practices, children's experiences in school, extracurricular activities, and church, and memories about birthdays and holidays.

Because we were particularly concerned about opportunity and mobility, we then asked young adults and their parents to recall their aspirations and expectations for the future in a series of questions including: "Walk me through the steps you went through when you were deciding what to do next. What kinds of choices did you have? How were your grades? Did you take the SATs? Did you plan to go to college or get a job? At what age did you start talking with your parents about going to college, and how was college talked about?" We also asked young adults and parents a series of questions about college tours, college preparatory classes, private college coaches or writing tutors, internships and jobs, and extracurricular activities. We asked about savings for college, financial aid, and college funds. We paid attention to the social resources available to young people, including mentors, guidance counselors, teachers, pastors, and other important adults. We also asked more "feeling" questions about trust, security, hope, and anxiety about their futures; about whether their lives had turned out as they had imagined they would; and the kinds of assistance and obstacles they had encountered along the way.

While we covered these topics in every interview, we also left space for interviewees to tell their own narratives and to identify important topics not touched upon by our interview guide. In some cases, the interview guide seemed laughably naive, such as when we began to ask Mary Sue—a young working-class woman abandoned by her mother at an early age and left with no company but a mouse—about piano lessons. In such situations, we realized how removed working-class kids are from our notions of a "normal" childhood, and we encouraged the respondents to tell their stories in their own words.

Allowing the interviewees to go off script enabled us to uncover salient categories of experience previously missing from our analysis of growing up. For example, our quantitative data on family structure distinguish between neo-traditional stability in the upper-middle-class and disruptive flux in the working class. However, Marnie, a divorced upper-middle-class mother, shed light on a different phenomenon: how upper-middle-class parents activate "air bags" for their children in stressful times (e.g., sending her daughter to boarding school, hiring staff to drive the children to extracurriculars, hiring professional counselors), thereby cushioning the kids from the potentially negative repercussions of divorce and single parenthood.

Our interviews lasted between one and three hours, and Jen often did follow-ups in person or over the phone. Respondents could end the interview at any point and could decline to answer any question, though virtually none did. With their permission, we digitally recorded and transcribed their stories. Jen wrote up brief summaries of each case, which we both discussed extensively with other members of our research team. On the basis of these shared appreciations, Bob drafted the stories as they appear in this book.

Keeping track of the working-class young adults proved difficult, as their housing situations changed rapidly, and their phones were often shut off for nonpayment. The best way to keep in touch with working-class kids turned out to be Facebook, as their accounts stayed active even though they changed their phone numbers frequently. Watching them post and interact on Facebook also gave us deeper information than a single interview could, and with their permission we used their updates and posts in our analysis.

We conducted each interview at a location chosen by the respondent. For upper-middle-class families, this often meant their homes, where we could see for ourselves the large backyards, safe streets, proudly displayed photographs of children in baseball uniforms and dance costumes, and comfortable daily rhythms of family dinners and casual conversations. Sometimes we went to working-class families' homes, which were equally informative. When we visited Lola and Sofia in Santa Ana, for example, we could not help noticing the young men on the sidewalk who eyed us warily as we drove through the neighborhood. Other times, we conducted the interviews in coffee shops, restaurants, or parks, eating local favorites like fried perch and watching children play while we talked.

Often, we learned most from what happened when the tape wasn't rolling. For example, in the very early stages of the project, the literature on family structure became a stark reality for us when one working-class kid after another told us we couldn't interview their fathers because they were in prison, addicted to drugs, abusive, or simply missing from their lives (thereby throwing a wrench into our neat quartet research design). The absence of the voices of working-class dads proved to be an unexpected and powerful piece of data for us. We also learned, for a split second, about what it felt like to be young, black, and working-class, when Michelle drove carefully through Clayton County with Jen, fearing that the police would pull her over for the slightest infraction and warning Jen of the dangers of tough neighborhoods. Just the simple act of scheduling an interview with working-class respondents—who lacked reliable transportation, money for gas, stable work hours, and child care—showed us how hard it is to plan for the future amid constant insecurity and uncertainty.

Building trust is essential to this kind of endeavor. To protect our respondents, we informed them of the purpose of the study—to understand the experience of kids growing up today—and promised to keep their identities confidential when retelling their stories. Thus while the stories you read in this book are true in every detail, we have used pseudonyms, and we have sometimes removed potentially identifying information, such as the names of schools or workplaces, while saying enough—"an Ivy League college" or "a major Wall Street firm"—to let the reader understand the context. All of the quotations are in the respondents' exact words.[1] In compliance with federal regulations for human subject research, at the outset of each interview we explained how we would use the information they shared, and we obtained a signed release form, authorizing us to use the material as we have done.

Jen is exceptionally experienced in recruiting and interviewing young adults about their life stories,[2] and she has a rare gift for putting people at ease. She found nearly all of the informants willing to let her into their homes and share their stories. Part of this openness probably comes from the fact that in our society, young white women like Jen are perceived as both nonthreatening and nurturing. Jen also drew upon aspects of her own background to build common ground with our respondents. Jen (who appears even younger than she is) conducted these interviews just as she turned 30, finished grad school, interviewed for academic jobs, and became engaged. When talking to young adults, she was close enough to the transition to adulthood to understand their anxieties about finding a job, making choices about education and choosing a partner; when talking to parents, she genuinely sought advice on these same topics.

Jen is also a first-generation college graduate and has grown up straddling the working-class world of firefighters, prison guards, and farmers of her childhood and the upper-middle-class world of Wellesley and Harvard. This liminal background allowed her to switch comfortably between the worlds of her upper-middle-class and working-class respondents. She also chose to accept Facebook friend requests from respondents, which opened up her life to them as they had opened up their lives to her. This choice made her seem more like a normal human being and less like a detached researcher, further engendering trust and reciprocity. When she changed her Facebook status to married and posted wedding photos, many of our informants "liked" her new status.

In the end only five of our research sites appear in detail in this book, and only two to three families from each of those five sites are featured. Limiting our stories to five sites allowed us to present more historical, socioeconomic, and cultural context for our respondents' stories. We chose those sites because they collectively represented the diversity of America—North, South, East, Midwest, and West; large and small; rising and declining. We chose those families in part because they collectively represented America's ethnic diversity, while also revealing class differences within a given ethnic group and community. While the nuances of race, ethnicity, and local economies and cultures allow us to convey the complexities of American society, the differences across these categories (for example, race or region) are not nearly as marked or influential as the differences within them (that is, social class).

We also sought paired comparisons that would illustrate the substantive issues on which our systematic research showed growing class gaps nationwide—family, parenting, schooling, and community. For example, to introduce the chapter on family structure, we sought a pair of contrasting cases from a single site that were rich in detail on the parents' lives and family structure, while to introduce the chapter on education we needed a pair of cases from a single site that included abundant information about two contrasting, nearby high schools.

All these constraints—limited sites, ethnic and geographic diversity, class pairings, and substantive richness—meant that many vivid life stories were left on the cutting room floor. We wish we could also have told you about Nicole in Austin, a young woman who got pregnant in high school and managed to graduate while working the night shift at Pizza Hut; or Tyler in Duluth, whose dad is a college professor and who plays string bass and now studies at a leading Ivy institution; or Dylan, a working-class boy in Waltham, Massachusetts, removed from his home on the recommendation of the Department of Social Services (perhaps without adequate justification) and now working at a gas station and deeply distrustful of the entire world. (Jen may present these and other cases in subsequent publications of her own.) But to the best of our ability and knowledge, this inevitable editing of our raw material has not introduced substantive bias into our collection of life stories.

In any event, we offer these narratives as illustrations, not proof. Our objective for the ethnographic part of this research was not to provide a representative picture of America (which would have been impossible, given our small sample and convenience sampling), nor to provide verification that specific events happened exactly as our respondents recounted, but rather to explore the ways in which our categories of analysis—family structure, parenting practices, schools, neighborhoods, and communities—play out in different families, of different racial backgrounds, in different places. The hard data for the generalizations in this book are the social scientific findings that we summarize. Nevertheless, we believe that the life stories accurately portray the trends that are evident in the quantitative data.

What we found in our interviews is that upper-middle-class kids—even across differences of race, gender, and region—look and sound remarkably similar across the nation. The same goes for working-class kids. For example, a black working-class boy like Elijah in Atlanta shares many more life experiences (parental abandonment, jail, poor schooling, and so forth) with David, a white working-class boy in Port Clinton, than he does with Desmond, a black upper-middle-class boy in suburban Atlanta. This is not to say that race does not matter for children's outcomes; as we saw in Atlanta, both Desmond (upper-middle-class) and Elijah (working-class) face harmful prejudice and discrimination in their schools and neighborhoods. However, Desmond's mother's *class-based* parenting practices—intervening in institutions, thoughtfully building cognitive skills and self-confidence from early childhood, and even monitoring how Desmond dressed when he left the house—sheltered him from many of the harsh realities experienced by Elijah on a daily basis.

During the interview process, we often reflected on what we might be missing. Early on, when we realized that many working-class dads were absent from our story, Jen purposely interviewed two working-class fathers who were no longer in touch with their children in order to understand, rather than demonize, their inability to parent. In order to get a fuller picture of the communities we studied, we added additional informants to our mix: community leaders, school committee members, directors of nonprofits, even homeless kids living in a shelter. While we do not draw upon these interviews directly, their knowledge and insight shaped our analysis of our results.

Our sampling method—recruiting from workplaces, schools, and recreation venues—means that we did not encounter the few exceptionally successful working-class kids—those who triumphed over all odds and made it to a top university. On the other hand the most alienated and detached young people in these communities—those who don't work, don't go to school, and don't participate in communal leisure activities, those who are homeless, on the run, or in prison—also escaped our net. In fact, every one of the lower-class kids featured in this book has obtained a high school degree (or GED), whereas roughly one in four of all kids from poor backgrounds nationwide fail to make it that far up the educational ladder, and thus our sample omits that lower quartile of poor kids. Far from being cherry-picked to exaggerate the plight of poor kids in America, *the heartbreaking stories of poor kids in this book actually understate the tragic life experiences of those on the very bottom of our society*, the most deprived of American kids.

With one exception, we have not sought comments from our respondents on any of the stories in this book. The exception involves the life stories of Bob's classmates, who will (despite all our precautions) be easily identifiable to many people in Port Clinton. For that reason we sometimes sought their reactions to our renditions of their stories, though no one suggested substantively significant deletions or revisions.

Our Quantitative Research

To test whether Bob's recollections or other verbal accounts of Port Clinton in the 1950s and 1960s were biased by golden memories of yesteryear, and whether our in-depth stories of Don, Frank, Libby, Jesse, and Cheryl were representative of the entire class, in 2012 we conducted a written, anonymous survey of the entire class of 1959, then roughly aged 71.

Of the original graduating class of 150, by 2012, 26 were known to be deceased and 14 were untraceable (many of whom were likely also deceased). Of the 110 members whom we asked to complete the survey, 75 (68 percent) did so. Of those who did not, we estimate that about 15 were in failing health and thus unable to complete the survey, so a reasonable estimate is that three quarters of the original class members who could complete the survey actually did so.

Fortunately, we have some crucial information for *all* members of the class of 1959, including gender, race, class rank, and (from the high school yearbook) a full record of participation in sports and other extracurricular activities, including academic clubs and awards. We were thus able to conduct an exhaustive analysis to see whether our survey sample was biased in any demographic, academic, or other ways, compared to the full graduating class. The short, simple answer is that the survey sample was remarkably representative. Female achievers in both academics and extracurriculars were faintly overrepresented in the final sample, but not in any degree that would call into question the basic results; in all other ways, our survey sample appears virtually identical to the set of class members whom we failed to reach because of death, illness, untraceability, or simple refusal.

We conducted yet another probe of the representativeness of the sample, by seeking to track down two dozen students who had been members of the class of 1959 at some point but did not graduate with the class. Although the response rate for this group was unsurprisingly lower, we did complete surveys with eight of them, virtually all of whom in fact completed high school elsewhere. Thus, although we know of a few members of the class of 1959 who entered PCHS as freshmen but failed to complete high school, those dropouts were not numerous enough to bias any of the inferences that we have drawn from this survey.

In addition to a few open-ended questions about recollections of Port Clinton in the 1950s, the PCHS class of 1959 survey posed detailed, closed-ended questions about the respondents' family background, their experiences growing up, both in school and out, and their educational and occupational attainment and those of their spouses and children. In Chapter 1 we used results from the survey to describe social, economic, and familial conditions in Port Clinton in the 1950s. The central analytic questions of our statistical analysis involved social mobility—to what extent were the attainments of the class of 1959 predictable from their family background, and what factors mediated or moderated intergenerational inheritance of socioeconomic status.

Although we explored various indices of socioeconomic status, of both parents and children, by far the most robust and reliable patterns involved educational attainment, so our analysis of social mobility relied heavily on that measure: To what degree were the eventual educational attainments of the members of the class of 1959 predictable from their parents' education? (Since our conclusion is that intergenerational mobility was relatively high, using education as our measure is methodologically conservative; if we had used measures of economic affluence, for example, intergenerational mobility would have appeared even greater.)

As reported in Chapter 1, the results were surprisingly clear and simple:

- Academic achievement (as measured by class rank) was reasonably predictive of college attendance.

- Less educated parents were modestly less likely to encourage their kids to attend college, and parental encouragement in turn was modestly important in determining college attendance. That pattern (much weaker than the comparable link between class rank and college attendance) was virtually the only link between parental background and the children's eventual achievement.

- No other measure of parental affluence or family structure or neighborhood social capital (or indeed anything else that we had measured)—none of the factors that this book has shown are so important in producing today's opportunity gap—had any appreciable effect on college attendance or other educational attainment.

Multivariate models (path diagrams) laying out these results are available at www.robertdputnam.com/ourkids/research.

A few notes may be helpful for statistical mavens, though these brief comments are necessarily generic and will not satisfy all professional curiosity.

- All correlational analyses in the book have been run with standard demographic controls.

- All trends reported in this book are based on nationally representative samples, including all races. In virtually all cases, however, we have carried out identical analyses for whites only, and (where sample sizes permitted) for nonwhites only. These additional analyses confirmed in all essential cases that the trends do *not* simply reflect racial patterns, but are (at least in part) class-based.

- The growth of the opportunity gaps that appear in the scissors charts in this book is statistically significant in every case. In most such charts the trend lines have been LOESS-smoothed to reduce the visual impact of "noise" in the annual measures.

- Our central claims here concern trends in class disparities in the resources available to young Americans and in their achievements. We sometimes present cross-sectional data, however, that merely show class disparities at one point in time—today—without showing how those disparities have changed over time. The reason for this lacuna is simple: In such cases we have been unable to find any comparable evidence from earlier decades. For example, our data on mentoring today show massive class differences in access to mentors, but we know of no comparable data from earlier years on informal mentoring, so we have no quantitative evidence on how class differences might have changed, though we do refer to qualitative evidence on this point.

Finally, we have used a wide variety of publically available national datasets to conduct the analyses and construct the charts that appear in this book. A comprehensive overview of the datasets that we used is available at http://www.robertdputnam.com/ourkids/research.

Acknowledgments

FOR MANY YEARS CREATIVE, ENERGETIC SCHOLARS HAVE cultivated the fields of scholarship on whose results this book has relied. As a newcomer to the topics of social stratification, social mobility, and inequality, I have drawn heavily on their hard work and shrewd insights. Many have befriended me personally in the course of my research, but others I know only through their publications. As our country gathers itself to confront the opportunity gap, one fundamental national asset is this large and diverse corps of engaged experts on social and economic inequality.

Any list of names will be marred by unintentional omission, but entirely omitting names would be even worse. In addition to all those whose work is cited in the endnotes, this roster of experts includes Chris Avery, Jeanne Brooks-Gunn, Raj Chetty, Sheldon Danziger, Greg Duncan, Susan Dynarski, Kathy Edin, Paula England, Robert Frank, Frank Furstenberg, Claudia Goldin, David Grusky, Jennifer Hochschild, Michael Hout, Christopher Jencks, Lawrence Katz, Lane Kenworthy,

Glenn Loury, Douglas Massey, Sara McLanahan, Richard Murnane, Katherine Newman, Sean Reardon, Richard Reeves, Robert Sampson, Isabel Sawhill, Patrick Sharkey, Jack Shonkoff, Mario Small, Timothy Smeeding, Betsey Stevenson, Jane Waldfogel, Bruce Western, and William Julius Wilson.

Many friends and colleagues contributed to this book by offering insights and encouragement and commenting on successive drafts. In addition to some people whose contributions were noted in the previous paragraph, this group includes Joel Aberbach, Robert Axelrod, John Bridgeland, John Carr, Jonathan Cohn, Matthew Desmond, Ronald Ferguson, Matt Gillman, John Gomperts, David Halpern, Ross Hammond, Diana Hess, Nannerl Keohane, Robert Keohane, Gary King, Meira Levinson, Chaeyoon Lim, Michael McPherson, Dick Ober, Christin Putnam, Jonathan Putnam, Lara Putnam, Paul Solman, Luke Tate, Elsie Taveras, Dennis Thompson, and Mary Waters. Given all this expertise, I alone am clearly responsible for errors that remain in this book.

I am most indebted to the scores of parents and young adults who so generously entrusted us with the details of their lives. Their voices bravely told of the burdens and opportunities facing young people today and helped bring the statistical trends to life. Unfortunately, professional ethics and our strict commitment to anonymity preclude us from thanking them by name. Indeed, in most cases even I do not know their real names, so carefully did we guard their identities. But without their voices I would be dumb.

As described in "The Stories of Our Kids," Jen Silva was the star of our field research team, with help from Jasmin Sandelson. In each site they drew on the knowledge and contacts of generous local observers, to each of whom we are grateful. These include: in Alabama, David Joyner and Stephen Woerner; in Atlanta, Lawrence Phillips; in Austin, Joseph Kopser; in Bend, Abby Williamson and the late Melissa Hochschild; in Duluth, Holly Sampson; in Orange County, Paul Vandeventer; in Ohio, Ginny Park, Connie Cedoz, Gerri Gill, Jack Nitz, Jan Gluth, Chris Galvin, Pat Adkins, Gary Steyer, Don Sauber, Lori Clune, Darrell Opfer, Lawrence

Hartlaub, Paul Beck, Zack Paganini, Nathaniel Weidenhoft, Tiffany Perl, Maureen Bickley, and my classmates of the class of 1959; and in Philadelphia, Kathy Edin, Melody Boyd, Jason Martin, and Tracie Blummer.

This research project began nearly a decade ago with an unusually perceptive undergraduate term paper by Rebekah Crooks (now Rebekah Crooks Horowitz). Rebekah's key insight was that while intense civic engagement was characteristic of her Harvard classmates, it was not characteristic of the working class kids in her high school. Though not convinced that she was right, I encouraged her to test her ideas on some empirical data, and in her subsequent senior thesis her insight proved more broadly true than even she had initially conceived. Rebekah herself moved on to a career in a different field, but with her blessing, my research team and I pursued her idea—at first in a somewhat desultory manner, I confess, but then with mounting interest and concern as we uncovered more and more evidence in support of her central hypothesis of a growing class gap among American youth.

This project became ever more thoroughly a team product, since I benefited from the extraordinary intelligence and commitment of a close-knit and dedicated group of predoctoral and postdoctoral researchers. Members of this group produced wide-ranging, detailed reviews of vast bodies of literature; they searched far and wide for relevant sources of data and then explored those data with the most sophisticated techniques available; and most important, they subjected every line of argument and every shaky inference to thoughtful scrutiny. I mostly followed their advice, but not always, so the mistakes that remain in this book are mine alone.

I've never worked with a sharper, more conscientious group of colleagues. This group includes Josh Bolian, Brielle Bryan, Brittany Butler, Anny Fenton, Reuben Finighan, Kate Glazebrook, Hope Harvey, Elizabeth Holly, Rachel Horn, Barbara Kiviat, Cyrus Motanya, Katie Roberts-Hull, Jasmin Sandelson, Lois Shea, Wolfgang Silbermann, Eric Stephen, Laura Tach, Brian Tomlinson, James Walsh, Edwenna Werner, and Matt Wright.

In the culminating three years of the research, the core team was composed of the fabulous five: Evrim Altintas, Carl Frederick, Jen Silva, Kaisa Snellman, and Queenie Zhu. These five scholars are already becoming recognized as young leaders in the field of inequality studies, and theirs will be names to be reckoned with in the years ahead. I am very grateful to have been able to learn from them as their careers took off. Without them, this book would not have been written.

A substantial research project like ours requires substantial financial support. In this case we benefited from a consortium of institutions who shared our view that a problem this fundamental to America's future required both a wide-angle lens (to encompass insights from multiple disciplines and perspectives) and a close-focus microscope (to explore the life experiences of individual kids, their families, and their communities). This roster of generous supporters includes the Spencer Foundation, the Rockefeller Brothers Fund, the W. K. Kellogg Foundation, the Ford Foundation, the Legatum Institute, the Markle Foundation, the William T. Grant Foundation, the Annie E. Casey Foundation, the Bill and Melinda Gates Foundation, the Carnegie Corporation of New York, the Corporation for National and Community Service, and the University of Manchester. Harvard's Kennedy School of Government (and particularly Dean David Ellwood and Executive Dean John Haigh) have been unfailingly supportive, frequently offering help to assure that the convoy stayed afloat and reached its destination.

A strong research team requires a strong leader. For nearly 20 years Tom Sander has played that role on successive projects with me. Virtually every analytic generalization in this book rests on research that he supervised or directly conducted. Tom combines terrific peripheral vision (spotting relevant work in distant fields), intense integrity (kicking every tire of every car on the lot to be sure that we were not selling junk), and personal commitment to a more just and peaceful world. He has diligently overseen our efforts to acquire financial support for this project. Tom also leads our efforts to develop solutions, not just name problems.

Kylie Gibson (and her equally terrific predecessor and still senior counselor to our team, Louise Kennedy Converse) has handled the administrative side of our operations with consummate conscientiousness, skill, and sensitivity. Moreover, she has been centrally involved in all aspects of this project—from strategizing to editing. (In another life she could be a professional editor or an air traffic controller.) She has also supervised the other administrative members of our team, including Ruth Reyes, Saebom Soohoo, Tara Tyrrell, and Blake Worrall.

Toby Lester edited every line of this book with admirable professionalism. It is better, more mellifluous, and above all, more succinct because of his skill and diligence. Bob Bender and his colleagues at Simon & Schuster have helped make the finished product something of which we are all proud. Rafe Sagalyn, my literary agent for nearly two decades, has once again provided good friendship, sage advice, and the professional expertise that has made him one of the most widely admired people in the business. Anne Mellor and Peter Cerroni helped keep me sound in mind and body, while gracefully enduring my endless chatter about the plight of poor kids in America.

Lew Feldstein, a dear friend and mentor for more than two decades, is also one of the outstanding civic leaders in America. (He served for many years as head of the New Hampshire Charitable Foundation.) Lew pressed me ceaselessly to undertake this project, even when I had doubts about whether I could carry it off. He masterminded our search for financial support for the project, and he urged us to develop actionable ideas that might help civic activists narrow the opportunity gap. As many others have said, Lew is a real mensch.

My family has long been gracefully tolerant of my professional preoccupations, but on this project they became much more involved in the substance of the research. My two children (Jonathan and Lara), their partners (Christin, Doug, and Mario), and my seven grandchildren (Miriam, Gray, Gabriel, Noah, Alonso, Gideon, and Eleanor Wren) joined in lively, lengthy discussions of the challenges of growing up and raising kids in contemporary America. Because the group includes several budding social scientists and talented writers, they offered much useful advice in the writing of this book. And they muted the usual trash-talking when the performance of my team in our family fantasy football league plummeted during the writing of this book. (Wait 'til next year!) More seriously, what we learned during this project about less fortunate families made us all aware of the privileges and pleasures that we as a family enjoy.

Rosemary, the true social capitalist in the family, has made a career of teaching and nurturing kids—both in our own family and in the wider community. (She lives by the motto posted in our kitchen: "One hundred years from now, it won't matter . . . how much I had in my bank account. . . . But the world may be a little better because I was important in the life of a child.") Her role in this research project has far exceeded her role in my previous books. When she mentored a pair of troubled young women in our home town, or when she tutored home-less kids in a neighboring town, she brought home insights that appear in these pages. She read every word of every field interview that appears here, and she helped Jen Silva and me make sense of these young lives. She also read every word of this book many times, as the manuscript moved from rough outline to page proofs. For more than 50 years, I've been indebted to her in ways beyond words.

Notes

For the full, alphabetical bibliography, please visit http://www.robertdputnam.com/ourkids/research.

Chapter 1: The American Dream: Myths and Realities

1. Chrissie Hynde, "My City Was Gone," The Pretenders, *Learning to Crawl*, Sire Records, October 1982. Thanks to Harold Pollack for this citation.
2. Richard Ellmann, *James Joyce* (Oxford: Oxford University Press, 1965), 520. Thanks to James Walsh for this citation.
3. I'm indebted to Professor William Galston for this information.
4. *Daily News*, Port Clinton, OH, June 2, 1959, 1.
5. The life stories in this book change names to minimize intrusions into our respondents' privacy, though all of those who spoke with us have given permission to retell their stories. Except for that change of name, no other facts have been altered.
6. She also bowled in a Thursday night league.

7. The generalizations and statistics in this chapter come from a 2012 survey of surviving members of the class of 1959, as well as statistical and archival research into the recent history of Port Clinton and of surrounding Ottawa County.

8. A partial exception is that unlike the women of my class, who (as I discuss later) often dropped out of college to get married, their daughters typically finished college once they started.

9. Statistically speaking, only 16 percent of variance in educational attainment in the class of 1959 was associated with parental education, and that was almost entirely explicable by differences in parental encouragement. Net of parental encouragement, *no measure of economic or social privilege had any detectable effect on educational attainment*—not parental socioeconomic status, not parental unemployment, not family economic insecurity, not the student's need to work, not homeownership, not family structure, and not neighborhood characteristics. We have confirmed this basic pattern with the Wisconsin Longitudinal Study of all 1957 high school graduates in Wisconsin, the only other comparable dataset that we have found for the 1950s, so this remarkable degree of social mobility seems not to have been unique to Port Clinton. See http://www.ssc.wisc.edu/wlsresearch/.

10. More than 60 percent of the women in my class say even now that their educational and occupational choices in life were "not at all limited" by their gender.

11. Isabel Wilkerson, *The Warmth of Other Suns: The Epic Story of America's Great Migration* (New York: Random House, 2010).

12. On changing racial, gender, and class inequality, see Douglas S. Massey, *Categorically Unequal: The American Stratification System* (New York: Russell Sage Foundation, 2007).

13. Kendra Bischoff and Sean F. Reardon, "Residential Segregation by Income, 1970–2009," in *Diversity and Disparities: America Enters a New Century,* ed. John Logan (New York: Russell Sage Foundation, 2014), https://www.russellsage.org/publications/diversity-and-disparities, and Richard V. Reeves and Isabel V. Sawhill, "Equality of Opportunity: Definitions, Trends, and Interventions," prepared for the Conference on Inequality of Economic Opportunity, Federal Reserve Bank of Boston

(Boston, October 2014), http://www.bostonfed.org/inequality2014 /agenda/index.htm.

14. I rely on county data when no historical data are available that separate city and county; where we have both city and county data, there are no significant differences in trend and only minor differences in level. On factory closings in northwestern Ohio in the last two decades, see the excellent three-part series by Joe Vardon, "Shut Down and Shipped Out," *Toledo Blade*, September 26–28, 2010.

15. Based on student eligibility for free and reduced price lunch in Port Clinton schools, as reported in Ohio Department of Education, Office for Safety, Health and Nutrition, LUNCH MR 81 Report, ftp://ftp.ode .state.oh.us/MR81/.

16. In 2013 I published an op-ed about Port Clinton, entitled "Crumbling American Dreams," *New York Times* (August 3, 2013). A subsequent lively discussion in Port Clinton accelerated earlier efforts to begin to reverse the growing opportunity gap in town. By late 2014 the Port Clinton school system was singled out by the state of Ohio for its successful efforts to raise the test scores of low-income third-graders, while the local United Way, led by Chris Galvin, had begun a series of very promising child care and mentoring initiatives. Whether these efforts will be sustained is still uncertain, but they illustrate that it is possible to focus civic energy and creativity in a small town in ways that would be much harder in larger communities.

17. In other words, this book focuses on intergenerational mobility, not intra-generational mobility.

18. Benjamin I. Page and Lawrence R. Jacobs, *Class War? What Americans Really Think About Economic Inequality* (Chicago: University of Chicago Press, 2009). Scholars disagree about the degree to which Americans favor equality of outcomes, but all agree that equality of opportunity is a virtually universally shared value. See Jennifer L. Hochschild, *What's Fair?: American Beliefs About Distributive Justice* (Cambridge: Harvard University Press, 1981); Larry M. Bartels, *Unequal Democracy: The Political Economy of the New Gilded Age* (Princeton: Princeton University Press, 2008); Katherine S. Newman and Elisabeth S. Jacobs, *Who Cares?: Public Ambivalence and Government Activism from the New Deal to the*

Second Golden Age (Princeton: Princeton University Press, 2010); and Leslie McCall, *The Undeserving Rich: American Beliefs About Inequality, Opportunity, and Redistribution* (Cambridge: Cambridge University Press, 2013). See Andrew Kohut and Michael Dimock, "Resilient American Values: Optimism in an Era of Growing Inequality and Economic Difficulty," report for the Council on Foreign Relations (May 2013), accessed August 29, 2014, http://www.cfr.org/united-states/resilient -american-values/p30203, for evidence that "Americans' core values and beliefs about economic opportunity, and the nation's economic outlook, remain largely optimistic and unchanged."

19. Page and Jacobs, *Class War?*, 57–58.

20. Kay Lehman Schlozman, Sidney Verba, and Henry E. Brady, *The Unheavenly Chorus: Unequal Political Voice and the Broken Promise of American Democracy* (Princeton: Princeton University Press, 2012), 55–56.

21. Pew Economic Mobility Project Poll 2011. In fact, lower-income Americans are slightly more likely to give priority to equality of opportunity over equality of outcome. Of course, as many Americans understand, no such choice is strictly necessary in the real world, and later in this book we will explore how addressing inequality of outcome in one generation may be a prerequisite for addressing inequality of opportunity in the next. See McCall, *The Undeserving Rich*.

22. Ben S. Bernanke, "The Level and Distribution of Economic Well-Being," remarks before the Greater Omaha Chamber of Commerce, Omaha, NE (February 6, 2007), accessed August 29, 2014, http://www .federalreserve.gov/newsevents/speech/bernanke20070206a.htm.

23. Frederick Jackson Turner, *The Frontier in American History* (Tucson: University of Arizona Press, 1986; orig. pub., 1920), 212.

24. David M. Potter, *People of Plenty: Economic Abundance and the American Character* (Chicago: University of Chicago Press, 1969; orig. pub., 1954), 91–94.

25. That pattern corresponds to the distinctive pattern of American public spending compared to Europe, for we spend more on education and less on welfare state redistribution. See Anthony King, "Ideas, Institutions and the Policies of Governments: A Comparative Analysis: Parts I and II," *British Journal of Political Science* 3 (July 1973): 291–313; and Irwin

Garfinkel, Lee Rainwater, and Timothy Smeeding, *Wealth and Welfare States: Is America a Laggard or Leader?* (Oxford: Oxford University Press, 2010).

26. Richard Weiss, *The American Myth of Success: From Horatio Alger to Norman Vincent Peale* (New York: Basic Books, 1969), 33.

27. Precise figures depended on specific wording of the question, and the charts show some ups and downs, but no evidence of a clear long-term trend.

28. Page and Jacobs, *Class War?*; McCall, *The Undeserving Rich*. Page and Jacobs (p. 51) report that in 2007 three quarters of us believed that "it's still possible to start out poor in this country, work hard, and become rich." On the other hand, Gallup (as cited in McCall, p. 182) reported that the fraction of Americans "satisfied with the opportunity for a person in this nation to get ahead by working hard" fell from 76 percent in 2001 to 53 percent in 2012. Moreover, a poll in 2014 found that "only roughly 4-in-10 (42%) Americans say that the American Dream—that if you work hard, you'll get ahead—still holds true today, [whereas] nearly half of Americans (48%) believe that the American Dream once held true but does not anymore," while "most Americans (55%) believe that one of the biggest problems in the country is that not everyone is given an equal chance to succeed in life." Robert P. Jones, Daniel Cox and Juhem Navarro-Rivera, "Economic Insecurity, Rising Inequality, and Doubts About the Future: Findings from the 2014 American Values Survey," Public Religion Research Institute (PRRI), Washington, DC, September 23, 2014, at http://publicreligion.org/site/wp-content/up loads/2014/09/AVS-web.pdf.

29. Claudia Goldin and Lawrence F. Katz, "Decreasing (and then Increasing) Inequality in America: A Tale of Two Half-Centuries," in *The Causes and Consequences of Increasing Income Inequality*, ed. Finis Welch (Chicago: University of Chicago Press, 2001), 37–82.

30. Massey, *Categorically Unequal*, 5.

31. This general pattern applies both to personal income and to family income and to income before and after taxes. The growth in income inequality reflected not simply that some people had good years, and others bad years, but the emergence of the stably rich at the top and

the stably poor at the bottom. Inequality in wealth was even greater in absolute terms than inequality in income, but the increase in inequality after the great reversal of the 1970s was greater for income than for wealth. Claudia Goldin and Lawrence F. Katz, "The Future of Inequality: The Other Reason Education Matters So Much," *Milken Institute Review* (July 2009): 28. See also Anthony B. Atkinson, Thomas Piketty, and Emmanuel Saez, "Top Incomes in the Long Run of History," *Journal of Economic Literature* 49 (March 2011): 3–71, http://eml .berkeley.edu/~saez/atkinson-piketty-saezJEL10.pdf; Emmanuel Saez, "Striking it Richer: The Evolution of Top Incomes in the United States," 2013, accessed November 12, 2014, http://eml.berkeley.edu /~saez/saez-UStopincomes-2012.pdf; Emmanuel Saez and Thomas Piketty, "Income Inequality in the United States, 1913–1998," *Quarterly Journal of Economics* 118 (2013): 1–39; Massey, *Categorically Unequal.*

32. U.S Census Bureau, "Historical Income Tables: Households," Table H-4, accessed August 30, 2014, http://www.census.gov/hhes/www /income/data/historical/household/, cited in Jennifer Hochschild and Vesla Weaver, "Class and Group: Political Implications of the Changing American Racial and Ethnic Order" (paper prepared for Inequality Seminar, Harvard Kennedy School, March 26, 2014).

33. Testimony of Robert Greenstein, Executive Director, Center on Budget and Policy Priorities, prepared for the Subcommittee on Labor, Health and Human Services, Education, and Related Agencies, House Committee on Appropriations (February 13, 2008), citing Congressional Budget Office data.

34. David H. Autor, "Skills, Education, and the Rise of Earnings Inequality Among the 'Other 99 Percent,'" *Science* 344, 6186 (May 23, 2014): 843–851.

35. Emmanuel Saez, "Striking It Richer: The Evolution of Top Incomes in the United States (Updated with 2012 preliminary estimates)" (Econometrics Laboratory working paper, September 3, 2013), accessed August 30, 2014, http://eml.berkeley.edu/~saez/saez-UStopincomes-2012.pdf. The computations are family market pretax income including realized capital gains; incomes deflated using the Consumer Price Index.

36. Similar trends are visible in many (but not all) other advanced nations. See "An Overview of Growing Income Inequalities in OECD Countries: Main Findings" in *Divided We Stand: Why Inequality Keeps Rising*, OECD, 2011, http://www.oecd.org/els/soc/49499779.pdf. A useful recent overview of the facts and consequences of growing economic inequality in the United States compared to other advanced countries is Lane Kenworthy and Timothy Smeeding, "The United States: High and Rapidly-Rising Inequality," in *Changing Inequalities and Societal Impacts in Rich Countries: Thirty Countries' Experiences*, eds. Brian Nolan et al., (Oxford: Oxford University Press, 2014), 695–717.

37. Edward N. Wolff, *Top Heavy: A History of Increasing Inequality of Wealth in America and What Can Be Done About It* (New York: New Press, 2002); Edward N. Wolff, "Wealth Inequality," in *State of the Union: The Poverty and Inequality Report* (Stanford Center on Poverty and Inequality, January 2014); Michael Hout, "The Correlation Between Income and Happiness Revisited" (unpublished manuscript, 2013); Jennifer Karas Montez and Anna Zajacova, "Explaining the Widening Education Gap in Mortality Among U.S. White Women," *Journal of Health and Social Behavior* 54 (June 2013): 166–82.

38. Claude S. Fischer and Greggor Mattson, "Is America Fragmenting?," *Annual Review of Sociology* 35 (2009): 437. Measuring the growing segregation is in each case plagued by methodological complexities, but the basic facts are clear enough.

39. Bischoff and Reardon, "Residential Segregation by Income, 1970–2009"; Richard Fry and Paul Taylor, "The Rise of Residential Segregation by Income," *Pew Social and Demographic Trends* (Pew Research Center, August 1, 2012), accessed August 31, 2014, http://www.pewsocialtrends .org/2012/08/01/the-rise-of-residential-segregation-by-income/; Paul A. Jargowsky, "Concentration of Poverty in the New Millennium: Changes in Prevalence, Composition, and Location of High Poverty Neighborhoods," report by the Century Foundation and Rutgers Center for Urban Research and Education (2013), accessed August 21, 2014, http://tcf.org/assets /downloads/Concentration_of_Poverty_in_the_New_Millennium.pdf.

40. Susan E. Mayer, "How Did the Increase in Economic Inequality Between 1970 and 1990 Affect Children's Educational Attainment?,"

American Journal of Sociology 107 (July 2012): 1–32; Michael N. Bastedo and Ozan Jaquette, "Running in Place: Low-Income Students and the Dynamics of Higher Education Stratification," *Educational Evaluation and Policy Analysis* 33 (September 2011): 318–39; Caroline M. Hoxby and Christopher Avery, "The Missing 'One-Offs': The Hidden Supply of High-Achieving, Low Income Students," NBER Working Paper No. 18586 (Cambridge: National Bureau of Economic Research, December 2012).

41. Robert D. Mare, "Educational Assortative Mating in Two Generations: Trends and Patterns Across Two Gilded Ages" (unpublished manuscript, January 2013). Although I speak loosely here of the two "halves" of the century, in fact the turning point, both for intermarriage rates and for income inequality, came around 1970.

42. This is true even after accounting for the rising number of well-educated potential mates from which to pick. See Christine R. Schwartz and Robert D. Mare, "Trends in Educational Assortative Marriage from 1940 to 2003," *Demography* 42 (November 2005): 621–46; and Feng Hou and John Myles, "The Changing Role of Education in the Marriage Market: Assortative Marriage in Canada and the United States Since the 1970s," *Canadian Journal of Sociology* 33 (2008): 337–66.

43. For some evidence that our most intimate confidants are becoming more homogeneous in educational terms, see Jeffrey A. Smith, Miller McPherson, and Lynn Smith-Lovin, "Social Distance in the United States: Sex, Race, Religion, Age, and Education Homophily Among Confidants, 1985 to 2004," *American Sociological Review* 79 (June 2014): 432–56. For evidence that de facto segregation by education is increasing in the workplace, see Michael Kremer and Eric Maskin, "Wage Inequality and Segregation by Skill," NBER Working Paper No. 5718 (Cambridge: National Bureau of Economic Research, August 1996). Theda Skocpol, *Diminished Democracy: From Membership to Management in American Civic Life* (Norman: University of Oklahoma Press, 2003), has made a powerful case that civic organizations no longer bring together people from different social and economic backgrounds as once they did.

44. Jacob A. Riis, *How the Other Half Lives: Studies Among the Tenements of New York* (New York: Charles Scribner's Sons, 1890).

45. Michael Hout, "Economic Change and Social Mobility," in *Inequalities of the World*, ed. Göran Therborn (New York: Verso, 2006); Elton F. Jackson and Harry J. Crockett, Jr., "Occupational Mobility in the United States: A Point Estimate and Trend Comparison," *American Sociological Review* 29 (February 1964): 5–15; Peter M. Blau and Otis Dudley Duncan, *The American Occupational Structure* (New York: John Wiley, 1967); David L. Featherman and Robert M. Hauser, *Opportunity and Change* (New York: Academic Press, 1978); Robert M. Hauser and David L. Featherman, "Trends in the Occupational Mobility of U.S. Men, 1962–1970," *American Sociological Review* 38 (June 1973): 302–10; Massey, *Categorically Unequal*.

46. Stephan Thernstrom, *Poverty and Progress: Social Mobility in a Nineteenth Century City* (Cambridge: Harvard University Press, 1964); Stephan Thernstrom, *The Other Bostonians: Poverty and Progress in the American Metropolis, 1880–1970* (Cambridge: Harvard University Press, 1973); Avery M. Guest, Nancy S. Landale, and James L. McCann, "Intergenerational Occupational Mobility in the Late 19th Century United States," *Social Forces* 68 (December 1989): 351–78; Joseph P. Ferrie, "The End of American Exceptionalism? Mobility in the United States Since 1850," *Journal of Economic Perspectives* 19 (Summer 2005): 199–215; David B. Grusky, "American Social Mobility in the 19th and 20th Centuries," *CDE Working Paper 86–28* (Madison: Center for Demography and Ecology, University of Wisconsin–Madison, September 1986), accessed August 31, 2014, http://www.ssc.wisc.edu/cde/cdewp/86–28.pdf.

47. Emily Beller and Michael Hout, "Intergenerational Social Mobility: The United States in Comparative Perspective," *Future of Children* 16 (Fall 2006): 19–36; Michael Hout and Alexander Janus, "Educational Mobility in the United States Since the 1930s," in *Whither Opportunity? Rising Inequality, Schools, and Children's Life Chances*, eds. Greg J. Duncan and Richard J. Murnane (New York: Russell Sage Foundation, 2011).

48. Daniel Aaronson and Bhashkar Mazumder, "Intergenerational Economic Mobility in the United States, 1940 to 2000," *Journal of Human Resources* 43 (Winter 2008): 139–72; and Bhashkar Mazumder, "Is Intergenerational Economic Mobility Lower Now than in the Past?," *Chicago Fed Letter 297* (Federal Reserve Bank of Chicago, April 2012),

found evidence that relative mobility increased into the 1950s, but then declined at an accelerating rate for cohorts born in the second half of the twentieth century. By contrast, Raj Chetty, Nathaniel Hendren, Patrick Kline, Emmanuel Saez, and Nicholas Turner, "Is the United States Still a Land of Opportunity? Recent Trends in Intergenerational Mobility," NBER Working Paper No. 19844 (Cambridge: National Bureau of Economic Research, January 2014), find virtually no change at all in relative mobility in recent years. The conclusion by Chetty and his colleagues rests on the unconventional methodological assumption that the annual income of people as young as 26 is a reliable indicator of their lifetime income. However, other research casts doubt on that assumption, since into their 30s offspring from upper-class backgrounds may be obtaining advanced education or getting started in a professional career (and thus earning relatively little compared to their lifetime income), whereas at the same age kids from lower-class backgrounds are more apt to be stuck in dead-end jobs for life. In his mid-20s my son (a law clerk at that time) had an income roughly one fifth of mine, and on Chetty's method, my son would count as an example of dramatic downward mobility. However, by his mid-40s my son's income as a senior lawyer in Manhattan was roughly five times mine, definitely not an example of downward mobility. Because of this potential "life cycle bias," most scholars of social mobility advise restricting the analysis to people aged 40 and older, thus generating the "rearview mirror" problem described in the text. On this point, see Bhashkar Mazumder, "Fortunate Sons: New Estimates of Intergenerational Mobility in the United States Using Social Security Earnings Data," *The Review of Economics and Statistics* 87 (May 2005): 235–55; Steven Haider and Gary Solon, "Life-Cycle Variation in the Association Between Current and Lifetime Earnings," *American Economic Review* 96 (September 2006): 1308–20; and Pablo A. Mitnik, Victoria Bryant, David B. Grusky, and Michael Weber, "New Estimates of Intergenerational Mobility Using Administrative Data," SOI Working Paper (Washington DC: Statistics of Income Division, Internal Revenue Service, 2015). If these latter experts are correct, then it is premature to judge the lifetime mobility of the young people on whom our research focuses.

49. Our approach to estimating future mobility by looking at class differences at various life stages of young people today echoes the approaches pioneered by Timothy M. Smeeding, *From Parents to Children: The Intergenerational Transmission of Advantage* (New York: Russell Sage Foundation, 2012) and the Social Genome project directed by Isabel Sawhill, Ron Haskins, and Richard Reeves of the Brookings Institution, http://www.brookings.edu/about/centers/ccf/social-genome-project.

50. For a thorough overview of the literature on social class, see eds. David B. Grusky with Katherine Weisshaar, *Social Stratification: Class, Race, and Gender in Sociological Perspective* (Boulder: Westview, 2014). David B. Grusky, Timothy M. Smeeding, and C. Matthew Snipp, eds., "Monitoring Social Mobility in the Twenty-First Century," *ANNALS of the American Academy of Political and Social Science* 657 (January 2015), esp. Richard Reeves, "The Measure of a Nation," 22–26; Michael Hout, "A Summary of What We Know about Social Mobility," 27–36; and Florencia Torchek, "Analyses of Intergenerational Mobility: An Interdisciplinary Review," 37–62.

51. Massey, *Categorically Unequal*, 252.

Chapter 2: Families

1. The following account of Bend's past and present is drawn from a lengthy unpublished report, "Social Capital, Diversity, and Inequality: Community Field Studies, Final Report on Bend, Oregon," by Dr. Abigail Fisher Williamson, completed in June 2008 and based on nearly 50 interviews with civic leaders, civic activists, and other residents conducted in several visits between 2002 and 2006, as well as extensive exploration of newspaper and statistical archives. The quotations of Bend residents on pp. 48–49 are drawn from this report. The contemporary life stories were collected in lengthy interviews conducted by Dr. Jennifer M. Silva in 2012. For points in this paragraph, see Williamson report, p. 3, drawing on *The Bulletin* (Bend, Oregon).

2. To the casual visitor Bend and Port Clinton (described in Chapter 1) appear utterly different—Bend booming, Port Clinton busted. In the early 1970s, Ottawa County in Ohio and Deschutes County in Oregon

had virtually identical populations (~39,000), but four decades later Deschutes County had a population almost four times (~158,000) that of Ottawa County (41,000). At a deeper level, however, both represent a trend toward local income inequality between rich newcomers (retirees and vacation home owners and the developers and others who serve them) and poor old-timers (manual workers who have lost jobs in the dying timber and manufacturing industries). The cross-site similarities in the relative circumstances of rich kids and poor kids suggest that that class contrast is not tied, ultimately, to a single type of local economy.

3. Because of the housing boom Bend was hard hit by the Great Recession. Named in a 2007 report by National City Corp. (now PNC) and Global Insight (now IHS Global Insight) as "the most overpriced housing market in America," during 2009 it experienced the largest price drop in the nation, with house prices falling by almost half (47 percent) between 2006 and 2011 and unemployment in Deschutes County reaching 17 percent, but by 2013 recovery was well under way, especially in the housing market. Data from Zillow, accessed February 27, 2014, http://www.zillow.com/; and United States Department of Labor, Bureau of Labor Statistics, *Labor Force Statistics from the Current Population Survey*, accessed February 27, 2014, http://www.bls.gov/cps/home.htm.

4. In the aftermath of the crash of 2008 youth unemployment rose sharply from 11 percent in 2007 to 19 percent at the time of our interviews in Bend in 2012. "Youth Unemployment Rises While Overall Rates Decline," *Oregon Public Broadcasting*, July 17, 2012, accessed February 27, 2014, http://www.opb.org/news/article/youth-unemployment-rises -while-overall-rates-decline/.

5. "The Story of a Decade," *The Bulletin* (Bend, Oregon), May 19, 2002, 114.

6. U.S. Census Bureau, American Community Survey, 2008–2012, as compiled by Social Explorer, accessed through Harvard University Library.

7. Jerry Casey, "State Releases High School Graduation Rates," *The Oregonian*, July 2, 2009, accessed February 27, 2014, http://www .oregonlive.com/education/index.ssf/2009/06/high_school_dropout_ rates.html#school.

8. Our account of trends in marriage and family structure draws heavily on the extraordinary work of historical and sociological synthesis produced by a remarkable group of scholars over the last decade or two. See eds. Maria J. Carlson and Paula England, *Social Class and Changing Families in an Unequal America* (Stanford: Stanford University Press, 2011); Andrew J. Cherlin, *The Marriage-Go-Round: The State of Marriage and the Family in America Today* (New York: Vintage, 2009); Frank F. Furstenberg, Jr., "Transitions to Adulthood: What We Can Learn from the West," *ANNALS of the American Academy of Political and Social Science* 646 (2013): 28–41; Sara McLanahan, "Diverging Destinies: How Children Are Faring Under the Second Demographic Transition," *Demography* 41 (2004): 607–27; and Sara McLanahan and Wade Jacobsen, "Diverging Destinies Revisited," in *Families in an Era of Increasing Inequality: Diverging Destinies*, eds. Paul R. Amato, Alan Booth, Susan M. McHale, and Jennifer Van Hook (New York: Springer, forthcoming 2015); Frank F. Furstenberg, "Fifty Years of Family Change: From Consensus to Complexity," *ANNALS of the American Academy of Political and Social Science* 654 (July 2014): 12–30; Wendy D. Manning, Susan L. Brown, and J. Bart Stykes, "Family Complexity Among Children in the United States," *ANNALS of the American Academy of Political and Social Science* 654 (July 2014): 48–65; Karen Benjamin Guzzo, "New Partners, More Kids: Multiple-Partner Fertility in the United States," *ANNALS of the American Academy of Political and Social Science* 654 (July 2014): 66–86. See also June Carbone and Naomi Cahn, *Marriage Markets: How Inequality Is Remaking the American Family* (New York: Oxford University Press, 2014).

9. Andrew J. Cherlin, "Demographic Trends in the United States: A Review of Research in the 2000s," *Journal of Marriage and Family* 72 (June 2010): 406.

10. Representative critics of this traditional marriage, especially from a feminist point of view, include Judith Stacey, *Unhitched: Love, Marriage, and Family Values from West Hollywood to Western China* (New York: New York University Press, 2011); Stephanie Coontz, *The Way We Never Were: American Families and the Nostalgia Trap* (New York: Basic Books, 2000); Nancy Chodorow, *The Reproduction of Mothering* (Berkeley:

University of California Press, 1978); Arlie Hochschild, *The Second Shift: Working Parents and the Revolution at Home* (New York: Avon, 1990); and John R. Gillis, *A World of Their Own Making: Myth, Ritual, and the Quest for Family Values* (Cambridge: Harvard University Press, 1996).

11. In the 1950s and 1960s, 52–60 percent of premarital pregnancies were resolved by a shotgun marriage, but by the early 1990s that had fallen to 23 percent, according to the U.S. Census Bureau, "Trends in Premarital Childbearing, 1930 to 1994," by Amara Bachu, *Current Population Reports* (Washington, DC, 1999), 23–197. For careful analysis of rates of premarital conception and shotgun marriage from (roughly speaking) the 1940s to the late 1970s, see Paula England, Emily Shafer, and Lawrence Wu, "Premarital Conceptions, Postconception ("Shotgun") Marriages, and Premarital First Births: Educational Gradients in U.S. Cohorts of White and Black Women Born 1925–1959," *Demographic Research* 27 (2012): 153–66. From roughly the late 1950s to the late 1970s, premarital conception among less educated white women rose from about 20 percent to about 30 percent, while the rate among white college grads remained steady at about 10 percent. Among black women, the equivalent changes were from about 50 percent to about 70 percent for less educated black women and from about 25 percent to about 35 percent for black college graduates. Among women who conceived before marriage, the rate of shotgun marriages fell over this period from about 65 percent to about 45–50 percent for white women and from about 30 percent to about 5–10 percent among black women.

12. Statistics for these claims:

- Premarital sex: The fraction of Americans who believed that premarital sex was "not wrong" doubled from 24 percent to 47 percent in the four years between 1969 and 1973 and then drifted upward through the 1970s to 62 percent in 1982. Robert D. Putnam and David E. Campbell, *American Grace* (New York: Simon & Schuster, 2010), 92–93.

- Shotgun marriages: In the 1960s roughly half (52 percent) of all brides were pregnant, whereas 20 years later, only one quarter (27 percent) were. Patricia H. Shiono and Linda Sandham Quinn,

"Epidemiology of Divorce," *Future of Children: Children and Divorce* 4 (1994): 17.

- Divorce: The annual divorce rate for married women aged 15–44 more than doubled between 1965 and 1980. Shiono and Quinn, "Epidemiology of Divorce," 17.

- Single-parent families: In the first half of the twentieth century most single-parent families were such because of the death of a parent, but that fraction sharply declined from the 1930s to the 1970s. Leaving orphans aside, the fraction of 16-year-olds living with two biological parents declined from 85 percent in the 1960s to 59 percent in the 1990s. David T. Ellwood and Christopher Jencks, "The Spread of Single-Parent Families in the United States Since 1960," in *The Future of the Family*, eds. Daniel Patrick Moynihan, Timothy M. Smeeding, and Lee Rainwater (New York: Russell Sage Foundation, 2004), 25–65.

13. George A. Akerlof, Janet L. Yellen, and Michael L. Katz, "An Analysis of Out-of-Wedlock Births in the United States," *Quarterly Journal of Economics* 11 (1996): 277–317.

14. Cherlin, *The Marriage-Go-Round*; David Popenoe, *War over the Family* (New Brunswick, NJ: Transaction, 2005); Paul R. Amato, "Institutional, Companionate, and Individualistic Marriages: Change over Time and Implications for Marital Quality," in *Marriage at the Crossroads: Law, Policy, and the Brave New World of Twenty-first-Century Families*, eds. Marsha Garrison and Elizabeth S. Scott (Cambridge: Cambridge University Press, 2012), 107–25; Robert N. Bellah, Richard Madsen, William M. Sullivan, Ann Swidler, and Steven M. Tipton, *Habits of the Heart: Individualism and Commitment in American Life* (Berkeley: University of California Press, 1985).

15. U.S. Department of Labor, Office of Policy Planning and Research, *The Negro Family: The Case for National Action*, by Daniel P. Moynihan (Washington, DC, 1965).

16. Landmark scholarly recognition was McLanahan, "Diverging Destinies."

17. Steven P. Martin, "Growing Evidence for a 'Divorce Divide'? Education and Marital Dissolution Rates in the U.S. Since the 1970s," working

paper (University of Maryland–College Park, 2005), accessed May 12, 2014, https://www.russellsage.org/sites/all/files/u4/Martin_Growing%20 Evidence%20for%20a%20Divorce%20Divide.pdf; Steven P. Martin, "Trends in Marital Dissolution by Women's Education in the United States," *Demographic Research* 15 (2006): 552; Frank F. Furstenberg, "Fifty Years of Family Change: From Consensus to Complexity," *AN-NALS of the American Academy of Political and Social Science* 654 (July 2014): 12–30.

18. For a careful summary of these studies, see Sara McLanahan and Christine Percheski, "Family Structure and the Reproduction of Inequalities," *Annual Review of Sociology* 34 (August 2008): 257–76.

19. An entire issue of the journal *Future of Children* is devoted to the issue of fragile families: "Fragile Families," *Future of Children* 20 (Fall 2010): 3–230. Also see Sara McLanahan, "Family Instability and Complexity After a Nonmarital Birth: Outcomes for Children in Fragile Families," in *Social Class and Changing Families in an Unequal America*, eds. Carlson and England, 108–33; Sara McLanahan and Irwin Garfinkel, "Fragile Families: Debates, Facts, and Solutions," in *Marriage at the Crossroads*, eds., Garrison and Scott, 142–69; McLanahan and Percheski, "Family Structure and the Reproduction of Inequalities," 257–76; Marcia J. Carlson, Sara S. McLanahan, and Jeanne Brooks-Gunn, "Coparenting and Nonresident Fathers' Involvement with Young Children After a Nonmarital Birth," *Demography* 45 (May 2008): 461–88; and Sara McLanahan, Laura Tach, and Daniel Schneider, "The Causal Effects of Father Absence," *Annual Review of Sociology* 39 (July 2013): 399–427.

20. Cherlin, *The Marriage-Go-Round.*

21. Figures 2.2 and 2.6 are drawn from McLanahan and Jacobsen, "Diverging Destinies Revisited." "High" education represents mothers in the top quartile of the education distribution; "low" education category represents mothers in the bottom quartile. Greg J. Duncan, Ariel Kalil, and Kathleen M. Ziol-Guest, "Increasing Inequality in Parent Incomes and Children's Schooling" (unpublished manuscript, October 2014) have recently shown that the class (income) gap in maternal age at any birth has grown even more rapidly than the class (income) gap in maternal age at first birth, so that Figure 2.2 understates the aggregate growth of the

class gap in maternal age for all children. Moreover, they find that this class gap in maternal age at birth now contributes roughly as much to the overall opportunity gap as the class gap in family structure.

22. Karen Guzzo and Krista K. Payne, "Intentions and Planning Status of Births: 2000–2010," *National Center for Family & Marriage Research*, FP-12-24 (Bowling Green State University, 2012). See also S. Philip Morgan, "Thinking About Demographic Family Difference: Fertility Differentials in an Unequal Society," in *Social Class and Changing Families in an Unequal America*, eds. Carlson and England, 50–67. Recent data show large and increasing differences by education and income in unintended fertility: Heather Boonstra et al., *Abortion in Women's Lives* (New York: Guttmacher Institute, 2006); Laurence B. Finer and Stanley K. Henshaw, "Disparities in Rates of Unintended Pregnancy in the United States, 1994 and 2001," *Perspectives on Sexual and Reproductive Health* 38 (2006): 90–96.

23. Kelly Musick et al., "Education Differences in Intended and Unintended Fertility," *Social Forces* 88 (2009): 543–72; Finer and Henshaw, "Disparities in Rates of Unintended Pregnancy in the United States, 1994 and 2001," 90–96; Paula England, Elizabeth Aura McClintock, and Emily Fitzgibbons Shafer, "Birth Control Use and Early, Unintended Births: Evidence for a Class Gradient," in *Social Class and Changing Families in an Unequal America*, eds. Carlson and England, 21–49; McLanahan, "Family Instability and Complexity After a Nonmarital Birth," 108–33.

24. Martin, "Growing Evidence for a 'Divorce Divide'?"

25. Zhenchao Qian, "Divergent Paths of American Families," in *Diversity and Disparities: America Enters a New Century*, ed. John Logan (New York: Russell Sage Foundation, 2014).

26. Cherlin, "Demographic Trends in the United States," 408.

27. Wendy D. Manning, "Trends in Cohabitation: Twenty Years of Change, 1972–2008," *National Center for Family & Marriage Research* FP-10-07 (2010), accessed April 18, 2014, http://www.bgsu.edu/content/dam/BGSU/college-of-arts-and-sciences/NCFMR/documents/FP/FP-10-07.pdf.

28. Kathryn Edin and Timothy Nelson, *Doing the Best I Can: Fathering in the Inner City* (Berkeley: University of California Press, 2013), 40.

29. McLanahan, "Family Instability and Complexity After a Nonmarital Birth," 117. See also Cherlin, "Demographic Trends in the United States," 408, for slightly lower estimates of the breakup rate of cohabiting parents.

30. Furstenberg, "Fifty Years of Family Change," 21.

31. Edin and Nelson, *Doing the Best I Can*.

32. McLanahan, "Family Instability and Complexity After a Nonmarital Birth"; Edin and Nelson, *Doing the Best I Can*; Kathryn Edin, Timothy Nelson, and Joanna Reed, "Daddy, Baby; Momma Maybe: Low-Income Urban Fathers and the 'Package Deal' of Family Life," in *Social Class and Changing Families in an Unequal America*, eds. Carlson and England, 85–107; Karen Benjamin Guzzo, "New Partner, More Kids: Multiple-Partner Fertility in the United States," *ANNALS of the American Academy of Political and Social Science* 654 (July 2014): 66–86.

33. Laura Tach, Kathryn Edin, Hope Harvey, and Brielle Bryan, "The Family-Go-Round: Family Complexity and Father Involvement from a Father's Perspective," *ANNALS of the American Academy of Political and Social Science*, 654 (July 2014): 169–84.

34. McLanahan and Percheski, "Family Structure and the Reproduction of Inequalities," 258–59.

35. Figure 2.5 includes both single mothers and single fathers. About 4 percent of children—most of them from lower-income backgrounds—are being raised primarily by their grandparents. We discuss this aspect of family structure in Chapter 3.

36. Finer and Henshaw, "Disparities in Rates of Unintended Pregnancy in the United States, 1994 and 2001"; Federal Interagency Forum on Child and Family Statistics, *America's Children: Key National Indicators of Well-Being, 2013*, "Births to Unmarried Women," accessed April 23, 2014, http://www.childstats.gov/americaschildren/famsoc2.asp.

37. "Trends in Teen Pregnancy and Childbearing," Office of Adolescent Health, U.S. Department of Health and Human Services, November 21, 2014, http://www.hhs.gov/ash/oah/adolescent-health-topics/repro ductive-health/teen-pregnancy/trends.html, as consulted December 1, 2014, citing B. E. Hamilton, J. A. Martin, M. J. K. Osterman, and S. C. Curtin, *Births: Preliminary Data for 2013* (Hyattsville, MD: National Center for Health Statistics, 2014), accessed November 14, 2014,

http://www.cdc.gov/nchs/data/nvsr/nvsr63/nvsr63_02.pdf; Pamela J. Smock and Fiona Rose Greenland, "Diversity in Pathways to Parenthood: Patterns, Implications, and Emerging Research Directions," *Journal of Marriage and Family* 72 (June 2010): 579; Furstenberg, "Fifty Years of Family Change." Teen births are often a precursor to later non-marital births, so teen births are worth worrying about, even though they are not a major contributor to the problems facing poor children. Marcia J. Carlson and Paula England, "Social Class and Family Patterns in the United States," in *Social Class and Changing Families in an Un-equal America*, eds. Carlson and England, 4–5.

38. McLanahan, "Diverging Destinies."
39. Suzanne M. Bianchi, John P. Robinson, and Melissa A. Milkie, *Changing Rhythms of American Family Life* (New York: Russell Sage Foundation, 2007); John F. Sandberg and Sandra L. Hofferth, "Changes in Children's Time with Parents: A Correction," *Demography* 42 (May 2005): 391–95.
40. Timothy M. Smeeding, "Public Policy, Economic Inequality, and Poverty: The United States in Comparative Perspective," *Social Science Quarterly* 86 (December 2005): 955–83; Sara McLanahan, "Fragile Families and the Reproduction of Poverty," *ANNALS of the American Academy of Political and Social Science* 621 (January 2009): 111–31; and Furstenberg, "Transitions to Adulthood," show that a similar class divergence in marriage patterns appears also in many advanced Western countries, though not to the same extent. "Multi-partner fertility" is much more common in the U.S., per Cherlin, *The Marriage-Go-Round*; and Furstenberg, "Transitions to Adulthood."
41. Cherlin, "Demographic Trends in the United States," 411–12.
42. Our analysis of the Monitoring the Future data archive. For an earlier and somewhat more optimistic analysis of these data through the 1990s, see Arland Thornton and Linda Young-Demarco, "Four Decades of Trends in Attitudes Toward Family Issues in the United States: The 1960s Through the 1990s," *Journal of Marriage and Family* 63 (November 2001): 1009–37.
43. Cherlin, "Demographic Trends in the United States," 404.
44. McLanahan and Percheski, "Family Structure and the Reproduction of Inequalities."

45. England, McClintock, and Shafer, "Birth Control Use and Early, Unintended Births."

46. Kathryn Edin and Maria J. Kefalas, *Promises I Can Keep* (Berkeley: University of California Press, 2005), summarized in Smock and Greenland, "Diversity in Pathways to Parenthood," 582–83.

47. Linda M. Burton, "Seeking Romance in the Crosshairs of Multiple-Partner Fertility: Ethnographic Insights on Low-Income Urban and Rural Mothers," *ANNALS of the American Academy of Political and Social Science* 654 (July 2014): 185–212.

48. Ruth Shonle Cavan and Katherine Howland Ranck, *The Family and the Depression* (Chicago: University of Chicago Press, 1938).

49. "The Great Depression," Eyewitness to History, accessed April 23, 2014, http://www.eyewitnesstohistory.com/snprelief1.htm; "The Human Toll," Digital History, accessed April 23, 2014, http://www.digitalhistory.uh .edu/disp_textbook.cfm?smtID=2&psid=3434. Matthew Hill, "Love in the Time of Depression: The Effect of Economic Downturns on the Probability of Marriage" (paper presented at UCLA, All-UC/Caltech Economic History Conference, April 22, 2011), accessed October 21, 2014, http://www.ejs.ucdavis.edu/Research/All-UC/conferences/2011 -spring/Hill_LoveDepression042011.pdf, confirms that local male joblessness in the 1930s had a strong negative effect on marriage rates, and reviews literature from other periods in American history reporting a similar negative relationship between hard times and marriage rates.

50. Glen H. Elder, Jr., *Children of the Great Depression: Social Change in Life Experience* (Boulder: Westview, 1999).

51. Phillips Cutright, "Illegitimacy in the United States: 1920–1968," from *Growth and the American Future,* Research Reports, vol. 1, *Demographic and Social Aspects of Population Growth,* eds. Charles F. Westoff and Robert Parke (Washington DC: US Government Printing Office, 1972), 381; Amara Bachu, *Trends in Premarital Childbearing: 1930 to 1994,* Current Population Reports (Washington, DC: U.S. Census Bureau, 1999), 23–197, accessed December 1, 2014, http://www.census.gov /prod/99pubs/p23-197.pdf.

52. Carlson and England, "Social Class and Family Patterns in the United States," 7.

53. For emphasis on other "behavioral" explanations, including differences in sexual initiation, use of contraception, self-efficacy, and the ability to self-regulate, see England, McClintock, and Shafer, "Birth Control Use and Early, Unintended Births."

54. For the argument that the pre-1996 welfare system encouraged family breakup, see Charles Murray, *Losing Ground: American Social Policy, 1950–1980* (New York: Basic Books, 1984); National Research Council, Robert A. Moffitt, ed., *Welfare, the Family, and Reproductive Behavior: Research Perspectives* (Washington, DC: National Academies Press, 1998); and McLanahan and Percheski, "Family Structure and the Reproduction of Inequalities," 263–64. Also relevant to this debate is the finding of Juho Härkönen and Jaap Dronkers, "Stability and Change in the Educational Gradient of Divorce: A Comparison of Seventeen Countries," *European Sociological Review* 22 (December 2006): 501–17, that more extensive welfare state policies are associated with *lower* divorce rates, *especially* among less educated couples, suggesting that welfare state generosity reduces strain on lower-income couples.

55. Jennifer Glass and Philip Levchak, "Red States, Blue States, and Divorce: Understanding the Impact of Conservative Protestantism on Regional Variation in Divorce Rates," *American Journal of Sociology* 119 (January 2014): 1002–46.

56. Nicole Shoenberger, "Young Men's Contact with Criminal Justice System," *National Center for Family & Marriage Research* FP-12-01, accessed April 24, 2012, http://www.bgsu.edu/content/dam/BGSU/college-of-arts-and-sciences/NCFMR/documents/FP/FP-12-01.pdf. See also Bryan L. Sykes and Becky Pettit, "Mass Incarceration, Family Complexity, and the Reproduction of Childhood Disadvantage," *ANNALS of the American Academy of Political and Social Science* 654 (July 2014): 127–49.

57. Becky Pettit and Bruce Western, "Mass Imprisonment and the Life Course: Race and Class Inequality in U.S. Incarceration," *American Sociological Review* 69 (2004): 151–69; Christopher Wildeman, "Parental Imprisonment, the Prison Boom, and the Concentration of Childhood Disadvantage," *Demography* 46 (2009): 265–80.

58. John Hagan and Holly Foster, "Intergenerational Educational Effects of Mass Imprisonment in America," *Sociology of Education* 85 (2012):

259–86. On the effects of parental incarceration on children's mental health, see Kristin Turney, "Stress Proliferation Across Generations? Examining the Relationship Between Parental Incarceration and Childhood Health," *Journal of Health and Social Behavior* 55 (September 2014): 302–19; and Sykes and Pettit, "Mass Incarceration, Family Complexity, and the Reproduction of Childhood Disadvantage.

59. For a careful summary of these studies, see McLanahan and Percheski, "Family Structure and the Reproduction of Inequalities."

60. Sara McLanahan and Gary Sandefur, *Growing Up with a Single Parent: What Hurts, What Helps* (Cambridge: Harvard University Press, 1994); Wendy Sigle-Rushton and Sara McLanahan, "Father Absence and Child Wellbeing: A Critical Review," in *The Future of the Family*, eds. Moynihan, Smeeding, and Rainwater; Paul R. Amato, "The Impact of Family Formation Change on the Cognitive, Social, and Emotional Well-Being of the Next Generation," *The Future of Children* 15 (Fall 2005): 75–96.

61. Sigle-Rushton and McLanahan, "Father Absence and Child Wellbeing."

62. Bruce J. Ellis et al., "Does Father Absence Place Daughters at Special Risk for Early Sexual Activity and Teenage Pregnancy?," *Child Development* 74 (May 2003): 801–21; Kathleen E. Kiernan and John Hobcraft, "Parental Divorce During Childhood: Age at First Intercourse, Partnership and Parenthood," *Population Studies* 51 (March 1997): 41–55; Susan Newcomer and J. Richard Udry, "Parental Marital Status Effects on Adolescent Sexual Behavior," *Journal of Marriage and Family* 49 (May 1987): 235–40; Sara McLanahan, "Father Absence and the Welfare of Children," in *Coping with Divorce, Single Parenting, and Remarriage: A Risk and Resiliency Perspective*, ed. E. Mavis Hetherington (Mahwah, NJ: Lawrence Erlbaum, 1999), 117–45; Arline T. Geronimus and Sanders Korenman, "The Socioeconomic Consequences of Teen Childbearing Reconsidered," *Quarterly Journal of Economics* 107 (November 1992): 1187–1214.

63. Furstenberg, "Fifty Years of Family Change"; Laura Tach, "Family Complexity, Childbearing, and Parenting Stress: A Comparison of Mothers' and Fathers' Experiences," *National Center for Family and Marriage Research* WP-12-09 (Bowling Green State University, 2012); McLanahan and Garfinkel, "Fragile Families," 142–69; Furstenberg, "Transitions

to Adulthood"; McLanahan, "Family Instability and Complexity After a Nonmarital Birth," 108–33; Edin and Nelson, *Doing the Best I Can*; Carlson and England, "Social Class and Family Patterns in the United States," 6.

64. Sara McLanahan and Christopher Jencks, "Was Moynihan Right?: What Happens to the Children of Unmarried Mothers," *Education Next* 15 (Spring 2015): 16–22; McLanahan, Tach, and Schneider, "The Causal Effects of Father Absence," 399–427. There is, by contrast, as yet little consistent evidence that children from single-parent families do less well in terms of obtaining a college education or higher adult income.

65. Isabel V. Sawhill, *Generation Unbound: Drifting into Sex and Parenthood Without Marriage* (Washington, DC: Brookings Institution Press, 2014), 6.

66. Raj Chetty, Nathaniel Hendren, Patrick Kline, and Emmanuel Saez, "Where Is the Land of Opportunity? The Geography of Intergenerational Mobility in the United States," NBER Working Paper No. 19843 (Cambridge: National Bureau of Economic Research, January 2014).

Chapter 3: Parenting

1. Frederick Allen, *Atlanta Rising: The Invention of an International City, 1946–1996* (Marietta, GA: Longstreet, 1996).

2. Alan Berube, "All Cities Are Not Created Unequal," *Metropolitan Opportunity Series,* Brookings Institution, February 20, 2014, accessed May 7, 2014, http://www.brookings.edu/research/papers/2014/02/cities -unequal-berube.

3. Robert D. Bullard, Glenn S. Johnson, and Angel O. Torres, "The State of Black Atlanta: Exploding the Myth of Black Mecca," *Environmental Justice Resource Center at Clark Atlanta University* (February 25, 2010), accessed May 7, 2014, http://www.ejrc.cau.edu/State_of_Black _Atlanta_Exploding_the_Myth_of_Black_Mecca.pdf.

4. Atlanta also attracted large numbers of Asian Americans and Latinos after 2000, though those groups are still much outnumbered in Atlanta by blacks and whites. For data in this paragraph, see "State of Metropolitan America: On the Front Lines of Demographic Transformation,"

Metropolitan Policy Program (Washington, DC: Brookings Institution, 2010), accessed September 19, 2014, http://www.brookings.edu/~ /media/research/files/reports/2010/5/09%20metro%20america/metro _america_report.pdf.

5. Data for 1970–1990 from David L. Sjoquist, ed., *The Atlanta Paradox* (New York: Russell Sage Foundation, 2000), 26, Table 2.5; data for 2000–2010 from the Atlanta Regional Commission, "Census 2010," accessed September 19, 2014, http://www.atlantaregional.com/File%20 Library/About%20Us/the%20region/county_census2010.xls.

6. U.S. Census Bureau data. In 2010, the median household income in the city of Atlanta was $76,106 for whites, more than three times the figure of $23,692 for blacks, by far the greatest racial disparity among the central cities of the top ten metro areas and indeed greater than in almost any other major American city.

7. From 1970 to 2010, the percentage of black families in Atlanta subsisting on less than $25,000 (in inflation-adjusted 2010 dollars) barely changed, slipping from 31 percent to 30 percent, whereas the percentage of black families with incomes over $100,000 more than doubled, rising from 6 percent to 13 percent. Data are from the author's analysis of Steven Ruggles, J. Trent Alexander, Katie Genadek, Ronald Goeken, Matthew B. Schroeder, and Matthew Sobek, *"Integrated Public Use Microdata Series: Version 5.0* [Machine-readable database]," (Minneapolis: University of Minnesota, 2010).

8. Raj Chetty, Nathaniel Hendren, Patrick Kline, and Emmanuel Saez, "Where Is the Land of Opportunity? The Geography of Intergenerational Mobility in the United States," NBER Working Paper No. 19843 (Cambridge: National Bureau of Economic Research, January 2014).

9. This family's census tract is roughly 25 percent black, with a child poverty rate of 7 percent. It is well-to-do, but it is not Buckhead.

10. Michelle's successive residences tell a revealing story about how Atlanta has been changing, and her place in that evolution.

   • As a preschooler she lived just south of the city of Atlanta. At that time the area was 50 percent black and 29 percent child poverty. Now it is 63 percent black and 53 percent child poverty.

- During elementary school she moved about 15 miles further south. In 2000 her census tract was 40 percent black and 18 percent child poverty. It is now 82 percent black and 25 percent child poverty. She lived there in the midst of that transition.

- As she entered high school her family moved another 22 miles further south. In 2000 the area was undeveloped and rural, 10 percent black and 4 percent child poverty. It is now 31 percent black and 21 percent child poverty.

Thus, her family has moved further and further south in the Atlanta metro area into areas that are becoming blacker and poorer, even as they escaped from places that have now become even blacker and even poorer.

11. Because Elijah's life trajectory has been so complicated, and because we were unable to interview any of the adults in his life, we are unable to reconstruct his neighborhoods with precision, but they were without exception heavily black and poor.

12. Because Simone later became so involved with her children's schooling, school officials became aware of her talents, and an elementary school principal in Georgia recruited her as a substitute special education teacher. She subsequently went on to get a master's degree and was recently named Teacher of the Year in the district.

13. It is impossible at a distance of 15 years and across cultural lines to establish what lay behind the five-year-old Michelle's distress, although the events occurred around the time that both her parents were repartnering, which Michelle and Lauren describe as the most stressful experience of their lives. Moreover, Stephanie was changing jobs, as well as husbands, so it seems likely that stress within the family was unusually high. Michelle would later be diagnosed with a variety of learning disabilities, which may have played some role in the earlier episode.

14. The term "concerted cultivation" comes from sociologist Annette Lareau, as I discuss later in this chapter.

15. This is not a typographical error. Within ten seconds, Elijah says both that he wanted James to pull the trigger and that he didn't.

16. This childhood chronicle of murders may sound incredible. However, in 1994 (the year that Elijah arrived as a three-year-old) New Orleans had

421 homicides, or more than one per day, most of them concentrated in the area where Elijah's grandparents lived—the highest annual homicide rate in any major American city in recent decades.

17. The firm Elijah briefly worked for was a direct sales company, sometimes alleged to be a scamlike operation exploiting ill-educated young workers.

18. Institute of Medicine, *From Neurons to Neighborhoods: The Science of Early Child Development*, eds. Jack P. Shonkoff and Deborah A. Phillips (Washington, DC: National Academies Press, 2000). This section relies heavily on the excellent selection of working papers and issue briefs compiled at the Center on the Developing Child at Harvard University, http://developingchild.harvard.edu/. I am grateful to the center's founding director, Professor Jack P. Shonkoff, M.D., for guidance and encouragement, though I remain solely responsible for this summary of the field. Other key citations include Paul Tough, *How Children Succeed: Grit, Curiosity, and the Hidden Power of Character* (New York: Houghton Mifflin Harcourt, 2012); Gary W. Evans and Michelle A. Schamberg, "Childhood Poverty, Chronic Stress, and Adult Working Memory," *The Proceedings of the National Academy of Sciences* 106 (April 21, 2009): 6545–49; James J. Heckman, "Skill Formation and the Economics of Investing in Disadvantaged Children," *Science* 312 (June 2006): 1900–1902; James J. Heckman, "An Effective Strategy for Promoting Social Mobility," *Boston Review* (September/October 2012); Eric I. Knudsen, James J. Heckman, Judy L. Cameron, and Jack P. Shonkoff, "Economic, Neurobiological, and Behavioral Perspectives on Building America's Future Workforce," *The Proceedings of the National Academy of Sciences* 103 (July 5, 2006): 10155–62; and Jack P. Shonkoff, Andrew S. Garner, The Committee on Psychosocial Aspects of Child and Family Health, Committee on Early Childhood, Adoption, and Dependent Care, and Section on Developmental and Behavioral Pediatrics, "The Lifelong Effects of Early Childhood Adversity and Toxic Stress," *Pediatrics* 129 (January 1, 2012): e232–46.

19. National Scientific Council on the Developing Child, "Young Children Develop in an Environment of Relationships," Center on the Developing Child Working Paper No. 1 (2004).

20. Marilyn Jager Adams, *Beginning to Read: Thinking and Learning About Print* (Cambridge: MIT Press, 1990); Kaisa Aunola, Esko Leskinen, Marja-Kristiina Lerkkanen, and Jari-Erik Nurmi, "Developmental Dynamics of Math Performance from Preschool to Grade 2," *Journal of Educational Psychology* 96 (December 2004): 699–713; Arthur J. Baroody, "The Development of Adaptive Expertise and Flexibility: The Integration of Conceptual and Procedural Knowledge," in *The Development of Arithmetic Concepts and Skills: Constructing Adaptive Expertise Studies,* ed. Arthur J. Baroody and Ann Dowker (Mahwah, NJ: Lawrence Erlbaum, 2003), 1–34; Herbert P. Ginsburg, Alice Klein, and Prentice Starkey, "The Development of Children's Mathematical Thinking: Connecting Research with Practice," in *Handbook of Child Psychology: Child Psychology and Practice*, 5th ed, Vol. 4, eds. Irving E. Sigel and Anne Renninger (New York: John Wiley and Sons, 1998), 401–76; Elizabeth P. Pungello, Janis B. Kupersmidt, Margaret R. Burchinal, and Charlotte J. Patterson, "Environmental Risk Factors and Children's Achievement from Middle Childhood to Early Adolescence," *Developmental Psychology* 32 (July 1996): 755–67; Hollis S. Scarborough, "Connecting Early Language and Literacy to Later Reading (Dis)Abilities: Evidence, Theory, and Practice," in *Handbook of Early Literacy Research*, eds. Susan B. Neuman and David K. Dickinson (New York: Guilford, 2001), 97–110; Stacy A. Storch and Grover J. Whitehurst, "Oral Language and Code-Related Precursors to Reading: Evidence from a Longitudinal Structural Model," *Developmental Psychology* 38 (November 2002): 934–47; Harold W. Stevenson and Richard S. Newman, "Long-term Prediction of Achievement and Attitudes in Mathematics and Reading," *Child Development* 57 (June 1986): 646–59; Grover J. Whitehurst and Christopher J. Lonigan, "Child Development and Emergent Literacy," *Child Development* 69 (June 1998): 848–72.

21. Tough, *How Children Succeed*; Walter Mischel, Yuichi Shoda, and Monica Larrea Rodriguez, "Delay of Gratification in Children," *Science* 244 (May 26, 1989): 933–38; Angela L. Duckworth and Martin E. P. Seligman, "Self-Discipline Outdoes IQ in Predicting Academic Performance of Adolescents," *Psychological Science* 16 (December 2005): 939–44; James J. Heckman, Jora Stixrud, and Sergio Urzua, "The Effects of

Cognitive and Noncognitive Abilities on Labor Market Outcomes and Social Behavior," *Journal of Labor Economics* 24 (July 2006): 411–82; Flavio Cunha and James Heckman, "The Technology of Skill Formation," *American Economic Review* 97 (May 2007): 31–47.

22. Center on the Developing Child, "Science of Neglect," InBrief Series, Harvard University, 1, accessed May 7, 2014, http://developingchild .harvard.edu/index.php/download_file/-/view/1340/.

23. Charles A. Nelson, Nathan A. Fox, and Charles H. Zeanah, *Romania's Abandoned Children: Deprivation, Brain Development, and the Struggle for Recovery* (Cambridge: Harvard University Press, 2014).

24. American Academy of Pediatrics, Early Brain and Childhood Development Task Force, "A Public Health Approach to Toxic Stress" (2011), accessed May 7, 2014, http://www.aap.org/en-us/advocacy-and-policy /aap-health-initiatives/EBCD/Pages/Public-Health-Approach.aspx.

25. Vincent J. Felitti et al., "Relationship of Childhood Abuse and Household Dysfunction to Many of the Leading Causes of Death in Adults: The Adverse Childhood Experiences (ACE) Study," *American Journal of Preventive Medicine* 14 (May 1998): 245–58; Vincent J. Felitti and Robert F. Anda, "The Relationship of Adverse Childhood Experiences to Adult Medical Disease, Psychiatric Disorders and Sexual Behavior: Implications for Healthcare," in *The Impact of Early Life Trauma on Health and Disease: The Hidden Epidemic*, eds. Vincent J. Felitti and Robert F. Anda (Cambridge: Cambridge University Press, 2010), 77–87.

26. Heckman, "An Effective Strategy for Promoting Social Mobility."

27. Gene H. Brody et al., "Is Resilience Only Skin Deep? Rural African Americans' Socioeconomic Status-Related Risk and Competence in Preadolescence and Psychological Adjustment and Allostatic Load at Age 19," *Psychological Science* 24 (July 2013): 1285–93.

28. "John Henry," accessed May 8, 2014, http://www.springsteenlyrics.com /lyrics/j/johnhenry.php.

29. Poor kids (<200% Federal Poverty Line): 4% parent death; 11% parent imprisoned; 10% saw parental physical abuse; 12% saw neighborhood violence; 10% mentally ill family member; 13% alcohol/drug problem family member. Not-poor kids (>400% FPL): 2%; 2%; 3%; 4%; 6%; 6%. Data from "National Survey of Children's Health," Data Resource

Center for Child and Adolescent Health, Child and Adolescent Health Measurement Initiative (2011/12).

30. Kirby Deater-Deckard, *Parenting Stress* (New Haven: Yale University Press, 2004); Keith Crnic and Christine Low, "Everyday Stresses and Parenting," in *Handbook of Parenting*, 2nd ed.: Vol. 5: *Practical Issues in Parenting*, ed. Marc H. Bornstein (Mahwah, NJ: Lawrence Erlbaum, 2002), 243–68, esp. 250.

31. Jeewook Choi, Bumseok Jeong, Michael L. Rohan, Ann M. Polcari, and Martin H. Teicher, "Preliminary Evidence for White Matter Tract Abnormalities in Young Adults Exposed to Parental Verbal Abuse," *Biological Psychiatry* 65 (February 2009): 227–34.

32. National Scientific Council on the Developing Child, *Excessive Stress Disrupts the Architecture of the Developing Brain: Working Paper 3* (2005/2014): 4, 6; Center on the Developing Child, "The Impact of Early Adversity on Children's Development," InBrief Series, Harvard University, accessed June 6, 2014, http://developingchild.harvard.edu /index.php/resources/briefs/inbrief_series/inbrief_the_impact_of_early _adversity/.

33. Ian C. G. Weaver, Nadia Cervoni, Frances A. Champagne, Ana C. D'Alessio, Shakti Sharma, Jonathan R. Seckl, Sergiy Dymov, Moshe Szyf, and Michael J. Meaney, "Epigenetic Programming by Maternal Behavior," *Nature Neuroscience* 7 (August 2004): 847–54. In fact, the Meaney research helped to call into question the hoary distinction between nature and nurture, since licking and grooming in one generation appears to be transmitted genetically to the next, but the epigenetic dimensions of the research are less immediately relevant to our interests here.

34. Philip A. Fisher, Megan R. Gunnar, Mary Dozier, Jacqueline Bruce, and Katherine C. Pears, "Effects of Therapeutic Interventions for Foster Children on Behavioral Problems, Caregiver Attachment, and Stress Regulatory Neural Systems," *Annals of the New York Academy of Sciences* 1094 (December 2006): 215–25.

35. Byron Egeland, "Taking Stock: Childhood Emotional Maltreatment and Developmental Psychopathology," *Child Abuse & Neglect* 33 (January 2009): 22–26. Egeland was building on the classic work in attachment

theory by Mary Ainsworth, "Attachment as Related to Mother-Infant Interaction," in *Advances in the Study of Behavior* (New York: Academic Press, 1979), 1–51.

36. Yann Algan, Elizabeth Beasley, Frank Vitaro, and Richard E. Tremblay, "The Long-Term Impact of Social Skills Training at School Entry: A Randomized Controlled Trial" (Paris: Centre National de la Recherche Scientifique, November 28, 2013). https://www.gate.cnrs.fr/IMG/pdf/MLES_14_nov_2013-1.pdf.

37. Gary W. Evans, "The Environment of Childhood Poverty," *American Psychologist* 59 (February/March 2004): 77–92 and works cited there; Jamie L. Hanson, Nicole Hair, Dinggang G. Shen, Feng Shi, John H. Gilmore, Barbara L. Wolfe, and Seth D. Pollack, "Family Poverty Affects the Rate of Human Infant Brain Growth," *PLOS ONE* 8 (December 2013), report that directly increasing the income of poor parents has measurable positive effects on children's cognitive performance and social behavior, strongly suggesting that the link between social class and child development is causal, not spurious.

38. S. J. Lupien, S. King, M. J. Meaney, and B. S. McEwen, "Can Poverty Get Under Your Skin? Basal Cortisol Levels and Cognitive Function in Children from Low and High Socioeconomic Status," *Development and Psychopathology* (2001): 653–76; G. W. Evans, C. Gonnella, L. A. Marcynyszyn, L. Gentile, and N. Salpekar, "The Role of Chaos in Poverty and Children's Socioemotional Adjustment," *Psychological Science* 16 (2005): 560–65.

39. Pilyoung Kim, Gary W. Evans, Michael Angstadt, S. Shaun Ho, Chandra S. Sripada, James E. Swain, Israel Liberzon, and K. Luan Phan, "Effects of Childhood Poverty and Chronic Stress on Emotion Regulatory Brain Function in Adulthood," *The Proceedings of the National Academy of Sciences* 110 (November 12, 2013): 18442–47.

40. Amedeo D'Angiulli, Anthony Herdman, David Stapells, and Clyde Hertzman, "Children's Event-Related Potentials of Auditory Selective Attention Vary with Their Socioeconomic Status," *Neuropsychology* 22 (May 2008): 293–300.

41. Hanson et al., "Family Poverty Affects the Rate of Human Infant Brain Growth."

42. For citations to the large body of evidence that maternal verbal interaction with children is strongly correlated with maternal education, see Erika Hoff, Brett Laursen, and Twila Tardif, "Socioeconomic Status and Parenting," in *Handbook of Parenting*, 2nd ed.: Vol. 2: *Biology and Ecology of Parenting*, ed. Marc H. Bornstein (Mahwah, NJ: Lawrence Erlbaum, 2002), 238–39.

43. Betty Hart and Todd R. Risley, *Meaningful Differences in the Everyday Experience of Young American Children* (Baltimore: Paul H. Brookes, 1995); Anne Fernald, Virginia A. Marchman, and Adriana Weisleder, "SES Differences in Language Processing Skill and Vocabulary Are Evident at 18 Months," *Developmental Science* 16 (March 2013): 234–48.

44. Greg J. Duncan and Richard J. Murnane, *Restoring Opportunity: The Crisis of Inequality and the Challenge for American Education* (New York: Russell Sage Foundation, 2014), 32.

45. Jeanne Brooks-Gunn, Flavio Cunha, Greg J. Duncan, James J. Heckman, and Aaron J. Sojourner, "A Reanalysis of the IHDP Program" (unpublished manuscript, Infant Health and Development Program, Northwestern University, 2006); Pedro Carneiro and James J. Heckman, "Human Capital Policy" in *Inequality in America: What Role for Human Capital Policies?*, eds. James J. Heckman, Alan B. Kruger, and Benjamin M. Friedman (Cambridge: MIT Press, 2003), 77–239.

46. Meredith L. Rowe, "Child-Directed Speech: Relation to Socioeconomic Status, Knowledge of Child Development and Child Vocabulary Skill," *Journal of Child Language* 35 (February 2008): 185–205.

47. Urie Bronfenbrenner, "Ecological Systems Theory," *in Annals of Child Development*, Vol. 6, ed. Ross Vasta (Greenwich, CT: JAI Press, 1989), 187–249; Sharon Hays, *The Cultural Contradictions of Motherhood* (New Haven: Yale University Press, 1996); Julia Wrigley, "Do Young Children Need Intellectual Stimulation? Experts' Advice to Parents, 1900–1985," *History of Education Quarterly* 29 (Spring 1989): 41–75; Maryellen Schaub, "Parenting for Cognitive Development from 1950 to 2000: The Institutionalization of Mass Education and the Social Construction of Parenting in the United States," *Sociology of Education* 83 (January 2010): 46–66.

48. Scott Coltrane, *Family Man: Fatherhood, Housework, and Gender Equity* (Oxford: Oxford University Press, 1996).

49. Various studies have used different measures of socioeconomic status (SES), including occupational status and income, but education (and especially mother's education) is by far the strongest SES predictor of differences in parenting.

50. Annette Lareau, *Unequal Childhoods: Class, Race, and Family Life; Second Edition, With an Update a Decade Later* (Berkeley: University of California Press, 2011). See also Jessica McCrory Calarco, "Coached for the Classroom: Parents' Cultural Transmission and Children's Reproduction of Educational Inequalities," *American Sociological Review* 79 (September 2009): 1015–37.

51. Hoff, Laursen, and Tardif, "Socioeconomic Status and Parenting," 231–52.

52. Hart and Risley, *Meaningful Differences in the Everyday Experience of Young American Children.* The three categories of parental socioeconomic status in Figure 3.2 come directly from Hart and Risley.

53. Kirby Deater-Deckard, *Parenting Stress* (New Haven: Yale University Press, 2004); Hoff, Laursen, and Tardif, "Socioeconomic Status and Parenting," 239; Ronald L. Simons, Les B. Whitbeck, Janet N. Melby, and Chyi-In Wu, "Economic Pressure and Harsh Parenting," in *Families in Troubled Times: Adapting to Change in Rural America,* eds. Rand D. Conger and Glen H. Elder, Jr. (New York: Aldine De Gruyter, 1994), 207–22; Rand D. Conger and M. Brent Donnellan, "An Interactionist Perspective on the Socioeconomic Context of Human Development," *Annual Review of Psychology* 58 (2007): 175–99.

54. Frank F. Furstenberg, Thomas D. Cook, Jacquelynne Eccles, Glen H. Elder, Jr., and Arnold Sameroff, *Managing to Make It: Urban Families and Adolescent Success* (Chicago: University of Chicago Press, 1999). Although Stephanie attributes parenting styles to race, in fact, the more important determinant is class.

55. Jane Waldfogel and Elizabeth Washbrook, "Income-Related Gaps in School Readiness in the United States and the United Kingdom," in *Persistence, Privilege, and Parenting: The Comparative Study of Intergenerational Mobility,* eds. Timothy M. Smeeding, Robert Erikson, and

Markus Jantti (New York: Russell Sage Foundation, 2011). Extracurricular involvement is discussed in Chapter 4.

56. Betty Hart and Todd R. Risley, "The Early Catastrophe: The 30 Million Word Gap by Age 3," *American Educator* 27 (Spring 2003): 4–9; Helen Raikes et al., "Mother-Child Bookreading in Low-Income Families: Correlates and Outcomes During the First Three Years of Life," *Development* 77 (July 2006): 924–53; Robert H. Bradley, Robert F. Corwyn, Harriette Pipes McAdoo, and Cynthia Garcia Coll, "The Home Environments of Children in the United States, Part II: Relations with Behavioral Development Through Age Thirteen," *Child Development* 72 (November 2001): 1868–86.

57. Jane Waldfogel and Elizabeth Washbrook, "Early Years Policy," *Child Development Research* 2011 (2011): esp. 5. See also other literature reviews cited there.

58. Jane Waldfogel, *What Children Need* (Cambridge: Harvard University Press, 2006), 161. For further confirmation, see Kelly Musick and Ann Meier, "Assessing Causality and Persistence in Associations Between Family Dinners and Adolescent Well-Being," *Journal of Marriage and Family* 74 (June 2012): 476–93.

59. This chart is based on the annual DDB Needham Life Style surveys described in Robert D. Putnam, *Bowling Alone: The Collapse and Revival of American Community* (New York: Simon & Schuster, 2000), 420–24. The question was simply agree or disagree: "Our whole family usually eats dinner together." Questions on family dinners have occasionally been asked in other surveys, such as the 2003 and 2007 National Surveys of Children's Health, but only in a few years and only since 2000, so they are much less useful in detecting long-term trends. Figure 3.3 is limited to parents with children under 18 at home and weighted to account for differences in single-parent and two-parent families.

60. Sabino Kornrich and Frank Furstenberg, "Investing in Children: Changes in Parental Spending on Children, 1972–2007," *Demography* 50 (February 2013): 1–23; Neeraj Kaushal, Katherine Magnuson, and Jane Waldfogel, "How Is Family Income Related to Investments in Children's Learning?," in *Whither Opportunity? Rising Inequality, Schools and*

Children's Life Chances, eds. Greg J. Duncan and Richard J. Murnane (New York: Russell Sage Foundation, 2011), 187–206.

61. Rand D. Conger, Katherine J. Conger, and Monica J. Martin, "Socio-economic Status, Family Processes, and Individual Development," *Journal of Marriage and Family* 72 (June 2010): 685–704, esp. 695.

62. Evrim Altintas, "Widening Education-Gap in Developmental Childcare Activities in the U.S.," *Journal of Marriage and Family* (forthcoming 2015), is the source of Figure 3.5. Unlike prior work on this topic, the data in Figure 3.5 have been adjusted to account for the very low time investment in child care by nonresidential fathers; since a large and growing fraction of kids in lower-education households are being raised by single mothers, this adjustment has a substantial effect on the size and growth of the class gap. For earlier work on this topic, see Garey Ramey and Valerie A. Ramey, "The Rug Rat Race," Brookings Papers on Economic Activity (Economic Studies Program, Brookings Institution, Spring 2010), 129–99; Meredith Phillips, "Parenting, Time Use, and Disparities in Academic Outcomes," in *Whither Opportunity? Rising Inequality, Schools and Children's Life Chances*, eds. Duncan and Murnane, 207–28; and Ariel Kalil, Rebecca Ryan, and Michael Corey, "Diverging Destinies: Maternal Education and the Developmental Gradient in Time with Children," *Demography* 49 (November 2012): 1361–83. The latter show that the education gap is largest in child care activities that are specifically important for a child's development at a particular age (play and basic care between ages 0–2, teaching/talking/reading between ages 3–5, and management/organizational activities between ages 6–13).

63. "Children with high-educated parents spend significantly less time watching TV and more time studying and reading compared to children of low-educated parents," Sandra L. Hofferth and John F. Sandberg, "How American Children Spend Their Time," *Journal of Marriage and Family* 63 (May 2001): 295–308; John F. Sandberg and Sandra L. Hofferth, "Changes in Children's Time with Parents: A Correction," *Demography* 42 (2005): 391–95; Suzanne M. Bianchi and John Robinson, "What Did You Do Today? Children's Use of Time, Family Composition, and the Acquisition of Social Capital," *Journal of Marriage and Family* 59 (May 1997): 332–44.

64. Jay Belsky et al., "Are There Long Term Effects of Early Child Care?," *Child Development* 78 (March 2007): 681–701; Peg Burchinal et al., "Early Care and Education Quality and Child Outcomes," Office of Planning, Research and Evaluation, U.S. Department of Health and Human Services (Washington, DC: OPRE Research to Policy Brief, 2009); Eric Dearing, Kathleen McCartney, and Beck A. Taylor, "Does Higher Quality Early Child Care Promote Low-Income Children's Math and Reading Achievement in Middle Childhood?," *Child Development* 80 (September 2009): 1329–49; Erik Ruzek, Margaret Burchinal, George Farkas, and Greg J. Duncan, "The Quality of Toddler Child Care and Cognitive Skills at 24 Months: Propensity Score Analysis Results from the ECLS-B," *Early Childhood Research Quarterly* 29 (January 2014): 12–21; Julia Torquati, Helen Raikes, Catherine Huddleston-Casas, James A. Bovaird, and Beatrice A. Harris, "Family Income, Parent Education, and Perceived Constraints as Predictors of Observed Program Quality and Parent Rated Program Quality," Nebraska Center for Research on Children, Youth, Families and Schools (Lincoln, NE: CYFS, 2011). Methodologists are steadily improving measures of day care quality and methods for dealing with selection bias (mothers who choose higher-quality day care may be better mothers in other respects, too, so we can't be sure it's the day care that matters). The summary given in the text is our best judgment, given all the evidence available today.

65. Lisa Gennetian, Danielle Crosby, Chantelle Dowsett, and Aletha Huston, "Maternal Employment, Early Care Settings and the Achievement of Low-Income Children," Next Generation Working Paper No. 30 (New York: MDRC, 2007).

66. "The State of Pre-School 2011: State Preschool Yearbook," National Institute for Early Education Research (Rutgers Graduate School of Education, 2011): 9, accessed May 13, 2014, http://nieer.org/sites/nieer/files/2011yearbook.pdf. See also Marcia K. Meyers, Dan Rosenbaum, Christopher Ruhm, and Jane Waldfogel, "Inequality in Early Childhood Education and Care: What Do We Know?," in *Social Inequality*, ed. Kathryn M. Neckerman (New York: Russell Sage Foundation, 2004).

67. Keith Crnic and Christine Low, "Everyday Stresses and Parenting," in *Handbook of Parenting*, 2nd ed.: Vol. 5: *Practical Issues in Parenting*, ed.

Bornstein, 243–68; Deater-Deckard, *Parenting Stress,* and sources cited there.

68. Figure 3.6 is based on DDB Needham Life Style data. Financial anxiety is measured by four agree-disagree statements: "No matter how fast our income goes up, we never seem to get ahead" (agree); "Our family is too heavily in debt today" (agree); "We have more to spend on extras than most of our neighbors do" (disagree); and "Our family income is high enough to satisfy nearly all our important desires" (disagree). Those who rank in the top quartile on this composite index across all years and respondents are shown as "high" in Figure 3.6.

69. This observation was made during a private meeting between the author, President and Mrs. Bush, and the president's senior advisors in March 2007.

70. Sendhil Mullainathan and Eldar Shafir, *Scarcity: Why Having Too Little Means So Much* (New York: Times Books, 2013), 156.

71. Rand D. Conger and Glen H. Elder, "Families in Troubled Times: The Iowa Youth and Families Project," in *Families in Troubled Times,* eds. Conger and Elder, 3–21; Miriam R. Linver, Jeanne Brooks-Gunn, and Dafina E. Kohen, "Family Processes as Pathways from Income to Young Children's Development," *Developmental Psychology* 38 (September 2002): 719–34; Elizabeth T. Gershoff et al., "Income Is Not Enough: Incorporating Material Hardship into Models of Income Associations with Parenting and Child Development," *Child Development* 78 (January 2007): 70–95; Rand D. Conger and Brent M. Donnellan, "An Interactionist Perspective on the Socioeconomic Context of Human Development," *Annual Review of Psychology* 58 (2007): 175–99; Rand D. Conger, Katherine J. Conger, and Monica J. Martin, "Socioeconomic Status, Family Processes, and Individual Development," *Journal of Marriage and Family* 72 (June 2010): 685–704, esp. 693.

72. Marsha Weinraub, Danielle L. Horvath, and Marcy B. Gringlas, "Single Parenthood," in *Handbook of Parenting,* 2nd ed.: Vol. 3: *Being and Becoming a Parent,* ed. Marc H. Bornstein (Mahwah, NJ: Lawrence Erlbaum, 2002), 109–40; E. Mavis Hetherington and Margaret Stanley-Hagan, "Parenting in Divorced and Remarried Families," in *Handbook of Parenting,* 2nd ed.: Vol. 3: *Being and Becoming a Parent,* ed. Bornstein,

287–315; Sarah McLanahan and Christine Percheski, "Family Structure and the Reproduction of Inequalities," *Annual Review of Sociology* 34 (2008): 268. See also cites in Greg J. Duncan, Kjetil Telle, Kathleen M. Ziol-Guest, and Ariel Kalil, "Economic Deprivation in Early Childhood and Adult Attainment: Comparative Evidence from Norwegian Registry Data and the U.S. Panel Study of Income Dynamics," in *Persistence, Privilege, and Parenting: The Comparative Study of Intergenerational Mobility*, eds. Timothy M. Smeeding, Robert Erikson, and Markus Jantti (New York: Russell Sage Foundation, 2011), 212; Ariel Kalil, Rebecca Ryan, and Elise Chor, "Time Investments in Children Across Family Structures," *ANNALS of the American Academy of Political and Social Science* 654 (July 2014): 150–68.

73. Teresa Toguchi Swartz, "Intergenerational Family Relations in Adulthood: Patterns, Variations, and Implications in the Contemporary United States," *Annual Review of Sociology* 35 (2009): 191–212. For trends on grandparents raising grandchildren, see Gretchen Livingston and Kim Parker, "Since the Start of the Great Recession, More Children Raised by Grandparents," Pew Research Social and Demographic Trends (September 9, 2010), accessed May 13, 2014, http://www.pewsocialtrends.org/2010/09/09/since-the-start-of-the-great-recession-more-children-raised-by-grandparents/; Gretchen Livingston, "At Grandmother's House We Stay," Pew Research Social and Demographic Trends (September 4, 2013), accessed May 13, 2014, http://www.pewsocialtrends.org/2013/09/04/at-grandmothers-house-we-stay/; Ye Luo, Tracey A. LaPierre, Mary Elizabeth Hughes, and Linda J. Waite, "Grandparents Providing Care to Grandchildren: A Population-Based Study of Continuity and Change," *Journal of Family Issues* 33 (September 2012): 1143; and Rachel E. Dunifon, Kathleen M. Ziol-Guest, and Kimberly Kopko, "Grandparent Coresidence and Family Well-Being: Implications for Research and Policy," *ANNALS of the American Academy of Political and Social Science* 654 (July 2014): 110–26.

74. David Elkind, *The Hurried Child: Growing Up Too Fast Too Soon* (Cambridge, MA: Perseus, 2001); Paul Tough, *How Children Succeed*.

75. Gary Evans, "The Environment of Childhood Poverty," *American Psychologist* 59 (2004): 77–92.

76. Hanson et al., "Family Poverty Affects the Rate of Human Infant Brain Growth"; Greg J. Duncan and Richard J. Murnane, *Restoring Opportunity: The Crisis of Inequality and the Challenge for American Education* (New York: Russell Sage Foundation, 2014), 30 and the sources cited there.

Chapter 4: Schooling

1. Demographic data from U.S. Census Bureau, as compiled by Social Explorer, accessed through Harvard University Library; Gustavo Arellano, *Orange County: A Personal History* (New York: Simon & Schuster, 2008), 13.

2. Orange County Community Indicators Project, *Orange County Community Indicators 2013* (Irvine, CA: 2013), accessed June 16, 2014, www.ocgov.com/about/infooc/facts/indicators.

3. Adam Nagourney, "Orange County Is No Longer Nixon Country," *New York Times*, August 29, 2010, accessed June 16, 2014, http://www.nytimes.com/2010/08/30/us/politics/30orange.html.

4. "Street Gangs in Santa Ana, CA," Streetgangs.com, accessed June 16, 2014, http://www.streetgangs.com/cities/santaana#sthash.rnESeLn4.dpbs.

5. U.S. Census Bureau, from Steven Ruggles, J. Trent Alexander, Katie Genadek, Ronald Goeken, Matthew B. Schroeder, and Matthew Sobek. Integrated Public Use Microdata Series: Version 5.0 [Machine-readable database] (Minneapolis: University of Minnesota, 2010).

6. All members of these two families are American citizens and all the children are native-born. Undocumented immigrants and their children obviously face additional challenges.

7. Fermin Leal and Scott Martindale, "OC's Best Public High Schools, 2012," *Orange County Register*, May 25, 2014, database accessed February 24, 2014, http://www.ocregister.com/articles/high-331705-college-schools.html?data=1&appSession=530132967931354. Rankings are generated from data taken from the California Department of Education. Calculations applied by the *Register*. Academics represent 50 percent of the school's rank, College and Career Prep 25 percent, and Environment 25 percent.

8. Hispanics in this neighborhood have a median household income of nearly $115,000, compared to $105,000 for their non-Hispanic neighbors. Fewer than 5 percent of the kids in this census tract are below the poverty line. All data from U.S. Census Bureau as compiled by Social Explorer, accessed through Harvard University Library.

9. Clara was also a star athlete, so she was able to support her college education in part with fellowship aid, as well as her part-time earnings as a coach and referee.

10. Uniform Crime Reporting Statistics, accessed November 18, 2014, http://www.ucrdatatool.gov/Search/Crime/Local/RunCrimeTrendsInOneVar Large.cfm.

11. Another young woman from a nearby high school echoed these descriptions of drugs and violence in classrooms and teachers whose lessons consisted of copying sentences out of tattered textbooks.

12. These two schools are not absolutely the extremes. As measured by the California state Academic Performance Index, Troy ranks at the 90th percentile and Santa Ana at the 20th percentile.

13. Horace Mann, *Twelfth Annual Report of Horace Mann as Secretary of Massachusetts State Board of Education* (Boston: Dutton & Wentworth, 1848). On the Common School movement, see David Tyack, "The Common School and American Society: A Reappraisal," *History of Education Quarterly* 26 (Summer 1986): 301–6; Joel Spring, *The American School, 1642–2004*, 6th ed. (New York: McGraw Hill, 2005); Sarah Mondale and Sarah B. Patton, eds., *School: The Story of American Public Education* (Boston: Beacon, 2002); and Michael B. Katz, *The Irony of Early School Reform: Educational Innovation in Mid-Nineteenth Century Massachusetts* (Cambridge: Harvard University Press, 1968).

14. Claudia Goldin, "America's Graduation from High School: The Evolution and Spread of Secondary Schooling in the Twentieth Century," *Journal of Economic History* 58 (June 1998): 345–74; Claudia Goldin and Lawrence F. Katz, *The Race Between Education and Technology* (Cambridge: Harvard University Press, 2008).

15. Scholars debate in detail both the goals and the consequences of these reforms. Leading voices include Edward Danforth Eddy, *Colleges for Our Land and Time: The Land-Grant Idea in American Education* (New York:

Harper, 1957); Mary Jean Bowman, "The Land-Grant Colleges and Universities in Human-Resource Development," *Journal of Economic History* (December 1962): 523–46; Colin Burke, *American Collegiate Populations: A Test of the Traditional View* (New York: New York University Press, 1982); Harold M. Hyman, *American Singularity: The 1787 Northwest Ordinance, the 1862 Homestead and Morrill Acts, and the 1944 GI Bill* (Athens: University of Georgia Press, 2008); Suzanne Mettler, *Soldiers to Citizens: The G.I. Bill and the Making of the Greatest Generation* (Oxford: Oxford University Press, 2005); Glenn C. Altschuler and Stuart M. Blumin, *The GI Bill: A New Deal for Veterans* (Oxford: Oxford University Press, 2009); and John R. Thelin, *A History of American Higher Education* (Baltimore: Johns Hopkins University Press, 2011).

16. David F. Labaree, "Public Goods, Private Goods: The American Struggle over Educational Goals," *American Educational Research Journal* 34 (Spring 1997): 39–81.

17. Sean F. Reardon, "The Widening Academic Achievement Gap Between the Rich and the Poor: New Evidence and Possible Explanations," in *Whither Opportunity? Rising Inequality, Schools, and Children's Life Chances*, eds. Greg J. Duncan and Richard M. Murnane (New York: Russell Sage Foundation, 2011). In contrast to many other measures of child development that I report in this book, Reardon finds that the growth of the class gap is most marked when class is defined in terms of parents' income, not parents' education, though the gap by parental education remains larger than the gap by parental income. The evidence summarized here refers to differences between kids from the 90th percentile of family income and the 10th percentile.

18. For an extensive discussion of the role of cognitive skills (as measured by achievement test scores) and noncognitive skills in predicting adult outcomes, see James J. Heckman, "Schools, Skills, and Synapses," *Economic Inquiry* 46 (July 2008): 289–324 and the sources cited there.

19. James J. Heckman, "Promoting Social Mobility," *Boston Review*, September 1, 2012, accessed June 16, 2014, http://www.bostonreview.net/forum /promoting-social-mobility-james-heckman. Heckman adds, "A similar pattern appears for socio-emotional skills. One measure of the development of these skills is the 'anti-social score'—a measure of behavior

problems. Once more, gaps open up early and persist. Again, unequal schools do not account for much of this pattern." Greg J. Duncan and Katherine Magnuson, "The Nature and Impact of Early Achievement Skills, Attention Skills, and Behavior Problems," in *Whither Opportunity? Rising Inequality, Schools, and Children's Life Chances*, eds. Duncan and Murnane, 57, however, suggest that class gaps in attention and behavior problems do grow during the elementary school years.

20. The summertime widening appears for class gaps, but not for racial gaps. David T. Burkam, Douglas D. Ready, Valerie E. Lee, and Laura F. LoGerfo, "Social-Class Differences in Summer Learning Between Kindergarten and First Grade: Model Specification and Estimation," *Sociology of Education* 77 (January 2004): 1–31; Douglas B. Downey, Paul T. von Hippel, and Beckett A. Broh, "Are Schools the Great Equalizer? Cognitive Inequality During the Summer Months and the School Year," *American Sociological Review* 69 (October 2004): 613–35; Dennis J. Condron, "Social Class, School and Non-School Environments, and Black/White Inequalities in Children's Learning," *American Sociological Review* 74 (October 2009): 683–708; David T. Burkam, "Educational Inequality and Children: The Preschool and Early School Years," in *The Economics of Inequality, Poverty, and Discrimination in the 21st Century*, ed. Robert S. Rycroft (Santa Barbara: Praeger, 2013), 381–97; Seth Gershenson, "Do Summer Time-Use Gaps Vary by Socioeconomic Status?," *American Educational Research Journal* 50 (December 2013): 1219–48; Flavio Cunha and James Heckman, "The Technology of Skill Formation," *American Economic Review* 97 (May 2007): 31–47; Heckman, "Promoting Social Mobility."

21. Kendra Bischoff and Sean F. Reardon, "Residential Segregation by Income, 1970–2009," in *Diversity and Disparities: America Enters a New Century*, ed. John Logan (New York: Russell Sage Foundation, 2014), https://www.russellsage.org/publications/diversity-and-disparities.

22. Joseph G. Altonji and Richard K. Mansfield, "The Role of Family, School, and Community Characteristics in Inequality in Education and Labor-Market Outcomes," in *Whither Opportunity? Rising Inequality, Schools, and Children's Life Chances*, eds. Duncan and Murnane, 339–58. James E. Ryan, *Five Miles Away, a World Apart: One City, Two Schools,*

and the Story of Educational Opportunity in Modern America (New York: Oxford University Press, 2010), reports that most children attend their neighborhood school, and even participants in school choice programs usually attend nearby schools.

23. Annette Lareau and Kimberly Goyette, eds., *Choosing Homes, Choosing Schools: Residential Segregation and the Search for a Good School* (New York: Russell Sage Foundation, 2014).

24. Jonathan Rothwell, "Housing Costs, Zoning, and Access to High-Scoring Schools," Brookings Institution (April 2012). Other estimates of the good schools bonus in housing prices are substantial. See Sandra E. Black and Stephen Machin, "Housing Valuations of School Performance," in *Handbook of the Economics of Education*, vol. 3, eds. Eric Hanushek, Stephen Machin, and Ludger Woessmann (Amsterdam: Elsevier, 2011), 485–519, accessed June 16, 2014, http://EconPapers.repec.org/RePEc:eee:educhp:3-10.

25. David M. Brasington and Donald R. Haurin, "Parents, Peers, or School Inputs: Which Components of School Outcomes Are Capitalized into House Value?," *Regional Science and Urban Economics* 39 (September 2009): 523–29.

26. Lareau and Goyette, eds., *Choosing Homes, Choosing Schools*. For conflicting views on whether school choice narrows class and racial gaps, see Mark Schneider, Paul Teske, and Melissa Marschall, *Choosing Schools: Consumer Choice and the Quality of American Schools* (Princeton: Princeton University Press, 2000); Tomeka M. Davis, "School Choice and Segregation: 'Tracking' Racial Equity in Magnet Schools," *Education and Urban Society* 46 (June 2014): 399–433.

27. Jaap Dronkers and Rolf van der Velden, "Positive but Also Negative Effects of Ethnic Diversity in Schools on Educational Performance? An Empirical Test Using PISA Data," in *Integration and Inequality in Educational Institutions*, Michael Windzio, ed. (Dordrecht: Springer, 2013), 71–98 and the works cited there.

28. Useful entryways to the massive literature on this topic include James S. Coleman et al., *Equality of Educational Opportunity* (Washington, DC: U.S. Department of Health, Education & Welfare, Office of Education, OE-38001, and supplement, 1966), 325; Gary Orfield and Susan

E. Eaton, *Dismantling Desegregation* (New York: New Press, 1996); Claude S. Fischer et al., *Inequality by Design: Cracking the Bell Curve Myth* (Princeton: Princeton University Press, 1996); Richard D. Kahlenberg, "Economic School Integration," in *The End of Desegregation*, eds. Stephen J. Caldas and Carl L. Bankston III (Hauppauge, NY: Nova Science, 2003), esp. 153–55; Russell W. Rumberger and Gregory J. Palardy, "Does Segregation Still Matter? The Impact of Student Composition on Academic Achievement in High School," *The Teachers College Record* 107 (September 2005): 1999–2045; John R. Logan, Elisabeta Minca, and Sinem Adar, "The Geography of Inequality: Why Separate Means Unequal in American Public Schools," *Sociology of Education* 85 (July 2012): 287–301; and for a comprehensive recent overview, Gregory J. Palardy, "High School Socioeconomic Segregation and Student Attainment," *American Educational Research Journal* 50 (August 2013): 714–54. Reyn van Ewijk and Peter Sleegers, "The Effect of Peer Socioeconomic Status on Student Achievement: A Meta-Analysis," *Educational Research Review* 5 (June 2010): 134–50, found that the effect of the socioeconomic composition of a child's classroom on his or her test scores is twice as large as the effect of the socioeconomic composition of his or her school. This entire line of research was stimulated in the 1960s by concerns about the effects of racial segregation, and in that era class segregation heavily overlapped with racial segregation. During the past half century, however, class segregation has grown, while racial segregation has diminished, and it is now possible to compare the adverse effects of racial and class segregation. While racial segregation continues to be a major national problem, virtually all relevant studies have concluded that class segregation is at least as pernicious in its effects on student achievement. See Richard D. Kahlenberg, "Socioeconomic School Integration," *North Carolina Law Review* 85 (June 2007): 1545–94.

29. As with any discussion of contextual effects, this literature is fraught with methodological issues, especially selection bias. For example, since poor kids are not randomly assigned to schools, something about those who end up in high-income schools may predispose them to higher achievement, quite apart from the schools or their fellow students. Douglas Lee Lauen and S. Michael Gaddis, "Exposure to Classroom

Poverty and Test Score Achievement: Contextual Effects or Selection?," *American Journal of Sociology* 118 (January 2013): 943–79. One recent study that addresses such concerns still finds a significant effect of school socioeconomic composition: Victor Lavy, Olmo Silma, and Felix Weinhardt, "The Good, the Bad, and the Average: Evidence on the Scale and Nature of Ability Peer Effects in Schools," NBER Working Paper No. 15600 (Cambridge: National Bureau of Economic Research, 2009).

30. The literature on school finance is massive and fraught with many controversies. Compare Eric A. Hanushek and Alfred A. Lindseth, *Schoolhouses, Courthouses, and Statehouses: Solving the Funding-Achievement Puzzle in America's Public Schools* (Princeton: Princeton University Press, 2009); and Rob Greenwald, Larry V. Hedges, and Richard D. Laine, "The Effect of School Resources on Student Achievement," *Review of Educational Research* 66 (Autumn 1996): 361–96.

31. Eric A. Hanushek, John F. Kain, and Steven G. Rivkin, "Why Public Schools Lose Teachers," *Journal of Human Resources* 39 (Spring 2004): 326–54.

32. Based on unpublished analyses by Carl Frederick of 2011–2012 data on school quality measures for 85 percent of all public K–8 and high schools in the country, as compiled and published in 2014 by the Office of Civil Rights of the U.S. Department of Education, available at http://ocrdata.ed.gov/. With controls for other potentially confounding variables, including the racial composition of the high school, the fraction of the student body eligible for free or reduced-price lunches, a widely used proxy for student poverty, is uncorrelated with the ratio of counselors to students and is *positively* correlated with more teachers per 100 students. This pattern is true of both high schools and K–8 schools.

33. Palardy, "High School Socioeconomic Segregation and Student Attainment," emphasizes school academic climate and peer influences as two key mediating factors between socioeconomic segregation and student attainment and provides a useful recent overview of this broad literature.

34. Anne T. Henderson and Nancy Berla, *A New Generation of Evidence: The Family Is Critical to Student Achievement* (Washington, DC: National Committee for Citizens in Education, 1994), 1. Other recent overviews of the vast literature on the effects of parental engagement

include William H. Jeynes, "The Relationship Between Parental Involvement and Urban Secondary School Student Academic Achievement: A Meta-Analysis," *Urban Education* 42 (January 2007): 82–110; Nancy E. Hill and Diana F. Tyson, "Parental Involvement in Middle School: A Meta-Analytic Assessment of the Strategies That Promote Achievement," *Developmental Psychology* 45 (May 2009): 740–63; William Jeynes, "A Meta-Analysis of the Efficacy of Different Types of Parental Involvement Programs for Urban Students," *Urban Education* 47 (July 2004): 706–42; Frances L. Van Voorhis, Michelle F. Maier, Joyce L. Epstein, and Chrishana M. Lloyd with Therese Leung, *The Impact of Family Involvement on the Education of Children Ages 3 to 8: A Focus on Literacy and Math Achievement Outcomes and Socio-Emotional Skills* (New York: MDRC, 2013), accessed June 16, 2014, http://www.mdrc.org/sites /default/files/The_Impact_of_Family_Involvement_FR.pdf; and Mikaela J. Dufur, Toby L. Parcel, and Benjamin A. McKune, "Does Capital at Home Matter More than Capital at School? The Case of Adolescent Alcohol and Marijuana Use," *Journal of Drug Issues* 43 (January 2013): 85–102. For a recent debate about whether parental involvement is overrated, see Keith Robinson and Angel L. Harris, *The Broken Compass: Parental Involvement with Children's Education* (Cambridge: Harvard University Press, 2014); and Mai Miksic, "Is Parent Involvement Really a Waste of Time? Recent Polemic Versus the Research Record," CUNY Institute for Education Policy (Policy Briefing, April 23, 2014), accessed June 16, 2014, http://ciep.hunter.cuny.edu/is-parent-involvement-really -a-waste-of-time-recent-polemic-versus-the-research-record/.

35. Kyle Spencer, "Way Beyond Bake Sales: The $1 million PTA," *New York Times*, June 3, 2012, MB1; Rob Reich, "Not Very Giving," *New York Times*, September 5, 2013, A25. Although we have found no trend data for parental giving to "public privates," according to the National Association of Independent Schools, median parental donations per private school rose 63 percent from $548,561 to $895,614 over the last decade. Jenny Anderson, "Private Schools Mine Parents' Data, and Wallets," *New York Times*, March 26, 2012.

36. Russell W. Rumberger and Gregory J. Palardy, "Test Scores, Dropout Rates, and Transfer Rates as Alternative Indicators of High School

Performance," *American Educational Research Journal* 42 (Spring 2005): 3–42; Palardy, "High School Socioeconomic Segregation and Student Attainment." Perhaps high-income schools need to spend less on remediation and discipline than low-income schools, allowing them to invest more in academically rigorous courses, though I have found no evidence on that issue.

37. See note 32 of this chapter. The division in Figures 4.1, 4.2, and 4.4 between the four levels of school poverty corresponds roughly to quartiles of the distribution of schools. A more detailed analysis suggests that the key determinant of AP offerings is parental income, not race; controlling for poverty, urbanism, school size, and other factors, heavily minority schools actually offer more AP courses than mostly white schools. Kids from more affluent homes are much more likely to take AP exams than kids from less affluent homes, but that class gap has shrunk over the past decade. College Board, "10th Annual AP Report to the Nation," February 11, 2014, 6. On the other hand, the incidence of gifted-and-talented programs is completely uncorrelated with school poverty in K–8 schools and slightly *higher* in high-poverty high schools.

38. See Palardy, "High School Socioecomic Segregation," 741–42, and the literature cited there, and Robert Crosnoe, *Fitting In, Standing Out: Navigating the Social Challenges of High School to Get an Education* (New York: Cambridge University Press, 2011).

39. Palardy, "High School Socioeconomic Segregation," esp. 735.

40. Greg J. Duncan and Richard J. Murnane, *Restoring Opportunity: The Crisis of Inequality and the Challenge for American Education* (New York: Russell Sage Foundation, 2014), esp. 47–49; Toby L. Parcel and Joshua A. Hendrix, "Family Transmission of Social and Cultural Capital," in *The Wiley Blackwell Companion to the Sociology of Families*, eds. Judith Treas, Jacqueline Scott, and Martin Richards (London: John Wiley and Sons, 2014), 374.

41. Scott E. Carrell and Mark L. Hoekstra, "Externalities in the Classroom: How Children Exposed to Domestic Violence Affect Everyone's Kids," *American Economic Journal: Applied Economics* 2 (January 2010): 211–28.

42. David S. Kirk and Robert J. Sampson, "Crime and the Production of Safe Schools," in *Whither Opportunity? Rising Inequality, Schools, and Children's Life Chances*, eds. Duncan and Murnane.

43. Simone Roberts, Jana Kemp, Jennifer Truman, and Thomas D. Snyder, *Indicators of School Crime and Safety: 2012* (Washington, DC: National Center for Education Statistics, 2013), accessed June 16, 2014, http://nces.ed.gov/pubs2013/2013036.pdf. We have not found any statistical breakdown of gang presence or school violence by school poverty rates.

44. See note 32 of this chapter. In a multivariate analysis, the suspension rate is predicted by a school's poverty rate, black enrollment, urban setting, and large size. As with any measure of discipline, it is impossible to tell from the suspension data alone how much is due to underlying misbehavior and how much to disciplinary standards, but surveys of students themselves, as well as the reports from Lola and Sofia, make it implausible that the pattern in Figure 4.2 is entirely due to disciplinary discrimination.

45. Greg J. Duncan and Katherine Magnuson, "The Nature and Impact of Early Achievement Skills, Attention Skills, and Behavior Problems," in *Whither Opportunity? Rising Inequality, Schools, and Children's Life Chances,* eds. Duncan and Murnane, 65.

46. John Rogers and Nicole Mirra, *It's About Time: Learning Time and Educational Opportunity in California High Schools* (Los Angeles: Institute for Democracy, Education, and Access, University of California, Los Angeles, 2014).

47. Raj Chetty, John N. Friedman, and Jonah E. Rockoff, "The Long-Term Impacts of Teachers: Teacher Value-Added and Student Outcomes in Adulthood," NBER Working Paper No. 17699 (Cambridge: National Bureau of Economic Research, 2011), accessed June 16, 2014, http://www.nber.org/papers/w17699; Martin Haberman and William H. Rickards, "Urban Teachers Who Quit: Why They Leave and What They Do," *Urban Education* 25 (October 1990): 297–303; Hanushek, Kain, and Rivkin, "Why Public Schools Lose Teachers," 326–54; Donald Boyd, Hamilton Lankford, Susanna Loeb, and James Wyckoff, "Explaining the Short Careers of High-Achieving Teachers in Schools with Low-Performing Students," *American Economic Review* 95 (May 2005): 166–71; Palardy, "High School Socioeconomic Segregation and Student Attainment"; Duncan and Murnane, *Restoring Opportunity,* 49–50; Eric A. Houck, "Intradistrict Resource Allocation: Key Findings and Policy Implications," *Education and Urban Society* 43 (May 2011): 271–95.

48. George Farkas, "Middle and High School Skills, Behaviors, Attitudes, and Curriculum Enrollment, and Their Consequences," in *Whither Opportunity? Rising Inequality, Schools, and Children's Life Chances,* eds. Duncan and Murnane (2011), 84–85. Our analysis of data from the annual nationwide "Monitoring the Future" survey of high school seniors shows that while the fraction of students from college-educated homes who are on a college-prep track has remained steady at about 60 percent from 1976 to 2012, the fraction of students from high-school-educated homes in the college-prep track has risen steadily from 30 percent to more than 40 percent. In short, while a tracking gap remains, it has narrowed by about one third during the same period that other measures of the opportunity and achievement gap have sharply widened. Ability grouping within elementary school classrooms seems to have increased in the last decade or so, but we have found no evidence that this grouping disadvantages kids from poorer backgrounds. Tom Loveless, "The Resurgence of Ability Grouping and Persistence of Tracking: Part II of the 2013 Brown Center Report on American Education," Brookings Institution Report, Brown Center on Education Policy, 2013, accessed October 3, 2014, http://www.brookings.edu/research/reports/2013/03/18 -tracking-ability-grouping-loveless; Courtney A. Collins and Li Ga, "Does Sorting Students Improve Scores? An Analysis of Class Composition," NBER Working Paper No. 18848 (Cambridge: National Bureau of Economic Research, 2013).

49. National Center for Education Statistics, "Advance Release of Selected 2013 Digest Tables, Table 201.20: Enrollment in Grades 9 through 12 in Public and Private Schools Compared with Population 14 to 17 Years of Age: Selected Years, 1889–90 through Fall 2013," Institute of Education Sciences, U.S. Department of Education, Washington, DC, accessed October 3, 2014, http://nces.ed.gov/programs/digest/d13 /tables/dt13_201.20.asp; Thomas D. Snyder and Sally A. Dillow, "Digest of Education Statistics 2012," Table 41 (NCES 2014–015), National Center for Education Statistics, Institute of Education Sciences, U.S. Department of Education, Washington, DC, December 2013.

50. For a tasting menu of this massive literature, including more detailed findings about the correlates of particular sorts of extracurricular activities, see Jacquelynne S. Eccles, Bonnie L. Barber, Margaret Stone,

and James Hunt, "Extracurricular Activities and Adolescent Development," *Journal of Social Issues* 59 (December 2003): 865–89; Jennifer A. Fredericks and Jacquelynne S. Eccles, "Is Extracurricular Participation Associated with Beneficial Outcomes? Concurrent and Longitudinal Relations," *Developmental Psychology* 42 (July 2006): 698–713; Amy Feldman Farb and Jennifer L. Matjasko, "Recent Advances in Research on School-Based Extracurricular Activities and Adolescent Development," *Developmental Review* 32 (March 2012): 1–48; Nancy Darling, "Participation in Extracurricular Activities and Adolescent Adjustment: Cross-sectional and Longitudinal Findings," *Journal of Youth and Adolescence* 34 (October 2005): 493–505; Susan A. Dumais, "Cohort and Gender Differences in Extracurricular Participation: The Relationship Between Activities, Math Achievement, and College Expectations," *Sociological Spectrum* 29 (December 2008): 72–100; Stephen Lipscomb, "Secondary School Extracurricular Involvement and Academic Achievement: A Fixed Effects Approach," *Economics of Education Review* 26 (August 2007): 463–72; Kelly P. Troutman and Mikaela J. Dufur, "From High School Jocks to College Grads: Assessing the Long-Term Effects of High School Sport Participation on Females' Educational Attainment," *Youth & Society* 38 (June 2007): 443–62; Beckett A. Broh, "Linking Extracurricular Programming to Academic Achievement: Who Benefits and Why?," *Sociology of Education* 75 (January 2002): 69–95; Daniel Hart, Thomas M. Donnelly, James Youniss, and Robert Atkins, "High School Community Service as a Predictor of Adult Voting and Volunteering," *American Educational Research Journal* 44 (March 2007): 197–219 and studies cited therein.

51. Jonathan F. Zaff, Kristin A. Moore, Angela Romano Pappillo, and Stephanie Williams, "Implications of Extracurricular Activity Participation During Adolescence on Positive Outcomes," *Journal of Adolescent Research* 18 (November 2003): 599–630. This study controlled for academic ability, school disorder, family structure, parenting, family socioeconomic status, ethnicity, and peer effects.

52. Robert K. Ream and Russell W. Rumberger, "Student Engagement, Peer Social Capital, and School Dropout Among Mexican American and Non-Latino White Students," *Sociology of Education* 81 (April 2008): 109–39.

53. Peter Kuhn and Catherine Weinberger, "Leadership Skills and Wages," *Journal of Labor Economics* 23 (July 2005): 395–436.

54. Thomas Fritsch et al., "Associations Between Dementia/Mild Cognitive Impairment and Cognitive Performance and Activity Levels in Youth," *Journal of the American Geriatrics Society* 53 (July 2005): 1191–96. The risk of dementia among participants in two or more activities was about one third that of participants who had participated in fewer than two activities.

55. Zaff, Moore, Pappillo, and Williams, "Implications of Extracurricular Activity Participation During Adolescence on Positive Outcomes"; Betsey Stevenson, "Beyond the Classroom: Using Title IX to Measure the Return to High School Sports," *Review of Economics and Statistics* 92 (May 2010): 284–301; Vasilios D. Kosteas, "High School Clubs Participation and Earnings" (unpublished manuscript, March 22, 2010), accessed December 15, 2014, http://ssrn.com/abstract=1542360. See also J. M. Barron, B. T. Ewing, and G. R. Waddell, "The Effects of High School Athletic Participation on Education and Labor Market Outcomes," *Review of Economics and Statistics* 82 (2000): 409–21, and E. R. Eide, and N. Ronan, "Is Participation in High School Athletics an Investment or a Consumption Good?: Evidence from High School and Beyond," *Economics of Education Review* 20 (2001): 431–42.

56. Eccles, Barber, Stone, and Hunt, "Extracurricular Activities and Adolescent Development," 865–89.

57. Christy Lleras, "Do Skills and Behaviors in High School Matter? The Contribution of Noncognitive Factors in Explaining Differences in Educational Attainment and Earnings," *Social Science Research* 37 (September 2008): 888–902; Flavio Cunha, James J. Heckman, and Susanne M. Schennach, "Estimating the Technology of Cognitive and Noncognitive Skill Formation," *Econometrica* 78 (May 2010): 883–931; Elizabeth Covay and William Carbonaro, "After the Bell: Participation in Extracurricular Activities, Classroom Behavior, and Academic Achievement," *Sociology of Education* 83 (January 2010): 20–45.

58. Christina Theokas and Margot Bloch, "Out-of-School Time Is Critical for Children: Who Participates in Programs?," Research-to-Results Fact Sheet No. 2006–20 (Washington, DC: Child Trends, 2006).

59. Kristin Anderson Moore, David Murphey, Tawana Bandy, and P. Mae Cooper, "Participation in Out-of-School Time Activities and Programs," *Child Trends Research Brief No. 2014–13* (Washington, DC: Child Trends, 2014). These figures include both school-related and community-based activities.

60. Kaisa Snellman, Jennifer M. Silva, Carl B. Frederick, and Robert D. Putnam, "The Engagement Gap: Social Mobility and Extracurricular Participation Among American Youth," *ANNALS of the American Academy of Political and Social Science* (forthcoming, 2015); Kaisa Snellman, Jennifer M. Silva, and Robert D. Putnam, "Inequity Outside the Classroom: Growing Class Differences in Participation in Extracurricular Activities," *Voices in Urban Education* 40 (forthcoming, 2015).

61. Ralph B. McNeal, Jr., "High School Extracurricular Activities: Closed Structures and Stratifying Patterns of Participation," *Journal of Educational Research* 91 (January/February 1998): 183–91.

62. See note 32 in this chapter. In a multivariate analysis, the number of sports teams is reduced by a school's poverty rate, minority enrollment, and urban setting. In other words, organized sports are more common in affluent, white, suburban, and rural schools. School size makes no difference.

63. Pamela R. Bennett, Amy C. Lutz, and Lakshmi Jayaram, "Beyond the Schoolyard: The Role of Parenting Logics, Financial Resources, and Social Institutions in the Social Class Gap in Structured Activity Participation," *Sociology of Education* 85 (April 2012): 131–57; Elizabeth Stearns and Elizabeth J. Glennie, "Opportunities to Participate: Extracurricular Activities' Distribution Across and Academic Correlates in High Schools," *Social Science Research* 39 (March 2010): 296–309; Palardy, "High School Socioeconomic Segregation and Student Attainment," 737.

64. Kate I. Rausch, "Pay-to-Play: A Risky and Largely Unregulated Solution to Save High School Athletic Programs from Elimination," *Suffolk University Law Review* 39 (2005–2006): 583–611.

65. Bob Cook, "Will 'Pay to Play' Become a Permanent Part of School Sports?," *Forbes*, August 22, 2012, accessed June 17, 2014, http://www.forbes.com/sites/bobcook/2012/08/22/will-pay-to-play-become-a-permanent-part-of-school-sports/.

66. "Pay-to-Play Sports Keeping Lower-Income Kids out of the Game," C. S. Mott Children's Hospital National Poll on Children's Health, Vol. 15, no. 3 (Ann Arbor: University of Michigan, May 14, 2012); "Huntington Bank Annual Backpack Index 2007–2013," accessed May 11, 2014, http://mms.businesswire.com/media/20130723005089 /en/376266/1/2013HuntingtonBackpackIndexSupplyList.pdf? download=1.

67. Eric Dearing et al., "Do Neighborhood and Home Contexts Help Explain Why Low-Income Children Miss Opportunities to Participate in Activities Outside of School?," *Developmental Psychology* 45 (November 2009): 1545–62; Bennett, Lutz, and Jayaram, "Beyond the Schoolyard: The Role of Parenting Logics, Financial Resources, and Social Institutions in the Social Class Gap in Structured Activity Participation," 131–57.

68. Jeremy Staff and Jeylan T. Mortimer, "Social Class Background and the School-to-Work Transition," *New Directions for Child and Adolescent Development* 119 (Spring 2008): 55–69; Jeylan T. Mortimer, "The Benefits and Risks of Adolescent Employment," *Prevention Researcher* 17 (April 2010): 8–11; Kelly M. Purtell and Vonnie C. McLoyd, "A Longitudinal Investigation of Employment Among Low-Income Youth: Patterns, Predictors, and Correlates," *Youth & Society* 45 (June 2013): 243–64.

69. Altonji and Mansfield, "The Role of Family, School, and Community Characteristics in Inequality in Education and Labor-Market Outcomes," 339–58, find that while family factors are much more important than neighborhood and school factors, the latter are important. However, they do not attempt to determine how important factors under the control of schools (like class size or teacher experience) might be, as compared to peer effects, academic climate, and so on. Palardy, "High School Socioeconomic Segregation and Student Attainment," 740, finds that "controlling for family and academic background and school inputs, students who attend a high SEC [socioeconomic composition] school have a 68% higher probability of enrolling in a 4-year college than students who attend a low SEC school." In short, differences between low-income and high-income high schools make a major difference, quite apart from the personal background of the student and

the resources made available to the school. The factors that explain this pattern are peer influences and school emphasis on academic preparation, along with teacher morale.

70. One important example of this much needed kind of thinking is Duncan and Murnane, *Restoring Opportunity*.

71. Richard J. Murnane, "U.S. High School Graduation Rates: Patterns and Explanations," *Journal of Economic Literature* 51 (June 2013): 370–422. See also Russell Rumberger and Sun Ah Lim, "Why Students Drop Out of Schools: A Review of 25 Years of Research," Policy Brief 15 (University of California, Santa Barbara: California Dropout Research Project, October 2008). As Murnane describes in detail, measuring high school dropout and completion rates is technically messy, so the detailed numbers in this section should be taken with more than a grain of salt, but the basic picture seems fairly accurate.

72. Murnane, "U.S. High School Graduation Rates," 370–422; James J. Heckman, John Eric Humphries, and Nicholas S. Mader, "The GED," NBER Working Paper No. 16064 (Cambridge: National Bureau of Economic Research, June 2010). Discounting for the GED boom of the late twentieth century, Murnane shows, the high school dropout rate stalled from 1970 to 2000, though in the early years of the twenty-first century the dropout rate began to fall, and the rate of regular high school completion resumed its pre-1970 growth. The reasons for this improvement after 2000 remain unclear, as does the degree to which it has or has not narrowed the class gap.

73. David Autor, *The Polarization of Job Opportunities in the U.S. Labor Market: Implications for Employment and Earnings*, The Center for American Progress and the Hamilton Project, accessed May 13, 2014, http://economics.mit.edu/files/5554.

74. Martha J. Bailey and Susan M. Dynarski, "Gains and Gaps: Changing Inequality in U.S. College Entry and Completion," NBER Working Paper No. 17633 (Cambridge: National Bureau of Economic Research, December 2011); Mark E. Engberg and Daniel J. Allen, "Uncontrolled Destinies: Improving Opportunity for Low-Income Students in American Higher Education," *Research in Higher Education* 52 (December 2011): 786–807.

75. Using more recent data and a slightly different metric, Robert Bozick and Erich Lauff, *Education Longitudinal Study of 2002 (ELS: 2002): A First Look at the Initial Postsecondary Experiences of the High School Sophomore Class of 2002* (NCES 2008–308), U.S. Department of Education (Washington, DC: National Center for Education Statistics, October 2007), report that by 2006, 40 percent of low-income students enrolled in a postsecondary institution immediately after high school graduation, compared to 84 percent of students with family incomes over $100,000.

76. "Bridging the Higher Education Divide: Strengthening Community Colleges and Restoring the American Dream," The Century Foundation Task Force on Preventing Community Colleges from Becoming Separate and Unequal (New York: The Century Foundation Press, 2013), 3–4.

77. Michael N. Bastedo and Ozan Jaquette, "Running in Place: Low-Income Students and the Dynamics of Higher Education Stratification," *Educational Evaluation and Policy Analysis* 33 (September 2011): 318–39; Susan Dynarski, "Rising Inequality in Postsecondary Education," *Brookings Social Mobility Memo* (February 13, 2014), accessed June 17, 2014, http://www.brookings.edu/blogs/social-mobility -memos/posts/2014/02/13-inequality-in-postsecondary-education; Sean Reardon, "Education," in State of the Union: The Poverty and Inequality Report, 2014, Stanford Center on Poverty and Inequality, Stanford University, 2014, 53–59, accessed October 3, 2014, http://web.stanford .edu/group/scspi/sotu/SOTU_2014_CPI.pdf.

78. According to Sandy Baum and Kathleen Payea, "Trends in For-Profit Postsecondary Education: Enrollment, Prices, Student Aid and Outcomes," College Board, Trends in Higher Education Series, 2011, 22 percent of full-time bachelor's students at for-profit institutions graduate within 6 years, compared to 55 percent for public universities and 65 percent for nonprofit institutions. David J. Deming, Claudia Goldin, and Lawrence F. Katz, "The For-Profit Postsecondary School Sector: Nimble Critters or Agile Predators?," *Journal of Economic Perspectives* 26 (Winter 2012): 139–64, show that the outcomes from for-profit institutions are worse, even holding constant the students' background characteristics. See also Suzanne Mettler, *Degrees of Inequality: How the*

Politics of Higher Education Sabotaged the American Dream (New York: Basic Books, 2014).

79. Estimates in this chart are drawn from "Family Income and Unequal Educational Opportunity, 1970 to 2011," *Postsecondary Education Opportunity* 245 (November 2012). The basic trends shown in Figure 4.5 are broadly consistent with the results in Bailey and Dynarski, "Gains and Gaps," which are methodologically more reliable, but limited to two points in time (roughly 1982 and 2003). Even though estimates in Figure 4.5 probably overstate the level of college graduation among the kids from the richest quartile by about 10 percentage points, I use this chart because it gives a more continuous picture of the trends over time. (The chart also shows the equivalent Bailey-Dynarski datapoints as "open" symbols.) See also Patrick Wightman and Sheldon Danziger, "Poverty, Intergenerational Mobility, and Young Adult Educational Attainment," in *Investing in Children: Work, Education, and Social Policy in Two Rich Countries*, eds. Ariel Kalil, Ron Haskins, and Jenny Chesters (Washington, DC: Brookings Institution Press, 2012), 208–36.

80. Figure 4.6 is drawn from the Educational Longitudinal Study of 2002–2012, which has followed a nationally representative sample of the sophomore class of 2002 for a decade: http://nces.ed.gov/surveys/els2002/ and Erich Lauff and Steven J. Ingels, *Education Longitudinal Study of 2002 (ELS: 2002): A First Look at 2002 High School Sophomores 10 Years Later* (NCES 2014–363), U.S. Department of Education (Washington, DC: National Center for Education Statistics, 2013), accessed June 17, 2014, http://nces.ed.gov/pubs2014/2014363.pdf. Socioeconomic status (SES) here is measured by a combination of parental income, parental education, and parental occupational status. The raw data from the ELS 2002 have been adjusted to account for the fact that a substantial number of lower-SES kids in that birth cohort had dropped out of school prior to the tenth grade. Analysis of the eighth-grade class of 1988 (passing through the system 12 years before the 2002 sophomores) suggests that 3 percent of students from the top SES quartile dropped out between the eighth grade and the tenth grade, but that 14 percent from the bottom SES quartile had done so. See Steven J. Ingels et al., *Coming of Age in the 1990s: The Eighth-Grade Class of 1988 12 Years Later (NCES*

2002–321), U.S. Department of Education (Washington, DC: National Center for Education Statistics, 2002), accessed June 17, 2014, http://nces.ed.gov/pubs2002/2002321.pdf.

81. The raw ELS 2002 data show a dropout rate of 7 percent in the bottom quartile of the 2002 sophomores, but that figure substantially understates the actual dropout rate, since most of their eighth-grade peers who failed to finish high school had already dropped out prior to the sophomore year interviews.

82. College financing is a separate topic and this is not the place to review that rapidly expanding debate; see the discussion of savvy in Chapter 5. See Michael Hout, "Social and Economic Returns to College Education in the United States," *Annual Review of Sociology* 38 (August 2012): 379–400. See also Duncan and Murnane, *Restoring Opportunity*, 16–17, citing James J. Heckman and Alan B. Krueger, *Inequality in America: What Role for Human Capital Policies?* (Cambridge: MIT Press, 2005), who observe that, "Analysts differ in their assessments of the relative importance of college costs and academic preparation in explaining the increasing gulf between the college graduates rates of affluent and low-income children in our country."

83. Test scores refer to eighth-grade mathematics achievement scores. Family socioeconomic status (SES) is measured by a composite score on parental education and occupation and family income. "High" refers to test scores or SES in the top quartile, "low" to test scores or SES in the bottom quartile, and "middle" to test scores or SES in the middle two quartiles. College graduation means obtained BA within 12 years after completing the sophomore year. Source: MaryAnn Fox, Brooke A. Connolly, and Thomas D. Snyder, "Youth Indicators 2005: Trends in the Well-Being of American Youth," U.S. Department of Education, National Center for Education Statistics, 2005, p. 50, based on data from the National Education Longitudinal Study of 1988 (NELS:88/2000), Fourth Follow-up.

84. Philippe Belley and Lance Lochner, "The Changing Role of Family Income and Ability in Determining Educational Achievement," *Journal of Human Capital* 1 (Winter 2007): 37–89.

Chapter 5: Community

1. H. G. Bissingher, "Main Line Madcap," *Vanity Fair,* October 1995, 158–60, 165–82.

2. U.S. Census Bureau, as compiled by Social Explorer, accessed through Harvard University Library.

3. Kristen Lewis and Sarah Burd-Sharps, "Halve the Gap by 2030: Youth Disconnection in America's Cities," Social Science Research Council, Measure of America project, 2013, accessed October 3, 2014, http://ssrc-static.s3.amazonaws.com/moa/MOA-Halve-the-Gap-ALL-10.25.13.pdf.

4. Although I may have coined the term "air bag" in this context, I am not the first person to notice the phenomenon. The anthropologist Sherry Ortner reports that "I heard, from [upper-middle-class] parents and grown children alike, about an amazing array of what I came to think of as "rescuing mechanisms" on behalf of children who seemed to be in trouble: counseling, therapy, rehab programs, tutoring, booster courses, abortions for pregnant daughters, expensive legal services for sons in trouble with the law." Sherry B. Ortner, *Anthropology and Social Theory: Culture, Power, and the Acting Subject* (Durham: Duke University Press, 2006), 99.

5. My colleague Kathryn Edin played an essential role in our study of inner-city Philadelphia, guiding our understanding and our work, and generously sharing her deep knowledge of the area, as well as some of her unpublished writings.

6. Melody L. Boyd, Jason Martin, and Kathryn Edin, "Pathways to Participation: Youth Civic Engagement in Philadelphia," unpublished manuscript (Harvard Kennedy School, 2012). See also Kathryn Edin and Maria J. Kefalas, *Promises I Can Keep: Why Poor Women Put Motherhood Before Marriage* (Berkeley: University of California Press, 2005).

7. For recent accounts of these pendulum swings, see Robert D. Putnam, *Bowling Alone: The Collapse and Revival of American Community* (New York: Simon & Schuster, 2000) on the empirical side; and E. J. Dionne, Jr., *Our Divided Political Heart: The Battle for the American Idea in an Age of Discontent* (New York: Bloomsbury USA, 2012) on the philosophical side.

8. For an introductory overview of this massive literature, see Putnam, *Bowling Alone*, 287–363.

9. Peter V. Marsden, "Core Discussion Networks of Americans," *American Sociological Review* 52 (February 1987): 122–31; Claude S. Fischer, *To Dwell Among Friends: Personal Networks in Town and City* (Chicago: University of Chicago Press, 1982); Karen E. Campbell, Peter V. Marsden, and Jeanne S. Hurlbert, "Social Resources and Socioeconomic Status," *Social Networks* 8 (March 1986): 97–117; Marjolein I. Broese Van Groenou and Theo Van Tilburg, "Network Size and Support in Old Age: Differentials by Socio-Economic Status in Childhood and Adulthood," *Ageing and Society* 23 (September 2003): 625–45; Ivaylo D. Petev, "The Association of Social Class and Lifestyles: Persistence in American Sociability, 1974 to 2010," *American Sociological Review* 78 (August 2013): 633, 651.

10. The specific question in the Benchmark survey was "About how many close friends do you have these days? These are people you feel at ease with, can talk to about private matters, or call on for help." This national survey included 30,000 respondents in 2000; for more details and access to the raw data, see http://www.hks.harvard.edu/saguaro /communitysurvey/ and http://www.ropercenter.uconn.edu/data_access /data/datasets/social_capital_community_survey.html. See also Campbell, Marsden, and Hurlbert, "Social Resources and Socioeconomic Status," 97–117.

11. See Mark S. Granovetter, "The Strength of Weak Ties," *American Journal of Sociology* 78 (May 1973): 1360–80; Mark Granovetter, *Getting a Job: A Study of Contacts and Careers* (Cambridge: Harvard University Press, 1974); Nan Lin, Walter M. Ensel, and John C. Vaughn, "Social Resources and the Strength of Ties: Structural Factors in Occupational Status Attainment," *American Sociological Review* 46 (August 1981): 393–405; Joel M. Podolny and James N. Baron, "Resources and Relationships: Social Networks and Mobility in the Workplace," *American Sociological Review* 62 (October 1997): 673–93.

12. Thanks to Lee Rainie and Keith Hampton of the Pew Research Center for providing access to these data. Across the full list of 22 diverse occupations that the researchers asked about, network breadth was best

predicted by education, followed by age (highest in late middle age) and small-town residence. Race and gender were not predictive.

13. Annette Lareau, "Invisible Inequality: Social Class and Childrearing in Black Families and White Families," *American Sociological Review* 67 (October 2002): 747–76.

14. Ann L. Mullen, *Degrees of Inequality: Culture, Class, and Gender in American Higher Education* (Baltimore: Johns Hopkins University Press, 2010); Jenny M. Stuber, *Inside the College Gates: How Class and Culture Matter in Higher Education* (Lanham, MD: Lexington, 2011); Elizabeth A. Armstrong and Laura T. Hamilton, *Paying for the Party: How College Maintains Inequality* (Cambridge: Harvard University Press, 2013); Anthony Abraham Jack, "Culture Shock Revisited: The Social and Cultural Contingencies to Class Marginality," *Sociological Forum* 29 (June 2014): 453–75.

15. Analysis of Monitoring the Future surveys, 1976–2012, the DEA's annual national survey of drug usage among American teens. See also Jennifer L. Humensky, "Are Adolescents with High Socioeconomic Status More Likely to Engage in Alcohol and Illicit Drug Use in Early Adulthood?," *Substance Abuse Treatment, Prevention, and Policy* 5 (August 2010): 19; and Megan E. Patrick, Patrick Wightman, Robert F. Schoeni, and John E. Schulenberg, "Socioeconomic Status and Substance Use Among Young Adults: A Comparison Across Constructs and Drugs," *Journal of Studies on Alcohol and Drugs* 73 (September 2012): 772–82.

16. Putnam, *Bowling Alone*; Miller McPherson, Lynn Smith-Lovin, and Matthew E. Brashears, "Social Isolation in America: Changes in Core Discussion Networks Over Two Decades," *American Sociological Review* 71 (June 2006): 353–75. For a methodological critique of the McPherson et al. findings, see Claude S. Fischer, "The 2004 GSS Finding of Shrunken Social Networks: An Artifact?," *American Sociological Review* 74 (August 2009): 657–69; and Claude S. Fischer, *Still Connected: Family and Friends in America Since 1970* (New York: Russell Sage Foundation, 2011). For evidence tending to confirm the shrinkage hypothesis (though not necessarily the related claim that complete social isolation has increased), see Miller McPherson, Lynn Smith-Lovin, and Matthew E. Brashears, "Models and Marginals: Using Survey Evidence to

Study Social Networks," *American Sociological Review* 74 (August 2009): 670–81; and Anthony Paik and Kenneth Sanchagrin, "Social Isolation in America: An Artifact," *American Sociological Review* 78 (June 2013): 339–60.

17. Petev, "The Association of Social Class and Lifestyles," 633, 651.

18. Jeffrey Boase and Barry Wellman, "Personal Relationships: On and Off the Internet," in *The Cambridge Handbook of Personal Relationships*, eds. Anita L. Vangelisti and Daniel Perlman (Cambridge: Cambridge University Press, 2006), 709–23; Lee Rainie and Barry Wellman, *Networked: The New Social Operating System* (Cambridge: MIT Press, 2012).

19. Kathryn Zichuhr and Aaron Smith, "Digital Differences," Pew Internet and American Life Project (April 13, 2012), accessed August 21, 2014, http://pewinternet.org/~/media//Files/Reports/2012/PIP_Digital _differences_041312.pdf.

20. Eszter Hargittai and Amanda Hinnant, "Digital Inequality: Differences in Young Adults' Use of the Internet," *Communication Research* 35 (October 2008): 602–21; Fred Rothbaum, Nancy Martland, Joanne Beswick Jannsen, "Parents' Reliance on the Web to Find Information About Children and Families: Socio-Economic Differences in Use, Skills and Satisfaction," *Journal of Applied Developmental Psychology* 29 (March/April 2008): 118–28; Eszter Hargittai and Yuli Patrick Hsieh, "Digital Inequality," in *The Oxford Handbook of Internet Studies*, ed. William H. Dutton (Oxford: Oxford University Press, 2013), 129–50.

21. Danah Boyd, *It's Complicated: The Social Lives of Networked Teens* (New Haven: Yale University Press, 2014), 172–73.

22. Eszter Hargittai, "The Digital Reproduction of Inequality," in *Social Stratification*, ed. David Grusky (Boulder: Westview, forthcoming), 936–44.

23. Evidence of the effects of mentoring can be found in Jean Baldwin Grossman and Joseph P. Tierney, "Does Mentoring Work?: An Impact Study of the Big Brothers Big Sisters Program," *Evaluation Review* 22 (June 1998): 403–26; David L. DuBois, Bruce E. Holloway, Jeffrey C. Valentine, and Harris Cooper, "Effectiveness of Mentoring Programs for Youth: A Meta-Analytic Review," *American Journal of Community Psychology* 30 (April 2002): 157–97; David L. DuBois et al., "How

Effective Are Mentoring Programs for Youth? A Systematic Assessment of the Evidence," *Psychological Science in the Public Interest* 12 (August 2011): 57–91; Lance D. Erickson, Steve McDonald, and Glen H. Elder, Jr., "Informal Mentors and Education: Complementary or Compensatory Resources?," *Sociology of Education* 82 (October 2009): 344–67. David L. DuBois and Naida Silverthorn, "Characteristics of Natural Mentoring Relationships and Adolescent Adjustment: Evidence from a National Study," *Journal of Primary Prevention* 26 (2005): 69–92, report that informal mentoring led to improvements in a broad array of positive and negative adolescent behavior: completion of high school, college attendance, working 10 or more hours a week, binge drinking, using drugs, smoking, gang memberships, fighting, risk taking, self-esteem, life satisfaction, depression, suicidal thoughts, general health, general physical activity, having an STD, using birth control, and using condoms.

24. Civic Enterprises in association with Hart Research Associates, "The Mentoring Effect: Young People's Perspectives on the Outcomes and Availability of Mentoring," report for MENTOR: The National Mentoring Partnership (January 2014), accessed August 21, 2014, http://www .mentoring.org/images/uploads/Report_TheMentoringEffect.pdf. This report offers extensive evidence of the value of both formal and informal mentoring for at-risk kids. We are grateful to John Bridgeland of Civic Enterprises and to Hart Research Associates for making the survey data (a nationally representative sample of 1,109 youth aged 18–21) available to us for secondary analysis, for which we alone are responsible. Respondents were told, "One way that a young person can receive mentoring is through a structured program. . . . An example of a structured mentoring program is Big Brothers Big Sisters. A second type of mentoring is when an adult comes into a young person's life and they naturally develop an informal mentoring relationship. The adult could be a friend of the family or a teacher with whom the young person maintains a relationship outside of the classroom [other than your parents or whoever raised you]. In both structured and informal mentoring relationships, the adult is supportive and works with the young person to build a relationship by offering guidance, support, and encouragement to help the young person's positive and healthy development over a period of time."

Respondents were asked whether they had ever had either sort of mentor and, if so, were asked about each mentoring relationship in detail.

25. Erickson, McDonald, and Elder, "Informal Mentors and Education: Complementary or Compensatory Resources?," 344–67. This research, the most statistically sophisticated study so far, finds that the effects of informal mentoring, when it happens, are even greater for less privileged kids, but that fact is more than offset by the greater frequency of informal mentoring in the lives of privileged kids.

26. Most of the formal mentoring relationships reported in the survey were school-linked. Formal mentoring through churches was rarer and (more important for our purposes) concentrated among upper- not lower-socioeconomic-status kids.

27. In our discussion of mentoring, "rich" and "poor" refer to the top and bottom quartiles of a composite measure of socioeconomic status.

28. Robert J. Sampson, *Great American City: Chicago and the Enduring Neighborhood Effect* (Chicago: University of Chicago Press, 2012), 356, emphasis in original. The study of neighborhood effects has been tormented by complicated methodological concerns, especially what is termed "selection bias." Since people generally choose where to live, if people in a given neighborhood have distinctive characteristics, it is possible that they brought those traits with them to the neighborhood, rather than those traits being "caused" by the neighborhood context. The best contemporary studies, however, have been attuned to that risk, and our discussion here is based on findings that seem robust in the face of that methodological issue. In fact, cross-sectional studies may actually underestimate true neighborhood effects by ignoring the impact of long-term effects. On these methodological issues, see Sampson, *Great American City*, especially Chapters 12 and 15; Robert J. Sampson and Patrick Sharkey, "Neighborhood Selection and the Social Reproduction of Concentrated Racial Inequality," *Demography* 45 (February 2008): 1–29; and Tama Leventhal, Véronique Dupéré, and Elizabeth Shuey, "Children in Neighborhoods," in *Handbook of Child Psychology and Developmental Science*, 7th ed., Vol. 4, eds. Richard M. Lerner, Marc H. Bornstein, and Tama Leventhal (Hoboken, NJ: Wiley, forthcoming 2015). At the center of these debates is the "Moving to

Opportunity" experiment of the 1990s that followed a randomly selected group of poor families who were enabled to move to low-poverty neighborhoods and then carefully compared to a control group of similar families who did not so move. For an overview of the complex and mixed results, see Jens Ludwig, et al., "Neighborhood Effects on the Long-Term Well-Being of Low-Income Adults," *Science* 337 (2012): 1505–10; and Lisa Sanbonmatsu et al., "Moving to Opportunity for Fair Housing Demonstration Program—Final Impacts Evaluation" (Washington, DC: U.S. Department of Housing and Urban Development, 2011).

29. Velma McBride Murry et al., "Neighborhood Poverty and Adolescent Development," *Journal of Research on Adolescence* 21 (March 2011):114–28. Yet unpublished work by Raj Chetty, Nathaniel Hendren, and their colleagues using evidence from the Moving to Opportunity study discussed in the previous note confirms that neighborhood effects are largest on younger children.

30. Patrick Sharkey and Felix Elwert, "The Legacy of Disadvantage: Multigenerational Neighborhood Effects on Cognitive Ability," *American Journal of Sociology* 116 (May 2011): 1934–81.

31. A randomized controlled study in Maryland estimated that perhaps two-thirds of the effect of neighborhood poverty on children's outcomes was attributable to poor schools. Heather Schwartz, *Housing Policy Is School Policy: Economically Integrative Housing Promotes Academic Success in Montgomery County, MD* (New York: Century Foundation, 2010). Another carefully controlled study found that growing up in a high poverty neighborhood increases the likelihood of dropping out of high school: David J. Harding, "Counterfactual Models of Neighborhood Effects: The Effect of Neighborhood Poverty on High School Dropout and Teenage Pregnancy," *American Journal of Sociology* 109 (2003): 676–719. On school-community networks, see Anthony S. Bryk, Penny Bender Sebring, Elaine Allensworth, Stuart Luppescu, and John Q. Easton, *Organizing Schools for Improvement: Lessons from Chicago* (Chicago: University of Chicago Press, 2010); and Mark R. Warren, "Communities and Schools: A New View of Urban Education Reform," *Harvard Educational Review* 75 (2005): 133–73.

32. A recent, comprehensive overview of neighborhood effects on children is Leventhal, Dupéré, and Shuey, "Children in Neighborhoods."

33. Cynthia M. Duncan, *Worlds Apart: Poverty and Politics in Rural America*, 2nd ed. (New Haven: Yale University Press, 2014).

34. On collective efficacy, see Sampson, *Great American City*, Chapter 7, quote at p. 370.

35. Figure 5.4 depicts the simple correlation between trust and poverty, but the correlation remains robust and substantial with controls for personal finances, education, citizenship, ethnicity, crime rates, income inequality, ethnic diversity, language, commuting time, residential mobility, homeownership, gender, region, and age. See Robert D. Putnam, "*E Pluribus Unum*: Diversity and Community in the 21st Century: The 2006 Johan Skytte Prize Lecture," *Scandinavian Political Studies* 30 (June 2007): 137–74, especially Table 3. The same pattern also applies to how often neighbors speak with one another.

36. See Putnam, *Bowling Alone*, 138; and Orlando Patterson, "Liberty Against the Democratic State: On the Historical and Contemporary Sources of American Distrust," in *Democracy and Trust*, ed. Mark E. Warren (Cambridge: Cambridge University Press, 1999), 187–91.

37. Putnam, *Bowling Alone*; Wendy M. Rahn and John E. Transue, "Social Trust and Value Change: The Decline of Social Capital in American Youth, 1976–1995," *Political Psychology* 19 (September 1998): 545–65; April K. Clark, Michael Clark, and Daniel Monzin, "Explaining Changing Trust Trends in America," *International Research Journal of Social Sciences* 2 (January 2013): 7–13; Jean M. Twenge, W. Keith Campbell, and Nathan T. Carter, "Declines in Trust in Others and Confidence in Institutions Among American Adults and Late Adolescents, 1972–2012," *Psychological Science* 25 (October 2014): 1914–23.

38. Sampson, *Great American City*; Leventhal, Dupéré, and Shuey, "Children in Neighborhoods"; Dafna E. Kohen, V. Susan Dahinten, Tama Leventhal, and Cameron N. McIntosh, "Neighborhood Disadvantage: Pathways of Effects for Young Children," *Child Development* 79 (January 2008): 156–69; Gopal K. Singh and Reem M. Ghandour, "Impact of Neighborhood Social Conditions and Household Socioeconomic Status on Behavioral Problems Among U.S. Children," *Maternal and Child Health Journal*

16 (April 2012): 158–69; Véronique Dupéré, Tama Leventhal, and Frank Vitaro, "Neighborhood Processes, Self-efficacy, and Adolescent Mental Health," *Journal of Health and Social Behavior* 53 (June 2012): 183–98; Elizabeth T. Gershoff and Aprile D. Benner, "Neighborhood and School Contexts in the Lives of Children," in *Societal Contexts of Child Development: Pathways of Influence and Implications for Practice and Policy*, eds. Elizabeth T. Gershoff, Rashmita S. Mistry, and Danielle A. Crosby (Oxford: Oxford University Press, 2014), 141–55.

39. Leventhal, Dupéré, and Shuey, "Children in Neighborhoods"; Rand D. Conger and M. Brent Donnellan, "An Interactionist Perspective on Socioeconomic Context of Human Development," *Annual Review of Psychology* 58 (2007): 175–99; Glen H. Elder, Jr., Jacquelynne S. Eccles, Monika Ardelt, and Sarah Lord, "Inner-City Parents Under Economic Pressure: Perspectives on the Strategies of Parenting," *Journal of Marriage and Family* 57 (August 1995): 771–84; Véronique Dupéré, Tama Leventhal, Robert Crosnoe, and Eric Dion, "Understanding the Positive Role of Neighborhood Socioeconomic Advantage in Achievement: The Contribution of the Home, Child Care, and School Environments," *Developmental Psychology* 46 (September 2010): 1227–44; Candice L. Odgers et al., "Supportive Parenting Mediates Neighborhood Socioeconomic Disparities in Children's Antisocial Behavior from Ages 5 to 12," *Development and Psychopathology* 24 (August 2012): 705–21.

40. Frank F. Furstenberg et al., *Managing to Make It: Urban Families and Adolescent Success* (Chicago: University of Chicago Press, 1999).

41. Gershoff and Benner, "Neighborhood and School Contexts in the Lives of Children," 143; Jason M. Bacha et al., "Maternal Perception of Neighborhood Safety as a Predictor of Child Weight Status: The Moderating Effect of Gender and Assessment of Potential Mediators," *International Journal of Pediatric Obesity* 5 (January 2010): 72–79; Beth E. Molnar, Steven L. Gortmaker, Fiona C. Bull, and Stephen L. Buka, "Unsafe to Play? Neighborhood Disorder and Lack of Safety Predict Reduced Physical Activity Among Urban Children and Adolescents," *American Journal of Health Promotion* 18 (May 2004): 378–86; Deborah A. Cohen, Brian K. Finch, Aimee Bower, and Narayan Sastry "Collective Efficacy and Obesity: The Potential Influence of Social Factors on

Health," *Social Science & Medicine* 62 (2006): 769–78; H. Mollie Greves Grow, Andrea J. Cook, David E. Arterburn, Brian E. Saelens, Adam Drewnowski, and Paula Lozano, "Child Obesity Associated with Social Disadvantage of Children's Neighborhoods," *Social Science & Medicine* 71 (2010): 584–91.

42. Centers for Disease Control and Prevention (CDC), "Physical Activity Levels Among Children Aged 9–13 Years—United States, 2002," *Morbidity and Mortality Weekly Report* 52 (August 22, 2003): 785–88; Penny Gordon-Larsen, Melissa C. Nelson, Phil Page, and Barry M. Popkin, "Inequality in the Built Environment Underlies Key Health Disparities in Physical Activity and Obesity," *Pediatrics* 117 (February 2006): 417–24; Billie Giles-Corti and Robert J. Donovan, "Relative Influences of Individual, Social Environmental, and Physical Environmental Correlates of Walking," *American Journal of Public Health* 93 (September 2003): 1583–89; Jens Ludwig et al., "Neighborhoods, Obesity, and Diabetes—A Randomized Social Experiment," *New England Journal of Medicine* 365 (2011): 1509–19.

43. Paul A. Jargowsky, "Concentration of Poverty in the New Millennium: Changes in Prevalence, Composition, and Location of High Poverty Neighborhoods," report by the Century Foundation and Rutgers Center for Urban Research and Education (2013), accessed August 21, 2014, http://tcf.org/assets/downloads/Concentration_of_Poverty_in_the _New_Millennium.pdf; Ann Owens and Robert J. Sampson, "Community Well-Being and the Great Recession," *Pathways Magazine* (The Stanford Center on Poverty and Inequality, Spring 2013): 3–7; Patrick Sharkey and Bryan Graham, "Mobility and the Metropolis: How Communities Factor into Economic Mobility," Pew Charitable Trust report (December 2013), accessed August 21, 2014, http://www .pewtrusts.org/~/media/legacy/uploadedfiles/pcs_assets/2013/Mobility andtheMetropolispdf.pdf; Jonathan T. Rothwell and Douglas S. Massey, "Geographic Effects on Intergenerational Income Mobility," *Economic Geography* 90 (January 2015): 1–23.

44. Robert D. Putnam and David E. Campbell, *American Grace: How Religion Divides and Unites Us* (New York: Simon & Schuster, 2010), especially Chapter 13. Statistics in this paragraph come from the 2006 Faith Matters national survey, described in that book.

45. John M. Wallace and Tyrone A. Forman, "Religion's Role in Promoting Health and Reducing Risk Among American Youth," *Health Education and Behavior* 25 (December 1998): 721–41; Mark D. Regnerus and Glen H. Elder, Jr., "Staying on Track in School: Religious Influences in High- and Low-Risk Settings" (paper presented at the annual meeting of the American Sociological Association, Anaheim, CA, August 2001); Chandra Muller and Christopher G. Ellison, "Religious Involvement, Social Capital, and Adolescents' Academic Progress: Evidence from the National Education Longitudinal Study of 1988," *Sociological Focus* 34 (May 2001): 155–83; Christian Smith and Robert Faris, "Religion and American Adolescent Delinquency, Risk Behaviors, and Constructive Social Activities," a research report of the National Study of Youth and Religion (Chapel Hill, NC, 2002), accessed August 21, 2014, http://eric.ed.gov/?id=ED473128; Jonathan K. Zaff, Kristin A. Moore, Angela Romano Pappillo, and Stephanie Williams, "Implications of Extracurricular Activity Participation During Adolescence on Positive Outcomes," *Journal of Adolescent Research* 18 (November 2003): 614; Jennifer L. Glanville, David Sikkink, and Edwin I. Hernandez, "Religious Involvement and Educational Outcomes: The Role of Social Capital and Extracurricular Participation," *Sociological Quarterly* 49 (Winter 2008): 105–37. These studies control for many other factors that might make the correlations spurious. The best studies of selection bias in the case of religious engagement conclude that, if anything, this bias tends to obscure, not exaggerate, the effects of religion: Mark D. Regnerus and Christian Smith, "Selection Effects in Studies of Religious Influence," *Review of Religious Research* 47 (September 2005): 23–50; Jonathan H. Gruber, "Religious Market Structure, Religious Participation, and Outcomes: Is Religion Good for You?," *Advances in Economic Analysis & Policy* 5 (December 2005).

46. Eric Dearing et al., "Do Neighborhood and Home Contexts Help Explain Why Low-Income Children Miss Opportunities to Participate in Activities Outside of School?," *Developmental Psychology* 45 (November 2009): 1545–62. Author's analysis of Social Capital Community Benchmark Survey (2000); out of seventeen different types of organizations, only self-help, veterans, and seniors groups are less class biased in their membership than religious groups.

47. Putnam and Campbell, *American Grace*, 252–53. The same generational trend of increasing class bias in church attendance appears in the General Social Survey, the National Educational Studies, and in the Roper Political and Social Trends archive, with either education (relative or absolute) or income as a measure of socioeconomic status, though more clearly with education. Attendance measures differ from archive to archive, but the trends by education are similar. The growth of the class gap is sharper for men than for women, and if anything, sharper among blacks than among whites and among evangelical Protestants than among other traditions. If all races are analyzed together, this trend is masked, because nonwhites are poorer, less educated, and more religious, but the growing class gap appears in each race, considered separately.

48. See Barrie Thorne, "The Crisis of Care," in *Work-Family Challenges for Low-Income Parents and Their Children*, eds. Ann C. Crouter and Alan Booth (Mahwah, NJ: Lawrence Erlbaum, 2004): 165–78; and Markella B. Rutherford, *Adult Supervision Required: Private Freedom and Public Constraints for Parents and Children* (New Brunswick, NJ: Rutgers University Press, 2011).

Chapter 6: What Is to Be Done?

1. Raj Chetty, Nathaniel Hendren, Patrick Kline, and Emmanuel Saez, "Where Is the Land of Opportunity? The Geography of Intergenerational Mobility in the United States," *Quarterly Journal of Economics* 129 (November 2014); Raj Chetty, Nathaniel Hendren, Patrick Kline, Emmanuel Saez, and Nicholas Turner, "Is the United States Still a Land of Opportunity? Recent Trends in Intergenerational Mobility," *American Economic Review Papers & Proceedings* 104 (May 2014): 141–47. See also note 48 in Chapter 1.

2. Isabel V. Sawhill, "Trends in Intergenerational Mobility," in *Getting Ahead or Losing Ground: Economic Mobility in America*, eds. Ron Haskins, Julia B. Isaacs, and Isabel V. Sawhill (Washington, DC: Brookings Institution, 2008).

3. Wendy in Port Clinton is the sole parent who herself came from an affluent background. Simone's father attended NYU. Earl's father

attended college for a year before entering the construction business, but by the time Earl himself was ready for college that business had gone bust, leaving Earl to fend for himself.

4. Arthur M. Okun, *Equality and Efficiency: The Big Tradeoff* (Washington, DC: Brookings Institution Press, 1975).

5. Claudia Goldin and Lawrence F. Katz, "The Legacy of U.S. Educational Leadership: Notes on Distribution and Economic Growth in the 20th Century," *American Economic Review* 91 (May 2001): 18–23; Eric A. Hanushek and Ludger Woessmann, "The Role of Cognitive Skills in Economic Development," *Journal of Economic Literature* 46 (September 2008): 607–68; Elhanan Helpman, *The Mystery of Economic Growth* (Cambridge: Harvard University Press, 2010); Martin West, "Education and Global Competitiveness: Lessons for the United States from International Evidence," in *Rethinking Competitiveness*, ed. Kevin A. Hassett (Washington, DC: AEI Press, 2012).

6. Claudia Goldin and Lawrence F. Katz, *The Race Between Education and Technology* (Cambridge: Harvard University Press, 2008), 98; Michael Handel, "Skills Mismatch in the Labor Market," *Annual Review of Sociology* 29 (2003): 135–65; James J. Heckman et al., "The Rate of Return to the HighScope Perry Preschool Program," *Journal of Public Economics* 94 (February 2010): 114–28; Pedro Carneiro and James J. Heckman, "Human Capital Policy," in *Inequality in America: What Role for Human Capital Policies?*, eds. James J. Heckman, Alan B. Krueger, and Benjamin M. Friedman (Cambridge: MIT Press, 2003).

7. Daron Acemoglu and David Autor, "What Does Human Capital Do? A Review of Goldin and Katz's *The Race Between Education and Technology*," *Journal of Economic Literature* 50 (June 2012): 426–63.

8. Harry J. Holzer, Diane Whitmore Schanzenbach, Greg J. Duncan, and Jens Ludwig, "The Economic Costs of Childhood Poverty in the United States," *Journal of Children and Poverty* 14 (March 2008): 41–61.

9. Clive R. Belfield, Henry M. Levin, and Rachel Rosen, *The Economic Value of Opportunity Youth* (Washington, DC: Corporation for National and Community Service, 2012), accessed October 6, 2014, http://www.dol.gov/summerjobs/pdf/EconomicValue.pdf. Opportunity youth

comprise the lowest 17 percent of young people in terms of preparation for work and life.

10. Katharine Bradbury and Robert K. Triest, "Inequality of Opportunity and Aggregate Economic Performance," (paper prepared for the conference on Inequality of Economic Opportunity, Federal Reserve Bank, Boston, October 2014). "Metropolitan area" is defined operationally as the "commuting zone" around a central city. I am grateful to Bradbury and Triest for calculating these specific estimates of the implications of their broader quantitative findings. Other relevant recent studies are Chang-Tai Hsieh, Eric Hurst, Charles I. Jones, and Peter J. Klenow, "The Allocation of Talent and U.S. Economic Growth." Working Paper 18693 (Cambridge: National Bureau of Economic Research, 2013); and Gustavo A. Marrero and Juan G. Rodriguez, "Inequality of opportunity and growth," *Journal of Development Economics* 104 (2013): 107–22.

11. James J. Heckman, "An Effective Strategy for Promoting Social Mobility," *Boston Review* (September/October 2012); James J. Heckman, Seong Hyeok Moon, Rodrigo Pinto, Peter A. Savelyev, and Adam Yavitz, "The Rate of Return to the High/Scope Perry Preschool Program," Forschungsinstitut zur Zukunft der Arbeit/Institute for the Study of Labor Discussion Paper No. 4533 (Bonn, Germany: IZA, October 2009), accessed September 26, 2014, http://ftp.iza.org/dp4533.pdf. Other researchers, while agreeing that the rate of return from early childhood education is favorable, view the Heckman estimate as perhaps too high, based as it is on a single landmark study begun in the 1960s of the Perry Preschool in Ypsilanti, Michigan.

12. On the related issue of the economic effects of inequality of income (not inequality of opportunity), the textbook theory once was that such inequality contributed to economic growth by providing incentives for effort and savings for investment that boost growth. More recent evidence strongly suggests the reverse—that high levels of inequality impede sustainable growth. See (among many other sources) Alberto Alesina and Dani Rodrik, "Distributive Politics and Economic Growth," *Quarterly Journal of Economics* 109 (May 1994): 465–90; Andrew G. Berg and Jonathan D. Ostry, "Inequality and Unsustainable Growth: Two Sides of the Same Coin?," IMF Staff Discussion Note 11/08 (Washington,

DC: International Monetary Fund, April 8, 2011); Joseph E. Stiglitz, *The Price of Inequality: How Today's Divided Society Endangers Our Future* (New York: W. W. Norton, 2012); and Jonathan D. Ostry, Andrew Berg, and Charalambos G. Tsangarides, "Redistribution, Inequality, and Growth," IMF Staff Discussion Note 14/02 (Washington, DC: International Monetary Fund, February 2014). In mid-2014, Standard and Poor's trimmed its forecast of U.S. economic growth by 0.3 percent because of the large gaps between the rich and poor in the United States and forecast more turbulent economic times ahead because of inequality. Peter Schroeder, "S&P: Income Inequality Slowing Economy," *The Hill*, August 5, 2014, accessed October 6, 2014, http://thehill.com/policy /finance/214316-sp-income-inequality-slowing-economy. Economists disagree about the reasons why extreme inequality might reduce growth— perhaps because it limits aggregate demand because of the high savings rate of the rich, perhaps because of supply-side constraints on adequately skilled labor, perhaps because high inequality triggers financial instability, and perhaps because of political distortions and popular unrest that impede economic growth.

13. Robert A. Dahl, *On Democracy* (New Haven: Yale University Press, 1998).

14. Meira Levinson, *No Citizen Left Behind* (Cambridge: Harvard University Press, 2012); Sidney Verba, Kay Lehman Schlozman, and Henry E. Brady, *Voice and Equality: Civic Voluntarism in American Politics* (Cambridge: Harvard University Press, 1995); Kay Lehman Schlozman, Sidney Verba, and Henry E. Brady, *The Unheavenly Chorus: Unequal Political Voice and the Broken Promise of American Democracy* (Princeton: Princeton University Press, 2012); Andrea K. Finlay, Constance Flanagan, and Laura Wray-Lake, "Civic Engagement Patterns and Transitions over 8 Years: The AmeriCorps National Study," *Developmental Psychology* 47 (November 2011): 1728–43; Jonathan F. Zaff, James Youniss, and Cynthia M. Gibson, "An Inequitable Invitation to Citizenship: Non-College-Bound Youth and Civic Engagement," Report prepared for PACE (Washington, DC: Philanthropy for Active Civic Engagement, October 2009).

15. Data on 2008 and 2010 civic engagement are from the Census Bureau's Current Population Survey; for these purposes "college-educated" means

any youth aged 20–25 currently enrolled in postsecondary education or holding a postsecondary degree. We simply counted the number of types of activity a youth reported from our list of six. See also "Understanding a Diverse Generation: Youth Civic Engagement in the United States," CIRCLE Research Report (Tufts University, November 2011), accessed October 6, 2014, http://www.civicyouth.org/wp-content/up loads/2011/11/CIRCLE_cluster_report2010.pdf.

16. Laura Wray-Lake and Daniel Hart, "Growing Social Inequalities in Youth Civic Engagement? Evidence from the National Election Study," *PS: Political Science and Politics* 45 (July 2012): 456–61; Amy K. Syvertsen, Laura Wray-Lake, Constance A. Flanagan, D. Wayne Osgood, and Laine Briddell, "Thirty-Year Trends in U.S. Adolescents' Civic Engagement: A Story of Changing Participation and Educational Differences," *Journal of Research on Adolescence* 21 (September 2011): 586–94. Data on 2008 and 2010 electoral turnout are from the Census Bureau's Current Population Survey.

17. Wray-Lake and Hart, "Growing Social Inequalities in Youth Civic Engagement? Evidence from the National Election Study," show this same pattern of gaps narrowing "downward" for measures of campaign involvement.

18. Analysis by Carl Frederick of the Monitoring the Future survey data of high school seniors, 2005–2012.

19. Kay Lehman Schlozman, Sidney Verba, and Henry E. Brady, "Weapon of the Strong? Participatory Inequality and the Internet," *Perspectives on Politics* 8 (June 2010): 487–509.

20. Schlozman, Verba, and Brady, *The Unheavenly Chorus,* quote at 83.

21. Larry M. Bartels, *Unequal Democracy: The Political Economy of the New Gilded Age* (Princeton: Princeton University Press, 2008); Martin Gilens, *Affluence and Influence: Economic Inequality and Political Power in America* (Princeton: Princeton University Press, 2012); Jan E. Leighley and Jonathan Nagler, *Who Votes Now? Demographics, Issues, Inequality, and Turnout in the United States* (Princeton: Princeton University Press, 2013).

22. Dahl, *On Democracy,* 76.

23. American Political Science Association Task Force on Inequality and American Democracy, "American Democracy in an Age of Rising Inequality," *Perspectives on Politics* 2 (December 2004): 651.

24. William Kornhauser, *The Politics of Mass Society* (Glencoe, IL: Free Press, 1959), 212. For a comprehensive overview of the mass society theorists, see Christian Borch, *The Politics of Crowds: An Alternative History of Sociology* (New York: Cambridge University Press, 2012).

25. Hannah Arendt, *The Origins of Totalitarianism* (New York: Harcourt, Brace, 1951), 310, as quoted in Borch, *The Politics of Crowds*, 181.

26. Pope Francis, in "Apostolic Exhortation *Evangelii Gaudium* [The Joy of the Gospel], to the Bishops, Clergy, Consecrated Persons and the Lay Faithful on the Proclamation of the Gospel in Today's World," Vatican Press, 2013, accessed October 6, 2014, http://w2.vatican.va/content /dam/francesco/pdf/apost_exhortations/documents/papa-francesco_es ortazione-ap_20131124_evangelii-gaudium_en.pdf; Pope Francis in an interview en route to Rio de Janeiro, Brazil: John L. Allen, "Pope on Plane: No to a 'Throw-Away' Culture," *National Catholic Reporter*, July 22, 2013, accessed October 6, 2014, http://ncronline.org/blogs/ncr -today/pope-plane-no-throw-away-culture.

27. On the moral philosophy of equality of opportunity, essential reading includes Lawrence A. Blum, "Opportunity and Equality of Opportunity," *Public Affairs Quarterly* 2 (October 1988): 1–18; John H. Schaar, "Equality of Opportunity, and Beyond," in *Equality: Selected Readings*, eds. Louis P. Pojman and Robert Westmoreland (New York: Oxford University Press, 1997), 137–47; William Galston, "A Liberal Defense of Equality of Opportunity," in *Equality*, eds. Pojman and Westmoreland, 170–81; Bernard A. O. Williams, "The Idea of Equality," in *Equality*, eds. Pojman and Westmoreland, 91–101; John Rawls, *A Theory of Justice*, rev. ed. (Cambridge: Belknap Press of Harvard University Press, 1999); John E. Roemer, *Equality of Opportunity* (Cambridge: Harvard University Press, 2000); Will Kymlicka, *Contemporary Political Philosophy: An Introduction*, 2nd ed. (New York: Oxford University Press, 2002), 53–101; T. M. Scanlon, "When Does Equality Matter?" (paper presented at a conference on equality at the John F. Kennedy School of Government, Cambridge, MA, April 2004), accessed October 6, 2014, http://www.law.yale.edu/documents/pdf/Intellectual_Life/ltw-Scanlon .pdf; and Richard Arneson, "Equality of Opportunity," *The Stanford Encyclopedia of Philosophy*, October 8, 2002, accessed October 6, 2014, http://plato.stanford.edu/entries/equal-opportunity/.

28. In an interesting essay by Serena Olsaretti, "Children as Public Goods?," *Philosophy and Public Affairs* 41 (Summer 2013): 226–58, she argues that we have an obligation to parents to help them raise their children, because those children will contribute to our future well-being. My argument rests instead on our moral obligation not to the *parents*, but to the *kids* themselves.

29. For a useful synthesis of approaches to the problem of the opportunity gap, see Lane Kenworthy, "It's Hard to Make It in America: How the United States Stopped Being the Land of Opportunity," *Foreign Affairs* 91 (November 2012): 103–9. I am especially indebted to Tom Sander for a thorough review of policy options to address the opportunity gap.

30. For a treatment of the growing class gap that often coincides with my account descriptively, but that offers a quite different diagnosis, see Charles Murray, *Coming Apart: The State of White America, 1960–2010* (New York: Crown Forum, 2012).

31. For evidence of the powerful influence of religious communities on the attitudes and behavior of their members, see Robert D. Putnam and David E. Campbell, *American Grace: How Religion Divides and Unites Us* (New York: Simon & Schuster, 2010), especially chapter 13.

32. Isabel V. Sawhill, *Generation Unbound: Drifting into Sex and Parenthood Without Marriage* (Washington, DC: Brookings Institution Press, 2014), 91–93, citing Robert G. Wood, Sheena McConnell, Quinn Moore, Andrew Clarkwest, and JoAnn Hsueh, "The Effects of Building Strong Families: A Healthy Marriage and Relationship Skills Education Program for Unmarried Parents," *Journal of Policy Analysis and Management* 31 (Spring 2012): 228–52; JoAnn Hsueh, Desiree Principe Alderson, Erika Lundquist, Charles Michalopoulos, Daniel Gubits, David Fein, and Virginia Knox, "The Supporting Healthy Marriage Evaluation: Early Impacts on Low-Income Families," *SSRN Electronic Journal* (2012), accessed October 11, 2014, www.ssrn.com/abstract=2030319; Adam Carasso and C. Eugene Steuerle, "The Hefty Penalty on Marriage Facing Many Households with Children," *The Future of Children* 15 (Fall 2005): 161; Ron Haskins, "Marriage, Parenthood, and Public Policy," *National Affairs* (Spring 2014): 65–66; Maria Cancian and Ron Haskins, "Changes in Family Composition: Implications for Income,

Poverty, and Public Policy," *ANNALS of the American Academy of Political and Social Science* 654 (July 2014): 42–43.

33. Sawhill, *Generation Unbound*, 3.

34. Evidence for the following two paragraphs is from Sawhill, *Generation Unbound* 9, 105–44. For a somewhat different view about the problem, see Andrew J. Cherlin, *Labor's Love Lost: The Rise and Fall of the Working Class Family in America* (New York: Russell Sage Foundation, 2014), Chapter 7.

35. Elizabeth O. Ananat, Anna Gassman-Pines, and Christina M. Gibson-Davis, "The Effects of Local Employment Losses on Children's Educational Achievement," in *Whither Opportunity? Rising Inequality, Schools, and Children's Life Chances*, eds. G. Duncan and R. Murnane (New York: Russell Sage, 2011), 299–315.

36. Kenworthy, "It's Hard to Make It in America," 97–109; Greg Duncan, Pamela Morris, and Chris Rodrigues, "Does Money Matter? Estimating Impacts of Family Income on Young Children's Achievement with Data from Random-Assignment Experiments," *Developmental Psychology* 47 (September 2012): 1263–79. See also Rebecca A. Maynard and Richard J. Murnane, "The Effects of a Negative Income Tax on School Performance: Results of an Experiment," *Journal of Human Resources* 14 (Autumn 1979): 463–76; Neil J. Salkind and Ron Haskins, "Negative Income Tax: The Impact on Children from Low-Income Families," *Journal of Family Issues* 3 (June 1982): 165–80; Pamela Morris et al., *How Welfare and Work Policies Affect Children: A Synthesis of Research* (New York: MDRC, 2001); Gordon B. Dahl and Lance Lochner, "The Impact of Family Income on Child Achievement," *American Economic Review* 102 (August 2005): 1927–56; and Greg J. Duncan, Ariel Kalil, and Kathleen M. Ziol-Guest, "Early Childhood Poverty and Adult Achievement, Employment and Health," *Family Matters* (Australia Institute of Family Studies) 93 (2013): 26–35, accessed October 11, 2014, http://www.aifs.gov.au/institute/pubs/fm2013/fm93/fm93c.pdf.

37. For a useful overview of the EITC and child tax credit and possible reforms, see Thomas L. Hungerford and Rebecca Thiess, "The Earned Income Tax Credit and the Child Tax Credit: History, Purpose, Goals, and Effectiveness" (report, Economic Policy Institute, September 25,

2013), accessed October 10, 2014, http://www.epi.org/publication /ib370-earned-income-tax-credit-and-the-child-tax-credit-history-pur pose-goals-and-effectiveness/.

38. Jeremy Travis, Bruce Western, and Steve Redburn, eds., *The Growth of Incarceration in the United States: Exploring Causes and Consequences* (Washington, DC: National Academies Press, 2014).

39. Jane Waldfogel, *What Children Need* (Cambridge: Harvard University Press, 2006), 45–62, quote at 45. She emphasizes that it is *full-time* work during a child's *first* year that has been shown to be detrimental, not work later in a child's life and not part-time work during the first year.

40. A 2008 report found that the United States had the least generous paid parental leave policies of any of the 21 high-income countries investigated and ranked next to last in terms of total length of leave offered parents. See Rebecca Ray, Janet C. Gornick, and John Schmitt, "Parental Leave Policies in 21 Countries: Assessing Generosity and Gender Equality" (Washington, DC: Center for Economic and Policy Research, 2008). More recent evidence confirms this low ranking: OECD Family Database, PF2.1 Key characteristics of parental leave systems, October 14, 2014, http://www.oecd.org/els/soc/PF2_1_Parental_leave_systems _1May2014.pdf.

41. For a review of the evidence on day-care quality, see Waldfogel, *What Children Need,* 72–81, and Lisa Gennetian, Danielle Crosby, Chantelle Dowsett, and Aletha Huston, "Maternal Employment, Early Care Settings and the Achievement of Low-Income Children," Next Generation Working Paper No. 30 (New York: MDRC, 2007).

42. Educare Learning Network, "A National Research Agenda for Early Education," April 2014, accessed October 10, 2014, http://www .educareschools.org/results/pdfs/National_Research_Agenda_for_Early _Education.pdf. Early returns on evaluation of Educare are promising; see N. Yazejian and D. M. Bryant, "Promising Early Returns: Educare Implementation Study Data, March 2009" (Chapel Hill: FPG Child Development Institute, UNC, 2009) and "Educare Implementation Study Findings—August 2012," accessed December 16, 2014, http:// eln.fpg.unc.edu/sites/eln.fpg.unc.edu/files/FPG-Demonstrating-Results -August-2012-Final.pdf.

43. Jane Waldfogel and Elizabeth Washbrook, "Early Years Policy," *Child Development Research* 2011 (2011): 1–12; Amy J. L. Baker, Chaya S. Piotrkowski, and Jeanne Brooks-Gunn, "The Home Instruction Program for Preschool Youngsters (HIPPY)," *The Future of Children* 9 (Spring/Summer 1999): 116–33; Darcy I. Lowell, Alice S. Carter, Leandra Godoy, Belinda Paulicin, and Margaret J. Briggs-Gowan, "A Randomized Controlled Trial of Child FIRST: A Comprehensive Home-Based Intervention Translating Research into Early Childhood Practice," *Child Development* 82 (January 2011): 193–208; "Policy: Helping Troubled Families Turn Their Lives Around," Department for Communities and Local Government, accessed October 10, 2014, https://www.gov.uk /government/policies/helping-troubled-families-turn-their-lives-around /activity. See also Tondi M. Harrison, "Family Centered Pediatric Nursing Care: State of the Science," *Journal of Pediatric Nursing* 25 (October 2010): 335–43.

44. OECD, *Education at a Glance: OECD Indicators 2014* (OECD Publishing, 2014), chart C.21, p. 320.

45. James J. Heckman, "Skill Formation and the Economics of Investing in Disadvantaged Children," *Science* 312 (June 2006): 1900–1902; Arthur J. Reynolds, Judy A. Temple, Dylan L. Robertson, and Emily A. Mann, "Age 21 Cost-Benefit Analysis of the Title I Chicago Child-Parent Center Program," Executive Summary (National Institute for Early Childhood Education Research, June 2001).

46. Recent entries in the vast literature evaluating early childhood education include David Deming, "Early Childhood Intervention and Life-Cycle Skill Development: Evidence from Head Start," *American Economic Journal* 1 (July 2009): 111–34; Jens Ludwig and Douglas L. Miller, "Does Head Start Improve Children's Life Chances? Evidence from a Regression-Discontinuity Design," *Quarterly Journal of Economics* 122 (2007): 159–208; and Alexander Gelber, "Children's Schooling and Parents' Behavior: Evidence from the Head Start Impact Study," *Journal of Public Economics* 101 (2013): 25–38. Encouraging results have also been found in the Infant Health Development Program. See Greg J. Duncan, Jeanne Brooks-Gunn, and Pamela K. Klebanov, "Economic Deprivation

and Early-Childhood Development," *Child Development* 65 (April 1994): 296–318; John M. Love and Jeanne Brooks-Gunn, "Getting the Most Out of Early Head Start: What Has Been Accomplished and What Needs To Be Done," in *Investing in Young Children: New Directions in Federal Preschool and Early Childhood Policy*, eds. W. Steven Barnett and Ron Haskins (Washington, DC: Brooking Institution, 2010), 29–37.

47. Greg J. Duncan and Richard J. Murnane, *Restoring Opportunity: The Crisis of Inequality and the Challenge for American Education* (New York: Russell Sage Foundation, 2014), 53–69.

48. William T. Gormley, Deborah Phillips, and Ted Gayer, "Preschool Programs Can Boost School Readiness," *Science* 320 (June 27, 2008): 1723–24; William T. Gormley, Jr., Ted Gayer, Deborah Phillips, and Brittany Dawson, "The Effects of Universal Pre-K on Cognitive Development," *Developmental Psychology* 41 (November 2005): 872–84; William Gormley, Jr., Ted Gayer, Deborah Phillips, and Brittany Dawson, "The Effects of Oklahoma's Universal Pre-K Program on School Readiness: An Executive Summary" (Georgetown University: Center for Research on Children in the U.S., November 2004).

49. Douglas S. Massey, Len Albright, Rebecca Casciano, Elizabeth Derickson, and David N. Kinsey, *Climbing Mount Laurel: The Struggle for Affordable Housing and Social Mobility in an American Suburb* (Princeton: Princeton University Press, 2013), 195.

50. Bruce D. Baker, David G. Sciarra, and Danielle Farrie, "Is School Funding Fair? A National Report Card" (The Education Law Center and Rutgers Graduate School of Education, 2012).

51. U.S. Department of Education, "For Each and Every Child—A Strategy for Education Equity and Excellence," a report to the Secretary (Washington, DC: The Equity and Excellence Commission, 2013), accessed October 11, 2014, http://www2.ed.gov/about/bdscomm/list/eec/equity -excellence-commission-report.pdf.

52. Steven Glazerman, Ali Protik, Bing-ru Teh, Julie Bruch, and Jeffrey Max, "Transfer Incentives for High-Performing Teachers: Final Results from a Multisite Experiment (NCEE 2014–4003)" (Washington, DC: National Center for Education Evaluation and Regional Assistance,

Institute of Education Sciences, U.S. Department of Education, November 2013), accessed October 11, 2014, http://ies.ed.gov/ncee/pubs/20144003/pdf/20144003.pdf.

53. Duncan and Murnane, *Restoring Opportunity.*

54. Erika A. Patall, Harris Cooper, and Ashley Batts Allen, "Extending the School Day or School Year: A Systematic Review of Research (1985–2009)," *Review of Educational Research* 80 (September 2010): 401–36.

55. Key studies of the effectiveness of charter schools include Caroline M. Hoxby and Sonali Muraka, "Charter Schools in New York City: Who Enrolls and How They Affect Their Students' Achievement," NBER Working Paper No. 14852 (Cambridge: National Bureau of Economic Research, April 2009); Atila Abdulkadiroglu, Joshua Angrist, Susan Dynarski, Thomas J. Kane, and Parag Pathak, "Accountability and Flexibility in Public Schools: Evidence from Boston's Charters and Pilots," NBER Working Paper No. 15549 (Cambridge: National Bureau of Economic Research, November 2009); Philip Gleason, Melissa Clark, Christina Clark Tuttle, and Emily Dwoyer, "The Evaluation of Charter School Impacts: Final Report (NCEE 2010–4029), National Center for Education Evaluation and Regional Assistance, accessed October 11, 2014, http://ies.ed.gov/ncee/pubs/20104029/; Ron Zimmer et al., "Charter Schools: Do They Cream Skim, Increasing Student Segregation?," in *School Choice and School Improvement,* eds. Mark Berends, Marisa Cannata, and Ellen B. Goldring (Cambridge: Harvard Education Press, 2011); and Joshua D. Angrist, Susan M. Dynarski, Thomas J. Kane, Parag A. Pathak, and Christopher R. Walters, "Who Benefits from KIPP?," *Journal of Policy Analysis and Management* 31 (Fall 2012): 837–60.

56. Mark R. Warren, "Communities and Schools: A New View of Urban Education Reform," *Harvard Educational Review* 75 (Summer 2005), accessed October 12, 2014, http://www.presidentsleadershipclass.org/images/uploads/ca_files/Communities_and_Schools.pdf. On the importance of community social capital for effective school reform, see Anthony S. Bryk, Penny Bender Sebring, Elaine Allensworth, Stuart Luppescu, and John Q. Easton, *Organizing Schools for Improvement: Lessons from Chicago* (Chicago: University of Chicago Press, 2010).

57. "What is a Community School?," Coalition for Community Schools, accessed October 12, 2014, http://www.communityschools.org/about schools/what_is_a_community_school.aspx.

58. Colleen Cummings, Alan Dyson, and Liz Todd, *Beyond the School Gates: Can Full Service and Extended Schools Overcome Disadvantage?* (London: Routledge, 2011); Colleen Cummings et al., "Evaluation of the Full Service Extended Schools Initiative: Final Report," Research Brief No. RB852 (Department for Education and Skills, June 2007), accessed October 12, 2014, http://webarchive.nationalarchives .gov.uk/20130401151715/http://www.education.gov.uk/publications /eOrderingDownload/RB852.pdf; Joy G. Dryfoos, "Evaluation of Community Schools: Findings to Date" (report, 2000), accessed October 12, 2014, http://www.communityschools.org/assets/1/asset manager/evaluation%20of%20community%20schools_joy_dryfoos .pdf; Martin J. Blank, Atelia Melaville, and Bela P. Shah, "Making the Difference: Research and Practice in Community Schools" (report of the Coalition for Community Schools, May 2003), accessed October 12, 2014, http://www.communityschools.org/assets/1/page /ccsfullreport.pdf; Child Trends, "Making the Grade: Assessing the Evidence for Integrated Student Supports" (report, February 2014), accessed October 12, 2014, http://www.childtrends.org/wp-content /uploads/2014/02/2014–07ISSPaper2.pdf.

59. Will Dobbie and Roland G. Fryer, Jr., "Are High Quality Schools Enough to Close the Achievement Gap? Evidence from a Social Experiment in Harlem," NBER Working Paper No. 15473 (Cambridge: National Bureau of Economic Research, November 2009).

60. James S. Coleman and Thomas Hoffer, *Public and Private High Schools: The Impact of Communities* (New York: Basic Books, 1987); Anthony S. Bryk, Peter B. Holland, and Valerie E. Lee, *Catholic Schools and the Common Good* (Cambridge: Harvard University Press, 1993); G. R. Kearney, *More Than a Dream: The Cristo Rey Story: How One School's Vision Is Changing the World* (Chicago: Loyola Press, 2008). See also Derek Neal, "The Effects of Catholic Secondary Schooling on Educational Achievement," *Journal of Labor Economics* 15 (January 1997): 98–123, and William H. Jeynes, "Religion, Intact Families, and the Achievement Gap," *Interdisciplinary Journal of Research on Religion* 3 (2007): 1–24.

61. Don Peck, "Can the Middle Class Be Saved?," *Atlantic,* September 2011, accessed October 11, 2014, http://www.theatlantic.com/magazine /archive/2011/09/can-the-middle-class-be-saved/308600/; Ron Haskins and Isabel Sawhill, *Creating an Opportunity Society* (Washington, DC: Brookings Institution Press, 2009).

62. James J. Kemple, "Career Academies: Long-Term Impacts on Work, Education, and Transitions to Adulthood," MDRC Report (June 2008), accessed October 12, 2014, http://www.mdrc.org/publication/career -academies-long-term-impacts-work-education-and-transitions-adult hood.

63. Harry J. Holzer, "Workforce Development as an Antipoverty Strategy: What Do We Know? What Should We Do?," *Focus* 26 (Fall 2009), accessed October 11, 2014, http://www.irp.wisc.edu/publications/focus /pdfs/foc262k.pdf; William C. Symonds, Robert Schwartz, and Ronald F. Ferguson, "Pathways to Prosperity: Meeting the Challenge of Preparing Young Americans for the 21st Century" (report for the Pathways to Prosperity project, Harvard School of Graduate Education, 2011); Ben Olinsky and Sarah Ayres, "Training for Success: A Policy to Expand Apprenticeships in the United States" (report for the Center for American Progress, December 2013), accessed October 12, 2014, http://cdn .americanprogress.org/wp-content/uploads/2013/11/apprenticeship_re port.pdf; Robert I. Lerman, "Expanding Apprenticeship Opportunities in the United States" (report for the Hamilton Project, Brookings Institution, 2014); David Card, Jochen Kluve and Andrea Weber, "Active Labour Market Policy Evaluations: A Meta-Analysis," *Economic Journal* 120 (November 2010): F452–F477; Katherine S. Newman and Hella Winston, *Learning to Labor in the 21st Century: Building the Next Generation of Skilled Workers* (New York: Metropolitan, forthcoming 2015). YouthBuild has shown positive results in nonexperimental research; see, for example, Wally Abrazaldo et al., "Evaluation of the YouthBuild Youth Offender Grants: Final Report," Social Policy Research Associates (May 2009). The Department of Labor has commissioned MDRC to conduct an experimental randomized control trial (RCT) on YouthBuild across 83 sites. Controlled experimental studies have found favorable results from such programs as Job Corps, Service and Conservation Corps, and National Guard Youth ChalleNGe; MDRC, "Building Better

Programs for Disconnected Youth," February 2013, accessed November 24, 2014, http://www.mdrc.org/sites/default/files/Youth_020113.pdf.

64. Arthur M. Cohen and Florence B. Brawer, *The American Community College,* 5th ed. (San Francisco: Jossey-Bass, 2008), 444. See also Sandy Baum, Jennifer Ma, and Kathleen Payea, "Trends in Public Higher Education: Enrollment, Prices, Student Aid, Revenues, and Expenditures," Trends in Higher Education Series, College Board Advocacy & Policy Center (May 2012): 3–31; Clive R. Belfield and Thomas Bailey, "The Benefits of Attending Community College: A Review of the Evidence," *Community College Review* 39 (January 2011): 46–68; and Christopher M. Mullin and Kent Phillippe, "Community College Contributions," Policy Brief 2013–01PB (Washington, DC: American Association of Community Colleges, January 2013). Recent blue-ribbon national reports on community colleges include American Association of Community Colleges, "Reclaiming the American Dream: Community Colleges and the Nation's Future," report from the 21st Century Commission on the Future of Community Colleges (April 2012), accessed October 12, 2014, http://www.insidehighered.com/sites/default/server _files/files/21stCentReport.pdf; and Century Foundation Task Force on Preventing Community Colleges from Becoming Separate and Unequal, "Bridging the Higher Education Divide: Strengthening Community Colleges and Restoring the American Dream" (New York: Century Foundation Press, May 2013), accessed October 12, 2014, http://tcf .org/assets/downloads/20130523-Bridging_the_Higher_Education_Di vide-REPORT-ONLY.pdf. I am especially grateful to Edwenna Rosser Werner for extensive background research on community colleges.

65. For guidelines on mentoring best practices, see MENTOR, "Elements of Effective Practice for Mentoring," 3rd ed., report of the National Mentoring Partnership, accessed October 12, 2014, http://www.men toring.org/downloads/mentoring_1222.pdf.

66. I refer here to Tenacity, a highly effective school-based mentoring program in Boston that uses tennis as its calling card; Skateducate, a Danish mentoring program based on skateboarding; and Quest, a summer-school-plus-mentoring program run by local Rotary Clubs in New England that brings together adults and disadvantaged kids around outdoor activities like fishing.

67. Nancy Andrews and David Erikson, eds., "Investing in What Works for America's Communities: Essays on People, Place and Purpose," report by the Federal Reserve Bank of San Francisco and Low Income Investment Fund, 2012, accessed October 12, 2014, http://www.frbsf .org/community-development/files/investing-in-what-works.pdf; Tracey Ross and Erik Stedman, "A Renewed Promise: How Promise Zones Can Help Reshape the Federal Place-Based Agenda," report of the Center for American Progress, May 2014, accessed October 12, 2014, http:// www.americanprogress.org/issues/poverty/report/2014/05/20/90026 /a-renewed-promise/.

68. Patrick Sharkey, "Neighborhoods, Cities, and Economic Mobility" (paper prepared for the Boston Federal Reserve conference on Inequality of Economic Opportunity, Boston, October 17–18, 2014), and sources cited there. Greg J. Duncan, Aletha C. Huston, and Thomas S. Weisner, *Higher Ground: New Hope for the Working Poor and Their Children* (New York: Russell Sage, 2009); Johannes Bos et al., "New Hope for People with Low Incomes: Two-Year Results of a Program to Reduce Poverty and Reform Welfare" (New York: MDRC, 1999); Aletha C. Huston et al., "New Hope for Families and Children: Five-Year Results of a Program to Reduce Poverty and Reform Welfare," Manpower Demonstration Research Corporation, 2003; Aletha C. Huston et al., "Work-Based Antipoverty Programs for Parents Can Enhance the School Performance and Social Behavior of Children," *Child Development* 72 (2001): 318–36; Howard S. Bloom, James A. Riccio, Nandita Verma, and Johanna Walter, "Promoting Work in Public Housing. The Effectiveness of Jobs-Plus. Final Report." Manpower Demonstration Research Corporation, New York: 2005.

69. Patrick Sharkey, "Neighborhoods, Cities, and Economic Mobility"; Xavier de Souza Briggs, Susan J. Popkin, and John Goering, *Moving to Opportunity: The Story of an American Experiment to Fight Ghetto Poverty* (New York: Oxford University Press, 2010); Leonard S. Rubinowitz and James E. Rosenbaum, *Crossing the Class and Color Lines: From Public Housing to White Suburbia* (Chicago: University of Chicago Press, 2000); Micere Keels, Greg J. Duncan, Stefanie Deluca, Ruby Mendenhall, and James Rosenbaum, "Fifteen Years Later: Can Residential Mobility Programs Provide a Long-Term Escape from Neighborhood

Segregation, Crime, and Poverty?" *Demography* 42 (February 2005): 51–73; Jens Ludwig, Brian Jacob, Greg Duncan, James Rosenbaum, and Michael Johnson, "Neighborhood Effects on Low-Income Families: Evidence from a Housing-Voucher Lottery in Chicago" (working paper, University of Chicago, 2010); Jennifer Darrah and Stefanie DeLuca, "'Living Here Has Changed My Whole Perspective': How Escaping Inner-City Poverty Shapes Neighborhood and Housing Choice," *Journal of Policy Analysis and Management* 33 (Spring 2014): 350–84.

70. Ralph Waldo Emerson, "Self-Reliance," in *Essays: First Series* (1841). Thanks to Thomas Spragens for alerting me to this passage.

71. Yvonne Abraham, "Doing Right by the Children in Chelsea," *Boston Globe*, August 31, 2014.

The Stories of Our Kids

1. Some quotations have been lightly edited to remove interjections, false starts, and repetition. For the sake of coherence, comments about the same subject from different parts of an interview have occasionally been placed together as a single statement. In no case do these edits alter the sense or tone of the quotation.

2. Jennifer M. Silva, *Coming Up Short: Working-Class Adulthood in an Age of Uncertainty* (New York: Oxford University Press, 2013).

Index

Page numbers in *italics* refer to figures and tables.

About the Author

ROBERT D. PUTNAM is the Malkin Professor of Public Policy at Harvard and is the author of 14 previous books, including the prize-winning *American Grace: How Religion Divides and Unites Us* and the bestselling *Bowling Alone: The Collapse and Revival of American Community.*

In addition to teaching both graduate and undergraduate courses at Harvard, Putnam is the cofounder of the Saguaro Seminar, a research initiative that brings together leading thinkers and practitioners to develop actionable ideas for civic renewal. In 2015, the Seminar is launching the Closing the Opportunity Gap initiative. The initiative will convene five working groups of roughly a dozen of the country's leading experts in each of five areas: family and parenting, early childhood, K–12 education, community institutions, and "on-ramps," such as community college or apprenticeships. In mid-2015 the groups will issue nonpartisan white papers distilling the best evidence-based ideas for narrowing the opportunity gap. To learn more, visit www.theopportunitygap.com.

Outside his academic life, Putnam recently celebrated his 51st wedding anniversary with his wife, Rosemary, and together they are the proud grandparents of seven grandchildren. When not cheering on the New England Patriots and the Boston Red Sox, he and his wife enjoy hiking and birding, both in the mountains near their New Hampshire home and around the world.